Mimi

August 2002

— end notes in this age of computer type setting —

— pp 30-31   limits of sincerity

— p 262 Gide, Verlaine sincerity

— p 35 "sincerity"

— p 36

p 47

— re Chanson d'Eve   Why does Carlo refer to
   Chapters of Von Lerberghe's poem?

Fauré and French Musical Aesthetics

This wide-ranging study of Gabriel Fauré and his contemporaries reclaims aesthetic categories crucial to French musical life in the early twentieth century. Its interrelated chapters treat the topics of sincerity, originality, novelty, self-renewal, homogeneity and religious belief in relation to Fauré's music and ideas. Taking a broad view of cultural life during the composer's lifetime and beyond, the book moves between specific details in Fauré's music and related critical, literary, and philosophical issues, ranging from Gounod to Boulez and from Proust to Valéry. Above all, the book connects abstract values to artistic choices and thus places such works as Fauré's Requiem, *La bonne chanson*, *La chanson d'Eve*, *L'horizon chimérique*, and the chamber music in a new light.

CARLO CABALLERO is Assistant Professor of Music at the University of Colorado. His recent essays have appeared in two edited collections, *Regarding Fauré* (1999) and *The Arts Entwined* (2000).

Music in the Twentieth Century

GENERAL EDITOR   Arnold Whittall

This series offers a wide perspective on music and musical life in the twentieth century. Books included range from historical and biographical studies concentrating particularly on the context and circumstances in which composers were writing, to analytical and critical studies concerned with the nature of musical language and questions of compositional process. The importance given to context will also be reflected in studies dealing with, for example, the patronage, publishing, and promotion of new music, and in accounts of the musical life of particular countries.

Recent titles

The Music of John Cage
James Pritchett
0 521 56544 8

The Music of Ruth Crawford Seeger
Joseph Straus
0 521 41646 9

The Music of Conlon Nancarrow
Kyle Gann
0 521 46534 6

The Stravinsky Legacy
Jonathan Cross
0 521 56365 8

Experimental Music: Cage and Beyond
Michael Nyman
0 521 65297 9
0 521 65383 5

The BBC and Ultra-Modern Music, 1922–1936
Jennifer Doctor
0 521 66117 X

The Music of Harrison Birtwistle
Robert Adlington
0 521 63082 7

Four Musical Minimalists: La Monte Young, Terry Riley, Steve Reich, Philip Glass
Keith Potter
0 521 48250 X

Fauré and French Musical Aesthetics

Carlo Caballero

CAMBRIDGE
UNIVERSITY PRESS

PUBLISHED BY THE PRESS SYNDICATE OF THE UNIVERSITY OF CAMBRIDGE
The Pitt Building, Trumpington Street, Cambridge, United Kingdom

CAMBRIDGE UNIVERSITY PRESS
The Edinburgh Building, Cambridge CB2 2RU, UK
40 West 20th Street, New York, NY 10011-4211, USA
10 Stamford Road, Oakleigh, VIC 3166, Australia
Ruiz de Alarcón 13, 28014 Madrid, Spain
Dock House, The Waterfront, Cape Town 8001, South Africa

http://www.cambridge.org

First published 2001

Printed in the United Kingdom at the University Press, Cambridge

Typeface Adobe Minion 10.5/13.5pt   *System* QuarkXPress™   [SE]

A catalogue record for this book is available from the British Library

ISBN 0 521 78107 8 hardback

for Rachel

Contents

Acknowledgments

It is a pleasure to recognize the friends, colleagues, and institutions who have contributed to the making of this book.

Whoever studies Fauré's music owes a debt of gratitude to Jean-Michel Nectoux. His pathbreaking research has established the documentary basis of all future work on the composer, and thanks to his books and essays we can now confidently speak of the chronology of Fauré's works, the state of his manuscripts, the scope of his contribution to French music, and the content of his social and intellectual life. I would like to thank M. Nectoux for his letters and our conversations. He always conscientiously answered my questions and has been the model of generous collegiality. I am also grateful to him for providing me with his beautiful edition of Fauré's Requiem, with the run of bulletins and studies published by the Société des Amis de Gabriel Fauré, and with other printed and recorded materials.

Brian Hart and I share sections of the same big historical puzzle, and more than once he slid pieces of esoteric evidence across the table to me. In long letters and conversations we often shared findings about critics and composers common to our projects. Brian's sense of humor and intelligence always added to the enjoyment of these exchanges, and I am above all indebted to him as a critical and unsparing reader of the original dissertation. I thank Edward R. Phillips, who provided me with photocopies and all manner of bibliographic quixotica. He never forgot to bundle in a dose of his incomparable black humor. Tracy Fernandez helped me isolate some important methodological problems at the earliest stages of my work and prompted the train of thought that led to the first chapter. He also gave us the espresso machine.

I acknowledge special debts to other colleagues: to the late William Austin, who responded so warmly to the talk on Fauré and sincerity that I delivered in Pittsburgh in 1992; to Steven Huebner, for pointing me to Dukas's review of *Werther*; to James Kidd, who was instantly enthusiastic about my project and who kindly put a copy of his own doctoral dissertation at my disposal; to Susan Richardson, who provided me with a typescript of her talk on Fauré's Requiem; to Keith Waters, who helped me improve the discussion of meter and style in the final chapter; and to Arnold Whittall, who supported this book and provided cogent editorial assistance. I also want to thank Michael Strasser, Brooks Toliver, Catrina Flint des

Médicis, and Mary Davis, all of whom located things for me in the Bibliothèque Nationale de France when I was on the wrong side of the Atlantic.

I am grateful to the Chancellor's Office of the University of Colorado at Boulder for the two-year postdoctoral fellowship that allowed me to make a research trip to Paris.

This book is based on my doctoral dissertation (University of Pennsylvania, 1996). Aside from the usual revisions, additions and subtractions, the final chapter of the book is entirely new. Several sections of chapter 5 appeared in a slightly different form in *Regarding Fauré*, a collection of essays edited by Tom Gordon (Gordon & Breach, 1999). Tom's exceptional editorial insight and precision ultimately improved this chapter as well as the earlier essay.

The faculty of music at Penn was always unstinting in individual and collective support for my work. Jeffrey Kallberg was an astute, broad-minded advisor, and I hope that some of his own habits of inquiry, particularly the spirit of independence I like so much in his work, contributed something to my own scholarship. I also thank Leonard Meyer for his thorough, constructive response to the last section of the third chapter, and Christopher Hasty for his warm interest and enthusiasm.

The translations are all my own, except on some rare occasions where I cite an English edition. For a number of passages from Proust's *A la recherche du temps perdu* I adopt the revised English translation by Moncrieff, Kilmartin and Enright. However, I have sometimes made my own translations from the French where I was not completely satisfied that Proust's three English collaborators had captured important structural or lexical details. Their superb edition is nonetheless so universally available in English-speaking countries that it seemed inconsiderate not to refer the reader to the appropriate pages for the passage in question. Therefore, for this work, I have explicitly indicated whether or not I translated each excerpt cited, and the reader is always pointed toward the appropriate pages in both the French editions and the standard translation.

No book on the history of the arts can be written without libraries and their keepers. I could not have proceeded without the diligent, painstaking work of the staffs of interlibrary loan offices of the University of Pennsylvania and the University of Colorado. Likewise, I thank Patti Maguire, who, during our time together at Harvard, procured obscure books and microfilms for me from the Center for Research Libraries. The databases of the Project for American and French Research on the Treasury of the French Language (ARTFL) sometimes aided my understanding of nineteenth-century usage, and particularly the history of the word "pantheism." I encountered the quotations from Victor Cousin, the Goncourt brothers, and Paul Bourget cited in the third part of chapter 5 by way of searches in the Treasury. I extend a firm electronic handshake to Mark Olsen, assistant director of the Project, for his friendly on-line support from Chicago.

To my parents, I am indebted for more than I can say. Their moral and financial support for my long education made everything possible. I want to thank my wife, Rachel Fetler, for exploring and performing with me the wonderful and sometimes refractory *mélodies* of Fauré. She was also the first to read every one of these chapters. With a sure hand and understandably sleepy eyes, she brushed the pages clean of mixed metaphors and all sorts of other intellectual junk. Her patience over the years has been preternatural.

Boulder, Colorado
May 2000

Introduction

Il faut un choix. Mais dans le choix des documents, un certain esprit dominera, – et comme il varie, suivant les conditions de l'écrivain, jamais l'histoire ne sera fixée.

"C'est triste," pensaient-ils.[1]
Flaubert, *Bouvard et Pécuchet*

Aesthetics and evidence

When we think about Fauré, we have to imagine a composer whose experience spanned two centuries and a cavalcade of artistic movements, fashions, and "isms." When Fauré was born in 1845, Cherubini had been dead only three years, and Fauré could have played some of his own earliest works in Rossini's salon. Before Fauré died in 1924, he had attended the première of *Le sacre du printemps*, studied the score of *Pierrot Lunaire* (he didn't care for it), and befriended Arthur Honegger. Varèse, whose diploma from the Conservatoire bears Fauré's signature, had already composed *Offrandes*, *Hyperprism*, and *Octandre*. Through this long, rich period in the history of music, with all its stylistic explosions, Fauré's own work changed, too. Yet there is an uncanny sameness in the way he realized certain personal techniques and modes of expression across six decades of activity. His contemporaries often remarked on his ability to resist powerful influences that drew other composers off a personal path. He participated in new cultural developments, but he was often regarded, like his friend Paul Dukas, as an "independent" artist. His ability to combine sameness and innovation is puzzling. Fauré's reticence, too, has been a stumbling-block for historians. Far from being the sort of artist to issue a manifesto, he reflected privately and commented obliquely in conversations. His music, often abstract, comes down to us as the most abiding statement of his thought and experience as an artist.

In navigating the open sea of Fauré's reticence, this book strikes a compromise by trying to attend to the most sympathetic vibrations between his extant words and his musical legacy. Drawing Fauré's music into my claims and arguments has been a constant concern, but I have sought above all to subject his rare pronouncements on art to close, repeated readings. There is every reason to take Fauré's critical legacy very seriously, and by putting it in the context of his professional and creative activities we may meet his reserve half way. In this way, it is possible to develop a historical context for Fauré's achievement. I have more particularly aimed to approach Fauré's understanding of his own work and of the art of music.

To speak of Fauré's aesthetics at all may appear implausible since theorizing about art was entirely contrary to his personal inclinations. He was not merely indifferent to the act of theorizing but almost embarrassed by it, especially where his own music was concerned. Unlike Saint-Saëns and Dukas, he left no philosophical essays on the nature of art or the principles of composition. Unlike Debussy and Ravel, he did not spike his critical articles and interviews with sarcastic sallies. Unlike Vincent d'Indy and Théodore Dubois, he wrote no pedagogical or historical volumes. Yet he was a teacher of composition, the director of France's national conservatory of music, an avid reader, a man of great culture. Fauré was, like Chabrier, Chopin, or Schubert, a literate musician who did not write much about music. It is true that he wrote a certain number of reviews for *Le Figaro*, and some of these reviews clearly manifest his opinions of his predecessors and contemporaries. But more often than not, he hid his deepest beliefs between the lines, or even suppressed them altogether in the interests of amiability or because of his sincere modesty before a novel achievement.

Fauré's reluctance to discuss general musical questions or the content of his own works extends even to his private letters. There, in rare moments when he begins to explain his artistic motivations or discuss a feature of his music, he tends to draw back, as if mortified by an indiscretion. For example, after vaguely explaining his compositional goals in "Le don silencieux," op. 92, to his wife, he exclaimed, "Here I am playing the pedant!"[2] Or again, in a friendly letter to Pierre Lalo, he reprimanded himself for mentioning his aims in the musical characterization of Penelope: "What a lot of chit-chat!!!"[3]

A musical historian offering a study of Wagner's aesthetics or Boulez's would cause less surprise than one who writes on Fauré's aesthetics. The abundance of written documents by Wagner or Boulez does not, of course, make those first two tasks particularly easy, but no one can complain of lacking primary material. In the title of this study, I chose to speak not of "Fauré's aesthetics" but more indirectly of "Fauré and French musical aesthetics." By conjunction rather than possession, I mean to acknowledge that Fauré did not leave the kind of detailed documents whose contents would allow for a systematic philosophical evaluation. Can we still assert, then, that Fauré had "an aesthetics"? Yes. For what does it mean to speak of a composer's aesthetics? In general, we mean not only his ideas about music in general and the music of his contemporaries, but also his ideas about his own music, his own creativity, his particular relation to other artistic visions. The aesthetics of a critic or philosopher will not reach into this second layer of meanings (unless, of course, the critic is a composer too). That is to say, when we speak of a critic's aesthetics, we draw our conclusions from the ideas expressed in his collected writings.[4] When we speak of a composer's aesthetics, we usually include his artistic legacy, and a book that evaluated a composer's letters and criticism but failed to consider his music would, on the whole, be unsatisfying as a study of his aesthetics. The most reliable traces of a composer's aesthetics might, far from any written decrees, lie in his music, or, more likely, in a composite space interpenetrated by notes and words.

Therefore the lack of systematic testimony from Fauré is not to be equated with a lack of aesthetic thought: an artist's creative work testifies to that thinking, too.[5] In a sense, Fauré's music might even be considered sufficient evidence of his aesthetics. However, we need not restrict ourselves to his music alone in recovering the foundations of his thinking. Fauré may have been laconic, but from time to time he could not help discussing his own and others' music. We shall see that on one or two occasions he even asked himself profound questions about his art. Other kinds of evidence may also be brought into play, including the record of his ambitions and activities in the Parisian musical world and his work as a teacher and as director of the Conservatoire. His œuvre, words, and actions all support the possibility of rendering a defensible account of his aesthetic orientation. Once we have come to terms with his ideals and stylistic practice, future researchers will be better able to explain how Fauré's music came to serve as a spiritual and technical model for at least two more generations of composers.

Overview

This book does not provide a biography of Fauré or a survey of his musical production. Jean-Michel Nectoux and Robert Orledge have already established the facts of Fauré's life and works on a solid documentary foundation. Rather, this book builds on that foundation by placing Fauré's musical achievement in the context of a cultural history at once broader and more detailed. Fauré's aesthetic thought is the starting point for each chapter, which then proceeds to larger premises, debates, and ideological warrants. This project is historical: the issues I have tackled are mostly those that concerned French critics and musicians of Fauré's own time, and I have approached them in their historical context. Where it seemed useful, I stretched the argument forward diachronically, as when writings by Pierre Boulez or Stanley Cavell allow us to reflect on the role of originality and sincerity over the course of the later twentieth century. The themes of the first five chapters, tied together by the concept of artistic vocation, are sincerity, novelty, originality, self-renewal, homogeneity, and religious belief. Sincerity and originality, though familiar ideas, had distinct meanings in Fauré's time which more recent historical developments have altered or obscured, and thus it is particularly important to map out their premises and implications. The recovery of these ideas, as well as some of those examined in the later chapters, often bears not only on Fauré's conception of his creative labors, but also on composers and critics who shared or rejected his views. Finally, each chapter connects abstract aesthetic categories to Fauré's choices in specific works, and thus I try to show how these categories might provide a basis for new analytical insights.

Chapter 1 argues that sincerity played a central role in the creation, criticism, and social production of French music between 1890 and 1930. Despite the centrality of this idea to French philosophy and criticism during the latter half of Fauré's life, the meaning of sincerity for the history of early twentieth-century music has never been studied. It is fair to say that music, of all the arts, dominated speculative aesthetics in France around 1900. In the novels of Proust as in the philosophy of Bergson, music came to embody an exemplary translation of the individual unconscious, and thus sincerity and music tended to merge. The privileged link between music and *la vie intérieure* made it possible for music to lay claim to sincere, transparent self-representation, whereas the same claim gave rise to epistemological conflicts in literature. Sincerity was essential to Fauré's conception of musical expression, and, among his contemporaries, he was consistently identified as "sincere." What did this mean? In Fauré's compositional practice and in his teaching, the idea of sincerity figured as a flexible, constructive response to the fragmentation of musical styles around the turn of the century. Opposed to fashion and yet welcoming stylistic difference, the call to sincerity placed historical and social conditions in a radically personal perspective and thus afforded composers a liberal means of discovering an individual relation to past or present music. This moral idea thus became central to the aesthetics of the era and left salient traces in the artistic practices of Fauré, Debussy, Messager, Dukas, and Kœchlin, as in the work of philosophers and writers such as Bergson, Combarieu, Valéry, and Proust.

Chapter 2 shows that Fauré tended to treat novelty and tradition as complementary rather than oppositional values. As Louis Aguettant once put it, Fauré's music is "a place where opposites are reconciled."[6] Fauré's seemingly paradoxical attitude toward innovation has caused a number of historians and analysts to lose him on the threshold of the twentieth century. Although the goal of this second chapter is to evaluate Fauré's views of innovation rather than to prove his qualities as an innovator, a number of musical examples there attest, in a very limited way, to an important phase in the development of his style during the last decade of the nineteenth century. The chapter more generally measures Fauré's artistic bearings by examining his relations with other composers, his pedagogical and administrative practices at the Conservatoire, and reactions to his musical innovations on the part of critics.

In studying the role of innovation in Fauré's career, we are forced to confront a distinction between novelty and originality. This difference was crucial to French aesthetics during Fauré's lifetime, but was subsequently lost or abandoned. Chapter 3 analyzes the relationship between originality and novelty. The concept of originality encompassed two levels of meaning. First, there is the material sense of stylistic novelty discussed in chapter 2. Newness in this sense, however, was subordinate to a "novelty of the spirit," which, in contrast to material novelty, is impossible to copy. It was this second meaning that Dukas dubbed a composer's "most original originality." It cannot be copied precisely because it is a manifestation of the unique moral and sensory temperament of the artist who possesses it. Such originality finally connotes nothing less than an artist's irreducible singularity as a human being and is a correlate of sincerity. The first section of chapter 3, centered on a close reading of Dukas's essay "La musique et l'originalité," takes up the definition, history, and cultural motivations of "radical originality." The following sections investigate the implications of this kind of originality for an artist's personal development and public reception. These sections focus on the problems raised by artistic influence and the process of self-renewal, which are closely related to originality. The final part of the chapter moves beyond the historical range of Fauré's lifetime to consider how the meaning of originality so changed in the later twentieth century as to become absorbed into the once subordinate category of novelty. The account of this ideological inversion continues as far forward as the most recent writings of Pierre Boulez, where we reach a point of reversal. Surprisingly, composers now seem to be rehabilitating originality as an important historical and aesthetic category.

Chapter 4 treats a topic that, like sincerity, has received little or no attention in studies of early twentieth-century music: homogeneity. I use this term to designate the consistency of a composer's musical style over time. The chapter unravels the meaning and cultural consequences of homogeneity in France and discusses Fauré's knack for reinventing himself musically within the bounds of almost unvarying technical and expressive propensities. Only through an understanding of the principles of sincerity and originality, as unfolded in the preceding chapters, can we reconcile Fauré's penchant for innovation with the homogeneity of his style. In the middle part of the chapter, the striking differences between the reception of new works by Fauré and Debussy from about 1900 to 1910 serve to point up some problems latent in the ideal of homogeneity. Insufficient homogeneity carried negative consequences for public reception; the main difficulty seemed to lie in listeners' uncertainty about the meaning of changes in a composer's style.

Proust, who greatly admired Fauré, made homogeneity the pre-eminent trait of his ideal musician, the fictional Vinteuil, and the novelist's detailed speculations on the composer's vocation in *La prisonnière* contribute to our understanding of why this quality was so important to Fauré's contemporaries as a mark of greatness. In the closing section of the chapter, I advance the idea that Proust's meditations on homogeneity may provide a new way of thinking about different forms of recurrence in Fauré's music. Compositions written in different periods of Fauré's life provide examples of these varieties of repetition, from self-quotation to vague reminiscence.

The concepts analyzed in the first four chapters – sincerity, novelty, originality, self-renewal and homogeneity – prove to be intimately bound up with one another; all address the process of self-expression in art. The fifth and sixth chapters consider other issues: the role of religion in Fauré's life and career, and the quality of elusiveness that seems to characterize so much of what Fauré was about as an artist.

The study of religious belief immediately throws the inquiry open to social history, politics, and symbolic representation, and the fifth chapter examines the relationships between Fauré's music and his personal commitments. It also compares his beliefs to the religious movements and controversies of his own lifetime. Fauré always avoided explicit avowals, but I argue that his beliefs and orientation can be outlined if not determined. Those beliefs also changed over time: beginning in a lukewarm Catholicism, he wavered between pantheism and agnosticism in his maturity and finally approached atheism in his last years. Fauré's statements on the nature of sacred music and the authority of the church are relatively abundant and allow us to trace his spiritual evolution indirectly. His music is even more revealing, and the second section of the chapter gives particular attention to his musical and textual choices in the Requiem, op. 48. The remainder of the chapter focuses on *La chanson d'Ève*, op. 95, a cycle of songs with complex spiritual implications. I argue for a pantheistic phase in Fauré's religious development around 1906 by analyzing Fauré's musical setting in detail and comparing it to Charles Van Lerberghe's original poems.

The sixth and final chapter attempts a summary of Fauré's aesthetics under the signs of evasion and ambiguity. The various elements of Fauré's music seem to work together to create a language of deliberate elusiveness. In the realm of harmony and counterpoint, he replaces strong harmonic progressions by fourth and fifth with weak progressions founded on a linear bass; he prefers tonicization to modulation; and his modal practice often concedes only what is strictly necessary to tonal unity. When these features are combined with a penchant for maintaining one or two figural patterns over a long time, a dignified reluctance to depend on obvious contrast, and a slowly graded dynamism, the musical result is kaleidoscopic, slippery, and wave-like. Copland referred more informally to "a certain ungetatable quality" in Fauré's music, "disconcerting to the uninitiated."[7] The first half of chapter 6 concentrates on one technical area in particular: Fauré's treatment of meter, which has gone relatively unnoticed in the literature. Yet even a rapid glance at some of Fauré's metrical techniques reveals an important aspect of the "ungetatable quality" of his art. In making metrical patterns the servant of the phrase rather than a series of continual downbeats, Fauré tends to confound regular metrical divisions and to deny accents except at selected points of harmonic reinforcement. The multivalence in Fauré's music sometimes makes two or three distinct metrical interpretations of the same phrase possible, but the composer characteristically disguises this complexity behind a bland façade of regular barlines. Notation does not contravene aural experience, however. The composer's harmonic, melodic, and metrical techniques work together to create passages of floating multivalence that throw the listener into a very Fauréan state of uncertainty.

The remainder of the chapter considers the theme of elusiveness in light of Fauré's character as a man and an artist. In this broader sense, Fauré's elusiveness extends to his attitude toward the poietic dimension of his work (its origins, conception, and craftsmanship); his distrust of titles and avoidance of extramusical referents in his instrumental music; and his tendency to erase or blur specific details drawn from the real world.

Unresolved: the case of Fauré

The greatness of Fauré's music is not at issue. What remains to be fathomed is the nature of his artistic adventure in a particular place at a particular time. Fauré's musical achievement embodies the interregnum in which he lived, and even people who like historical labels grope aimlessly when asked whether Fauré's music is late romantic, post-romantic, or modern. These categories are not interesting, but the specific nature of Fauré's achievement is. He created something new by driving traditional means to peculiar and untraditional ends. Consequently, his music appears too reckless for a traditionalist and not reckless enough for a revolutionary. Outside of France, Fauré figures inadequately in histories and analyses of nineteenth-century and twentieth-century music. British scholars have done him more justice than Americans, but his music too easily slips between the chrono-logical volumes of our histories. A pair of volumes published by Schirmer Books in 1990, *Nineteenth-Century Piano Music* and *Twentieth-Century Piano Music*, offers a rather literal example of this failure: Fauré figures in neither of these books despite the fact that he should be in both.[8] Even the collective nature of their authorship does not excuse the double oversight. To omit Fauré's piano music is to omit that of one of the most important composers to sustain and transform the legacy of Chopin and, in some respects, of Liszt, Schumann, and Mendelssohn, into the twentieth century. In this sense, one could contend that Fauré and Skryabin occupy similar his-torical positions.

As I look back on the various stages of this study, it seems to me that making a case for Fauré's historical importance must have been one of the latent motivations behind my research. In a private letter, Leonard B. Meyer once drew my attention to an interesting distinction that bears on this moti-vation. Meyer distinguishes between musical importance (for example, Mozart or Fauré) and historical importance (Weber, Webern). The distinc-tion is not meant to pigeonhole but to provide a historiographic starting point. Fauré's musical importance is more obvious than his historical importance, but his historical importance has been given so little attention that it is difficult to judge what it might be. This book does not make an explicit case for this latter kind of importance, but many of the ideas advanced in the following pages substantiate Fauré's historical importance and his influence on other musicians. This preliminary work only offers a point of departure for a more detailed examination of Fauré's place in twen-tieth-century music. The power of Fauré's style remains, to some extent, a source of unrealized potential. In 1995, Robin Holloway asked whether "somewhere, somehow, there lies within [Fauré's style] an elixir for the future."[9] The question is particularly pertinent when we seem to be looking toward an eclectic, post-tonal future, not a strictly atonal one. Looking backward, too, Holloway observes, "Fauré stands to Stravinsky . . . rather as Mahler to Schoenberg." This comparison is interesting precisely because it suggests the possibility that Fauré might be "as important historically as he is intrinsically."[10] Holloway challenges other listeners to hear Fauré's tech-nique and spirit, as he does, in *Orpheus, The Rake's Progress*, and even sec-tions of *Agon*.[11] There is good reason to pursue such unexpected likenesses, which may have a common basis in the free modal interchange that charac-terizes Fauré's music.

Fame came late to Fauré. Although a certain amount of interest in his work started to grow among amateurs and critics after 1887, the great turning point came in 1905, the last phase of his career. "It could be said that Fauré's great fame dates only from the moment when he was named director of the Conservatoire [i.e., 1905]," wrote André Messager. "This office naturally brings with it a certain amount of publicity for the works of the person who holds it, and thus his songs, piano pieces, and chamber music were rapidly disseminated."[12] Yet Fauré's ascent to a high position in the French musical world was no guarantee of artistic understanding, and misunderstanding continued into his very last years. Haloes of distinction descended on him, but his real importance as a composer, as opposed to a figurehead, was long an enigma to all but a select circle. Champions of Fauré's art, few in number, were not far off the mark when they sometimes called themselves "initiates." Beyond French borders, the Fauréan cult was even smaller. In 1961, Louis Aubert, once a pupil of Fauré's, approached this problem from the angle of musical style: "It's the perfection of his style that makes Fauré hermetic. He seldom allows the listener to take a breath. He offers him no concessions. There are none of those landings that would ordinarily dispel fatigue and allow the listener to relax . . . Everything in his music is elaborated in terms of beauty and beauty alone."[13] Earlier in the century, René Dumesnil considered the relative neglect of Fauré's music from a historical viewpoint:

> Two things undermined him, and greatly: first, his modesty, or rather the disdain in which he held glory during a period when it was easier than ever for mediocrity to raise a ruckus; second – and this was a consequence of that attitude – his reluctance to supplant his first successes as a composer of songs with the more substantial, large-scale works he composed later. For people who knew only his point of departure as a composer, he remained a "charming" musician, the composer of "La chanson du pêcheur," "Lydia," "Après un rêve."[14]

Dumesnil did not hesitate to add that these songs "deserved their renown" but claimed that they mattered less in the history of French music than *La chanson d'Ève* and *L'horizon chimérique*, than *Prométhée* and *Pénélope*, than the treasury of the late chamber music. He was on the mark in alluding to Fauré's often passive approach to his own reputation as one cause of indifference to his later works. As a pianist, at home and abroad, Fauré was docile in catering to the tastes of his singers and audiences, who almost always called for "the good old things."[15] It is characteristic, too, that he continued to arrange and participate in performances of his first and second piano quartets (dating from 1880 and 1887) even during the Great War, while leaving his later chamber music, including the masterpieces he composed in that very period, almost to providence. Certainly, Fauré's increasing deafness would explain this reluctance to perform new music. But his physical impairment cannot be cited as the only explanation, for on the one hand he occasionally participated in performances of his new works as late as 1919, and on the other hand, he admitted before he lost his hearing that he preferred to perform the first of his two piano quartets because "it is the one I play least badly."[16] It is probably significant that Saint-Saëns once remarked, "*When he wants to be*, Gabriel Fauré is an organist and a pianist of the first water."[17] Fauré could have been a stronger proponent of his own later music, whose value he knew. But his temperament restrained him from self-promotion.

Fauré, then, may be partly to blame for the impairment of his own reputation. But surely enough time has passed to extricate his legacy from the influence of his own modesty or lack of enterprise. In the past ten years, a high tide of new recordings has come in from all over Europe and North America. The increasing international interest on the part of interpreters bodes well for a matching response from scholars and amateurs.

Afterthought

In working out the themes of this study, a small amount of repetition across the chapters was difficult to avoid. This repetition is warranted, since it is the consequence of an attempt to ground the consistent and interrelated elements of Fauré's thought. I deliberately subject certain phrases or sentences of Fauré's to repeated examination. I have chosen to return to some passages in new contexts in order to bring out different implications. While aiming for breadth of historical span and depth in analyzing aesthetic categories, the conditional nature of most conclusions in a study such as this brings me back to my epigraph, provided by Flaubert's disheartened copy-clerks: "In the choice of documents, a certain frame of mind will prevail, and as it varies according to the writer's circumstances, history will never be fixed." This is the more true for the fact that Fauré lived through the era historians have christened the "golden age" of the press in France. The printed record of musical activity in his lifetime is vast, and no one can hope to exhaust it. Other scholars will thus bring new details to bear on Fauré's aesthetic orientation or will reinterpret the documents I have already marshaled. "How sad," Bouvard and Pécuchet remarked in the face of this perpetual instability and revision. But no: there is no sadness, only lucid pleasure in reimagining one of the richest eras in the whole history of music.

Western

1   The question of sincerity

[handwritten margin notes: "cf Soviet Russian descriptions of music as 'sincere'"]

[handwritten margin note: "again diss. style; telling us what he will do"]

[handwritten margin note: "visual arts? or art in general?"]

This chapter examines the role sincerity played in the creation, criticism, and social production of French music at the beginning of the twentieth century. Between 1890 and 1930, references to sincerity pervaded French writings on music as constantly as ideas about decadence, impressionism, or the conflicting currents of the classical and the modern. But in contrast to these categories, which have not only endured in more recent writing on music but also taken on new meanings, the question of sincerity has vanished from sight. It is an idea that belongs less characteristically to the domain of art than to ordinary moral behavior, and probably for this very reason studies of music have disregarded it. Yet the idea of sincerity has a definite history, a real aesthetic presence, specifically French, whose telling opens up new perspectives on a crucial phase in the history of music. Fauré becomes a central figure in this discussion because no composer more than he and no music more than his were hailed as sincere in France during the first quarter of the twentieth century.

Émile Littré, in the supreme French lexicon of the period, defined a sincere person as one who expresses truthfully what he feels or thinks. Littré also admitted the application of the word to things as well as people.[1] When Fauré's contemporaries called a musical work sincere, they meant, in short, that it expressed truthfully what its composer felt or thought. It would be easy to object at once that sincerity is not an *aesthetic* value but a moral one. In fact I do not wish to argue that sincerity can confer greatness on a work of art; it is not my intention here to defend any aesthetic theory. Rather, I offer the history of an idea and an understanding of its function in an aesthetic system that existed in the past. Within this system, the free intercourse of moral and aesthetic values was firmly entrenched; therefore, to insist on separating them would play the evidence false from a historical point of view. If we wish to understand how Fauré and his critics viewed the composer's artistic calling, we must provisionally set aside our prejudices, however valid, against so fragile a category as "sincerity."

Fauré's ideas form the starting point of the following account. But Fauré entrusted his most deeply held beliefs to the page only rarely and fleetingly; he preferred, it seems, to reserve such avowals for intimate conversation among friends or an inspired word of advice to a promising student. Fauré's reticence forces us to rely on those friends and loyal students, privileged witnesses, for many details and explanations. Charles Kœchlin and Émile Vuillermoz, among his pupils, and André Messager, Henri Duparc and Paul Dukas, close colleagues, all provide precious testimony, appraising sincerity both as a general phenomenon and as a quality eminently characteristic of Fauré's work. Moreover, by occasionally moving beyond this inner circle of witnesses to weigh the opinions of a Debussy, a Proust, a Bergson, we will come to see the broader horizon of this idea in French music and letters of the early twentieth century.

1 The composer's sincerity

While Fauré was working on his First Piano Quintet in 1903, he wrote a letter to his wife thanking her for encouraging his undertaking. "You're right to value [chamber music] as much as you do. Indeed, in it, as in symphonic music, you'll find real music and the sincerest translation of a personality."[2] Here Fauré links together three terms at the heart of our inquiry: sincerity itself, the act of translation, and the artist's personality. The translation of personality, or a personal sensibility, is the fundamental meaning of sincerity in composition. More precisely, musical sincerity is *the translation of the artist's inner life into music by force of innate creative necessities*. This definition arrives before the argument and all the historical nuances that will support it but states a working thesis. We should also take up the meaning of a fourth term, *sensibility*, which in the French of Fauré's time designated a "quality of feeling," feeling being generally distinguished from, though not exclusive of, the operations of mind or intelligence. In artistic production, sensibility signified the maker's ability to reproduce a unique, individual quality of feeling in the finished work.[3] We find Fauré using the word in this sense in a preface he wrote in 1916. There Fauré asks, rhetorically, "Isn't every artist free to *translate his thought, his sensibility*, by the means it pleases him to choose?"[4]

We should notice, in both of these short quotations by Fauré, the recurrence of the idea of "translation." Fauré used this verb repeatedly in his meditations on art, as did countless other composers and critics in early twentieth-century France. The notion of translation is important because it captures the movement from the realm of individual experience (the composer as human being) to the realm of public representation (the work of art). Sincerity, as an aesthetic and ethical value, entails an intimate correspondence between the composer – or more precisely, the real, historical human being – and his music. We *equate* the composer with the man rather than issuing grounds for distinguishing them, because this identification is one of the fundamental premises of artistic sincerity. When Fauré's critics call his music sincere, they affirm an ideal harmony between his music and his personality. The specific qualities of this personality are usually described as revealing a particular "sensibility." Thus Charles Kœchlin could assert that "beautiful works are those that . . . best translate the beautiful sensibility of their creator, or, if you prefer, those that give the whole measure of his personal character."[5] More specifically, Kœchlin evoked the reflection of Fauré's personal character in his creative work. He makes this premise explicit: "It is always the *man* that we find in the works of an artist: we benefit or suffer from the good or bad qualities of his inner being."[6] These observations may strike some as simple-minded. Yet Paul Dukas, the most erudite French composer of his generation and an inveterate skeptic, did not hesitate to follow the same line of thought. Kœchlin's ostensibly naïve considerations find unequivocal support in an essay Dukas wrote a few weeks after Fauré's death. Dukas places remarkable emphasis on Fauré's personal character:

> In every beautiful work, it is the man the work expresses that counts first and foremost.
>
> In this, what more luminous example to follow?
>
> Those who had the joy of sharing Fauré's intimacy know how faithfully his art reflected his being – to the extent that his music at times would seem to them the harmonious transfiguration of his own exquisite charm. Others did their utmost to rise above themselves or, if they collaborated with a poet, to surpass that collaborator. Fauré, with a unique grace, without constraint, gathers every external impression back into his inner harmony. Poems, landscapes, sensations that arise from the spur of the moment or the fleeting wave of memories – whatever sources his music springs from, it translates above all his own self according to the varied moods of the most admirable sensibility.[7]

The irresistible presence of Fauré's artistic personality in this passage signifies something beyond the conventions of a eulogy. Dukas, without using the word "sincerity," here elaborates his understanding of how a composer channels various "external impressions" and personal sensations through a unique quality of feeling, "sensibility," so that every source of inspiration returns to a single origin, the self, ultimately translated into music.

However, Dukas's description of this almost magical transmission immediately raises an important question. His allusion to poems and "external impressions" does not fully explain how a composer can remain "himself" when setting a poet's texts – the work of another mind – to music. By what grace does Fauré "gather every external impression back into his inner harmony"? We must pause to see how the proponents of sincerity responded to this problem, for if the composer of a song or opera speaks not in his own voice but through the mouth of another, then the whole concept of musical sincerity would suffer a drastic narrowing. We would find it difficult to talk about the "sincerity" of anything but "pure" or "absolute" music, which ostensibly conserves a singleness of voice. It was Kœchlin who took up what Dukas left unspoken and most explicitly addressed the question of sincerity in collaborative works of art. Kœchlin acknowledged that a partnership between a poet and a *misguided* composer – one who turns away from the real nature of his gifts (or, as Dukas said, willfully attempts to surpass his collaborator) – will very probably result in an inauthentic work. But collaboration in itself need not bring about a betrayal of a composer's inner voices. For Fauré in particular, Kœchlin claimed the widest possible domain for sincerity in his work, collaborative or otherwise. "What is peculiarly Fauré's is an absolute penetration of things and beings; we would not say that his music adapts itself to its subject, but rather that it constitutes the essence of it; a magic mirror, *his music becomes the subject itself*. A unique gift, to make the poets' thought live again; an inexplicable mystery, never to lose, for all that, his exceedingly recognizable personality."[8] This assertion itself looms as something of an inexplicable mystery, for Kœchlin maintains, in effect, that a composer's thought can *become the object it contemplates*. It might be tempting to dismiss such reflections as beyond the pale. Yet they embody assumptions representative of late nineteenth-century and early twentieth-century thought, and challenges to these assumptions by contemporary composers, critics, or aestheticians are rare. Cultural critics today are in a position to see that Fauré's musical culture essentialized sincerity. We shall see, with the work of Wilde and Valéry, a few direct intellectual attacks on the notion of an "essential self" which come close to undoing the whole ideological structure. As for Kœchlin's conclusions, in their historical context they are exceptional only in their bluntness, their explicit delineation of received ideas about creativity and originality. Why musicians went to such lengths to retain the prerogatives of sincerity and personal utterance will become apparent as we begin to see what was at stake.

These idealizations of sincerity obviously reflect a fundamental belief that musical expression answers its highest spiritual calling when it conveys the experience of a single subjectivity. From this belief follows a constant emphasis on the composer's "oneness of being," on his unique "inner self." For an example of this concern, we may call upon a short essay by the critic Gaston Carraud, whose observations on Fauré's personal style distinctly foreshadow what Kœchlin wrote about sincerity and collaborative works over a decade later. Carraud remarks how Fauré's style changes as he turns from one poet to another, and Carraud points out the variety of media and genres found in Fauré's work, but what matters most to this critic is that in everything the composer does, he "remains so constantly himself." "It is the manner of speaking that changes, not the spirit, which keeps a consistency such as one rarely sees in a body of work so diverse."[9] Dukas, of course, said much the same thing when he praised Fauré for always "translating himself" and filtering the different sources of his inspiration through his own sensibility.

To maintain a singleness of voice amid such variables as poetic inspiration, genres, forms, and the passage of time may be difficult for even a great composer, but at least the first three of these variables normally remain matters of personal choice. By the end of the nineteenth century, other contingencies posed hindrances to the expression of a unique subjectivity. Diverse stylistic trends, whose fluctuations remained beyond any individual artist's control, and the simultaneous attraction of a few outstanding artistic figures, made the quest to reveal a single sincere inner self in music ever more difficult. Even the luminaries themselves, Fauré and Debussy among them, felt the potential vulnerability of their status as independent and original creators. Early in 1911, in the course of an interview, Debussy spoke passionately on this topic, and his slightly defensive tone reveals a certain apprehension over his artistic independence: "Do not think that . . . I wish to position myself as the leader of a school or as a reformer! I simply try to express *as sincerely as I can* the sensations and sentiments I experience. The rest scarcely matters to me!"[10] Debussy brooded over the ongoing challenge of "remaining oneself," for he, like the imitators who rallied around his music in spite of all his protests, had faced parallel difficulties in his changing responses to Wagner's style. Self-critical in his own art, Debussy was quick to observe a lack of self-reliance in the music of others. In his critique of Georges Witkowski's First Symphony, for example, he rued the composer's excessive compliance with precepts Vincent d'Indy was then instilling in the students of the Schola Cantorum: "[Witkowski] heeds voices whose authority is redoubtable, and these, it seems to me, prevent him from hearing a more personal voice."[11]

A composer who consistently heard his "personal voice" through the din of contemporary trends, celebrities, and polemics would naturally attract attention. In his stylistic autonomy, Fauré stood out in this tumultuous early twentieth-century context. When the leading Belgian critic Octave Maus attended the first Parisian performances of *Pénélope* in 1913, he intentionally led off his review with praise for Fauré's independence and "the individual character [*particularisme*] of a completely personal accent," which Maus declared to cherish before anything else in the work. "We can only

rejoice in [this] example . . . at a time when the art of music is tossed among
so many different currents that it is in danger of being turned adrift."[12]
Carraud thought that Fauré was able to preserve this "personal accent"
because he "escaped, almost inadvertently, all the imperious influences that
contested one another at the end of the last century."[13] Thus, in the minds
of his contemporaries, Fauré's indifference to stylistic vogues was one aspect
of his sincerity.

sequitur?

In 1904 Paul Landormy conducted a series of interviews with composers
and academicians on "The Present State of French Music." Unfortunately,
Fauré was not one of the respondents. However, Henri Duparc's extensive
response touches our inquiry directly, for in it he renders explicit the opposition between a sincere self on the one hand and various forces construed
as external to this self on the other. We shall see that he and Fauré seemed
to share kindred views of self-expression and sincerity in music:

> For me, the musician speaks his own language in writing music and should
> not concern himself with anything but expressing his soul's emotions to
> other souls; music that is not the gift of oneself is nothing. In other words,
> the musician who, as he writes a work, worries about belonging to such and
> such a school – he may be a skillful craftsman, but he's no more than that . . .
> There are certain works that have no need to be either archaic or modern,
> because they are beautiful and sincere.[14]

A historical understanding of sincerity in French music hinges on this distinction between true self-expression, which may reveal itself by any style,
and the superficial expressions of a scattered, externally affiliated consciousness. Indeed, Duparc clearly implies that sincerity, as a factor in artistic
activity, outstrips all matters of mere style, which are subordinated to it.
Once a style, be it modern or traditional, becomes identified with a clique,
an institution, or the compositional model of a leading creative figure, it can
become an obstacle to sincerity. Imitators and disciples, in their zeal to
embrace a ready-made solution or adhere to a dogma, run the risk of betraying their own personalities; in scuttling their souls' own emotions, they
resemble those unnamed composers Dukas opposed to Fauré and described
as striving to "rise above themselves" rather than attending to their own
"inner harmonies." To convey "the deep sincerity of Fauré's art," meant,
therefore, invoking his autonomy as an artist: "belonging to no school, he
has no dogma but the search for beauty."[15]

The testimony of Fauré's contemporaries affords us a clear view of his
identity as a "sincere artist," and Fauré's brief comment to his wife about the
"translation of a personality" fits into the general conception of artistic sincerity I have tried to reconstruct from these more detailed accounts.

However, in order to enrich this image we should like to know better how Fauré himself understood sincerity in music. From his pen – so reluctant to theorize – we have only one description of sincerity more elaborate than the one that began this section. But we also have the evidence of his teaching, to which this other document is tied.

Fauré took over Massenet's class in composition at the Conservatoire upon the latter's resignation in 1896. At various times between 1896 and 1905, Fauré could count Ravel, Florent Schmitt, Nadia Boulanger, Émile Vuillermoz, Georges Enesco, Charles Kœchlin, Jean Roger-Ducasse, Alfredo Casella, and Louis Aubert among his students. By all accounts, Fauré seems to have instilled in them an uncompromising loyalty to their own individual tendencies. In an interview with Jean-Michel Nectoux, Boulanger conveyed the special quality of Fauré's teaching, which she considered from an almost ethical point of view:

> Liberal, to be sure, Fauré was liberal in the highest degree. I would say he had a profound sense of respect. Respect for himself and for others, respect for things and beings; respect he would show us, as if the very thought of influencing us had never even occurred to him; a respect that was his alone and that acted upon us and made us more conscious of "being" . . . We were aware of his desire to understand us and to say to each one whatever would allow him to find his own way more easily.[16]

Vuillermoz similarly stressed that his teacher never tried "to impose the seal of his own personality" upon his pupils. "His principal concern was, on the contrary, to allow the individual qualities of the young creators in his care to develop freely. He helped them when they were in trouble, but allowed their personal temperaments to assert themselves."[17] The testimony of Louis Aubert was the same: "We listened to him, we loved him, we were grateful to him for placing no constraint upon our emerging personalities."[18] In the late 1890s, such liberal practices were far from universal in France's conservatories. Composers, critics, and educators of the period often made a point of contrasting Fauré's openhanded approach with the methods of his more conservative predecessors at the Conservatoire. But more significantly, Fauré's program seemed liberal even beside that of his younger and more loudly innovative colleague, Vincent d'Indy. D'Indy had instituted a pioneering systematic and historical curriculum at the Schola Cantorum. At the same time, however, his outward pedagogical attitude remained autocratic, and critics of the period did not hesitate to compare him to a soldier of Christ leading the Church Militant.[19]

In 1899, after one of Fauré's students, Florent Schmitt, made an unsuccessful bid for the Prix de Rome, Fauré wrote an illuminating letter to

Schmitt's benefactor, Madame de Chaumont-Quitry. This is the second meditation on sincerity and artistic vocation we have from Fauré. He begins the following paragraph with reference to Schmitt, but he soon shifts to a more personal perspective.

> For my part, I would try to allay his worries about finding a direction, a path. His artistic conscience alone should guide him, the desire for expression in sentiment and perfection in form, without concern for immediate or distant success . . . To express what you have within you with sincerity and in the clearest and most *perfect* terms possible would always seem to me the summit of art.

As if embarrassed to have caught himself in a moment of speculation, Fauré immediately added, "But that's so simple it must seem foolish!"[20] Fauré here made a rare profession of artistic faith. He delicately cast doubt on the value of eyeing success or trying too hard to stand out. These worries on Schmitt's part, he implied, were premature and moreover generally at cross purposes with the finer goals named in the next sentence: sincerity, clarity, and perfection. Of these three qualities, sincerity is certainly the most distinctive, and it made for a valuable lesson as Fauré's students began their careers.

We can trace the profound consequences of Fauré's position in a letter Kœchlin wrote to Fauré on 15 June 1921. Kœchlin had just dedicated a violin sonata to his old teacher.

> I wanted to dedicate to you only a work in which I felt, genuinely, I had put something of myself, in a language of my own – and *music* nevertheless. Whether I managed this, the future will decide. For an artist the essential thing is to have written his work, to have done his best. And I can say that I never had before me a more perfect model . . . than that of your works. Not that I claim, in my sonata, either to match them or to imitate them; but they have enlightened me with their serene light and their absolute sincerity, which is to make the music one loves.[21]

This letter testifies to Fauré's success in transmitting his artistic values, built on sincerity, to his students. For Fauré and his circle, music is a translation of the self; the composer does best when he "makes the music he loves." Significantly, Kœchlin acknowledges Fauré's work as a model – but an ethical model rather than a stylistic one. He denies the act of imitation, technical mimicry, and invokes instead a luminous emanation, symbolizing the spiritual value of sincerity. I spoke earlier of the conflation of morality and aesthetics in this milieu: now it is clear that as an ethical value transposed into creative action, "sincerity" essentially left the composer free to choose his own stylistic means. As Fauré put it, "Every artist [is] free to translate his thought, his sensibility, by the means it pleases him to choose" (above, p. 12). Hence, further on in this same letter, Kœchlin explains his stylistic experiments in terms of his own sensibility. He disdains other pretexts for novelty and rejects innovation as an end in itself: "You know, of course, that in every instance I have only written harmonies or developments because they corresponded to the expression of what I felt – never to astonish the gallery or to strive for something more or less *new*." By emphasizing the idea of sincerity rather than laying down a particular stylistic doctrine, Fauré tried to show his students that the best music gives "the gift of oneself." Sincerity, exemplified in a constructive and tolerant approach to the development of his students' unique musical personalities, was perhaps the most valuable legacy of Fauré's teaching.

2 Why sincerity?

We are now in a position to consider how sincerity became a central aesthetic category in Fauré's time and why. One way to determine the significance of sincerity in musical practice is to identify what it opposed: what would constitute *insincerity* in composition?

In the foregoing discussion we already glimpsed some of sincerity's negative counterparts. Dukas referred dimly to those who "did their utmost to rise above themselves"; Debussy deplored any timid submission to authority or convention; Duparc considered the obedience to schools or trends beneath the dignity of a real composer; and Kœchlin rejected innovation as an end in itself. A common motive stands behind all of these faults: to try to be what one is not. For a particular shade of this deception, turn-of-the-century French society found a new word, *arrivisme*, and it is the *arriviste* who most often plays the foil to the sincere artist.

According to Robert's dictionary, an *arriviste* is an unscrupulous person who wants to make his mark in the world by any means that suit his purposes. The word, derived from the verb *arriver*, made its first appearance in 1893; within ten years the inevitable suffix came to consecrate it: *arrivisme*.[22] I can think of no illustration of *arrivisme* better suited to the present discussion than Proust's trenchant depiction of Charles Morel in *Le côté de Guermantes*. Marcel, the narrator, one day receives a visit from a young man, Morel, previously unknown to him. He is the son of Marcel's late uncle's personal manservant but looks nothing like a servant himself. He dresses "rather more lavishly than in good taste" and is quick to introduce himself, with a satisfied smile, as a "premier prix du Conservatoire." After a bit of conversation, Marcel sizes up his guest:

> I realized that Morel's son was very "arriviste." Hence that very day he asked
> me if I, being a bit of a composer myself and capable of putting a few lines to
> music, might not know of a poet really well-positioned in the upper crust
> [*dans le monde "aristo"*]. I named one. He didn't know this poet's work and
> had never heard his name, which he jotted down. Well, I found out that soon
> afterward he wrote the poet to tell him that, being a fanatical admirer of his
> works, he had set a sonnet of his to music and would be happy if the librettist
> would arrange a performance of it at the salon of Countess so-and-so. This
> was jumping the gun a bit and giving away his game. The poet, offended, did
> not respond.[23]

This passage is especially felicitous in the way it binds Morel's social climbing to his shallow understanding of his vocation as a composer. These, of
course, are opposite sides of the same coin. Morel, in his work as in his social
conduct, is an *arriviste* because he composes music at profit to himself and
with self-promotion first in mind.

Albert Bertelin, who knew Fauré from 1897 onward, wrote in a memoir,
"Any new endeavor, every step forward, elicited his sympathies, but he did
not like *arrivistes*."[24] Fauré himself used the neologism as early as 1910, in a
letter deploring "this era of operators [*faiseurs*] and *arrivistes*" in contrast to
the "noble, disinterested career" pursued by his father-in-law, the sculptor
Emmanuel Fremiet.[25] And in the very last letter he wrote, he tried to console
his wife with the thought that he – like her father, Fremiet – would die
having followed a "disinterested career" and having left behind the "pure
beauty" of his works. "In these hard times, *nonetheless shot through with
arrivisme*, doesn't all that count for something?"[26] Fauré implicitly opposed
a "disinterested career," here engaged in the pursuit of "pure beauty," to
arrivisme. The fictional Morel exemplifies the "interested" career, pledged to
something more immediately profitable than "sincerity" or "pure beauty."
Such artistic tradesmanship provoked Debussy's ready indignation, too, as
early as 1912, when he delivered a long reproof to composers chasing after
fashion and formulas rather than looking for music within themselves.

> You learn to crawl before you walk. This is something our epoch of frantic
> "arrivisme" deliberately forgets as it stockpiles works that serve only to fulfill
> the need to satisfy a fashion, necessarily unstable. And to think how many
> "arrivistes" haven't even "left" yet! When will we decide to shatter the idea, all
> too current, that it's as easy to be an artist as a dentist? . . . Let us try to relieve
> music, not of those who truly love her, but of those who would profit from
> her by usurping the good name of artists![27]

In a memoir written in 1923, Edouard Dujardin would make the conceptual opposition between sincerity and *arrivisme* explicit. Writing about the

era of the *Revue wagnérienne* (1885 to 1888) in France, he separated the young composers attracted to the Wagnerian cult at the Concerts Lamoureux into two categories: "Around Lamoureux gathered . . . most of our Wagnerians, young composers, the sincere ones and the *arrivistes* alike." Dujardin characterized the latter as "able to see in Lamoureux only the man who would play their pieces in concert, the man who would become the director of a great musical theater."[28]

Dujardin provides an example of a retrospective application of the word "arriviste." He wrote at a moment when *arrivisme* was at high tide, the *années folles* of the early 1920s. Arguments about *arrivisme* came into full prominence only after 1918, in the wake of a war that changed the direction of artistic tendencies and altered social structures. Paul Landormy, looking back on these years, wrote: "This was no longer the age of works pondered for many years, patiently polished and repolished. This was not the time for unhurried careers that bring a man glory in his old age or in the grave . . . The rush to success was general . . . Art took on an aggressive aspect it had never presented before."[29] While we might immediately presume that only the older and more conservative artists opposed this atmosphere of self-promotion, there was no clear-cut generational division. For instance, the cubist painter and poet Max Jacob, associated with Picasso and Apollinaire, had as little patience as Fauré or Debussy for *arrivistes*. When asked to define the nature of sincerity in artistic expression, Jacob responded, "Sincerity is a faith, a conviction in direct opposition to the charlatanism of the brigaded parties of pictorial *arrivisme*."[30]

Brash personal ambition, often designated by the word "tapage" – blatant or noisy publicity – certainly troubled composers and critics alike, but self-promotion, albeit louder than before, was hardly a newcomer to the Parisian musical scene. Not merely ambition, therefore, but relentless stylistic change, the displacement of one trend by another in quick succession, disturbed the atmosphere most momentously. Jacob's reference to "charlatanisme" – quackery – reveals the most notable consequence of this condition: the sense that a certain amount of new music perpetrated its novelty under false pretenses. These pretenses came in various shades: straining for effect, playing to the gallery, doting on fashion or convention, seeking to astonish – critics varied their accusations from case to case. Writing a preface to Georges Jean-Aubry's *La musique française d'aujourd'hui* in 1916, Fauré assessed this stylistic fragmentation coolly but also included a passing reproach:

> Under the favorable conditions of a continuing, voluptuous peace, which we
> believed could never be disturbed, a number of artists consumed by the fever

of the new, created – one after another, in the wake of impressionism –
intentionism, cubism and more, while certain musicians, less daring, tried to
suppress *feeling* in their works and substitute *sensation* in its place, forgetting
that sensation is in fact the first stage of feeling.[31]

Incidentally, those who recall no artistic movement by the name of intentionism ("intentionnisme") are not wrong. Fauré wryly cited a fictional
trend, which he borrowed from a speech Gounod delivered to the Institut
on 20 October 1883.[32] More pointed is Fauré's distinction between "feeling"
and "sensation," whereby he implies that sacrificing feeling to sensation
means sacrificing something deeply experienced to immediate, superficial
effects. Rather than moving to a direct affirmation of this point, however,
Fauré then seems to leave it aside; he begins a new paragraph, wondering
aloud if the crisis of war might not "restore us to ourselves." But this sentence, beginning so abstractly, then goes on to name "sincerity" and "the
disdain of grand effects" among the virtues that will contribute to the
renewal of French music after the battle. Fauré's critique of charlatanism in
music thus, as we should expect, takes aim at artists who calculate sensa-
tional "effects" instead of sincerely expressing a personal sensibility.

It is well to remember that a general crisis of personal autonomy in stylistic choice beleaguered artists long before the First World War. Fauré, with
his reference to "intentionism," slyly linked his own position back to
Gounod's. The older composer was far less lenient toward society than
Fauré and took it upon himself to criticize a number of "current opinions
. . . that form the immense heritage of accepted absurdities." Among these
"is one that consists in believing, or rather in making people believe, that
the sympathy and protection of society are necessary for an artist to *succeed*
[*arriver*] . . . There is only one protection that an artist should get worked
up about, for it is the only one worth any trouble at all, and that is absolute
sincerity toward oneself."[33] Sincerity was a key issue for Gounod, who in his
thinking on this topic may have been more Fauré's mentor than Saint-Saëns,
who seldom spoke of sincerity.[34]

In the presence of drastic stylistic fragmentation, the motivations of compositional choices readily came under suspicion. Establishing whether a
composer's motives were sincere or not became a routine practice in private
letters as in public criticism. Artists and critics began to wonder more
openly about the relationship between style and personality. Oscar Wilde,
whom Jean Pierrot has called "the prime theoretician of French decadence,"
early on recognized the fragile nature of artistic personality but manifested
this recognition by adopting a paradoxical attitude toward sincerity.[35] To
this end, he went out of his way to represent personal identity as fundamen-

tally malleable. *In*sincerity, he pointed out, "is merely a method by which we can multiply our personalities."[36] Put into artistic practice, insincerity would abolish the very idea of stylistic consistency and blur beyond recognition authentic reflections of the artist's personality in his work. To imagine this practice is therefore to imagine the overthrow of two of the most cherished principles of traditional (romantic) European aesthetics. Wilde, for all his speculation, remained on the outskirts of such a radical undertaking. Indeed, he did not hesitate to counter his own aphorisms. He brought the value of insincerity into question most forcefully in *The Picture of Dorian Gray*. "There is no such thing as a good influence, Mr. Gray," says Lord Henry. "All influence is immoral . . . because to influence a person is to give him one's own soul. He does not think his natural thoughts, or burn with his natural passions . . . He becomes an echo of someone else's music." Dorian Gray, the allegorical victim of the influences that finally consume his being, vividly personifies insincerity and certainly bears out Lord Henry's ironic warning. Similarly, we might say that a composer who works against his "inner harmonies" or who too slavishly follows in the steps of others risks becoming an echo of techniques and ideas absorbed from outside himself: the reverberation of someone else's music. Lord Henry therefore concludes, "The aim of life is self-development. To realize one's nature perfectly – that is what each of us is here for."[37] His sermon, of course, could not be more ironic. He urges self-development but divulges no solution to the fundamental problem – how to "realize one's nature perfectly" in a world of influences that tell us how to represent ourselves to ourselves. This paradoxical condition renders all appeals to the artist's "true self" incalculable; the self is already an echo of other selves. Wilde thus swiftly brings the very idea of sincerity to an abyss. Once sincerity itself qualifies as a pose, another "method by which we can multiply our personalities," we can go no further with the concept. But musicians of the period kept clear of pushing the concept to this extreme, perhaps because, as we begin to see, it was much too valuable to them.

Their apparent lack of sophistication came down to self-preservation. By the end of the war, those who wished to advocate recent music found themselves at pains to justify novelty of any kind. Certainly a large proportion of the public felt itself at a loss to distinguish the sincere artists from the posers and looked to musical authorities for guidance. Kœchlin, in his important contribution to the *Encyclopédie de la musique*, "Les tendances de la musique moderne française" (1921), confronted this problem directly. In the course of justifying polytonality as a legitimate musical procedure, he wrote,

> With new works, the public goes from one extreme to the other . . . "They are
> making fools of us," we hear over and over again, until one day people
> suddenly declare, "This is sublime" . . . Contemporary harmonies will often
> seem disconcerting – even to more than one professional colleague. However,
> let no one suppose that these inventions are some kind of bad joke; let no
> one think that the best of these composers wish to astonish the gallery. They
> do not lack sincerity.[38]

Kœchlin consistently defended novelty as a means of *personal* expression.
However, as we know, he disdained novelty as an end in itself, or something
gauged to shock the bourgeoisie.[39] A composer who resorts to novelty in
order to astonish his audience also does so in order to draw attention to
himself. He becomes an *arriviste*. In his excessive concern for public
response, he introduces obstacles between his inner life and his music. The
translation he produces will be muddled.

We may conclude that a style can, at opposite extremes, either represent
a personal sensibility sincerely translated into music or a superficial preoccupation with fashion and success. Fauré's contemporaries consistently
laid his musical style at the first of these two extremes. In the twentieth-
century musical press his work figured continuously as an achievement
that managed to be both novel and "sincerely translated" at the same time.
This coupling proved a decisive signifier of permanent musical value. In
1921, Kœchlin could look back upon Chabrier, Debussy, and Fauré as
masterful innovators, but their modernity was admirable because it was
sincere. In each of these composers, there was "an unaffected quality, especially free of self-importance, that never strives to show off erudition or
modernity." They achieved something new, yet, again, "they wrote what
they loved."[40]

Fauré's unassuming personal character and constructive leadership in
musical life only enhanced this reputation. "Never was there an artist more
hostile to puffery, to publicity, to all forms of self-exaltation, than Fauré,"
said Camille Bellaigue, who was intimately acquainted with Fauré's private
and professional conduct.[41] On the other hand, a critic who apparently
never knew Fauré intimately but who followed his career and recognized the
value of his work at the Conservatoire gave a similar appraisal:

> Rather more heedless than disdainful of publicity (so foreign was the very
> thought to his relaxed sense of spiritual self-respect), he created his work
> simply, without public fanfare, handing on the greater part of it to a
> publisher who never bothered much with it, and glory came to him without
> accessory, commanding attention little by little, everywhere, and not without
> amazing Fauré himself. This great artist was indeed strangely modest . . . No
> career was ever more devoid of *arrivisme*.[42]

Of course, the eulogistic tone of these passages cannot be ignored; Marnold and Bellaigue each made their observations very shortly after Fauré died. It is therefore important to find similar testimony at least as early as 1887, when Hugues Imbert interviewed Fauré and produced a lengthy critical and biographical notice, the first such essay devoted to the composer. In the first paragraph Imbert asserted, "If ever a man held publicity in high contempt, and kept his distance from all compromises with questionable public tastes, it is Gabriel Fauré." Imbert added, "He pursues his goal with true passion, without the slightest care for the world's opinion."[43] It is significant that Imbert did not choose to underscore this artistic attitude in his studies on Saint-Saëns, d'Indy, and others included in his *Profils de musiciens*. We may adduce a second example from the following year. In a review of Fauré's Requiem, Camille Benoît drew attention to the "personal imprint" Fauré gave his work, contrasting it with the music of those "malleable servants of prevailing taste" who "attune themselves to fashion" and "received ideas" – by which Benoît meant the music that the affluent, fashionable parishioners of La Madeleine were more accustomed to hearing.[44]

Fauré was still an obscure figure in 1888. When he was named to replace Dubois as Director of the Conservatoire in 1905, his position in musical life changed dramatically; he was launched into public, even national, notoriety. In these changed circumstances, his enduring personal modesty became something really unusual. At the moment of the nomination, Alfred Bruneau expressed pleasure at the sudden recognition it brought Fauré. That social and institutional ambitions had played little role in Fauré's preceding career evidently intensified this satisfaction. "None of our composers better warrants universal and fervent admiration than Gabriel Fauré. Without ever sacrificing anything to fashion, snobbery, puffery, or the peremptory needs of the throng; without ever lowering himself to covet, seek, or beg for cheap success, he built the edifice of his music patiently and honorably."[45] The next year, Pierre Lalo, reviewing the composer's new quintet, likewise saluted Fauré's sustained resistance to the enticements of fashion and publicity.[46] Over the next fifteen years such observations would become predictable yet continued to carry great authority; the perception that Fauré had achieved what he had done without compromising his personal and artistic integrity spoke directly to the preoccupations of an age increasingly fraught with *arrivisme*.

Many held up Fauré's disinterested career as a sane exemplar for younger composers in the frenetic twenties. Among such advocates, Kœchlin was perhaps most outspoken. We should recall that Kœchlin, four years Debussy's junior, was one of the most broad-minded musicians of his generation in France. The young Poulenc, spurned by Paul Vidal and unable to attract Ravel's interest, found a sympathetic teacher in Kœchlin, as did Henri Sauguet and the so-called École d'Arcueil that formed around Satie in 1923. Kœchlin wanted these exuberant twenty-year-olds to reflect on their own creative inclinations, to pursue their vocation sincerely rather than thoughtlessly committing themselves to the latest trend. In this he found the ideal model in his own teacher, "never donning a mask, never striving for effect, never wishing to seem anybody but himself."[47] During these years Kœchlin developed his own calling as a teacher and proposed a course of action to those who would listen to him. He spoke of "the moral quality of an art created by the artist for himself, for the sake of music, without concessions either to the tastes of the moment or to personal vanity."[48] In his biography of Fauré, published in 1927, he passionately maintained the uselessness of ignoring individual sensibility or bowing to the dictates of fashion:

> This kind of "novelty" declares itself the very opposite of art, since it is neither felt, nor created, nor personal . . . All lasting beauty is born, lives and survives – eternal, *outside of fashion*. The artist wants an aesthetic diametrically opposed to that of a "man of the world" whose eye (temporarily) becomes accustomed to some baroque line or illogical distortion, ugly in itself, simply because it is *chic* . . . If [Fauré] did not seek to retreat from all the trends that excited discussions among the snobs, which would have been a slavery in reverse, at least he was never pulled in by their undertows.[49]

This independence from fashion and public opinion leads to a focus on the work itself, on the composer's "inner harmony" and that "pure beauty" of which Fauré spoke in his letters. The composer should write his music "for the Muse alone, for pure beauty, for a dream of something better and of the beyond"; he should not look to the public or his colleagues, but proceed aloof to critics and future success. "Think only of the work, do not fear simple and modest means, be yourself" – this was Kœchlin's Fauréan message to a new generation of artists.[50]

Another student of Fauré's, Émile Vuillermoz, reviewing a new work by his former teacher in 1921, took the opportunity to admonish a group of young composers whose activities struck him as less than disinterested:

> At the present moment, when hasty innovators are turning aesthetics topsy-turvy in order to discover, faster than their rivals, the unknown treasure destined to enrich them, the Piano Quintet [Fauré's op. 115] brings us a wise reminder . . . In these four movements there are more victorious annexations [to modernity] than in all the trophies currently brandished by certain apprentices in music, anxious to organize a profitable revolution for their own benefit.[51]

Vuillermoz probably intended this sharp critique for "Les six," then at the height of their antics. No doubt the collaborative venture *Les mariés de la tour Eiffel*, organized by Cocteau the summer beforehand, had irritated Vuillermoz, who saw more love of self-advertisement than of art in such stunts. However, it is well known that "Les six" existed on the pages of a newspaper far more cohesively than in life. After their musical outfit had its brief heyday under Cocteau, each member of the group found (or returned to) an individual path. Had Vuillermoz gone to the trouble to interview Honegger, Milhaud or Auric, he would have found himself preaching to the converted. Milhaud, for example, who had been a student of Dukas and Gédalge at the Conservatoire, never concealed his profound admiration for Fauré. As early as 1923 he published a homage more persuasive in presenting Fauré as a positive artistic model than anything Vuillermoz had written. In this essay Milhaud evokes the influences of Franck, Wagner, Debussy and Russian music and marvels at Fauré's stylistic independence amid the changing currents. "What do [all these] matter to him?" asks Milhaud. "Fauré simply lets his heart sing and gives us the tenderest, the *sincerest* music imaginable."[52]

The details of the preceding citations suggest that at least three sufficient reasons led Fauré's contemporaries to single him out as a sincere composer. First, he remained aloof to fashion, to trends he did not need in order to express himself. Second, he did not, at least in anyone's judgment, put his art in the service of vanity or personal gain. And third, he did not innovate in order to goad the public, but only in order to express himself, to translate his sensibility; he was modern by "inner necessity." Lest this final reason be dismissed as redundant pleading, let us remember that some composers in the first two decades of the century certainly did innovate in order to provoke the public, and many more ran the risk of the accusation. Between 1900 and 1914, Richard Strauss was frequently the object of such criticism. In the most insightful judgments, this reproach was usually tempered by a sincere expression of respect and even awe for Strauss's craftsmanship and power. Such was the case, for example, with the English poet and critic Arthur Symons. Writing in 1905, he wanted to be clear that it was not the modernity of Strauss's style that disturbed him:

> Strauss chooses to disconcert the ear; I am ready to be disconcerted, and to admire the skill with which he disconcerts me. I mind none of the dissonances, queer intervals, sudden changes; but I want them to convince me of what they are meant to say. The talk of ugliness is a mere device for drawing one aside from the trail. Vital sincerity is what matters, the direct energy of life itself, forcing the music to be its own voice. Do we find that in this astonishingly clever music?
> I do not find it.[53]

Symons did not go so far as to accuse Strauss of pandering to his audiences; rather he suggested that the composer acted on cravings whose motives were "elaborate, intellectual and frigid" rather than passionate and personal.[54]

Although we could wish that Fauré himself left more evidence of his attitude toward modernity of style and musical *arrivisme*, one final witness in this indirect account may help us better understand the implications of his basic principles. André Messager, like Fauré, received his musical training and general education at the École Niedermeyer. In fact, in 1871 he became Fauré's very first pupil. The two young musicians, only eight years apart, became close friends. As Fauré recalled, "Our initial conversations – I dare not say lessons – were enough to convince us that we were meant to be friends, and since that time, this friendship, I'm proud and happy to say, has never abated."[55] Messager wrote primarily for the stage and served as the administrator and conductor at various times of the Paris Opéra, the Opéra-Comique, and Covent Garden. Fauré, the master of song and chamber music, and Messager, the man of the theater, bequeathed very different legacies, but they both held sincerity at the core of their artistic values.

In the course of an interview held in 1928, a year before he died, Messager reflected on recent musical trends. His statements confirm that sincerity was a central category in his aesthetics and had a direct bearing on his judgment of new works:

> [The young composers] want to prospect new claims . . . Let us respect this
> endeavor and their efforts. Are they on the right track? I have no idea. I'm
> not keen on everything they're offering us, but who can assure me that *I* am
> not wrong? . . . People reproach the young for not bothering to study the
> rules, for rushing toward success [*d'être pressés d'arriver*], for grasping after
> money – it's all possible! But let's not forget: *we have built the rules on*
> *celebrated works and not the other way around.* Rules of composition are only
> empirical products. But styles change . . . I couldn't care less if one composer
> writes a "polytonal" piece while another writes an "atonal" one. What is
> essential is that the work be sincere; if so, who has the right to hinder his
> hopes, his sensibility, his tendencies? No one has the authority to discourage
> an effort or block the work of an artist.[56]

It is neither rash nor difficult to align this statement with Fauré's views. In effect, the last part of Messager's declaration echoes and elaborates the response Fauré made to *Le Figaro* when he was asked in 1905 to indicate his intentions as the new director of the Conservatoire:

> I should like to put myself in the service of an art at once classical and
> modern, sacrificing neither contemporary taste to salutary traditions nor

traditions to the whims of fashion. But what I advocate above all is liberalism: I would not wish to exclude any serious ideas. *I'm not biased in favor of any school and there is no type of music I'm inclined to ban, provided it springs from a sincere and considered doctrine.*[57]

Messager's testimony helps us to understand the consequences of Fauré's stated position. Of all the contributions the idea of sincerity could make to the vitality of French twentieth-century music, this tolerance for stylistic change was the most compelling. Behind the noble, eulogizing vapors that waft through critical discourses about Fauré, there is indeed something of substance. Fauré's and Messager's profound liberality clearly set them apart from contemporaries such as Saint-Saëns and d'Indy, both of whom, in very different ways, placed limits on the possibilities of musical expression by insisting on fixed principles of form and style. The concept of sincerity, on the other hand, places no definite limits on style or expression. It is neutral to style, and this crucial property accounted in no small part for Fauré's success with his students, his beneficent influence on musical life, and his high repute with composers as young as Auric and Milhaud, some fifty years his juniors. Thus Fauré's simple rhetorical question – "Isn't every artist free to translate his thought, his sensibility, by the means it pleases him to choose?" – proved extremely consequential. His question subordinates outward stylistic allegiances to a personal standard of beauty, and what counted for Fauré were the individual qualities of the resulting work. By upholding the idea of sincerity instead of insisting on a fixed stylistic doctrine, Fauré prolonged his own creative life through an era of great change; at the same time he broad-mindedly prepared a favorable ground for the self-determined development of younger composers. Saint-Saëns and d'Indy, on the other hand, however noble their intentions, each fatally undermined his own capacity to influence younger composers by demanding obedience to specific stylistic norms.[58]

As an aesthetic and ethical category, sincerity responded to some of the strongest issues forced on composers working after the turn of the century. Its practice meant that a new generation might find personal routes through a stylistic emporium whose attractions included both the risk of the new and the lure of tradition. Opposed to fashion, fads and self-promotion, sincerity did not ignore historical and social factors but rather placed them in a radically individual perspective. A composer who managed to discover a relation to past or present music by such personal means – that is, in Fauré's words, "with the help of his sensibility and in the measure of his gifts"[59] – was a sincere artist.

3 Questioning sincerity

I have tried to show how certain historical conditions made sincerity a key aesthetic category in French musical culture during Fauré's lifetime. Since these same conditions likewise affected the endeavors of writers and visual artists, the question of sincerity naturally entered a wide arena of debate. Indeed, far from being a parochial concern, sincerity in this period took on a general cultural significance that might be compared to present-day discussions of gender in personal and social identity. Beyond what amounts to a fixation on the question of sincerity among artists and critics, perhaps the most telling emblem of the weight the concept bore in French culture was the publication, between 1905 and 1920, of at least five books touching on sincerity or exclusively devoted to it by professional philosophers.[60] In the absence of such philosophical work, we might be tempted to assume that composers latched onto the category of sincerity as a convenient term of praise without reflection on its equivocal nature.

To a certain degree, nonetheless, this accusation is true. If we examine one of these treatises, Gabriel Dromard's *Essai sur la sincérité*, we encounter processes of reasoning and an attention to nuance and implication quite unlike anything met with in musical writings. Seeking the greatest possible clarity, Dromard makes his hypotheses explicit: "The man of an ideal sincerity would be one who would reflect, both within his own consciousness and in his modes of expression, the whole substance and nothing but the substance of his ideas and feelings; one who would translate everything he feels and everything he conceives fully and faithfully, before himself as before others."[61] On the one hand, this definition jibes with views of sincerity held by contemporary musicians and even turns on the same essential action: translation. On the other hand, Dromard brings in a crucial modifier – *ideal* – by which he indicates from the outset of his study that it is *not possible* to realize such perfect sincerity toward oneself. If we cannot be perfectly sincere with ourselves, it follows that we cannot be perfectly sincere with others. "How can we appear as what we are, when what we *are* does not square with what we *believe* we are? How can we express our inner realities faithfully when we can by no means place ourselves outside of *sham and imaginary representations of these realities*?" Dromard acknowledges that we mask parts of ourselves from ourselves in order to act in everyday life and concludes that "from this absolute point of view, we can say without hesitation that sincerity toward others is impossible since the very basis of this sincerity is neither realized nor realizable" (pp. 7–8). In this conclusion he seems to second Wilde's paradoxical view of sincerity. Of course, maintaining this line would abolish Dromard's object of speculation and bring his study to a quick halt. He therefore purposefully moves away from absolute principles and toward pragmatic ones. He wishes to move beyond the basic insight that certain kinds of self-delusion are inevitable in order to recognize "that scrupulous introspection guided by a deep love of truth should certainly attenuate them" (p. 9). This practical conception of sincerity therefore entails not a perfect representation of the subject's inner realities before himself and others, but an adequate one. "For want of *seeing ourselves as we really are*, we can at least *show ourselves as we believe we are*" (p. 9).

The detailed nature of Dromard's reasoning, barely even sketched here, might sanction the charge of unreflectiveness against the composers and critics we have been reading. Yet Dromard's conclusions effectively return us to a truly subjective idea of sincerity, whereby the composer creates "adequate" representations of his inner life by writing what he loves and feels most deeply. This conclusion is almost identical to what contemporary musicians professed unsystematically. But we did not blow the dust off Dromard's book for nothing, because his chain of inferences points up the outstanding element missing from all accounts of sincerity in music – their silence as to how composers could possibly express their inner realities faithfully when, as Dromard said, "we can by no means place ourselves outside of sham and imaginary representations of these realities." Even that brilliant doubter, Paul Dukas, neglected to ask whether sincerity in music is possible at all. Although Dromard's careful interrogation of the concept of sincerity does not undermine contemporary assumptions about its role in music, his detailed reasoning (the book is 242 pages long) shows what composers felt they could take for granted.

Significantly, many of their peers in literature did not share this blind confidence in self-representation.[62] We already know that Wilde swept aside the concept of sincerity, in life as in art, with his characteristic irreverence for conventional virtues. Among French writers, Valéry, training his keen intellect on the more specific question of sincerity in literature, reached similar conclusions. Indeed, the most lucid document ever to refute the notion of sincerity in literary art is probably his brief essay on Stendhal, written in 1927. Though Valéry confronts his theme in a rigorous spirit, it is not without mockery that he diagnoses Stendhal's resolve to make a "real voice" speak through his prose as something that "leads him to try to amass in a work all the most expressive symptoms of *sincerity*."[63] Valéry professes to find Stendhal's inflections "three or four times too sincere" and unflinchingly maintains that efforts to be "true" unavoidably result in self-betrayal:

The truth we like best is changed from this, under the pen, imperceptibly toward the truth that is made to seem true. Truthfulness and the will to truthfulness together make up an unstable blend in which a contradiction ferments and from which an adulterated product will not fail to result.

In literature the truth is not conceivable . . . Whether the nudity exhibited be that of a sinner, a cynic, a moralist or a libertine, it is inevitably clarified, colored and camouflaged according to all the rules of mental theater . . . Hence one writes the avowals of some other, more remarkable, more sensitive, purer, blacker, keener, and even more *oneself* than one can be, because the self has gradations. Whoever confesses lies, and flees the real truth, which is null, or formless, and, in general, indistinct.[64]

Valéry's severity does not merely flaunt his habitual delight in negation; behind this skepticism lies a constructive inference by which he posits choice rather than truth as the working foundation of literary expression. Literary texts may embody an astonishing range of personal representations, but these are "always *chosen*, and chosen as well as possible."[65] When a writer decides to "confess," he is forced to choose both what he does and does not confess and the words by which he expresses any avowal. The impossibility of determining the sincere essence behind such literary representations results from one of the most important conditions of creativity, namely, the luxury of selection from several possibilities.

At this point, we could infer Dromard's rejoinder to Valéry and protest that creative choice does not in itself make adequate representations of inner realities impossible. However, let us pass over this objection and simply take stock of the glaring ideological differences between Valéry and his musical contemporaries. Where Valéry demolished the idea of sincerity in literature, Fauré or Dukas deemed it not merely possible but indispensable. These two positions, in their cultural co-existence, seem to present a paradox. Yet among contemporary French musicians there was a unique voice, a composer who spoke against the idea of sincerity in music and whose blatant dissent allows us better to understand this puzzling disparity of positions. Ironically, this voice belonged to one of Fauré's own students, Maurice Ravel.

While interviewing Ravel in 1927, the American critic Olin Downes made passing reference to the question of a composer's sincerity. Ravel remarked, "I don't particularly care about this 'sincerity.' I try to make art."[66] Ravel expressed his contempt for the idea of sincerity several times between 1924 and 1931. This brief comment already reveals the gist of his reasoning, which opposes two predicates: sincerity and art. Artists properly concern themselves with the latter, not the former; for Ravel, the pursuit of art remains as indifferent to sincerity as it does to created nature.

Sincerity, as we already know, may be defined so as to serve or oppose a variety of conditions and causes. For Fauré, Duparc, Debussy, and others, the opposite of a "sincere composer" was one disastrously enslaved to things outside of himself (in particular, conventions and fashions), or for whom vanity and self-promotion motivate creativity. Ravel understood sincerity differently. He equated it with facile spontaneity and believed it a false constraint on the prerogatives of artistic selection. Like Valéry, then, he considered choice the essential mechanism of artistic invention and valued it so deeply that he unabashedly preferred to present his own music as the fruit of artifice rather than of self-representation.

> I know that a self-conscious (and conscientious) artist is always right. I say self-conscious [*conscient*] and not sincere, because in the latter word there is something humiliating. An artist *cannot* be sincere. Falsehood, taken as the power of illusion, is the only superiority of man over animals, and when falsehood can claim to be art it is the only superiority of the artist over other men. When one allows oneself spontaneity one babbles and that's all.[67]

Ravel boldly acknowledged the artificiality of art – its power as a superior form of illusion.

In honoring the ideal of artifice to the exclusion of sincerity, Ravel aligned himself with two opponents of sincerity in literature with whom we are already familiar, Wilde and Valéry.[68] All three of these men made the notion of artifice central to their aesthetics, and this ideal, or the strategy behind it, tended to reduce sincerity to the instinctive or the natural. Ravel, accepting this reductive definition of sincerity, rebuffed it as a potential danger to art. "I consider sincerity to be the greatest defect in art, because it excludes the possibility of choice. Art is meant to correct nature's imperfections. Art is a beautiful lie."[69] Ravel echoes both the letter and the spirit of Wilde's beguiling dialogue on aesthetics, "The Decay of Lying," first published in 1889. In it, Wilde had entered an influential plea for the restoration of illusion to literature and art, which in his view had gone into shocking decline under the influences of Realism and Naturalism. "All bad art comes from returning to Life and Nature, and elevating them into ideals," he wrote. "Lying, the telling of beautiful untrue things, is the proper aim of art."[70] Yet even as Ravel echoed Wilde, he also signaled his rapport with Valéry. As I began to suggest a moment ago, in affirming "the possibility of choice" as the very foundation of creativity, Ravel anticipated Valéry's critique of Stendhal, written three years later.

Ravel, Valéry, and Wilde each combated established ideas about "naturalness" in art and artistic activity. Preferring instead to ground creativity in craftsmanship – a material practice – they laid stress on artifice or technique as the means to beauty and perfection. Although they held this aesthetic discourse in common, Ravel's repeated emphasis on the idea of "self-conscience" was peculiarly his own. By pitting sincerity against what is self-conscious, conscious, or simply conscientious in musical practice, he seemed to suggest that sincerity is akin to their opposite: the unconscious. Ravel's complaint against sincerity thus included an intellectual resistance to portrayals of musical creativity as a spontaneous and artless expression of the unconscious. Such ideas, we shall see, had their leading sources in the German metaphysical tradition, including the work of Schopenhauer and his disciples, a tradition introduced into France after 1880 and more widely known by the turn of the century. Ravel detested all veneration of spontaneity, which, as we see, he equated with babbling. He observed to the contrary that "in art, everything must be thought out," and sincerity only tends to abet "rambling and imperfect works."[71] Furthermore, the idea of music as a manifestation of *l'inconscient* would have been repugnant to Ravel because the French word can also mean "unwitting," "oblivious," or "unknowing": states of mind inimical to the self-conscious, conscientious, and fully knowing artifice of musical composition.

Yet if Ravel found "something humiliating" in sincerity, this awareness followed from his preference for a reductive definition. Sincerity, when viewed as spontaneous and unwitting egress of the self, certainly leaves much to be desired as a foundation for making art. Indeed, who would blame Ravel for feeling humiliated by such an idea? By making artifice and "falsehood" the "only superiority of man over animals," he seems to imply that sincerity is a habit of instinct best left to brutes and beasts. But it should already be clear the ideal of sincerity does not suppress self-criticism or painstaking craft. Those composers, like Fauré, who favored sincerity in musical practice understood it neither as a spontaneous effusion nor as a humiliating impediment to craft, but rather as a kind of spiritual progress, achieved over the course of a lifetime devoted to art. In the words of Jacques Rivière, "Sincerity is a never-ending effort to create one's soul as it is."[72] Neither facile nor spontaneous, the realization of such sincerity in art was itself a form of perfection, a spiritual practice, complementary to the material practice of craft. These distinctions allow us to see how Fauré and Ravel could both hold the idea of perfection at the core of their musical values even as they took opposite views of its relationship to sincerity. In disagreeing over sincerity, they responded to disparate meanings of the same word.[73]

When Ravel declared that "an artist cannot be sincere," he seemed to disallow the possibility of sincerity in art altogether, but apart from this single dictum, he otherwise more specifically insisted that sincerity leads to bad music ("rambling and imperfect works"). Since this latter and more frequent formulation evidently admits sincerity back into the realm of musical practice (albeit a defective practice) we are left to ponder a complication. If Ravel really meant to deny the possibility of sincerity in art completely, then his discourse against it would represent a viewpoint more radical than Valéry's, for, unlike Ravel, Valéry never extended his defiance of sincerity to all of art; he restricted his plea to literature. For Valéry, the barriers to sincerity seemed to lie in the very nature of language itself.

> The sincerest man in the world, expressing what he has seen, and singularly, what he has seen in a realm where he alone was able to see, inevitably taints the conditions of sincerity *merely by the use of the common language*, whose segmentation into *words* within the forms and combinatory laws of syntax joins its distortions to those, no less inevitable, brought on by the act of direct recollection.[74]

To generalize this rebuff to include music alongside literature would have been light work for Valéry. He certainly knew that musical works are conditioned by syntactic procedures, conventions and perceptual limitations of their own. But not only did he never propose any arguments against sincerity in musical practice, he appealed, as we shall see later, to music as a model for authentic feeling in poetry. Valéry was by no means the only thinker of the period to contest the idea of sincerity in literature, but he was probably the most explicit and unrepentant. That he of all writers would implicitly permit music a special compass, a reserve of self-expression forbidden to his own art, is significant.

   How is it that, despite Ravel's isolated efforts, and despite the cultural authority wielded by figures like Wilde and Valéry, the art of music placidly resisted the critiques that challenged the viability and possibility of sincerity in art or literature? I would propose that the extraordinary prestige music held in late nineteenth-century thinking allowed it to glide over such epistemological questioning noiselessly. As an art set apart from the others, music appropriated the trait of sincerity to itself and rarely incurred the charges brought against sincerity in literature. In the first two sections of this chapter we determined the nature of the composer's sincerity; we now need to concern ourselves with a major ideological foundation of those views – the *inherent sincerity of music*.

4 The sincerity of music

In nineteenth-century aesthetics, music was often given the privilege of transcending words. Music, in its non-representational aspects, was thought to break the confines of reason and intellectual signification intrinsic to verbal communication. The writer or poet who attempts to be sincere, we recall, "inevitably taints the conditions of sincerity merely by the use of the common language," with rules of syntax to be observed, and "segmentation into words." Valéry urges us to recognize that confession, in literature, means nothing more or less than deception, whose specific form is verbal fabrication. Turning this idea on its head, we would say that *whoever writes music, confesses,* and indeed returns exactly to that "real truth, which is null, or formless, and, in general, indistinct": the truth Valéry believed beyond the range of all literary confession. This drastic notional inversion ultimately informs René Dumesnil's explanation of sincerity in music (and with special reference to Fauré): "All music is a confession, an avowal. It cannot lie: it is transparent and cannot hide the innermost nature of the composer underneath the ambiguity of words."[75] The sincerity of music followed from what thinkers perceived as its indeterminate, almost unmediated character.

This contrast leads to a paradox, because music at once skips over the *precision* of all linguistic referents and yet does not fall prey to their *ambiguity* either. The alleged ambiguity – of words – would seem to be the imperceptible and fatal drift of "truth" beneath the pressure of the pen as it writes. Placed in the hand of a composer, however, this same pen seems to represent things unrepresentable in language and to do so loyally. In a study of musical aesthetics published in 1907, the French musicologist Jules Combarieu tried to get at the heart of this paradox. Combarieu gave music the privilege of "thinking without concepts" and of revealing the subject's inner personality:

> *To think without concepts*, not in order to discard the objects they represent, but on the contrary to penetrate them better; to dissolve this exterior personality encumbered with words and focused outwards, which masks and hides from us the inner depth of our own selves; to return to the state of nature, to the free determination of oneself, to the ingenuous and yet skillful play of our internal energies; to intellectualize the sensibility subtly and to reflect into the intelligence a diffused emotion, so as to produce, as it were, a delicate emanation from both – such appears to me to be the privilege of music.[76]

Given the lofty spiritual role Combarieu assigns to music, we might be tempted to view his work as a belated echo of Schopenhauer. Was it not Schopenhauer who most emphatically granted music the privilege of directly representing the affective life of man? We must acknowledge Schopenhauer's philosophical initiative, but at the same time we ought not let the familiarity of his views prevent us from looking beyond their influence to indigenous philosophical works, whose authors often asserted original ideas of more immediate consequence in French intellectual life. Combarieu interposes something distinctly foreign to Schopenhauer's aesthetics by asserting the reciprocal action of the intellect and sensibility in musical experience. This difference may appear slight, but it constructively enlarges the domain of music by subtly favoring music's capacity for "thought" over its role as a concentrated essence of "the will." This same recognition of intellectual processes is no less evident in Combarieu's brief definition of music as "the art of *thinking with sounds*."[77] Combarieu's effort to move in an individual direction becomes even clearer if we compare his work to that of Albert Bazaillas, whose *Musique et inconscience* appeared a year later, in 1908. Bazaillas, a professor of philosophy at the Lycée Condorcet, sought to remain earnestly and self-consciously loyal to Schopenhauer throughout the first half of his book:

> Music develops outside of all reflection or conscious intent: what is musical is spontaneous . . . Music allows us to experience the internal development of the sensibility, oscillating between two basic affective modes: pleasure and pain, calm and affliction; in its restless and unforeseeable progress it translates the contingent, irrational, and unstable elements at the root of all feeling . . . Music is not representational; it is not even imaginative; least of all is it speculative – music is purely emotional.[78]

Bazaillas posits an oscillation between different affective modes, but he suggests no communication between the intellect and sensibility. Indeed, his meticulous exclusion of all intellectual activity in favor of "purely emotional" causes evidently bars the very possibility of this exchange that so interested Combarieu, whom we may count among a number of French intellectuals who disputed both the overemphasis on emotional causes in Schopenhauer's writing on music and his exaggerations of musical spontaneity. In looking over Schopenhauer's metaphysical project, Combarieu thus firmly distanced himself from any "absolute Idea that exists prior to concrete realities and concepts" and refused to enter "that realm of clouds where, the mind, thinking to attain the first Principle that reveals the secret of things, only builds its own dream." Yet he also recognized that music presents the philosopher with a mysterious excess, something ineffable that cannot and should not be explained, lest it cease to be musical.[79]

Combarieu, in this endeavor to reshape the German idealist tradition, cuts a more representative figure than Bazaillas among early twentieth-century French aestheticians. Like most of his intellectual peers, Combarieu was especially loath to admit Schopenhauer's conception of the will. It is important to remember that by the time Schopenhauer's work began to make its mark in Parisian intellectual life, his disciple Eduard von Hartmann had already recast the idea of the will into something more general: the unconscious.[80] French philosophers and critics were quick to embrace this adjustment, perhaps finding in the very indefiniteness of the notion of the unconscious a handy incentive to intellectual variation. Indeed, with the persistence of such revisions and reshadings into the first decade of the new century, such phrases as "la vie intérieure" and "la réalité intérieure" found much greater favor than the less sonorous "inconscience." We find these two phrases, for example, scattered throughout Dromard's three books on sincerity. In musical criticism, an essay written by Adolphe Boschot in 1901 shows the same propensities. Boschot knew enough German philosophy to paraphrase Schopenhauer and Nietzsche when it suited him, but the words "volonté" or "inconscience" remain completely outside his own aesthetic vocabulary. Focused instead on "la réalité intérieure" and "l'intériorité" (in which he saw "the essential nature of music"), Boschot would write, "We may try to suggest this interior state by equivalents, by symbols or images, by verbal metaphors, but we will not convey it in its true reality; being musical, it is expressed through music."[81] In the general tide of prevailing terms, we may discern an ideological drift – a resistance to or refusal of the *abstractly impersonal* (the Will, with its disturbingly narrow scope for individual freedoms) in deference to the *ineffably personal* (a unique and profound interiority). This interiority, the cherished abode of the artist's "true personality," was the prime zone of contentions about sensibility and sincerity in French intellectual life. We begin to see why Valéry would have found it more difficult to deny sincerity to musical expression than to literary expression. Combarieu's call to self-determination, the divestment of masks, and his desire to bring the inner self up to scrutiny by abandoning an "exterior personality encumbered with words," together reveal the supreme value his culture ascribed to personal interiority and its access through music.

These same values informed the work of Henri Bergson, whose influence and immense popularity in France after the turn of the century would be difficult to exaggerate. Bergson's project highlights the degree to which musical experience could control nothing less than a philosophical methodology. Bergson wished to reveal and analyze those forms of consciousness he believed earlier philosophers, from Zeno of Elea to Kant, had neglected or distorted in their representations of human experience. For the most part, these earlier intellectual traditions had based their analyses of experience on spatial categories to the exclusion of temporal ones. Bergson, while acknowledging the constant interpenetration of time and space in lived experience, sought to build a counterdiscourse to the spatial tradition by making time the axis of his inquiry. It was certainly not divisible, measured time that seemed to Bergson to pose the most profound questions for human experience, but *la durée toute pure*, a temporality irreducibly continuous and heterogeneous, divisible only by changes in quality and not quantity. Of this *virtual* time the durations of our actual clocks cast only an undifferentiated shadow, a spatial and homogeneous representation.

Bergson further believed that ordinary language was inherently tied to spatial representations; no logical explanation would ever allow the subject to understand pure duration as an immediate datum of consciousness. Thus, Bergson, caught in a daunting paradox conceived within his own system, needed more than anything else to find a way to convey, in words, this very notion, pure duration, whose vital and distinctive mobility always freezes up under the cold scrutiny of spatial analysis. Yet if ordinary discourse can never comprehend *la durée pure*, thought Bergson, poetic utterance may sometimes approach it, and musical expression comes very close to resembling it. Aesthetic experience thus signaled a way out of his quandary. Because Bergson thought music possessed certain analogies with *la durée pure*, he constantly appealed to these analogies at critical moments in his writing. The very experience of listening to music sometimes stands in place of a proof we sense just beyond his possible articulation:

> Listen to a melody with your eyes closed and thinking of it alone, no longer matching the notes to an imaginary keyboard or page that might allow you to recall them one by one (for this allows them to become simultaneous and forfeit their ongoing fluidity in time to congeal in space): you shall rediscover undivided, indivisible, the melody or melodic fragment that you have thus re-invested in pure duration [*la durée pure*]. Now our inner duration [*durée intérieure*], projected from the first to the last moment of our conscious life, is something like this melody.[82]

The nature of pure duration is truly the stopping point in Bergsonian writing, what remains after all reasoning ceases. Musical metaphors allowed Bergson to elaborate what he could only begin to suggest by argument. Bergson's commentators have often remarked mistrustfully on the deftness with which he replaces analysis with analogy, but we must always remember that "the squandered wealth of his passion for metaphor" flows from the very source of his inquiry and its paradoxical method.[83] Bergsonian metaphors seek to guide us to the verge of the ineffable.

Within and beyond this communicative paradox, by which Bergson truly made music a surrogate for the unwritable, he regarded this art as a mysteriously adequate revelation of that same "inner life" which he, as a philosopher, wished to reach through speculative thought. Thus, in a discussion of music and philosophy with his colleague Lionel Dauriac, Bergson fixed on the latter's phrase, "la vie en profondeur," as denoting common ground between these two fields of knowledge:

> I think . . . we can give an exact sense to this expression. It designates that which art makes us experience at certain moments, and what philosophy – true philosophy – should make us experience continually. In this specific sense I would accept your comparison of philosophy to music.[84]

"La vie en profondeur," "la réalité intérieure," and "la vie intérieure" all play lexical variations on the same subjective interiority that once again returns us to the realm of music. When Bergson asks, "What makes the continuity of our inner life?" he finally answers, "Duration itself." Yet to convey the sense of this pure duration that forms the continuity of our inner lives, he resorts to a musical metaphor.[85] That is, when Bergson cannot represent his intuitions by argument or deduction, he struggles to reveal them in metaphors and thus induces a special order of speculation; he awakens that "fruitful perplexity" his disciple Vladimir Jankélévitch ascribed to musical experience. In this sense Bergsonian writing strives to imitate the very condition of music so as to glimpse human experience in all its essential fluidity, not analytically isolated and subject to spatial orderings, but pursued as "the indivisible and indestructible continuity of a melody whose past enters into its present and forms with it an undivided whole."[86]

In Bergson's philosophy we discover a double role for music. It both supplies a crucial metaphor for pure duration and vies with philosophy itself as a revelation of "la vie intérieure." Summoning a melody to sing this unrepresentable inner life for us in his prose, Bergson refers to musical experience in order to spur introspection. In this annexation of musical experience to philosophy Bergson primarily sought to illuminate "la vie intérieure" through a new temporal consciousness of reality, but he simultaneously entered the realm of sincerity. He gave music the prerogative of contact with a verbally unrepresentable interiority. It is most significant that Bergson always represents this inner consciousness as a melody, a metaphysical melody, "the continuous melody of our inner life, a persistent melody that will endure, indivisible, from the beginning to the end of our conscious existence." If we should doubt that this inner strain bears the sincere translation of a personality, Bergson's next words answer us. "Our personality," he concludes, "is precisely this."[87]

Bergson's work holds up a philosophical mirror to contemporary musical ideologies and gives a sense of their cultural suffusion. The essence of music, glimpsed on the threshold of the ineffable, seemed to lie forever beyond the grasp of definitive warrants. By predicating musical phenomena as both the source and manifestation of the composer's inner life – the musicality of his inner consciousness *and* its fluid translation – philosophers and musicians just about construed sincerity as an intrinsic property of musical creation. It is not surprising that these hermeneutic coils successfully safeguarded the idea of musical sincerity from negative critique.

Fauré himself once came up against the threshold of musical ineffability. While struggling with the material of his First Quintet, he wrote,

> So often the point where we are or the one we are aiming for is untranslatable. How many times have I asked myself what music is for? And what it is? And what I am translating? What feelings? What ideas? How can I express something of which I myself can give no account![88]

Like Bergson and Combarieu, Fauré sensed that music emanates from an inner reality whose depth resists explanation and to which we have only imperfect access. What he calls "untranslatable" is, of course, untranslatable into words; the absent account is verbal. In another letter, three years later, Fauré made his conception of music's prestige over words in this respect explicit. He explained to his wife that his music had no particular connections with external ideas or images, with one exception:

> It is only in the Andante of the Second Quartet that I can remember having translated – and almost involuntarily – the very distant memory of bells ringing, which at Montgauzy in the evenings . . . would reach us from a village called Cadirac when the wind blew from the west. Over this drone a vague reverie goes aloft, which, like all vague reveries, would be untranslatable *by literary means.* Yet isn't it often that something external thus lulls us into thoughts of a sort so imprecise that in truth they are not thoughts, and yet they are something in which we take pleasure? The desire for nonexistent things, perhaps. And that is indeed the domain of music.[89]

This testimony is utterly isolated in Fauré's writings, for only this once did he indicate an extramusical stimulus for one of his works. Coming from a composer who most characteristically expressed himself in the abstract realm of *musique pure*, this paragraph has the quality of a revelation. If we turn to the third movement of the Piano Quartet, op. 45, we can profit greatly by the insights Fauré afforded us (see Example 1). The droning fifths of bells, softened by distance, toll in the low register of the piano; in the viola, a vague reverie floats up, the pure interiority of a solitary voice: this would be a literal translation of Fauré's description. But Fauré contravenes this bifurcation of timbres by exchanging the instrumental roles further on

Example 1. Second Piano Quartet, op. 45, III, mm. 1–7.

(Example 2). In this striking mutation we have an example of Fauré's strong tendency to efface (dematerialize) any concrete impression: to move, as his view of music's phenomenal destiny suggests, toward "nonexistent things." Here, the violin's soft undulation amid plucked strings reproduces not the imagined sound of bells, as the piano did, but rather the musical idea first used to represent this sound. This passage, divested of its original echoic trappings, is truly the echo of an echo, a disembodied chiming filtered through that timbral interiority first intoned by the viola alone. Let us follow Fauré still further on this path, veering away from the "literally trans-latable" toward what music alone can represent.

Fauré began his Adagio by presenting two musical ideas in contrast with one another. The first example allows us to see how they differ in meter,

Example 2. Second Piano Quartet, op. 45, III, mm. 40–42.

mode, texture, and timbre. Indeed, these two phrases overlap only for a moment, as the viola begins to sing over the piano's dissolving arpeggio. Yet over the course of the movement these two elements gradually converge toward a magical synthesis that ultimately rests on a progressive "dematerialization" of the bells. The instrumental exchange shown in Example 2 marks only the first step in this process. Soon afterward, Fauré sequentially develops the initial tolling figure (marked with an open bracket in the examples) and thus displaces it still further from its origins in real or recollected vibrations (mm. 46–50, not shown). The tolling figure and the viola's alternately developed theme are fully reconciled only at the end of the movement, in the coda (Example 3). Fauré ushers in the coda by oscillating between an inversion of the tolling figure, newly harmonized with sevenths in the piano, and a threefold augmentation of the same inversion in the cello. Then, in an arrival (m. 101) whose opulence gives the lie to its motivic resourcefulness, this silky augmentation continues, and the muted strings unite their ethereal "bells" to the viola's first melody.[90]

Perhaps the most important point to bring away from this series of events is that the timbral etherealization of the bells goes hand in hand with purely musical processes – sequence, inversion, augmentation, and motivic fusion. This union allows us to rethink the meaning of "the untranslatable" in musical interiority, broadening it to include not only moods and reveries for which words fail, but also all those beautiful, specifically musical processes to which the other arts lack access.

If we return to Fauré's letter in this light – in the resonance of his Adagio – it becomes clear that any concessions to exteriority (for example, mimesis) remain slight beside his broader aesthetic designs. Fauré – while incidentally furnishing us the key to the atmosphere and virtual bells of his quartet –

Example 3. Second Piano Quartet, op. 45, III, mm. 94–102.

more significantly makes a claim for special expressive possibilities within the domain of music. In "thoughts of a sort so imprecise that in truth they are not thoughts," in things "untranslatable by literary means," Fauré recognized the stuff of musical imagination. He thus sanctioned, a year in advance, Combarieu's independent hypothesis that music "thinks without concepts." Music, in so doing, as Combarieu insisted, does not discard objects represented conceptually but rather penetrates them more profoundly, in a subtle intercourse between intelligence and sensibility. The virtual, reimagined, and fully spiritualized bells of Fauré's quartet bear out this idea, by which Combarieu urged an imaginative and personal journey into "the inner depth of our own selves" and the "ingenuous and yet skillful play of our internal energies."[91]

The broad dissemination of ideas about sincerity and musical interiority among Fauré's contemporaries would lead one to suppose that at least some of them would have been able to grasp his aesthetic intentions on the basis of his music alone. It is nonetheless surprising to discover just how transparently his most sophisticated listeners understood the process of creative translation. In the following excerpt, Reynaldo Hahn, freely speculating on Fauré's creative process in a lecture of 1914, came unbelievably close to what Fauré himself declared in his letter on the Second Quartet:

> His mind is attracted by a vision, by an image; his heart suffers a feeling; his refined sensuality thrills under the contact of an impression; immediately the emotion is translated into a musical formula, fixed in an instant; but soon reverie gains the upper hand, the image becomes general, the overtones of feeling reverberate, hum, and the inconstant dreamer, seduced by their echo, allows himself to be distracted and carried away.[92]

This sentence seems to follow the very trajectory of Fauré's Adagio, gliding from outside impressions into personal reveries and their echoes.

If we think back to the most objective element in Fauré's account, the tolling of distant bells, the word "extramusical" now rings false, the nature of the outside stimulus being musical at its source. Moreover, from a creative point of view, Fauré's recollection of a real past has become so distant that it persists only in the traces of a reverie, and music, this singular phenomenon, comes to deliver it on the threshold of the nonexistent. We nevertheless discern the presence of something more than pure music in the affective experience Fauré described to his wife. Memories of some unique atmosphere – that wind from the west, or perhaps, unspoken, the smells of wild grasses, glimmers of light on the high Pyrenees – drift back to him out of his childhood in Montgauzy. Something preceded Fauré's musical realization: the captivation of an unutterable and distant moment, suddenly and fleetingly recaptured.

It is difficult to think of such moments without invoking the name of one of Fauré's most ardent admirers, Proust, and his *A la recherche du temps perdu*. Proust plumbed the depths of experiences such as those Fauré associated with his childhood in Montgauzy – those moments when "something external . . . lulls us into thoughts of a sort so imprecise that in truth they are not thoughts, and yet they are something in which we take pleasure." When the novel's hero, Marcel, at a turning point in his vast narration, links the three great remembered experiences of his life together for the first time, he is guided toward this revelatory intuition by music, chiefly that of Vinteuil:

> Nothing resembled more than one of Vinteuil's beautiful phrases this peculiar pleasure I had sometimes experienced in my life, as, for example, before the bell-towers of Martinville or certain trees on the path to Balbec, or more simply, at the start of this work, in drinking a certain cup of tea.[93]

Indeed, it is Marcel's experiences with music that ultimately allow him to discover his true vocation as a writer. This great epiphany reflects Proust's declaration to Benoist-Méchin that music, besides being one of the greatest passions of his life, "ran like a golden thread through the whole of my *Recherche du temps perdu*."[94] At this moment in *La prisonnière*, however, the narrator's literary vocation has yet to be resolved. The ineffable beauty of Vinteuil's Septet affects him so deeply that he concludes that music reveals a person's irreducible individuality more authentically than any literature:

> This music seemed to me something truer than all known books. At times I thought that this was because what we feel in life not being felt in the form of ideas, its literary translation (that is, an intellectual one) accounts for it, explains it, analyzes it, but does not recompose it as does music, whose sounds seem to trace the modulations of our being, to reproduce that extreme inner point of our sensations, the part that gives us that peculiar rapture we rediscover from time to time and which, when we say "What a fine day! What beautiful sunshine!" we do not in the least communicate to others, in whom the same sunlight and the same weather evoke very different vibrations.[95]

We cannot fail to remark affinities between this passage and what Fauré wrote about his quartet. Like Fauré, Proust qualitatively differentiates a literary translation of lived experience from a musical one, the translation to which both artists accord a *purer* interiority. Furthermore, for Proust as for Fauré, this artistic insight, its pleasure or rapture, is born of a uniquely resonant outside impression, experienced and remembered: the bell-towers of

Martinville, the unforgettable sunlight of a certain day, or faraway bells tolling in the wind at Montgauzy.

It is significant that Proust often reflected Fauré's music back into the works of his fictional composer Vinteuil. But such specific interrelations need not absorb us at present. Fauré haunted the spiritual atmosphere and objective traits of Vinteuil's works not alone, but as part of a Proustian community of great composers, including Franck, Wagner, and Schumann. We are not chasing down the shadows of a specific phrase in Proust's fictional music, but rather asking what the whole phenomenon of musical creativity meant to him as a writer. The joyous phrases that conclude Vinteuil's Septet prompt in the narrator a subjective disposition whose grandeur seems to surpass any effort on our part to identify it with known works:

> I knew I would never forget it – this new shade of joy, this call to a superterrestrial joy. But would it ever be realizable for me? This question seemed to me all the more important because this phrase [of Vinteuil's music] had been the thing best able to characterize . . . those impressions that I would recover at distant intervals of my life as the landmarks, the starting points for the construction of a true life: the impression felt before the bell-towers of Martinville, before a row of trees near Balbec.[96]

Here, as in the thought of Combarieu, Bergson, and Jankélévitch, music frees up an extraordinary form of self-awareness, an introspection whose questionings will prove fruitful for Proust's narrator as he begins to glimpse and pursue his literary ideal. What especially fascinated Proust about music was its power to translate the concreteness of an impression of the world into a strangely true and immediate representation. Music miraculously closed the gap between the phenomenal sensuality of such impressions and their baffling ineffability:

> Like that cup of tea, so many sensations of light, the limpid clangors, the brazen colors that Vinteuil sent us from the world in which he composed, paraded before my imagination, insistently, but too quickly for me to grasp it, this certain something I might compare to the perfumed silkiness of a geranium . . . It was necessary to find in the geranium scent of his music not a material explanation, but the profound equivalent, the unknown and florid celebration . . . the way in which he "heard" and projected the universe outside of himself.[97]

In seeking this "profound equivalent" Proust turned away from "material explanation" and toward the composer's inner reality, the unique modes of expression by which the artist "projects the universe outside of himself." We infer that Vinteuil, like his historical doubles, in revealing "a unique world, one no other musician has ever caused us to see,"[98] expresses himself sincerely.

Of course, even as Proust honored music, he ultimately sought to appropriate its privileges to a literary enterprise. The moment the narrator of *A la recherche du temps perdu* resolves to write his story, to capture in words what tones have so often illuminated for him, music ceases to be an isolated miracle in Proust's aesthetics and becomes a working model for "the construction of a true life." Likewise, Bergson, despite his fascination with music, believed that the consummation of his own philosophical project would ultimately surpass all the arts in deepening our understanding of reality. Art shows us that "an extension of our faculties of perception is possible," but this is only a clue to the wider domain in which philosophy would bequeath "satisfactions comparable to those of art, but more frequent, more continuous, and indeed, more accessible to the multitude."[99] How could it be otherwise? It would stretch credulity to imagine that a philosopher like Bergson or a literary genius like Proust would strike the flags of their intellectual callings before the forces of music. Nevertheless, it was the art of music, with its profound correspondences with inner experience, its sincerity, that figured as an ideal model in both of their creative ventures.

Let us now consider the obvious but really significant fact that Vinteuil's great works are not operas, cantatas, or symphonic poems, but a sonata and a septet. Proust made Vinteuil a composer of chamber music for more than one reason, but among them we may single out the overdetermined ties between sincerity, aesthetic interiority, and pure music. If, as an art, music was an ideal medium of profound self-representation, then the more specific concept of pure music was the ideal within an ideal – "the most profound, the most 'inward' music imaginable," as Boschot said of chamber music.[100] Whilst music in general launches a return to the verbally inexpressible core of personal existence, music totally freed of words and imagery renders up the most unmediated, the purest possible expression of the artist's personality and sensibility. According to the precepts of early twentieth-century French thinking, *la musique pure* is music in supreme isolation from the representational and thus in profound accord with the spiritual. This is why Fauré designated chamber music and the symphony, the two exemplary provinces of "pure music," not as merely "sincere," but as "the *sincerest* translation of a personality." Likewise, Combarieu described the symphony as "a world of ideas untranslatable in words" and asserted that "when the work is strong and sincere, skillful and inspired, [all its details] foster a singular miracle, the miracle of expressing a personality."[101]

Like Fauré and Combarieu, Boschot willingly included the symphony alongside chamber music as an ideal manifestation of self-expression in music, but, in a significant refinement, he could not grant them absolutely equal status. After wavering a little, Boschot gave his preference to chamber music, and this choice reflected the special place chamber music generally held within the already rarefied domain of "pure music."[102] Kœchlin apparently took the same view, but, unlike Boschot, he imposed a defensible historical limit upon his thesis. He pointed to recent French music, to composers of Fauré's, Debussy's and Ravel's generations, who had cultivated pure music more continuously and successfully in chamber music than in orchestral music. In the latter medium, Kœchlin rightly observed, the role of programmatic and descriptive elements had come to dominate, while French chamber works remained untouched by them and thus truer to the idea of pure music.[103] The small number of players required for chamber music and its relatively limited palette of timbres also played a part in its ideological ascendancy. Timbral purity or intimacy, along with the focused sociability of the players and listeners gathered together, apparently rendered the chamber medium optimal for the representation of what was most personal in a composer's sensibility. Boschot said that such intimate works, "the expression of one soul speaking to another," require "an atmosphere of respect and sympathy, or better, friendship and affection."[104] Vuillermoz spoke of chamber music as if it could unmask the innermost secrets of a creator's soul:

> Chamber music has had the mysterious and uncanny prerogative of giving us an idea of what cannot be grasped and of directly revealing the rarest and worthiest aptitudes of a creative temperament. For the composer loath to reveal himself, a quartet is always a confidence if not a confession. From Beethoven to Ravel, we have never had a surer way to penetrate an artist's deepest musical intimacy, to know the scruples and enticements he scarcely avows to himself, to violate the mystery of his melodious soul . . . It would seem that the frail and penetrating voice of the strings thus isolated can only sustain an impeccable sincerity; with the first notes sounded by the four soloists, the mask most rigidly lashed to a countenance bent on a lyric drama or symphony falls, cut clean away by the hair of the bows.[105]

In his teacher's chamber music, Vuillermoz found "the essential Fauré." And when, fifteen years later, Fauré left as his final work a string quartet, published posthumously, it was predictable that critics would find in it "the keen and faithful evocation" of the "charm and goodness" that emanated from the man himself.[106]

Perhaps the most revealing oblation to pure music came not from a musician but from a poet. None other than Valéry clearly indicated non-representational art, and specifically pure music, as a model for the kind of expressiveness he was trying to realize in his own poetic work. Thus, in a special effort to frame his account of the birth of *La jeune Parque*, this poem with which he broke twenty years of artistic silence, he called upon the authority of a musical representation:

> Rather than literature, I would make the arts that reproduce nothing at all the objects of my satisfaction, the arts that do not counterfeit, that play only with our momentary qualities without recourse to our capacity for imaginary lives and the false precision we so readily grant them. These "pure" modes do not burden themselves with characters and events that adopt whatever is arbitrary and superficial from observable reality, which are the only things subject to imitation. On the contrary, these modes exploit, organize and compose the values of our sensibility's every strength, detached from all reference and all function as *signs*. Thus reduced to itself, the course of our sensations no longer has a chronological order, but a sort of intrinsic and instantaneous order that reveals itself by degrees.[107]

This expressive ideal, with its realization of an "intrinsic and instantaneous order," seems in all respects to aspire to the condition of Bergson's *durée pure*. Curiously, Valéry also adopts the Bergsonian strategy of averting further explanation by resorting to an example, which here, of course, is *la musique pure*, a "production of sensibility developed outside of all representation."[108] If Valéry deftly avoids the equivocal notion of sincerity as such, his reliance on the values of *sensibility* nonetheless implies his acquiescence to the idea of expressive authenticity in music. Because he so ruthlessly probed and rejected the concept of sincere self-representation in literature, such a concession to pure music must be considered extraordinary. Moreover, the art of music did not remain an untouched and abstract exemplar for Valéry but rather entered into his poetic practice. His two longest and most celebrated poems, *La jeune Parque* and *Le cimetière marin*, were both guided in certain respects by a musical idea of "composition," a term much favored by Valéry because it allowed him to emphasize the "attractions of 'formal' sensibility prior to all 'topics'" – what pure music and pure poetry could hold in common.[109] Significantly, he described *La jeune Parque* as "a quest, literally boundless, for what could be done in poetry by way of analogy to what is called 'modulation' in music."[110] In a parallel discussion of *Le cimetière marin*, he wrote of "striving to *compose* in the lyric domain." The abstract nature of such poetic composition is perfectly clear because Valéry directly compares his "lyric domain" to pure music: "I speak not of poems in which a narrative dominates and in which the ordering of events intrudes; these are composite works – operas, and not sonatas or symphonies."[111] In other words, his lyric compositions approach the non-representational purity of "sonatas or symphonies," and such "pure" productions of sensibility in music or poetry stand apart from works in which extrinsic elements intervene.

Valéry's persistent enthusiasm for an ineffable world of tone as a paradigm for lyric invention attests to the power of his culture's idealization of music, whose magnetism could charm even the most skeptical critics. Little wonder, therefore, that alongside eminent poets, novelists, and philosophers, composers themselves imputed an authoritative immediacy or candor to their own art. Fauré and his colleagues could think of music as intrinsically sincere because the premise of its linguistically unmediated character, already in place, effectively displaced the conceptual obstacles that critics associated with the idea of sincerity in other forms of self-expression.

Thus we have reached our conclusion and reviewed the principal evidence for "music's sincerity." We may understand why, of all means of artistic expression, *la musique pure* most perfectly embodied the trait of sincerity. For Fauré, who destroyed his only two symphonies, chamber music eventually became the fullest expression of pure music in his work. But we must not forget that Fauré himself did not bar any musical medium or genre from manifesting sincerity. Though pure music seemed to him its supreme abode, he thought that other kinds of music could attain to sincere self-expression as well. In an assessment of Messager, Fauré unwaveringly asserted that "there is no living form or medium to which a persistent, sincere genius cannot accord the eternity of Beauty."[112] In this precept, Fauré again showed himself more generous in his principles than many of his contemporaries. Messager, of course, wrote little in the way of pure music, but proved his genius in the ballet and comic opera. Fauré firmly believed that different creative personalities crave different forms of expression; each musician must "feel out the medium that suits him best, be it the theater or pure music."[113]

"The theater or pure music" – with this phrase Fauré deftly encompassed the range of musical expression by denoting what were thought to be its antipodes. Let us reconsider the differences between them as an epilogue to this section. Though Fauré loved the theater, many of his contemporaries distrusted it:

> In France, we cherish dramatic music too much. Dramatic music is an exterior and inferior type. It does not allow the artist to speak to us directly and freely express the beautiful spirit, the great spirit, that he must be, lest he be nothing at all.[114]

With these severe words, Duparc gave witness to a whole generation's residual exasperation with the musical ambience of the Second Empire, dominated as it was by the opera and ballet to the exclusion of all less spectacular media. Furthermore, even as chamber music and concert music struck deeper roots in Paris and, indeed, flourished by the end of the nineteenth century, musicians continued to view the theater with a mixture of reverence and consternation. The theater, an impersonal public space, a shifting scene of alluring masks and disguises that exhorts its creators, watchers and players endlessly to "multiply their personalities," was, after all, the place where Wilde had Dorian Gray venture his first great public act of insincerity.[115] Dramatic music, with its allures, became the most extreme endeavor by which one could measure the achievement of sincerity in self-expression. Debussy once said, "The theater offers favorable resources of gestures, cries, and movements that might come to the aid of an overwhelmed musician, but pure music does not offer a single prop to help him out of his difficulty."[116] If a composer of dramatic music can forgo such extrinsic props and rely wholly on his inner resources of feeling, his artistic sincerity will have withstood a formidable challenge indeed.

Hence critics often went out of their way to assert that Fauré "remained wholly himself" in his music for the theater. René Dumesnil wrote that Fauré was a true "musician of the theater precisely because he brings to the stage, without concessions to the supposed dramatic necessities, all his personal qualities, because on no account does he ever give up being himself."[117] With *Pénélope* – Fauré's decisive fulfillment as a composer for the stage – commentaries of this kind proliferated, and it is fascinating to see how contempt for "the supposed dramatic necessities" led those who best understood this opera to try to invest it back into the realm of pure music. On the occasion of the tenth-anniversary performance of Fauré's *Pénélope*, Paul Dukas wrote,

> We can rightfully ask no more [of composers] than that they express themselves according to a personal truth . . . It is by remaining faithful to this kind of truth and to his own musical genius that Gabriel Fauré has given us [with *Pénélope*] a unique work and an incomparable masterpiece, or certainly one that bears comparison only to his other masterpieces of pure music and to his marvelous songs.
>   As in the latter, in translating his poem, in drawing from it the harmonious reverberations on his sensibility, he first of all expresses *himself*, and, in expressing himself so completely, raises the theater to such heights of lyricism as fashion will never attain.[118]

Likewise, in a contemporaneous evaluation of modern French operas, Kœchlin insisted: "The essential thing is the place all these composers accord to *pure music* and the sincerity with which they tend to translate feelings without bidding for 'dramatic effect.'"[119] Under the commanding sign of interiority, the ideal of sincerity and the inwardness of pure music were literally put on stage. Superficial effects were cast out, along with "false props" and the trespass of fashion. The Paris Opéra was at last ready to represent, as if unfolding its own mythical destiny, the birth of architecture from the sounds of the lyre – for this was the theme of Valéry's *Amphion*, a ballet-melodrama realized in its lyric fullness with Honegger's musical collaboration. Finished in 1929, it reached the stage of the Opéra in 1931 with Ida Rubinstein in the title role. Perhaps this rarefied conception of the theater would have sustained an even more extraordinary spectacle which the two men contemplated but never managed to complete. "This would have begun with a text in prose," Honegger recalled, "then prose would have been relaxed towards a more and more rhythmic poetry, which, in turn, would have given way to music at the precise moment when the power of words came to a halt."[120] We could hardly find an allegory more befitting the triumph of Pure Music.

5 Conclusion

Practically everything we have confronted in this chapter reverts to the fundamental question of sincere expression in music and the difficulties of representing such expression in words. We have seen the same problem variously posed and probed by composers, writers, and philosophers. But, in the end, we may well ask if the question does not belong entirely to a past era whose quaint metaphysical theories muddled up its aesthetic categories and whose problems no longer actively concern us.[121]

On the contrary, I would like to suggest that the question of sincerity is an essentially *modern*, if not a postmodern, question. So long as suspicions of fraudulence and fabrication trouble our encounters with new works of art, the question of sincerity remains open. At the beginning of the twentieth century these suspicions compelled French composers and critics to defend new music as never before. Responsible critics tried to reassure audiences, confronted with multifarious and sometimes contradictory trends, that contemporary composers were not playing pretentious jokes on them, that stylistic innovations reflected sincere translations of unique personal sensibilities. The urgent need to defend new works and to probe their authenticity has not vanished from more recent musical criticism. Indeed, the listening public still makes efforts to distinguish the posers from the sincere artists, and, likewise, rival artistic factions continue to accuse one another of fraudulence.

Far from evaporating, the doubts raised by stylistic novelty and diversity intensified with the passing decades. Stanley Cavell could rightly claim, in 1965, that "the possibility of fraudulence, and the experience of fraudulence, is endemic in the experience of contemporary music."[122] For Cavell, the point was not "to condemn any given work as fraudulent, but to call attention to . . . the obvious but unappreciated *fact* that the experience of the modern is one which itself raises the question of fraudulence and genuineness" (p. 214). It is significant that Cavell, in defining the social and aesthetic significance of the breach between modern composers and audiences, chooses to concentrate his arguments around the concept of fraudulence. In defining "fraudulent" art, he indicates that it more or less skillfully produces "*the effect* of the genuine," or "some of its properties" (p. 190). Perhaps fraudulence is the most willful shade of insincerity, for the kind of work Cavell distinguishes as "fraudulent" may be identified with the trade of "false and shallow spirits" whom Kœchlin habitually opposed to "sincere artists."[123]

Cavell's emphasis on fraudulence seems to predicate the same relationship between sincerity and modernity as did the criticism of Fauré's era. But Cavell goes beyond the culture of twentieth-century music to question the very conditions of artistic production and reception, conditions that music, for him, merely happens to expose more directly than the other arts. Cavell insists that "the danger of fraudulence, and of trust," are essential to the experience of art (p. 189). The attention I have lavished on understanding how Fauré's culture sought to differentiate sincerity from insincerity in art finds justification in this assertion, for Cavell suggests that this very act of differentiation lies at the root of aesthetic experience. Although we may wait for "time to tell" whether our judgments of a work are valid, the act of differentiation precedes that telling and cannot be deferred. Kœchlin, writing in the twenties, a decade of social and artistic turmoil, wished to place the effort of differentiation between sincerity and insincerity at the center of a modern aesthetics; Cavell, forty years later, in another period of turmoil, renewed this intention:

> I've been insisting that we can no longer be sure that any artist is sincere – we haven't convention or technique or appeal to go on any longer: *anyone* could fake it. And this means that modern art, if and where it exists, *forces* the issue of sincerity, depriving the artist and his audience of every measure except absolute attention to one's experience and absolute honesty in expressing it. This is what I meant in saying that it lays bare the condition of art altogether. And of course it runs its own risks of failure, as art within established traditions does. (p. 211)

If these conclusions point to what Cavell calls "an unattractive critical situation," it is unattractive partly because the category of sincerity remains disconcerting, if not impracticable, to most philosophers. Indeed, it is surprising to find a modern intellectual like Cavell, surely unaware of his philosophically uncelebrated French forebears, making the idea of sincerity the key to determining "what kind of stake the stake in modern art is" (p. 212). In a summary declaration that Fauré and his students would have keenly appreciated, Cavell insisted that "the task of the modern artist, as of the modern man, is to find something he can be sincere and serious in; something he can mean" (p. 212). Such testimony hints at the surprising scope and continuity of "sincerity" as a factor in twentieth-century aesthetics.

It may of course be objected that we have passed from a modern age into a postmodern one. Yet the most sophisticated proponents of postmodernity concede that the very existence of a "postmodern moment" – its historical identity – cannot be ascertained within the "postmodern space," the operation of its ideologies. This can only leave the situation of modernity in eerie suspense. At the same time, I suspect that today's artists and audiences have *not* resolved the issues of authentic self-representation which modernity first "forced" upon art decades ago. The position of sincerity in the "postmodern space" remains at present either indeterminate or invisible. Until a postmodern critique seriously takes up the question of sincerity for the future of art and ethics, we remain far too near its *modern* implications to dismiss it.

The coupling of art and ethics, communicated so forcefully by Cavell's allusions to honesty in representing human experience, returns us to the double nature of sincerity: it is at once aesthetic and moral, individual and shared. In this chapter, I have intentionally emphasized the aesthetic and historical significance of the idea rather than its moral implications. Yet the moral values of sincerity are inescapable. It seems clear that sincerity is, in general, a virtue. While not all composers were able to achieve it, one can make a favorable case for its creative efficacy by comparing it to such providential concepts in musical criticism as genius or "historical destiny." Sincerity, as we have found it defined in early twentieth-century France, was held up to composers as a quality to be gradually realized and guarded, not a gift of grace.

Sincerity, then, is a practice and an ideal. By laying claim to both practical and theoretical objectives in art, it acquired a force that outweighed its fragility. The *ideal* of sincerity charted a difficult course on the periphery of trends, money, and celebrities. The *practice* of sincerity demanded an interrogation of one's innermost predilections, a return to the domain of inner consciousness. Proust spoke of this domain, far from worldly glory, most unforgettably in *La prisonnière*:

> Every artist seems . . . like the citizen of an unknown homeland that he
> himself has forgotten, different from the one from which another great artist
> will set out for this earth . . . Composers do not remember this lost
> homeland, but every one of them always remains unconsciously harmonized
> in a kind of unison with it; a composer is delirious with joy when he sings in
> tune with his homeland; he sometimes betrays it for love of glory, but then in
> searching for glory he flees it, and it is only in disdaining such gain that he
> finds it again, when he intones that individual song whose singleness of tone
> (for, whatever subject he treats, he remains identical to himself) proves the
> constancy of the elements that make up his soul.[124]

Thus Proust's narrator on the enigma of personal style. Fauré, Debussy,
Dukas, Kœchlin and others had likewise urged their fellow composers to
find this Proustian "singleness of tone." In the music of their peers, these
composers, like Proust, were listening for voices in tune with an "unknown
homeland" and themselves trying constantly to translate the harmonies of
their own universes into music. *La prisonnière* was published in 1923, a year
before Fauré's death, but he lived by the Proustian exhortation before it was
written. His pupils, whose formation at the Conservatoire preceded Proust's
words by some twenty years, would certainly have recognized something
familiar in this quotation. Indeed, in 1909, Vuillermoz referred to beauty in
music as "a virgin forest where every explorer must blaze a narrow path
alone to go in search of unsuspected treasures."[125] The spirit of this explor-
atory metaphor anticipates Proust's text and matches it in thought if not in
eloquence. Could it be significant that Kœchlin likewise called the world of
creative possibilities "the great virgin forest" in 1921?[126] The image of the
virgin forest may have had its source in Fauré, their teacher. That is speculation. But what is certain, Fauré's pupils left his classroom with a common
understanding of their vocation and its high responsibilities. Through his
belief in the aesthetic value of "the sincere translation of a personality," and
through the example of his own artistic practice, Fauré opened up an expansive possibility for his students: to approach, to discover and finally to sing
in tune with their own musical homelands.

2 Innovation, tradition

To begin this chapter, we ask what was Fauré's attitude toward novelty, toward "making something new" in music? Because newness is contingent upon the known as well as the unknown, we also ask, what was his attitude toward tradition, and how did he expect to act upon it? We shall find that Fauré's distinctive position in the music of his time and the difficulty many historians experience in classifying him come from his attitude toward tradition and novelty, which he considered as complementary rather than oppositional values. This attitude, of course, may be described as either liberal or conservative, and Fauré, like his contemporary Mallarmé, realized the culmination of certain long-standing French traditions in his work even as he took astounding but carefully calculated steps into unknown territory.

In approaching an understanding of the complementary values of innovation and tradition in Fauré's career, this chapter works from a distinction between *novelty* and *originality* which is sometimes forgotten today but was central to French aesthetics during Fauré's lifetime. We leave a proper historical account of the relation between the two concepts for the next chapter; let us for now imagine novelty and originality relating to one another as different parts of an organic system. A rooted plant, partly visible to the eye, offers us its palpable greenery, its novelty. But its leaves and flowers feed from roots hidden beneath the ground, a whole organism born from an obscure, originating kernel. This hidden realm is originality. The present discussion draws attention to the leaves, novelty in its materiality, with only incidental glimpses of the deeper level we shall uncover later. Inasmuch as novelty was a *tangible* idea for Fauré's contemporaries, it stands in contrast to the murkiness of ideas like sincerity and originality. Because of this concreteness, and also because aesthetic novelty is familiar to us in much the same form as it was a century ago, it is not difficult to understand. We shall establish Fauré's relation to this material phase of creativity in the brief exposition that follows. Having done so, we will be prepared to enter into a full understanding of the broader concept of originality, whose definitions, history, and cultural motivations become the focus of chapter 3.

Fauré's letters, public remarks and, of course, his music, leave no room for doubt about his attitude toward novelty. His impulses toward innovation[1] manifested themselves at the start of his adult career and did not decline. According to Jean-Michel Nectoux, "The desire to write things that were new was one of his main preoccupations."[2] Nectoux's close examination of Fauré's life and music has been most persuasive in upholding his conclusion. The first fruits of Fauré's desire to innovate may be seen in the three major works that marked the end of his compositional apprenticeship: the Violin Sonata, op. 13 (1875–76), the First Piano Quartet, op. 15 (1876–79), and the Ballade for piano and orchestra, op. 19 (1877–79). Fauré's own contemporaries, for the most part, valued vocal over instrumental music and took keener notice of the transformations he was operating upon French song in his settings of Leconte de Lisle, Baudelaire, and Silvestre – certainly no less remarkable for their smaller scale. Saint-Saëns, however, encouraged Fauré to write large-scale instrumental works and turned out a magnificent review of the Violin Sonata, where he made a strong case for Fauré's elusive combination of urbane charm with "unexpected audacities."[3] Forty-seven years later, when Fauré died, a critic for *Le temps* would look back on Fauré's accomplishment with the same thought: "Fauré innovated; he enriched our harmonic language, but with a sureness of hand and an innate taste that make one take real technical audacities for a natural occurrence."[4]

By 1879 the young composer was starting to develop his own consciousness of having realized new forms and procedures. This growing awareness may be seen in a letter he wrote concerning the Ballade, op. 19:

> By using methods at once *new* and *old*, I have found the means to develop, in a sort of interlude, the phrases of the second piece and at the same time to give the premises of the third, in such a way that the three parts have become a whole. Thus, it has all turned into a Fantasy that's a bit outside of the usual sort, or at least I hope so.[5]

The form of the Ballade resists any conventional label, and Nectoux has concluded that it is truly one of those rare works that "invents its own form."[6] In my opinion, the long ending of the Ballade is perhaps its most remarkable aspect; it inscrutably satisfies the desire for closure without pressing toward a conclusive climax or returning to the opening theme. The most robust accents resonate at the middle of the Ballade, and then the music dissolves into a long quietude of scales and trills, magically sustained for nineteen pages. This luxurious stillness, as James Parakilas has observed, was something new to music.[7] The Ballade, more than just "a bit" different from its predecessors in the genre, represented a moment of great experimentation in Fauré's work, and after the turn of the century, critics would cite it as a forerunner of musical impressionism. This retrospective insight was not without merit but was often left unexplained and proposed under historical misapprehensions. (Thus, in 1922 the Ballade was mistaken for a "recent work," written by Fauré in "palpable imitation" of Debussy.)[8] Possible links to "impressionism" in French music are intriguing but ultimately less compelling than the predictive qualities that the Ballade carries for innovative details in Fauré's *own* future works, especially the Fifth Barcarolle and the late Fantasy, op. 111, for piano and orchestra.

Fauré's search for novelty, his "almost obsessive interest in self-renewal,"[9] continued into his artistic maturity with marvelous results. He was fifty-nine when he stated the matter most succinctly: "It's perfectly natural that one would always want to write works that make progress over the preceding ones." Such was his aim in the First Quintet, which he was composing at the time.[10] Of course, Fauré's words, in this instance, could refer to perfecting what he had already done rather than creating something new. An intention to innovate is, however, unmistakable in a slightly later letter concerning "Le don silencieux." This song (1906) is one of Fauré's least known and most noteworthy; it is written from start to finish in the spare prosodic style that would imbue most of his subsequent *mélodies*. Making a rare self-analysis, Fauré commented, "Since it in no way resembles any of my previous works, nor anything else I know of, I am very happy." He proudly added that it achieved its musical expressiveness through purely harmonic and contrapuntal means. "There isn't even a main theme; it has a freedom of flow that would throw Théodore Dubois quite off balance."[11]

[handwritten margin note: is it the prosody that is spare?]

These two remarks written after the turn of the century are more assertive than Fauré's early letter concerning his Ballade. The difference in tone reminds us that at the age of thirty-four, when Fauré was writing the Ballade, he did not yet possess self-confidence equal to his underlying desire to write things "outside of the usual sort," for one aspect of Fauré's well-known modesty was precisely a lack of self-confidence. But toward the end of the century he became more and more fully persuaded of his own merits.[12] Years of encouragement and urging on the part of his friends and patrons played a fundamental role in this transformation. In 1891 he would present his *Cinq mélodies*, op. 58, his first motivically unified cycle of songs, to Winnaretta Singer in the following manner: "You will see that as in 'A Clymène' I have attempted a *form* that I take to be new, or at least I know nothing like it; indeed, to try to create *something new* is really the least I can do when I work for you, the person who is the least like anyone else in the world!"[13] Likewise, it was Saint-Saëns, and probably Marguerite Baugnies, too, who kept urging Fauré "to break a little bit with those habits of modesty which some are good enough to find exaggerated."[14]

Partly as a result of such prompting, Fauré decided to put in his name for the seat at the Institut left vacant at Gounod's death in 1893. He was not successful, but three years later he managed to get a teaching position at the

Conservatoire, where in 1892 Ambroise Thomas had bellowed, "Fauré? Never! If he is appointed I resign."[15] Passing over the threshold of the Conservatoire with a mere diploma from the less prestigious École Niedermeyer, with no Prix de Rome, without the Academician's green *veston*, Fauré was moving toward the hub of musical power from its outer edges, but his actions and integrity would eventually undermine the cultural standing of powerful insiders like Thomas and Dubois.

Fauré took his first official steps reluctantly and naively. He surely knew he had little chance for a chair in the Institut in 1893, but the terms in which he imagined the possibility of his eventual election reveal his delusion:

> Of all my probable rivals there is not one who *compels* the vote of the Academy, and if you will allow me to relay, under the *seal of secrecy*, Saint-Saëns's opinion, it is that I am the only one who, among the likes of Widor, Dubois, Joncières, Salvayre, and Godard, has brought something *new* to music![16]

The stylistic novelty that set Fauré's work apart from his rivals' was an obstacle to his election, not a rallying point! Fauré's innovations, subtle as they were, were not so discreet either in their immediate impression upon the ear or in their vexing implications for tonal syntax as to escape the censure of official musicians. It is not my point here to demonstrate Fauré's qualities as an innovator but rather show the importance of novelty to his vocation as an artist. Yet if we wish to return to the truth of details, to the notes on the page, a glance at a few excerpts from Fauré's work in this particular period yields interesting evidence. In 1892, when Fauré made his first bid for the composition class at the Conservatoire, his most recent publication had been the *Cinq mélodies*, op. 58. In these songs, as he said to Winnaretta Singer, he tried "to create something new." Let us consider the following measures from "A Clymène" (Example 4). This passage follows a dynamic climax in the remote key of E-flat minor and begins the path back to the tonic, E minor. What would have upset Ambroise Thomas here? In short, the melody, the harmony, and the poem. Fauré's treatment of the voice is not conventionally songful. The melody, anchored around the B-flat or A-sharp, stresses the tritone, and the sevenths above the bass (F-flat in measure 54, E-natural in measure 56) are not only left unresolved but are heightened by the luxurious fall of an octave. This melodic style, floating above an independent accompaniment (in the right hand, the falling third that turns back on itself is a recurring motive), might be accused of exacerbating Wagner's vices. Thomas would have noticed the parallel motion of the seventh chords in measures 53 to 54 (shown in the harmonic reduction). Moreover, the second seventh (F-flat) parries its dominant function for an

Example 4. "A Clymène," op. 58, no. 4 (1891), mm. 53–57, with harmonic reduction.

enharmonic twist (F-flat to E) that then binds a C-major chord to an F-sharp-major one.[17] And if this C-major harmony is only a feint, then is it not perversion of the very concept of "resolution" to bring the bass to its home dominant in measure 57 but leave the vocal part moored to its persistent tritone anchor? Let us also consider the suspicions that this particular poem from Verlaine's *Fêtes galantes* would have aroused. "A Clymène" is a love song written under the sign of Baudelairian *correspondances* – the very word Verlaine uses to predicate the fusion of music, color, and perfume "sur d'almes cadences."[18] Verlaine's ravished synaesthesia very much implicates Fauré in *modernité* and the poetics of late nineteenth-century French literature. For the official poets, such ideas about the intermingling of sensual and spiritual experiences still constituted a challenge to the notions of French "clarity" and "reason," rallied under the handy banner of the "classical" (though they would, in this oppositional guise, have been more appropriately labeled "academic").

"Green," the preceding song in this same set, likewise contains passages difficult to fault in strictly technical terms but whose novelty is unmistakable to the ear (Example 5). As in "A Clymène," the familiar motto of the entire cycle (falling third, rising second) winds through the upper voice of the piano part, but its expression through ninths and sevenths above the

Example 5. "Green," op. 58, no. 3 (1891), mm. 10–16.

bass make it a fluid element meandering over the musical surface, not a static point of reference. The voice-leading throughout the passage is linear and impeccable. But Fauré has refashioned dominant and tonic functions to respond to a highly personal sense of tension and release: his own harmonic flux. Here, gentle motion about a tonic bass (measures 10–13), suddenly gives way before a foreshortened progression to the dominant (measures 14–15).[19] This moment is difficult to recognize as an arrival at the dominant despite the fact that we have never really left the tonic, because the triads on F and G in measure 14 lack any conventional tonal explanation. The passage illustrates Fauré's crafty way of allying tradition and innovation. His outer parts, according to the best contrapuntal traditions, move in contrary motion from measure 13 through the whole of measure 14, and the F in the bass, the root of the first chord we find difficult to explain, has been anticipated through the preceding play of neighbor tones (F-sharp and G). Yet this logic does not lessen the shock of that "irrational" major ninth on F in measure 14; we are left with several contrapuntal rationales but no direct harmonic connection backwards or forwards.[20] Let us move to the next measure. Once Fauré recovers the dominant, he uses the submediant to put off a true tonic reprise (measure 15). This is a traditional deceptive cadence, and the G-flat in the vocal part should allow us to recognize a conventional substitution of vi for I. But among the ninths and sevenths we scarcely perceive the G-flat as the tonic when it arrives. Fauré repeats it in the soprano and tenor parts, but as the tonal underpinning changes the tonic glides toward pitches above and below it. Fauré's linear voice-leading gently disperses its functional force (measures 15–16).

Now there is no reason to assume that a composer would be refused the prestige of an official position on the basis of musical style alone; political and personal alliances played their usual role. Yet Fauré was very well-connected, for he had two staunch supporters in two different sections of the Académie des Beaux-Arts: his father-in-law, the sculptor Emmanuel Fremiet, and his former teacher, Saint-Saëns. Thus, the modernity of Fauré's work does appear to have played a significant role in his exclusion (and soon we shall see this reasoning confirmed in a revealing letter from Dubois to Fauré). In any event, before the *Cinq mélodies*, we need not restrict ourselves to imagining the disapproval of Ambroise Thomas or another established musician of previous generations. Camille Benoît, six years younger than Fauré and a student of César Franck's, admired Fauré's recent Requiem, but he, too, was dismayed when Fauré showed him "A Clymène":

> [Benoît] told me, with a severe and saddened brow, that I'd do better to pass on to other exercises and drop Verlaine because I was becoming far too *incoherent* and *obscure*! Well, you can see I'm very worried! I who thought myself too classical! Please don't spread around this terrifying assessment![21]

Fauré's irony does not disguise his self-confidence; Benoît's verdict does not seem to have worried him at all. What we might take more seriously is Fauré's banter about his own style seeming "too classical." He might well have asked himself whether his music had yet fully captured or measured up to the sensual pirouettes of Verlaine's verses. Had he strayed *far enough* from his classical grounding?

Indeed, what we have been considering in these examples are modifications of traditional voice-leading and tonal succession; we are far from revolution. We could expect to look to Théodore Dubois, always ahead of Fauré on academic paths, for an enlightening contrast in style. Dubois got the position at the Conservatoire in 1892, and it was he, too, who won Gounod's vacant seat in 1894. Yet if we turn to his songs we do not find the work of a colorless academician, which is what received knowledge would lead us to expect.[22] In Dubois's songs, there is considerable access to the vein of harmonic riches Fauré, Duparc, Debussy, Chabrier, and Chausson were exploring in the 1870s and 1880s.[23] Dubois's subsequent standing as an official musician and author of academic treatises may have undermined his worth in the eyes of later French musicians, but it is wrong to categorize his work as reactionary, at least in 1892. Dubois not only left his teacher Ambroise Thomas far behind in matters of harmony; he mined Massenet's style for fresh harmonic invention. We will remember how important Massenet was for Debussy, too, in this same period. The composer of *Manon* was one of the few immediate French ancestors Debussy was always willing to praise later in life. The technical and expressive features Debussy drew out of Massenet's style to create songs like "Nuit d'étoiles" and "Beau soir" are no less evident in Dubois's "Éclaircie" (1882) or "Baiser maternel" (1882–83). Dubois's "Nous nous aimerons" (1882), which is for the most part less harmonically adventurous than the two songs just mentioned, nonetheless closes on a tonic triad through which the lowered seventh is reiterated and allowed to vibrate in an inner voice. The device would later become a commonplace in Poulenc's songs. Fauré, something of a purist for final triads, never allowed himself to end a piece on this floating, purely harmonic sound. He may well have thought added sevenths and their like an easy indulgence, a mere ornamental "sensation." But treating chords timbrally rather than functionally was certainly a fresh idea, and one with a future.

Dubois's music raises the question of what so troubled the academicians about Fauré's work. The answer must lie beyond a surface of shared upper-tertian harmonic vocabularies. The most important difference between Fauré and Dubois, as borne out by comparison of their songs, lies not in the vocabulary of chords but in the way each composer handles the overall musical structure, specifically the middleground. If Dubois's harmonic language represents an advance on Gounod and Massenet, if he takes some superficial lessons from Wagner, too, he still breaks up his harmonic luxuriance with *explicit, regular cadences*. This difference leads one to believe that Fauré's capacity to suspend resolution for increasingly long spans of time troubled his contemporary listeners more than anything else, despite the fact that he accomplished most of his evasions and extensions through traditional means. Fauré's mature control of large-scale harmonic structures and his ability to move us powerfully from one tonal level to another were described by Jankélévitch in terms of experience and duration: "Fauré, like Debussy, knows how to stretch the endurance of the auditory memory to its extreme limits; he gauged the slightest affinities of tones and tonalities and measured the limits beyond which a tonality can no longer be distinguished . . . [In certain works] he constrains us to wait for the return of a prodigal key just up to the point of desire beyond which impatience would become insensibility."[24] Beyond this "prodigality," the intervallic twists of Fauré's vocal lines, his insight into the possibilities of expressive and independent instrumental accompaniment, and his handling of accented non-harmonic tones, gave his songs a distinctive modernity that outstripped Dubois's attractive and certainly not unadventurous harmonic practice.[25]

In 1896, when Fauré stood for the Institut a second time, Charles Lenepveu won the seat. Fauré had now begun to understand the travails and disappointments of professional life, and in the wake of this recent failure he wrote a resigned letter to Dubois that, in its final paragraph, could not hide a certain sourness behind the veneer of humility:

> If you know of some bias against me which is keeping me isolated from the official musical world, as your colleagues in the musical section left me to understand at the time of the most recent election to the Institut (I'm referring to the rankings), or even if you just have a general sense of such a thing, tell me in all sincerity. If that's the case, I shouldn't bother anyone, or myself, in the future but just continue along in my corner, perpetrating my probably detestable and certainly inferior work!

Dubois, whom Fauré knew as a friend as well as a highly ranked colleague, answered very frankly,

> I am not aware that any bias is serving to keep you isolated from the official world. The rankings of the Institut mean nothing; for proof, you need only note that Lenepveu, who belongs to this official world, was ranked last by his colleagues and yet was elected. Since you ask me to be sincere, I had the feeling that your music was judged too vague, too modulating, too *cherchée*. This does not prove, as you tend to affirm very modestly, that it is either detestable or inferior. Your music is what you want it to be, that of an extremely talented artist, very committed, an enemy of the banal. But you cannot demand that it please all comers or bear a grudge against those who have a different aesthetic.

Fauré's response (to Dubois's response) was to affirm his good conscience as an artist, but he also expressed amazement that "the faults people reproach me for are precisely the ones I hate the most, and music moves me all the more when the means employed are clear, correct, exact and even concise. I suppose that only proves that most of the time we know ourselves badly!"[26] Fauré seems to have looked upon his own technical methods as fundamentally traditional ("I who thought myself too classical...") and was at first dumbfounded by the opinions of those who saw his music in a different light. These experiences hardened him to institutional politics, but he retained enough good humor to joke with Saint-Saëns, "My only hope would be to succeed you in forty years, and I swear I like you much more than the Institut!"[27] In the end it would take an unusual combination of circumstances to put this outsider with "modernist tendencies" at the head of one of the official centers of French musical life, the Conservatoire.[28]

Fauré began to feel an *inward* persuasion of his merits in this same period, a persuasion above and beyond outside encouragement. His persistence in trying to gain official recognition would seem to bespeak a certain self-assurance, but we must remember that it was the result of material needs as well; Fauré was hard-pressed to support his family, and a position at the Conservatoire would have been a blessing. What seems more certain and most significant is that between the time of his first bid for the Institut and his second, Fauré did not pull back from artistic exploration but moved onto a trajectory of even more rapid innovation. The harmonic and contra-puntal audacities of the Fifth Barcarolle (1894), the passion and complexity of *La bonne chanson* (1892–94), put him at the forefront of French moder-nity. Of course, such compositions also removed him still further from general academic approval. "Avant que tu ne t'en ailles," the sixth song of *La bonne chanson,* is one of many examples that bears out this stylistic evolution.

Fauré's song is a masterful realization of Verlaine's poem. The poet divided his quatrains into alternating couplets that interweave two distinct, coherent poems within a larger one.

> Avant que tu ne t'en ailles,
> Pâle étoile du matin,
>   – Mille cailles
> Chantent, chantent dans le thym. –
>
> Tourne devers le poète,
> Dont les yeux sont pleins d'amour;
>   – L'alouette
> Monte au ciel avec le jour. –
>
> Tourne ton regard que noie
> L'aurore dans son azur;

> – Quelle joie
> Parmi les champs de blé mûr! –
>
> Puis fais luire ma pensée
> Là-bas, – bien loin, oh, bien loin!
>   – La rosée
> Gaîment brille sur le foin. –
>
> Dans le doux rêve où s'agite
> Ma mie endormie encor . . .
>   – Vite, vite,
> Car voici le soleil d'or. –[29]

In the main set of couplets the lover contemplates the morning-star; in the indented set he interrupts his contemplation with rapt, exclamatory descriptions of the birds, dew, and fields awakening to sunlight. Fauré's inspired translation of Verlaine's alternating pattern results in an extremely novel form for the song as a whole.[30] Verlaine's method of composition allows the poem to be read either straight through or by choosing one of the two sets of couplets and ignoring the alternate ones. Fauré chooses to put aside his customary continuity of mood and texture and instead leaps from one set of couplets to the other in abrupt juxtapositions; gradually, however, the contrasts are attenuated until the two sets of couplets interlock for the burst of sunlight at the end of the poem.

Prior to this great moment of unity, each set of the indented (exclamatory) couplets seems to call forth music more daring and elaborate than the last. When we reach the fourth set ("La rosée / Gaîment brille sur le foin"), we find a passage that would have outraged members of the Institut (Example 6).[31]

In the light of preceding events in the song, we may view this passage as an extravagant harmonic parenthesis surrounded on either side by the dominant of D-flat (m. 53 and m. 65, the latter instance displaced up an octave). This "parenthesis," of course, encloses the contrasting tone and content of the interrupting couplets. Verlaine's double-couplet structure presented Fauré with special opportunities to exercise his talent for suspending and regaining tonal stability, and Example 6 is one illustration. As I have tried to show in the analytic diagram, the foundation of the passage is complex but not unintelligible; it comprises a series of harmonies linked by neighbor tones and roots a third apart. The final chord of the parenthesis (last beat of m. 64) is resolved as a German sixth back to the dominant of D-flat.[32] Fauré unsettles this already complex harmonic background with a musical surface of extreme richness. The pianist's right hand traces strange, syncopated scalar fragments. These scales form ruthless appoggiaturas against the bass,

Example 6a. *La bonne chanson*, op. 61: "Avant que tu ne t'en ailles" (composed in 1892, published in 1894), mm. 53–65.

Example 6b. Harmonic analysis and background structure of Example 6a.

and the texture of the accompaniment, ordinary at first sight, is splintered into something dry, unstable, almost vertiginous. Here as elsewhere in Fauré's work, the intensity and persuasion of the moment inspires a mingling of fantasy and reason. Fantasy is evident by a dozen details, down to the coloration of non-harmonic tones; reason, in his handling of multivalent tonal and formal forces. The two surrounding dominants shown in the analysis may be taken as symbols of Fauré's method; despite the wide, visionary landscape conjured up between them, the harmonic pillars are never shattered.[33]

Fauré's innovations met with hostility even among some of his admirers and supporters. Surely Fauré knew, or strongly suspected, that *La bonne chanson* would give Saint-Saëns great pause when, in a letter of 1893, he cheerfully offered to show him "proofs of my most recent, *extravagant* songs."[34] Saint-Saëns's first response, according to Emmanuel Fauré-Fremiet, was bewildered, if not stunned: "'Fauré has gone completely out of his mind.'"[35] A more exact critique came from the critic Camille Bellaigue, who had known Fauré since 1871 and sincerely treasured Fauré's songs of the next two decades. Bellaigue would later admire *Pénélope*, too (through some mental swerve whose details remain unknown). But in a review of 1897 he lodged stern complaints against the musical surface of *La bonne chanson*:

> Here, all the sonorous materials seem to contradict one another: the voice
> contradicts the accompaniment, the melodic notes the harmonies, the
> harmonies each another, and the notes of the vocal line one another, too.[36]

Bellaigue even singled out three measures (41–43) of the very song we just examined, "Avant que tu ne t'en ailles," for a paragraph of detailed protest that reaches beyond the musical surface into a larger structural question. "And what about tonality?" he asks, "what becomes of it in this music unleashed to the whim of incessant modulations?" Fauré's musical answer, of course, is not to Bellaigue's liking. After a discussion of the three horrible measures, he concludes, "In this practice, each key winds up lasting only a half-measure; I should say keys can no longer be said to be established at all. The ground is laid for each but without a one ever being realized."[37] Bellaigue's complaints reveal his deafness to the middleground harmonic implications of Fauré's song but also bear out the hypothesis I offered earlier: that it was the very span and complexity of Fauré's evasions that most upset his listeners.

We may judge by "Avant que tu ne t'en ailles" or another example: Fauré seems to have had no thought of giving up his personal impulses in order to gain wider recognition. Nectoux has gone so far as to wonder whether Fauré's official, professional disappointments in the 1890s caused him to plunge into his creative work with a touch of provocation – an intriguing speculation.[38] Having considered only a short stage of Fauré's development (and the music of the following two decades would be far more adventurous), we already have good evidence of Fauré's intention and ability to create "something new" and the steadiness with which he pursued that goal. Let us, then, change our perspective to pursue a different issue.

For Fauré, the freedom to innovate was not absolute but grounded in a principle of self-expression; innovation was desirable and justifiable not for its own sake but as the outcome of a composer's efforts "to translate his thought, his sensibility, by the *means* it pleases him to choose" (see p. 12). At a fundamental level, Fauré's intention to translate his own sensibility into music put innovation in a broader aesthetic context. We recall the development of this context from the previous chapter: the difference between novelty as a means of expression and novelty as an end in itself measured nothing less than the gap between art and *chic*. We know that some of Fauré's students remembered this distinction well.[39] But just as the *fantaisie* of Fauré's style is intimately linked to its *raison*, just as the two can only be separated for moments of partial analysis, likewise Fauré's desire for innovation should not be isolated from other impulses in his thinking which modified or tempered it. Here we must cite not only the principle of self-expression, but also his stated respect for tradition.

It seems clear, first of all, that Fauré's passion for innovation worked in harmony with his interest in music of the past, not against it. More than most other composers of his generation, Fauré knew the older repertories, even the most remote; his respect for these traditions was not aloof but grounded in wide-ranging knowledge. Like his schoolmates Eugène Gigout and André Messager, he grasped the special value of his education at Louis Niedermeyer's school, and his experience there left permanent traces in his development.[40] Toward the end of his life, Fauré would write,

> Perhaps it might raise a few eyebrows if I said how much a musical constitution can enrich itself through frequent contact with the masters of the sixteenth and seventeenth centuries, and indeed what resources may spring from the study and practice of Gregorian chant. Indeed, would anyone dare affirm that certain melodic lines and harmonic discoveries of recent vintage haven't any of their roots in this past from which we think ourselves so distant and detached?[41]

Plainchant and the polyphonic masterpieces of the Renaissance had been part of Fauré's everyday experience between 1854 and 1865. From the age of nine, under Niedermeyer's tutelage, he learned this music by singing, playing, listening, and accompanying. He considered himself fortunate to have been educated at a school founded on principles so extraordinary for their time. "In that period," Fauré recalled with some amusement in 1922, "Bach's masterpieces, which constituted our daily bread, still had not infiltrated the organ class at the Conservatoire, and there in the piano classes students were laboring over Henri Herz's concertos, while Adolphe Adam shone the full splendor of his light upon the composition students." Nearby, the pupils at Niedermeyer's school were immersed in Palestrina, Arcadelt, Lasso, Victoria, Couperin, Rameau, Bach, Handel, Gluck, Mozart, Haydn, Beethoven, and Mendelssohn.[42]

If, as James Kidd has shown, this schooling had great consequences for Fauré's stylistic orientation, especially his use of modality, it also decisively shaped his goals as an educator. Roger-Ducasse remembered how Fauré preferred to instruct his composition pupils through a broad range of examples taken from masterpieces in a given medium. Turning to opera, for example, Fauré would bring out scores by Monteverdi, Rameau, Gluck, Mozart, Meyerbeer, Rossini, Wagner, Musorgsky, and Debussy for study and discussion. This list reveals an impressive historical scope and catholicity of taste. "Without Fauré," Roger-Ducasse mused, "I wonder, would we have remained indifferent and scornful towards the charms of 'Sombres forêts' from Rossini's *William Tell*, which he regarded as the model of an authentic melody?"[43] We, in turn, might well ask: without Niedermeyer and Saint-Saëns, would Fauré have remained indifferent to the works of

Monteverdi, Rameau, Gluck, and Rossini altogether? Would he have known them well enough to communicate their values convincingly to his own students decades later? When, after ten years of teaching composition at the Conservatoire, Fauré became its director, he continued to pursue a broad historical orientation and, operating along administrative lines, instituted a series of reforms aiming to encourage greater knowledge and esteem for the music of preceding centuries. Fauré put great stock in Louis Bourgault-Ducoudray's course in the history of music, which had been at best tolerated under Thomas and made only slight progress under Dubois. With Fauré's new policy, attendance at Bourgault-Ducoudray's lectures suddenly became compulsory for the students in harmony and composition, and performances of historical repertory were given in the classroom so that lectures would be complemented by musical experience.[44] With these and other reforms, Fauré sought to expand the students' field of knowledge and cultivate awareness of different styles of performance as appropriate to different kinds of music. With the same objective, Fauré asked the faculty to enlarge the repertory that the students brought to the official examinations and exercises, and he took the lead in this effort with the programs he chose for the yearly public recitals. These repertorial adjustments were carried out on temporal and geographical planes at once – which is to say that the canon of the institution was finally expanded beyond the historical and national traditions of a mid-century French opera-house. Fauré's policies quickly diffused and swiveled the spotlight fixed for so long on Meyerbeer and Thomas. Now Caccini, Lully, Cesti, Clérambault, Bach, Schubert, Wagner, Debussy, and many other composers formerly unadmitted or undervalued began to share this light and to play a sanctioned role in the training of the nation's most promising young musicians.[45]

Now, in several respects these actions reveal the conservative tenor of Fauré's thinking, in the specific sense that he sought to preserve and to make available the musical traditions of the past. However, he did not on that account oppose change and novelty. Clearly we must not overstate one side of Fauré's thinking, conservative or liberal, to the detriment of the other. Even as Bach and Cesti filtered into the new curriculum, Wagner, Musorgsky, and Debussy did, too. To Fauré's mind, tradition did not take the place of the modern but supplemented it, gave it a context and foundation. We may recognize a familiar attitude behind Fauré's view of the past and the future; it is a position based on the humane, enduring, and finally sensible idea that "our individual activity is mediated and sustained by the continuities of shared traditions which reciprocally it sustains, mediates, and (re)constructs."[46] In this light let us recall the key statement with which, in 1905, Fauré set the tone of his entire administration at the Conservatoire:

"'I should like to put myself in the service of an art at once classical and modern, sacrificing neither contemporary taste to salutary traditions nor traditions to the whims of fashion.'"[47]

If Fauré's highly disciplined education gave him thorough knowledge of past masters and respect for their achievements, he was not, for all that, inclined to the sort of reverence that made for a passive and retrospective historical consciousness. He was candid about the healthy limits of admiration. In prefacing his own edition of Bach's organ music, Fauré commented, "What really harms masterpieces is to fence them around with such excessive respect as to end up making them boring."[48] This realistic, unacademic frame of mind explains his personal antagonism to the brand of historicism self-righteously flaunted by the more reactionary parties of the Schola Cantorum. In a little-known letter to Auguste Mangeot, Fauré went so far as to allude to the Schola as "this institution as deadly dull as it is self-glorifying."[49] Ultimately, he did not consider the constructive value of tradition to lie in constraint but rather in a kind of extended moral support. Fauré thought that each generation of artists would build upon the foundation of the past without necessarily sinking back into it.

In 1923, Fauré's ex-pupil Émile Vuillermoz published *Musiques d'aujourd'hui*, a collection of reviews and essays. Fauré agreed to write the preface. He apparently detected a particular consciousness of history in Vuillermoz's writing, perhaps a resultant of his own teaching, and Fauré made a special point of underlining this attitude for the benefit of less alert readers. Vuillermoz's zeal for contemporary music was evident to Fauré, who granted the importance of welcoming artistic innovation but added,

> He [Vuillermoz] is, at bottom, too musical and too broadly educated not to admit that, following the example of our greatest predecessors, each one of us must, with the help of our sensibility and in the measure of our gifts, try to add a stone to the great edifice and, with that, define the limits of ambition.[50]

This is first of all a critique of personal pride. Fauré implicitly questions the ambitions of any artist who would set out to destroy what he calls "the great edifice" rather than simply "adding a stone" and enjoying the effort of a personal contribution. The conservative intent of this statement is clear. But, characteristically, Fauré modulates it in a progressive direction; he calls upon the artist to try to add *something new* to the accumulated edifice of art, to carefully place his unique and solid stone.[51] He specifies the means by which the artist accomplishes that goal, that is, "with the help of his sensibility and in the measure of his gifts."

Zealots of a chimerical modernity who claimed to foresee the demolition of the "great edifice," we must remember, created a great stir in Paris and across Europe between 1910 and 1922.[52] Fauré, without passing judgment on a particular artist or clique, seems to have been moved to affirm his own vision of what an artist's vocation should be. Binding together the fragments of this vision from letters and prefaces, we find it centered on the act of creation as if on an act of love; Fauré could admit no role for arbitrary rebellions, hate, or willful destruction in artistic endeavor. His ideal is, above all, cumulative not destructive. Innovation is born out of a personal sensibility whose uniqueness does not for all that efface an inexorable relation to the past.

The consideration of novelty as a specific manifestation of creative originality leads us back to its source in artistic sincerity. In effect, what we hear as novelty is a *concrete result* of sincere self-expression; it becomes more and more salient and self-possessed with the progressive realization of individual sensibility in tone. This premise explains how Fauré was able to cultivate freedom and innovation while still honoring historical tradition; for him, reconciling tradition and innovation did not mean retreating into inhibited orthodoxy. He once described this interaction of innovation and tradition rather extravagantly:

> All who in the immense realm of the human mind have seemed to bring something new, to transmit thoughts in a language till then unknown, have but translated, through their personal sensibility, what others had already thought and said before them, and likewise the form of their language, brilliant or daring as it might be, only sums up the efforts, the gains, the successive advances, the past has bequeathed us.[53]

He might have added: "And there is no new thing under the sun." Fauré's terms seem to put innovation at a distinct disadvantage. Was he in a biblical mood, echoing the principles of Ecclesiastes? Fauré here cloaks novelty in an apparently austere, conservative framework (as he often does in his late compositions). Reading these guarded words, we may also detect "that slightly veiled smile which is the only sensible attitude" – the benign skepticism Fauré identified with his own view of life.[54] On any reading, the historical perception embodied in his sentence may be linked not only to a venerable past but also to a bountiful future. His student Nadia Boulanger, who in turn taught so many, would similarly comment: "Each successive stage brings something new which has its own value, but there is no genius without ancestors." In Western music, from Scarlatti to Beethoven to Dutilleux, she mused, "the language is common, but each person is unique and either has powers of invention or doesn't." Boulanger was always proud to stress the sway of Fauré's spiritual guidance over the formation of her own thinking; it seems significant that she specifically refused the notion of "geniuses without ancestors" and rather suggested that understanding the advent of artistic novelty meant recognizing that "an imaginative person has an option on the unknown."[55]

What could that option, beyond any "powers of invention," be? Boulanger was always trying to get at this mystery. "One day a man like Dutilleux appears on the scene, whose personality is very marked. But there again, how would you define it? He only used seven notes like everyone else, and even if he used quarter-tones and demi-quarter tones it would have been the same."[56] I would suggest that for Fauré such imaginative and inventive individuals had done nothing else but translated, from age to age, "through their personal sensibility, what others had already thought and said before them." Such artists always bring something new to art *through a personal reserve* whose precise qualities no ancestor can either aid or hinder. Therein lies their option on the unknown, to be blended with powers of technique and imagination. At the heart of Fauré's observation on novelty and tradition in "the immense realm of the human mind" there is the qualifying phrase about personal sensibility or translation, crucially skewing the summation, just as in his preface to Vuillermoz's book.

For Fauré and Boulanger, artists are durably linked to one another from generation to generation: there is more or less rapid change but seldom, if ever, a break.[57] Yet there is something else again. As the collective flame of artistic traditions spreads from brand to brand, it catches on a unique ember that remains with its possessor and burns with a passion and color all its own. In the history we are trying to imagine, the only "remainders" truly irreducible to the structural continuities of its own telling are those unique embers, the sensibilities particular to each and every artist. Tracking down these vital differences, the individual sources of surface novelty, now brings us to the problem of originality.

3 Originality, influence, and self-renewal

"Originality" points to those qualities of works or composers that make them distinct from forebears and contemporaries. Baudelaire spoke of originality when he declared, "An artist, a man who is truly worthy of this great title, has to possess something essentially *sui generis* by dint of which he is *himself* and no one else."[1] We are perhaps so accustomed to originality as a creed of nineteenth-century artistic production that we take it for granted; it is a concept familiar to critic, scholar, and amateur alike. But if we think harder, we realize that works of art must manifest originality in different ways at different times. The potential for differences within the concept, its heterogeneity, should lead us to ask whether one kind of originality was valued over another in a specific time or place. Active questioning releases the idea from its bland generality; in beginning to reflect nuances of meaning according to shifting contexts, "originality" gains historicity.

The following passage offers a foretaste:

> In [Fauré's work], we find above all a striking and wondrous originality in melody and harmony. Hear two measures of Fauré, and you can put a signature to them immediately. His music does not resemble any other music, old or recent, and yet it is neither bizarre, nor contorted, nor pretentious, nor vague, nor hostile, nor decadent. It is beautiful, natural, sincere and new.[2]

This paragraph shows how originality, as a general aesthetic desideratum, can be squeezed through the contingencies of a given time, place, and rhetorical purpose into something singular. We are not surprised when Bruneau begins by indicating "a music like no other," an art with a clear signature, as original. But then he leads us into an opposition of specific vices and virtues; he moves from generalities into terms whose specificity is loaded. The long string of adjectives designates those preconditions of originality and novelty Bruneau believed to be prevalent yet inadequate or false. He damns the etiquettes of decadence and fashion, the temptations of aesthetic cowardice or belligerence, opposing all of these to the "sincerity" and "naturalness" he identifies with Fauré's achievement. Such qualities and oppositions are far from generic, and might even be lost on us. They require historical exegesis.

Knowing the aesthetic issues that tend to characterize histories of music in the nineteenth and twentieth centuries, we might start by putting forward the following queries about the relative value of musical originality in its various forms. Is it deemed better to be original by creating new forms and genres, or by reworking traditional ones? Is it better to explore a new syntax within familiar forms, or to discover new forms for a familiar syntax? Or is it most significant that all new aspects – form, syntax, and medium – seem to give rise to one another and proceed in parallel? These questions would appear to be good starting points for exploring the varied dispositions of originality in music during the period of Fauré's maturity. Yet these were not the questions being asked.

We shall see that French musicians of the period seemed to invest the concept of artistic originality with a double meaning. Originality will of course manifest itself in the novelty of a composition; that is, original music immediately and appreciably distinguishes itself as such by saying something new. And as we know from the previous chapter, this meaning of the word was important to Fauré. Yet it was secondary. To return to the metaphor I used at the start of the discussion there: innovation is the foliage, not the root. What was considered life-giving and most fundamental was the radical originality constituted by an artist's irreducible singularity as a human being.[3]

The series of questions I posed a moment ago were seldom asked of originality as such precisely because they could be posed more directly as questions of stylistic novelty. They speak to the leaves (the "letter" of originality), not the roots (the spirit): they tackle the work of art in its material existence rather than at its inscrutable source. The topic of originality, in other words, tended to elicit a line of inquiry focused on the composer more than the work – on the intangible spirit beyond or behind all composition. "Originality" in the most general sense does contain both meanings. To speak of a composer's originality, as Carl Dahlhaus has observed, is to evoke "a combination of novelty and a formation *ab origine*, that is, a formation out of that inner self whose individuality cannot be duplicated."[4] Material newness, however, finally figures as the consequence of an essential and more powerful domain, a composer's "most original originality." We shall try to establish what this kind of originality meant to Fauré and his contemporaries, and to investigate its implications for an artist's personal development and public reception. Here the questions of artistic influence and self-renewal will be discussed in their relation to the premises of originality. In the final section of this chapter, we shall move beyond the historical range of Fauré's lifetime to consider what happened to originality in the later twentieth century. This extended historical and conceptual analysis is perhaps the most useful way to bring home the importance of originality as

[handwritten margin note: seems to be an artificial distinction]

a historical category. We shall find, in the end, that originality appears to have a future far more like its past than we might have imagined.

1 Originality: letter and spirit

In a letter to Hugues Imbert in 1887, Fauré briefly commented on his own situation and his French contemporaries': "The composers who really interest me the most are my peers, d'Indy, Chabrier, Chausson, Duparc, etc. . . . those, in short, who arrived at a moment when it is more difficult than ever to be an original composer."[5] In speaking of this "difficult moment," Fauré revealed his consciousness of an artistic challenge facing his own generation; what this challenge, linked to a particular moment in history, made especially difficult was originality. Characteristically, Fauré remained silent about the nature of the historical conditions causing the difficulty.

The answer is not central to our present discussion, but we cannot afford to pass over it either. In seeking to identify the alleged difficulty, we may ask ourselves if there was not a force so ubiquitous and commanding that all the composers whom Fauré named and admired in his letter would have felt it, a force, moreover, whose high-water mark came in the period around 1887. Indeed there was. For a French composer maturing between 1885 and 1895, the dominant problem was Wagner. (The extravagant reception of Wagner's art and ideas among French writers and musicians, alternately besotted and vexed with the German master, bequeaths us a vast pool of documentation.[6] Our present inquiry does not require we dip into it. Yet, in the manner of one of Wagner's verbose operatic narrators, we set aside the Wagnerian problem only to come back to it repeatedly later on.)

The content of Fauré's letter shows us that he considered originality a great factor in his artistic calling. This inference may serve us as a ground for exploring originality as a force shaping Fauré's work. Several other important passages from Fauré's writings will supplement this one over the course of the chapter. Yet Fauré's remarks on originality were always brief and are strewn across disparate contexts. To attempt to deduce, from them alone, the integral significance of originality for his artistic practice would be like charting a constellation through clouds that rove and gape but never completely scatter; the astronomer can wait for a clear night, but we will have to consider secondary evidence in order to delineate the larger significance of Fauré's remarks. The resulting degree of interpretative uncertainty must be acknowledged, but it is the necessary price we must pay for attempting the kinds of historical exposition that may be discussed, corroborated or challenged.

The kind of text that, ideally, would allow us to define the terms of our historical inquiry from the start would be one less fragmentary, a clear and affirmative discourse on the sources of originality in music and the conditions that allow it to develop. Such a discourse would provide ideas that might be related back to Fauré after proper explication. If we lack this kind of account from Fauré himself, we are fortunate to have one as close to his personal tendencies and beliefs as "La musique et l'originalité," an essay written by Paul Dukas for the *Revue hebdomadaire* of September 1895. Even better: Dukas's speculations in this essay also tell us what he thought about the consequences of Wagner's influence and the means he proposed to confront it, bringing Wagnerism and originality into a tangible relationship for us.

We know that Fauré felt a deep artistic sympathy and personal affection for Dukas. According to Fauré's younger son, "it was undoubtedly Paul Dukas, among the younger composers, whom [Fauré] liked best . . . To him alone could Fauré confide the fullness of his thought."[7] They eventually became neighbors, living around the corner from one another in the sixteenth arrondissement, and Dukas was a regular visitor in Fauré's later years. The intimate relationship between Fauré and Dukas goes back at least to 1907, when the latter arrived in Lausanne for a two-week working holiday with Fauré. Already before Dukas arrived, Fauré wrote his wife, "Dukas [is] an artist I esteem enormously from *every point of view*."[8] Toward the end of the visit, Fauré wrote again, "Dukas grows on you as you get to know him. He is a *serious* type, gifted with a true philosophical spirit and a well-stocked mind."[9] More specifically, Fauré praised Dukas's work as a critic, as we see from this letter of 1923:

> We are taking infinite pleasure, Mme. Hasselmans and I, in re-reading your old articles for *La revue hebdomadaire*. No, *you* simply don't realize just how remarkable, instructive, and zesty they are. We wish you would take stock of their importance, their value, and the *useful purpose* that would be served if you took the trouble to bring them together in a book and publish them. I defy you to tell me who, during the past twenty-five years, has spoken more learnedly and pleasantly of music and has presented more novel insights in a more personal form.[10]

Fauré's assessment of Dukas's intellectual qualities is just: the legacy of Dukas's reviews and essays survives as the most penetrating, fair, and prescient of the entire period.

*

Dukas begins "La musique et l'originalité" by announcing his explicit concern with defining "true originality" in music. He also wants to identify certain factors that seem to undermine originality and prevent it from being achieved as often as it might be. He begins his analysis negatively, by denying that originality is simply a result of patient labor. He traces that belief back to a naïve reading of Poe's famous essay on the genesis of "The Raven."[11] Dukas regarded Poe's account as exuberantly paradoxical, "inciting the kind of smile that all brilliant mystification demands among those who, not capable of being fooled by it, are its foregone accomplices."[12] According to Dukas, patience and tenacity are certainly prerequisites to the making of art, but they cannot guarantee an original work. On the contrary, to take writers like Poe or Buffon (whom Dukas cites as an earlier and more pedantic legislator of "patient" aesthetics) at their word may lead to works characterized by nothing more than "painstaking correctness." Dukas certainly respected the perfection of musical craft as the means to an end, but he censured the self-exaltation of those who would insist on the idea that technical proficiency in and of itself leads to musical greatness:

> In an art where combinations play so great a role, the special mastery they
> require, some believe, would be the fruit of patience, and patience alone.
> What follows from this are an extraordinary abundance of false masters
> whose entire genius lies solely in the mechanical dexterity they acquired by
> attentive study of the counterpoint and the methods of real creators. (p. 622)

For Dukas the existence of such middling works finally serves to prove his larger point: "If the tenacity required for the realization of a great idea is an absolute condition for delivering it to the world, that tenacity can never beget it" (p. 288). Thus, the patience of the human will, toiling for positive knowledge and expertise in handling the materials of art, does not suffice to create an original work.

Nor, therefore, will the imitation of even the greatest composers. Dukas immediately cites Wagner's influence as a case in point. "The imitation of Wagner, limited to the more or less servile reproduction of the exterior methods of his music, which I indicated in an earlier article as one of the foremost preoccupations of music today, seems to me equivalent to the mere borrowing of a formula" (p. 623). Holding such imitation to reproduce external effects without the support of correlative inner resources, Dukas condemns it as another recourse to vain *method*; like proficient but unmotivated counterpoint, this Wagnerian practice is a technique suspended over a void. Inasmuch as Wagnerism becomes a doctrine of compulsory emancipation from operatic conventions, Dukas regards it as a creative imposition:

> It is wrong to make this borrowing the prerequisite of all musical freedom.
> On the contrary, I think that a forthright originality, though it might not
> throw off this yoke under which, indiscriminately, we presume all heads must
> bow, would at least be able to carry it freely and without fatigue. (p. 623)

If certain "hostile critics" would complain about the lack of originality in French music, Dukas answers them by ascribing this lack to habits of "compulsory imitation" which may be most blatantly exemplified by Wagnerian tendencies, but also emerge more generally as the urge to represent (and re-present) any prevailing trend.[13]

Dukas then says that we recognize "true creators" by their willingness "to shake off the yoke of authority" and take responsibility for their own artistic decisions (p. 288). He proceeds to a definition of originality:

> If we wished to define musical originality, we could indeed designate it "the result of an auditory impression not yet experienced." There is no doubt that, to arouse such an impression in the listener, the skillfulness of the combinations and their effect, more or less favorable, will remain unavailing if they do not arise from an inner necessity, from a living sensation [*d'une nécessité intime, d'une sensation vive*] freed of all alien influence and all worry over imitation.[14] (p. 623)

The definition limits itself to the *effect* of originality upon the listener, but it is notable that Dukas lends less weight to the definition than to his afterthoughts, and even frames it with a conditional verb (*Si l'on voulait . . . on pourrait . . .*). With his reference to "the skillfulness of the combinations and their effect," Dukas obviously points to the most willed and material phase of composition, but, as he continues, what completes them, what allows technique to gain the spiritual consequence of originality, are "necessity" and "a living sensation," both within the artist. We are familiar with such "inner necessity" from our analysis of interiority as a source of sincere self-expression. The "living sensation" to which Dukas refers would seem to denote an immediate experience of the world later transformed, through sensibility, into the aesthetic.

The proposed bond between the artist's originality and his inner necessities and sensations moreover implies that in art, sincerity and originality share common ground. Dukas makes their convergence plain when he identifies a composer's personality with his originality – in other words, when he identifies the man with the artist:

> Indeed, one property of great musical individuality is to correspond very closely to the particulars of the moral and sensory temperament of its possessor. It is the direct expression of his personality as a man revealed through special faculties resulting from his gifts as an artist. (p. 625)

One may summarize the confluence by saying that sincerity and originality both are founded on individual expression, and both know degrees of achievement through personal growth. Though they appear to work in concert, however, there *is* a difference between them, for originality is ultimately shown to *draw upon an inborn trait*. Dukas speaks of musicians as uncommonly gifted or as competent; he ponders the legacies of greater and lesser originalities; finally, he feels forced to explain the most extraordinary instances of artistic originality as reflecting the full realization of a *natural gift*. This premise was not at all uncommon; we may cite examples from across our historical range. In 1894, Gustave Larroumet, former director of the ministry of Beaux-Arts, wrote, "An artist's first duty is to be himself, in other words to realize that bit of originality nature dealt out to him."[15] This statement, published a year before Dukas's essay, put sincerity and originality in much the same relation to one another, with originality figuring as a fact of nature and sincere self-expression as a method to realize it. At the other end of our historical range, in 1926, we read in Benoist-Méchin's book on Proust:

> Every musician of genius receives a *donnée première* (Descartes would have called it "*innée*"), a sort of internal mode of operation [*régime*], constantly recognizable, whose speed or slowness opens to him a world of forms imprinted with what we rightly call "his originality."[16]

In every case, originality is already present in the individual, awaiting disclosure. In contrast to sincerity, then, originality cannot simply be brought into being through moral development. Yet, despite its inherence, originality is still subject to development: it will remain an unrealized potential if desire or effort are lacking on the part of the possessor.

In a characteristic qualification, Dukas now insists on reminding us that even the least talented person still has his own special temperament or unique way of being. "Not all are equally gifted," he admits,[17] but he did not let his reverence for the gifts of a Mozart, Beethoven, or Wagner prevent him from recognizing the very fact of human individuality – that everyone is, in some way, "original." Even an imitative work, he thinks, so long as it makes some minimal claim to art, cannot help but reflect a facet of its creator's uniqueness, if only by presenting other people's ideas in a different light. For Dukas, therefore, "There is no music that is absolutely impersonal" (p. 627). Still, because not all music is "original" or "personal" to the same degree, he seeks to explain how certain artists succeed in projecting the fullness of their originality well beyond the general order of individual uniqueness. In the domain of creative production, consequently, what finally seems to be most important about originality for Dukas is not where it comes from but how it is developed. Originality flows from the unconscious and all our personal qualities, but everyone has an unconscious, everyone has a unique inner depth. The passion or temperament to realize this uniqueness completely and artistically, however, is something rarer. Because the process of realizing one's originality is a relatively free process, responsive to individual choice, it becomes a topic far better suited to discussion – and action – than the problem of first causes.

Dukas therefore places the greatest emphasis on the process of self-development. He observes that artists often realize the full artistic expression of their personalities only gradually and sometimes with great difficulty:

> [There are] truly gifted musicians who have not yet thrown off the yoke of imitation to which even the greatest composers submitted as they started out, and these budding musicians await the listener whose approval could help them to discern an originality, still latent, often needing only a little encouragement to dare reveal itself completely. But – it must be admitted – this encouragement is seldom forthcoming from the listener, and artists must resort to encouraging *themselves*. (p. 628)

Latent originality, to emerge and grow, needs only encouragement or, lacking that, steady self-assurance. Here, the expressed need for self-reliance does not surprise us. Dukas previously emphasized the role of self-reliance in bolstering the artist's independence – his crucial efforts to transgress authority and assume full responsibility for his own creative endeavor. The original artist, gradually moving beyond imitation and the search for mastery at the beginning of a career, comes to write music that depends less and less on things outside himself. His desire to express his own modes of existence, his "inner necessities," will guide him. In the end he may attain an originality so vivid and profound as to seem the overflowing translation of his true self alone. Dukas saw examples of such achieved "translation" in Wagner and Beethoven – and in the mature Fauré. Twenty-eight years after writing this essay, Dukas applied its principles to Fauré's *Pénélope*: "In translating his poem, in drawing from it its harmonious reverberations on his sensibility, he first of all expresses *himself*, and, in expressing himself so completely, raises the theater to such heights of lyricism as fashion will never attain."[18] In *Pénélope*, Dukas deemed Fauré's creative self-realization to be as "complete" as imaginable. This plenitude is the sign of artistic triumph.

It is telling that Fauré, at the end of his own life, singled out this same kind of growth in Beethoven. Identifying Beethoven's sixteen quartets with the unfolding of a lifetime's achievement, Fauré declared his deep admiration for "the slow but uninterrupted ascent of his inner life, of this thought, style, technique, from involuntary imitation to free creation."[19] By this admiration, Fauré invoked the same pattern of self-realization which Dukas and others had begun to ascribe to his work, too. Fauré's comment on Beethoven is fleeting but suggestive. We may draw two main inferences. First, the allusion to Beethoven's "inner life" ["cette vie intérieure"] gives us some idea of where Fauré located one source of such growth, that is to say, close to the "inner necessities" and "living sensations" of which Dukas spoke. Dukas and Fauré both ultimately refer to a seat of experience that sustains creative self-renewal and originality from within. And again like Dukas, Fauré explicitly portrays Beethoven's career as a passage from "involuntary imitation" to "free creation." This progress, he says, is "slow but uninterrupted." He does not begrudge Beethoven some "involuntary imitation" in his earliest music but rather, by his wording, seems to suggest that this kind of imitation is a perfectly natural precedent to the "free creation" that will come later. Fauré indicates a basic curve of progress in originality: this image will prove significant when we consider the question of influence in the next section.

But Fauré does not actually say what would allow a composer to find his own ascending curve. Dukas was more explicit: for a composer to attain the fullest possible realization of his originality, he must ponder inwardly; he must try to know himself.

Sincerity is the familiar premise of this injunction. Both Fauré and Dukas referred the challenge of external influence to the efficacies of individual sensibility and self-examination. If Fauré thought his generation had arrived "at a moment when it is more difficult than ever to be an original composer," he also affirmed a particular solution to the problem. For Fauré, to reach the summit of art always meant returning to the expressive needs of one's sensibility, and he consistently recommended this habit to his students (see chap. 1, pp. 17–19). After the initial phase of imitation, this decision, this self-determination, becomes imperative. To persist in imitating others, even the strongest, in the hope of discovering originality through extrinsic means, will prove unavailing at best, self-destructive at worst. In Dukas's words,

> After the advent of a great genius, the mania to resemble him by imitation
> begets works useless to the imitator and prejudicial to the model. This
> tendency, moreover, is destructive of originalities, perhaps minor but
> sometimes real, that would emerge from the sincere expression of individual
> temperaments. If only every person had the courage to affirm his own nature
> in music rather than deliberately placing it in the service of another, however
> powerful, we would see the emergence of works less ambitious, perhaps, but
> doubtless much more interesting, too. It would only be a question of daring,
> beginning by convincing oneself completely that there is no such thing as
> collective originality. (pp. 626–27)

Whether the master imitated be Wagner or another mattered little to Dukas; the waste, the misdirection of human potential, remained the same. Such musical servitude depressed him. He was truly convinced that irrevocable losses could be prevented if every artist simply heeded his own heart and followed his own inclinations.

If it seems that originality in music can only be sincere, this must be because originality is a by-product of sincerity, and because sincerity more than anything else can counter external influence. This line of thought appears to have suggested an elegant distinction to Dukas. He proposed that there are really two forms of originality: a novelty of style, objective and therefore subject to imitation, and a novelty of the spirit, which is radically subjective and *in*imitable. Thus:

> In the work of a disciple, the *inner cause* of a particular objective effect and the spontaneous impulse of the creative mind are lacking; the disciple succeeds only in evoking a more or less perfect body, but one unendowed with the spark of life. The master, after all, always remains the master; whatever wrongs the spread of his techniques might cause him, *his most original originality*, I dare say, remains inviolable all the same. (p. 625, emphasis mine)

Unlike the objective signs of a composer's originality (that is, the "body" of the music), what can never be stolen is its motivating "spark of life." His "most original originality" mirrors his own special temperament, and another artist can no more imitate it than become someone else. All the peculiarities of Wagner's style, for example, are like "so many signs by which we perceive all the traits of his nature as a man – they are the figuration of the inner energies of his being." Without those inner causes that are Wagner's alone, there will always be "something ludicrous in seeing the expression of this special temperament reproduced loyally by artists who have entirely dis-similar ones" (p. 626). Perceptible novelty, then, depends on something prior, on the unique subjectivity that creates the music: the harmonies of a soul as yet unheard. These personal harmonies represent the kind of origi-nality that mattered most to Dukas. He carefully defined originality as "the result of an auditory impression not yet experienced" (p. 623), he acknowl-edged the role of "new combinations" in creating such impressions, but he insisted on the material resources of these impressions far less than on their fundamental correspondence to a unique personality. Along similar lines, Édouard Schuré would write, "Every person possesses an original soul, an original mind, like no other. In the mystery of this mind or soul lies the secret of talent and of genius. The main thing is to find the secret for ourselves."[20] For Schuré as for Dukas, to surprise this secret, "to seize it and make it speak," requires a practice of self-knowledge. Behind all combinations of sounds yet to be imagined, we may say, what is truly "original" is the self.

2 The equanimity of influence

Let us begin with an example of artistic influence – an example that returns us to the power of Wagnerian affinities. In 1909, Albéric Magnard published a *tragédie en musique*: *Bérénice*, his third and last opera. There is a remarkable preface by Magnard at the head of the score – including the following *défi* on the second page:

> My score is written in the Wagnerian style. Devoid of the genius necessary to create a new form of lyric theater, I have chosen from among existing styles the one which best suited my altogether classical tastes and altogether traditional musical culture. I have only sought to get as close as possible to pure music.[21]

Magnard was not the kind of a man to beg a question. But his well-earned reputation for gruff honesty hardly prevents these words from taking us by surprise. His self-appraisal, with its blunt admission of debts to Wagner, would be noteworthy even if it were only a gesture of deference. But, in fact, Magnard is insisting on the truth; *Bérénice*, like his previous two operas, depends on Wagnerian precedents.

When we turn to the work itself, nonetheless, we discover a musical and dramatic art considerably farther removed from Wagner than such recent works as *Fervaal* and *L'Étranger* by d'Indy, or *Le Roi Arthus* by Chausson.[22] How puzzling, then, that Magnard's preface really tells us so little about the individuality of his own work (except to give us the premises of a most unusual libretto). This is a deeply personal opera whose indisputable debts to Wagner suggest idiosyncratic adaptations, not echoes. The disparity between Magnard's description of debt and his actual achievement lessens when we reach the sentence declaring his intention "to get as close as possible to pure music." Such an ambition should put us on guard against a too literal reading of his preceding words. For how can an opera that tries "only to get as close as possible to pure music" really have anything fundamental to do with Wagnerian dramaturgy? The Wagnerian music-drama is by definition a compromise that demands the forfeit of "pure" music. The curtains are up, so to speak, when Magnard immediately goes on to cite his use of fugue in Titus's meditation and "the sweet harmony of a canon at the octave in all the outpourings of love." Wagner would have pushed aside such associations, tending as they might to fulfill a musical need at the expense of competing scenic and dramatic elements in a work for the stage. Magnard, however, succeeds in doing precisely what he says he does: he joins the claims of pure music to signifying mediations from the orchestra, leitmotivic structure, and a model of uninterrupted action, all inherited from Wagner. In this special success, the work is, in my judgment, more than adequate to its own declared intentions. Even as Magnard openly cites his debt to a progenitor, he seems aware that a larger success protects his finished achievement from being shown up as unoriginal.

With this example I want to call attention to a remarkable attitude: the mixture of serenity and stylistic self-awareness in Magnard's preface. The stable quality of this mixture, which I might describe as equanimity, goes against the belief that the sheer force of artistic legacies *must* induce states of creative and psychological anxiety. This latter is Harold Bloom's view, one of the most prevalent theories of influence in the second half of the twentieth century.

The contradiction between his dark outlook on creation and Magnard's is noteworthy. Bloom's views, so frequently cited and adopted over the past twenty-five years, are impossible to reconcile with the *début-de-siècle* aesthetics of sincerity and sensibility we are discussing, for in the Bloomian universe there is no "true self," only an anxiously related one. We shall resist the temptation to adopt Bloom's thesis. The anxieties of influence and "ratios of revision" proposed by Bloom as reactions to "strong predecessors" are liable to become theoretical barriers to historical understanding by imposing a grossly undifferentiated moralizing discourse upon the past.[23] We should already be suspicious of Bloom's unique, monumental partition of literary history: "Shakespeare belongs to the giant age before the flood, before the anxiety of influence became central to poetic consciousness."[24] Bloom's is a poor lens for viewing the dynamic interrelations between teaching, sharing, and influence – relations that are not stable across cultural and historical boundaries. Despite the great *internal* coherence of Bloom's arguments, his premises are extremely restricted, particularly when construed as a view of artistic creation: "Poetry is the anxiety of influence, is misprision, is a disciplined perverseness," he writes. "Poetry is misunderstanding, misinterpretation, misalliance."[25] In all, Bloom is hardly concerned with a poet's "inner life" as a factor in creativity; he very nearly negates interiority and originality as ideas altogether. This is only being self-consistent: Bloom takes the concept of originality to the same abyss where Wilde led sincerity; he dispatches it without any fuss and concentrates all his intellectual resources on the idea that every great poem is a misinterpretation of another prior poem.

Where would this leave Paul Dukas, our theorist of originality? If an artist's every creative act happens in relation to creative acts outside of himself, then it is difficult to see where there would be a foothold for any radically original embodiment in the process. The closest that Bloom comes to granting such a possibility, a possibility of originality, is to say that poems "arise out of an illusion of freedom." But this illusion is, after all, an illusion, and it reflects "the mind in creation," whereas Bloom is concerned with the poem on paper – "a made thing . . . an achieved anxiety."[26] Achieved originality, then, is perpetually displaced.[27]

Following Bloom, we might point out that Magnard has revealed his strength as a creator by appropriating Wagner through a misinterpretation. ("Laius and Oedipus at the crossroads," Bloom would add enthusiastically.) But could this patricide have been what Fauré meant, even unconsciously, when he spoke of Magnard's "strength and dignity"? And again, if self-appropriation of the progenitor's traits incurs "immense anxieties of indebtedness," where are they?[28] Magnard, here as elsewhere, seems to mull over his indebtedness rather dispassionately. In a preface invoking the great "ancestors" of his creative project – Racine, Wagner, and to a lesser extent Corneille, Virgil, and Berlioz – we could expect anxiety, but it is not there. Magnard expresses himself in tones assertive, jesting and pensive by turns. Fauré found the preface "full of wit and good humor."[29] Perhaps the older composer recognized a kindred spirit in Magnard and his attitude toward Wagner. We recall that Fauré, while working on the first act of *Pénélope*, mentioned the need to indicate dramatic agents musically, and he was fully aware of his situation: "That's the Wagnerian system," he said to his wife, "but there's none better."[30]

It seems less and less likely that Bloom would rank Magnard, despite his admirable misprision of Wagner, among the "strong" composers. Magnard and Fauré, for their very composure and judiciousness, are doomed to stand (or stumble) among the "weak." Let us admit that Bloom's codes could provide one starting point for a critique of the aesthetic premises we find in Fauré, Magnard, or Dukas. But Bloom's theory will not serve us constructively in assessing artistic values so far removed from his own that even the lapse of the intervening fifty years hardly begins to measure it. The composers we are discussing did not cherish interiority and originality as illusions, but as realities transmitted into the finished work. The equanimity we just noted in Magnard and Fauré comes not from weakness, laziness, or indifference but from conviction, sometimes fully conscious, in the transformative energies of such inner resources as Dukas described for us in his essay. Certainly the effects of influence on creative labor cannot be brushed aside, for commitment to a Dukasian ideal of originality does not expunge their presence and persistence, but there is no reason to assume, as a matter of principle, that every experience of artistic influence was always and already fraught with torment.

D'Indy, who was Magnard's most important teacher, once posed this question: "Can an artist, in spite of every influence, ever render anything but the art he bears within himself?"[31] We may admit the element of self-delusion, "the illusion of freedom" that, for Bloom, must always haunt such a conviction. But let us also admit the great power of that illusion and our own *incapacity* as critics to draw the line between illusion and reality in a personal artistic practice. There is no casuistry behind d'Indy's question, just as we find none in Magnard's preface to *Bérénice*. Fauré joins them in looking upon masterpieces, past and present, as profoundly supportive enrichments to a creative life, not as menacing progenitors and competitors.[32]

If this kind of confidence is common – to us, surprisingly common – among French composers working around the turn of the century, the story of artistic influence still cannot be told from one point of view. Debussy's struggle with the Wagnerian inheritance provides a case in point. Though mastered and made personal, this inheritance led Debussy to articulate a constant and self-conscious concern with remaining artistically "unfettered," an edginess that seems to lend itself to Bloomian analysis. Rather different from Fauré in this respect, Debussy regarded his artistic kinships with apprehension.[33] But even Fauré would remark in a moment of dissatisfaction, "It's true that this rogue of a man [Wagner] seems to have used up all the formulas."[34] And perhaps Fauré's comment to Hugues Imbert about working "at a moment when it is more difficult than ever to be an original composer" also has something about it of what Bloom would call "the exhaustions of being a latecomer" – though without any of Bloom's fatalism.[35] We need not deny the consequences of self-appropriation, the "anxieties of indebtedness," or even the efficacy of Bloom's theories in laying open specific artistic interrelationships in order to justify exploring a space of indebtedness shaped by calm rather than anxiety. The distance between our own critical predilections and those of Fauré's era already suggests that this project might prove enlightening. Let us consider two tendencies (among, no doubt, several others) that helped to produce a sense of relative equanimity in the experience of influence in artistic creation and reception. These are, first, the consideration of age and, second, confidence in the power of sincerity.

When critics confronted music evidently influenced by other music, the creator's age, in years or span of development, became a primary motive for special discrimination. The almost universal expectation that an artist show stylistic progress over time led to the practice of bringing different standards of judgment to bear on different stages of maturity. The signs of influence therefore had different meanings in earlier and later works. Imperfect stylistic assimilation and self-expression figured as accepted liabilities of artistic youth, but as a composer matured he found himself at the mercy of higher critical standards.

Let us recall that Fauré did not look askance at what he called "involuntary imitation" in Beethoven's first compositions. One explanation for this indulgence may be the allowances made for the limited artistic experience of youth. Fauré, like most of his contemporaries, respected the virtue of stylistic evolution to extract and refine personal essences. A period of imitation at the start of an artist's career was viewed as acceptable and, indeed, almost unavoidable. In this expectation, therefore, we find a reprieve from the normal requirements of stylistic uniqueness. If a composer makes the efforts necessary to realize his talents and has the desire for sincere self-expression, he will pass out of this initial phase; his true originality will gradually emerge "with the help of his sensibility and in the measure of his gifts."[36] In certain imperfect, early efforts of Beethoven, Fauré discerned the origins of the extraordinary trajectory that would end in "free creation."

To concede rights of inadequacy to young artists was simply a way of encouraging them in their vocation and allowing them the time necessary to refine their technical and expressive abilities. The philosopher Yvon Belaval has noted that the inexperienced artist often finds it helpful to copy and imitate other artists in order to hone technical skills. This is an old and familiar form of training. "But," says Belaval, "once [the creator] possesses such aptitudes, artistic sincerity consists in placing [those skills] in the service of his personal vision."[37] Undoubtedly, the transition between early experience and mature self-discovery was a crucial phase in the life of any artist, and this transition was an important theme in late nineteenth-century French criticism. The following review by Téodor de Wyzéwa represents a constructive encounter between a critic and a painter whose work, at the time, could be fairly located in this stage of transition:

> [Jacques-Émile] Blanche undoubtedly got up the preliminary education of his eyes in the study of impressionist paintings – thus his care over precisely graduated hues, the elimination of asphaltus, and various technical devices. But he has held on to a special character, the obvious merit of sincerity. He has not sought any coloristic complications except those of his own visions; beneath the adroitness of his methods, his impression remains completely faithful.[38]

Wyzéwa was assessing the work of a twenty-five-year-old artist. This passage exemplifies the sort of allowances critics made for talented newcomers. In Blanche's work, the influences of other painters are still too striking to be ignored, but they are redeemed by "the obvious merit of sincerity." In the work of a mature artist, however, a critique beginning with the same sentence, with a pointed account of external influence, would probably not end well. When critics like Wyzéwa responded with thoughtful forbearance, young artists benefited. Of course, this attitude differs significantly from Harold Bloom's: "All that a critic, as critic, can give poets is the deadly encouragement that never ceases to remind them of how heavy their inheritance is."[39] In contrast, the critic of Fauré's time often sought to assume the role of one of those spiritual accomplices Dukas mentioned in his essay – the desired "listener whose approval could help [the artist] to discern an originality, still latent, often needing only a little encouragement to dare reveal itself completely" (above, p. 83).

Dukas had insisted that originality arise "from a living sensation freed of all alien influence and all worry over imitation." So sweeping a claim, verging on the absolute, is unrealistic but characteristic of his personal idealism. When contemplating the fact of Wagner's influence, he admitted, more pragmatically, that some composers would, after all, be able to bear what they learned from that "alien" source "freely and without fatigue" (above, p. 80). "La musique et l'originalité" is an abstract, speculative essay; when Dukas faced the concrete task of reviewing a new work, he, too, was prepared to make allowances for a young or maturing composer. Vincent d'Indy was certainly close to maturity when Fervaal was staged in 1897, but he had begun the project while he was in his thirties and very much under the spell of Parsifal. Dukas, in an admirably balanced review of the work, did not shy away from a detailed discussion of Wagner's influence on d'Indy's opera. "Complex and fashioned from sundry elements, among which Wagnerian practices have an important place, but not an exclusive one," Fervaal was not yet a fully personal work – but Dukas clearly thought it was no pastiche either.[40] He looked upon d'Indy's opera as a promise of greater things to come, a serious effort by a composer still in a process of self-discovery – and thus deserving of a certain leniency:

> M. d'Indy has not shown us everything he is capable of or had his last word. We await the work freed from all Wagnerian alloying, the work whose outlines we already divine in Fervaal; he will undoubtedly write that work, and I think that his next piece for the stage will be the fulfillment of the magnificent promises we find here.[41]

In the end, Dukas recognizes a partial triumph in Fervaal – an admiration he is unquestionably the more willing to assert for "the profound sincerity that emanates from the work."[42]

In the writings of d'Indy himself, we find a strong variant of the premise that the young be granted certain stylistic indulgences. The image of a glorious originality forced into being all at once is something d'Indy liked to expose as wishful thinking. His experience as a composer and a teacher confirmed him in this conviction: originality will emerge out of native gifts "in due course." The effort to set oneself apart stylistically, the search for what French writers in this period called "distinction," too often became a search for prestige at the expense of continuing self-development. Prudence stands behind d'Indy's admiring sketch of Fauré's career:

> No less direct than sincere in his art, he did not search for originality at all costs in his first efforts, as the impotent so often do, for he knew that originality shows itself in due course in those spirits endowed with it.
> Nor did he ever affect to shun, out of prejudice, the artistic traditions established by our great predecessors. In precisely this way he came to create a style absolutely his own, impossible to confuse with any other.[43]

D'Indy thought that the various artistic patrimonies Fauré inherited did not prevent him from developing his own style. And here – though Fauré and d'Indy diverged on many issues – we must certainly recognize a confluence. Having considered Fauré's views on history, novelty, and education in the previous chapter, we can see how the two composers' different perspectives on the past also complement one another. D'Indy stressed alliances with tradition; Fauré, personal sensibility. Fauré named talent and sensibility as sources for self-expression, but he showed his respect for working in awareness of chosen traditions, too, as testified by his reference to the "great edifice" of art. D'Indy, on the other hand, did not altogether neglect personal interiority. For example, while stressing Beethoven's late treatment of the variation as a link with established forms, he also voiced his admiration for the "inner thought" that could rejuvenate those forms.[44]

"No less direct than sincere in his art, he did not search for originality at all costs in his first efforts." D'Indy's assertion already reveals the second factor contributing to relative equanimity in experiences of artistic influence: the more general conception of artistic originality as a direct outgrowth of sincerity. Why berate an artist for relying on other masters in his earliest efforts if, as many musicians clearly believed, the practice of sincere self-translation will gradually allow him to find his own direction? The negotiation of inner and outer worlds through the premises of sincerity diminished concerns over influence at *every* stage of a composer's career. Only these premises can explain how a critic could make an exhortation such as the following without a strong sense of paradox: "The artist should keep his personality intact amidst outside influences, in contact with which it will still be possible for it to develop itself."[45] But how? The closest the practitioners and advocates of sincerity come to answering this important question is to offer us something like a confession of the very quandary it expresses. Their aesthetic practice, which appears so idealistic at times, is also a compromise, a

pragmatic recognition that all great artists are influenced, and all strive for sincerity. In an imperfect world, it is the composer's responsibility to bring sincerity and influence into a fruitful relation, a relation that allows him to produce art he can believe in.

*

Let us consider a whimsical scene from André Gide's *Caractères*:

> Michel used to exasperate Édouard by constantly repeating that in art it was above all essential to be sincere.
> "What do you mean by sincerity?" Édouard finally asked.
> "Sincerity begins where imitation ends."
> "How many artists think they are sincere the moment they cease to be aware that they are imitating!"[46]

This dialogue seems to be a scoffing critique of sincerity, and Gide wittily draws out the want of rigor we sometimes find in discussions of the topic. Certainly, Gide was aware of widespread critical deficiencies in his contemporaries. But Édouard's deflation of Michel's "artistic doctrine" is not quite what it seems on first reading. He censures not sincerity as a principle, but a particular kind of sincerity. The concluding aphorism is of utmost significance. Édouard does not reproach artists their desire for sincerity; rather he pities their self-delusion. This delusion results from a self-examination that does not go deep enough: "How many artists *think* they are sincere . . ." but are not, for their imaginations outrun their achievement.

In Édouard's voice, the author probably allowed himself the last word. Gide the diarist, novelist, and moralist urged upon himself and upon others a process of soul-searching which was endless and required the strength to flee the illusions we create for ourselves.[47] If, after an inner debate, Édouard rails against a sincerity without depth, his Gidian exasperation probably comes from two directions: exasperation with those who think themselves sincere when they do not yet know how to know themselves, and exasperation with deficient critical practices that threatened to reduce sincerity to a cliché in talk about art. At the same time, the dialogue reminds us that there is more to sincerity than simply ceasing to imitate. Difference alone ["distinction"] does not signify true originality or attest to sincerity. There must also be that inner necessity to which Dukas pointed.

To a greater degree than we should expect, composers could rely on their belief in sincerity to extricate themselves from obsessions with impossible conditions of absolute independence. A passage from one of Fauré's most interesting reviews goes some way toward confirming this inference. The occasion was the revival of Massenet's *Werther* at the Opéra-Comique in 1903:

I should like to point out that this work dates from a period when the dominating influence of new principles had spread out over our music and that M. Massenet underwent this influence, if not to the same degree as some, at least as much as the majority of his colleagues, and it seems clear that with *Werther* [1892], after *Esclarmonde* [1889], he once again paid his tribute to the divinity of the day.

Whether M. Massenet accomplished this evolution altogether naturally, by the only law of progress that is enjoined upon every artist of worth, or whether, lacking an irresistible calling, he became Wagnerian because Wagnerism was then in vogue, matters little.

What on the other hand does matter is that he managed to give a rare unity to *Werther*, that in it he distributed the musical interest more generously and more equally among the voices and orchestra, and also that in it he never ceased to reveal "himself": by the grace of ideas, something so natural to him; by the allure of sonorities; by the sincere emotion of certain pages, and maybe even by the more artificial emotion of certain others.[48]

This critique is remarkable for its lack of worry over poetic influence. Massenet himself apparently felt no particular anxiety over the work and composed it very much as he composed his other operas. What Bloom would dub the "heavy inheritance" of *Werther* gives way, in Fauré's view, before the composer's sincere intentions and native originality. Fauré's discussion begins with a long, indirect evocation of the weightiest and most perilous influence of all, Wagner, and does not veil the fact that Massenet "paid his tribute to the divinity of the day." Yet Massenet's tribute does not become grounds for disapproval. A few pages ago, in discussing de Wyzéwa's favorable review of the young Jacques-Émile Blanche, I suggested that a critique of an older artist beginning with a bare account of external influences would probably not end so well. Jules Massenet's reputation had been sealed with *Manon* in 1884, and already in 1878 he had been elected to the Institut. So how can we explain Fauré's favorable review of a *mature* work whose "influenced" condition appeared obvious to him?

It is true that Fauré was a more forbearing critic than, say, Dukas. It may also be true that Fauré was less concerned about the *signs* of an artistic influence than its *effects*. But, beyond any apparent indulgence, there is logic to Fauré's assessment of Massenet, and to follow this logic, we need to examine in detail the movement of ideas across the three paragraphs cited above.

Despite any apparent swerves from Dukasian precepts, the principles behind Fauré's review in fact greatly resemble those of "La musique et l'o-riginalité." The ideal of artistic sincerity remains as central here as anywhere else: it is at the crux of Fauré's assessment of *Werther*. Note how the first two paragraphs are carefully shaped to punctuate the culminating third, which finally fulfills the rhetorical expectations Fauré has carefully built up. In the third paragraph we learn what matters most to Fauré are the quality of Massenet's actual achievement and his sincerity. The way Fauré introduces sincerity into this discussion is extremely important, for he gives it the extraordinary power to redeem the presence of another artist's influence. Wagnerian influences may be discovered in Massenet's opera, and Massenet may have absorbed this influence through complaisance rather than through an "irresistible vocation"; despite all that, he *"never ceased to reveal 'himself'"* in the finished music. Massenet's unique voice pealed through – and that, alongside the other successful qualities of the opera, was the artistic fact to which Fauré attached greatest value.[49] We may note, with some surprise, that Carl Dahlhaus recently expressed the same view: "Massenet had a genius for assimilating techniques without belying his own nature, and the leitmotiv technique he applies so openly, without thereby turning into a Wagnerian, sets up a close bond between the duets or dialogue scenes."[50]

In short, not only is Fauré's review of *Werther* far from anxious, but in it the ideological power of sincerity, firmly subjugating outside influences, proves greater than we had dared imagine. This case history is a bit strange. Surely that is part of its interest: it shows Fauré, a composer firmly identified with the ideal of sincere self-expression, praising the same quality in a composer with whom it was seldom if ever associated. Needless to say, there is an element of humor in Fauré's claim that Massenet "reveals 'himself'" not just by "the sincere emotion of certain pages" but also by "the more artificial emotion of certain others." Yet this comment takes on real substance. In later paragraphs of the review, Fauré declares his preference for the first act of the opera over the other two and reserves his greatest praise for its final scene, where Charlotte and Werther converse in the moonlight. This judgment ushers in another significant moment in the review wherein Fauré again sums up his praise by couching it in the language of sincerity. "Here M. Massenet reveals himself constantly, completely, with his most precious gifts, his most captivating qualities, his extraordinary sureness of hand."[51] But,

> he also reveals himself with his unfortunate exaggerations, and thinking, no doubt, to move us the better, he does not hesitate, at the end of this same act, to abruptly punch us in the chest with that sweet and exquisite phrase – the sigh of ineffable tenderness that at first had charmed us so much – using the violence of the orchestra's most brutal *fortissimo*.
>
> This procedure, which M. Massenet seems to have abused at all times, undoubtedly comes from "a reason of his heart," which to my reason, alas, is unknown![52]

Fauré's irritation with this device, which may indeed be found in Massenet's other operas, indicates something of what he had in mind in speaking of "artificial emotions." Yet if this emotion is "insincere" in its effects, it is, in at least two senses, sincere in its causes. First, as Fauré intimates, certain "artificial emotions" characterized Massenet himself. (Fauré may have been thinking of Massenet's great penchant for flattery.) Second, the musical and dramatic technique in question is a consistent feature of Massenet's style. Wagnerism did not mask Massenet's "most captivating qualities," but neither did it save him from his most "unfortunate exaggerations." Thus, he "reveals himself constantly, completely" and just as Fauré said, for better or for worse.

One feature of Fauré's review remains difficult to reconcile with what we know about the principles of sincerity: his statement about Massenet's later evolution. How could it "matter little" whether that evolution grew from inner necessity or from adaptations to an artistic trend? We should expect, on the contrary, that it mattered a great deal. Because Fauré makes the opposition between these two alternatives so clear, we can hardly attribute to carelessness such seeming indifference to Massenet's creative footing. I would favor allowing this contradiction to stand unresolved, for it reminds us that a historian's best theories can never encompass the full scope of historical acts. The surviving testament of one mind, let alone an era, is too diverse to be contained in this way.

For those who insist on a resolution, it is also possible to find one. Two circumstances put this detail in harmony with the aesthetic principles outlined elsewhere in this study. First, Fauré's indifference concerns only this specific work, an opera he judged among Massenet's finest achievements. Fauré may well have felt it pointless to take the most successful French operatic composer of the period to task for a possible inadequacy behind one of his most popular works. I emphasize that this inadequacy is only *possible*, because Fauré does not say whether he thinks Massenet's evolution came out of an "irresistible vocation" or not. The question is left open. In either case, Fauré apparently preferred to consider the actual merits and shortcomings of the work rather than its relation to Wagnerism, for, in the end, those merits and shortcomings seemed to Fauré to have so much to do with Massenet and so little to do with Wagner. Second, Fauré's terms of comparison in the crucial sentence do remain compelling. On the one hand, he recognizes an evolution accomplished "*altogether naturally*, by the only law of progress that is enjoined upon every artist of worth," which is "an irresistible calling," the principle of becoming as fully oneself as possible. On the other hand, he poses the alternative quite specifically as an indigence or lack

– and a lack filled in casually.[53] Although the difference between these two paths of artistic evolution may, at least in this case, "matter little," the difference still does matter in some degree. The first way is "natural"; the other, a substitute. If the second did not hinder the creation of an excellent work in *Werther*, it might well fall apart in less talented hands. Artistic choices informed by "an irresistible calling" – those which are affirmative and natural – implicitly remain the surest and most preferable. Influence in creative work was, here as elsewhere, a force seldom subject to absolute judgments.

3 Perpetuating originality: the ideal of self-renewal

When Fauré alluded to the difficulty of "being an original composer" in his correspondence with Hugues Imbert (above, p. 78), he was writing in 1887, at the height of Wagner's Parisian splendor; his concern was unsurprising. The concern with originality would persist, however, and resurface years after the Wagnerian tide went out. In 1904, as he was working on the First Quintet, op. 89, he wrote to his wife:

> Yesterday I worked well again. But how hard it is to write good music that doesn't owe anything to anyone and that might interest a few people. And as Saint-Saëns says, the difficulty is renewed with each new composition. And it's perfectly natural that one would always want to write works that make progress over the preceding ones [*faire des œuvres en progrès sur les précédentes*].[54]

The implicit topics of his paragraph are, first, originality and, second, self-renewal, which may be defined as the perpetuation of originality. Fauré's letter gets to the core of what, in his mind, made writing original music such a challenge. He begins with the obvious, by evoking the independence that characterizes an original composer. Fauré describes good music as "not owing anything to anyone," and, hence, like Dukas he expresses an ideal, an absolute summit that artists approach but never fully attain. What is desired is perfect independence in self-expression; what is achieved is "good music," music that is markedly different from other music – even that which it most closely resembles. Yet, in composing, "the difficulty is renewed with each new composition"; therefore stylistic independence is not a static achievement; the composer will aim to *renew* his originality as he imagines each new work. This is the desire Fauré believes "perfectly natural" – "toujours faire des œuvres en progrès sur les précédentes."

Dukas's essay and our other sources have indicated that certain virtues, such as independence and self-reliance, were considered supports to a gifted artist trying to create original music. Fauré's letter of 1904 further suggests that only when bound to a process of self-renewal will these qualities allow the artist to *perpetuate* his success. Through this process, he will be able to create not just one original work but a succession of them over a lifetime.

Self-renewal is therefore a dynamic reverberation of originality which reveals itself over time in personal, artistic progress. Originality, progress, self-renewal – these are all abstract ideas, but they had concrete effects, both personal and public. We shall consider two examples from Fauré's music to show both sides of these effects. The content and structure of *L'horizon chimérique*, op. 118, will serve to tell us about the inward, spiritual effects of self-renewal – in short, how Fauré thought about his own developing vocation as a composer, even in old age. We shall then consider the implications of stylistic self-renewal for public reception through the earlier example of Fauré's First Quintet, op. 89.

Ongoing evolution mattered deeply to Fauré. In his comments on *Werther*, he referred to "the only law of progress that is enjoined upon every artist of worth." In writing on Beethoven's string quartets, he admiringly singled out the way they reflected Beethoven's personal evolution. And, to the end of his own life, in his own music, Fauré sought the same quality. One of the most satisfying moments of his whole public career was probably the première of his Second Quintet for Piano and Strings, op. 115, in May 1921. Philippe Fauré-Fremiet tells us that despite the fluency and beauty of Fauré's later chamber works, they mostly elicited respect rather than enthusiasm at the time. But the Second Quintet was an exception: at the première, the performers were "incandescent, *white-hot*" with their own amazement and conviction, and "the public was carried away from the first bars in a continuous impulse of surprise and dazzlement."[55] In 1921 Fauré might have begun thinking about resting on his laurels; he was seventy-six, and he had just retired from the Conservatoire. Yet the conviction of his performers and the enthusiasm of his audience apparently left him with precisely the opposite feeling. His son recounts, "When he was back home, at the moment he was ready to retire, he said to us as he sat on his bed, 'Of course, an evening like this is a joy. But what's really almost *maddening* about it is that afterwards you mustn't settle down again; you must try to do even better.'"[56] That fall, Fauré wrote what would be his last set of songs, *L'horizon chimérique*. I would suggest that this work tells us something about what he meant when he spoke of the "maddening" need to surpass oneself.

The poem Fauré placed last in *L'horizon chimérique* begins in a vein of loss:

Vaisseaux, nous vous aurons aimés en pure perte;
Le dernier de vous tous est parti sur la mer.
Le couchant emporta tant de voiles ouvertes
Que ce port et mon cœur sont à jamais déserts.

[Ships, in vain we'll have loved you;
every last one of you has gone out to sea.
The sunset bore away so many open sails
that this harbor and my heart are forever deserted.]

Standing on the shore and looking out to the horizon at twilight, the poet knows he is "among those whose desires are on the earth" (l. 9). The song ends in a mixture of hope and desperation as the poet still addresses the ships:

Mais votre appel, au fond des soirs, me désespère,
Car j'ai de grands départs inassouvis en moi.

[But in the depths of evenings your call drives me to despair,
For within me I have great departures still unsatisfied.]

The poems of *L'horizon chimérique* are by Jean de La Ville de Mirmont, a gifted young poet who died in the Great War. As Charles Panzéra has observed, the communion of two artists at opposite extremes of human experience, a poet in his twenties and a composer nearly eighty, lends a special poignancy to this whole collection.[57] It is, however, unclear at all times whether Fauré, in setting these poems, reflects the dreams of the late poet, too soon silenced, or rather lets them become a vehicle for his own mingled hopes and desires. What is clear, Fauré shrewdly selected and re-ordered the poems to his liking. The two lines just cited, the end of the composer's cycle but the middle of the poet's, seem to have captured Fauré's imagination most of all and compelled a musical realization that broadens and intensifies them beyond what we would expect from reading them on the page. Indeed, this final effusion (from the word "Mais") is so powerful and positive as to seem, retrospectively, to put the rest of the song completely under its sway (Example 7).

Fauré traces a poetic path from emptiness and remembrance to spacious, open-armed desire.[58] Those sails vanishing over the horizon are perhaps the thousand pages Fauré has already sent out into the world. Crowded with memories and a sense of approaching night, this song may be the last one of all. But the final couplet reopens the question: "Mais votre appel . . ." Desperate or elated, Fauré faces the challenge of self-renewal again: another voyage, another work. In Fauré's hands, the ending looks vibrantly into the

Example 7. *L'horizon chimérique*, op. 118, no. 4: "Vaisseaux, nous vous aurons aimés," mm. 18–28.

future. At least we may be permitted to think so, since he then embarked on
two major works, the Piano Trio and the String Quartet. Significantly, the
vocal climax is not on "désespère" but "inassouvis"; defiance and resignation collide on this word to create one of the most heartfelt moments in all
his *mélodies*. This D-major ending, its "great departures still unsatisfied,"
would seem to furnish a musical embodiment for the remarks Fauré made
to his family after the première of the Second Quintet.

Fauré dedicated *L'horizon chimérique* to the young baritone Charles
Panzéra, who gave the première of the work at the Société Nationale on 13
May 1921, the day after Fauré's seventy-seventh birthday. Panzéra sang this
work again the following month in the prestigious concert of national
homage to Fauré held in the Sorbonne. Fauré admired Panzéra's art from
the start and gave him advice on interpreting his songs. Thus it is interesting to consider a comment Panzéra made many years later. He wrote that
the final phrase of "Vaisseaux," "synthesizing the entire cycle, restores the
work to its starting point."[59] What did he mean? Panzéra was an interpreter
of extraordinary sensitivities. The comment, though fleeting, is not facile;
both the music and the poetry bear it out in a number of ways. If we look
back to the "starting point," that is, the first song of the cycle, its opening
line envisions precisely the kind of psychological horizon that the last song's
"unsatisfied departures" dare to imagine in the face of memory and physical groundedness.

> La mer est infinie et mes rêves sont fous.
> [The sea is endless and my dreams are mad.]

Thus the "great departures still unsatisfied" now, in the first song, look out
again on a new morning; this is the circle Panzéra referred to. How does
Fauré set these words? (Example 8.)

The accompaniment, as if inhaling, almost floats up to its target, "fous."
Fauré substitutes the flat mediant for the expected dominant harmony, and
with this delightful shift brings out the all-important word behind the
singer's A. The ascent and the harmonic recoloration also mark the latent
contrast in the line between outer scene ("La mer est infinie") and subjective feeling – the mad potentiality of the dreams the poet will exultantly send
out. Their giddy voyage becomes the poetic conceit of the entire poem,
which Fauré sets in a rugged, pandiatonic D major:

> La mer est infinie et mes rêves sont fous.
> La mer chante au soleil en battant les falaises

Example 8. *L'horizon chimérique*, op. 118, no. 1: "La mer est infinie . . .", mm. 1–4.

Et mes rêves légers ne se sentent plus d'aise
De danser sur la mer comme des oiseaux soûls.

Le vaste mouvement des vagues les emporte,
La brise les agite et les roule en ses plis;
Jouant dans le sillage, ils feront une escorte
Aux vaisseaux que mon cœur dans leur fuite a suivis.

Ivres d'air et de sel et brûlés par l'écume
De la mer qui console et qui lave des pleurs,
Ils connaîtront le large et sa bonne amertume;
Les goëlands les prendront pour des leurs.

[The sea is endless and my dreams are mad.
The sea sings to the sun while beating the cliffs,
and my light dreams are even more ecstatic
to dance on the sea like drunken birds.

The vast motion of the waves carries them along,
the breeze tumbles them and rolls them in its folds;
they will be an escort, playing in the wake
of ships whose flight my heart pursued.

Drunk on the air and the salt and bitten
by seafoam that consoles and cleanses with tears,
they will know the open sea and its good bitterness;
the seagulls will take them for their own.]

From start to finish, this first song seems to answer the questions the last one poses. "La mer est infinie" is a call to life; if we turn the pages back to it after "Vaisseaux, nous vous aurons aimés," it seems to justify our feeling that that final cry, though bittersweet, was not bleak.[60] Jankélévitch found *L'horizon chimérique* free of pathos and, emphasizing its continuity, he gamely juxtaposed the first and last lines of Fauré's work: "The sea is endless and my dreams are mad . . . For within me I have great departures still unsatisfied."[61] For Jankélévitch this music embodies the spirit of adventure, of the desire to be "always elsewhere."

The obvious rise from first to fifth degree in the opening phrase of "La mer est infinie" also calls attention to a curious mirroring that exists between the beginning and end of the cycle, and this link is made more obvious by the common key of D major. In effect, the vocal lines of the first and last songs are palindromes writ large. The ascent from D to A which begins "La mer est infinie" (Example 8) corresponds to the descent from A to D at the end of "Vaisseaux" (Example 7, mm. 25–27). In both cases the ascent or descent also summarizes the larger melodic path the song gradually traverses. In "La mer est infinie," for example, the voice rests successively on the supertonic (m. 11), mediant (m. 16), subdominant (m. 18), and dominant degree (m. 20), to which it remains anchored to the very end of the song. "Vaisseaux" does just the opposite, prolonging the dominant degree in the treble until the desired harmonic and structural descent is fulfilled in the last phrase. This, I suggest, is the second way in which the end of the cycle, with its long-awaited tonic, may be said to "restore" us to the beginning, where the same note awaits flight toward "mad dreams" again. Even the urgent rising seventh at the close of the last song (m. 26) has a parallel in the falling seventh at the end of the first (mm. 26–27).[62]

We may draw a circle from the last to the first note of *L'horizon chimérique*.[63] We need not dwell on whether Panzéra, who provided only a slender stem for our allegory, would have noticed all these poetic and musical interrelationships. The rightness of his insight remains impressive, especially when we consider Fauré's stated goals of self-renewal. Fauré would, with the Piano Trio, op. 120, try to satisfy his desire for another creative adventure – and succeed in spite of old age and rapidly declining health. Both the Trio and the posthumous String Quartet, op. 121, remind us that the circle, the great spiral, of expectation and memory symbolized by *L'horizon chimérique* could until death be traversed again and again.

Fauré's need for self-renewal went hand in hand with his concern for a novelty whose conditions and motivations we considered carefully in the previous chapter. This section puts novelty in the background and brings a specifically personal, even spiritual, capacity for self-renewal to the fore. The kind of artistic development Fauré praised in others and worked out for himself meets our ears as "something new" but also coincides with those forms of inner, subjective growth Dukas described in his essay on originality.

We turn now to the public reception of Fauré's personal vision. What response could he anticipate from his audience, and what did they expect of him? For answers, we look to the genesis and reception of Fauré's First Piano Quintet, op. 89, a piece that had resisted him for a long time and with which he was struggling again in 1904, precisely when he spoke of his desire "to write works that make progress over the preceding ones" (above, p. 97). The Quintet had been an on-and-off project for eighteen years, which gives it a much longer genesis than any other work by Fauré. He first planned it as a third piano quartet in 1887 after the rapid completion of the Second Quartet, op. 45, in the previous year. But the Requiem and two projects for the theater occupied him in the short term, and it was not until 1890 or 1891 that he began the new piece in earnest. His notebooks from those years contain material for three large-scale movements; according to Philippe Fauré-Fremiet, the exposition of the first movement was completely written out.[64] Eugène Ysaÿe, on a visit to Paris, tried the movement out with Fauré and was overwhelmed by its beauty. But for unknown reasons Fauré set aside this promising start until the latter half of 1894, and then at that point his return to the project was haunted by a desire to start the first movement all over again or at least revise it severely. Then came a long silence. His extant letters speak no more of the Quintet until 1903.[65]

In the end, he would rewrite the first movement and compose the others over three working vacations in Switzerland between 1903 and 1905. Yet as his letters from Switzerland in 1903 reveal, this return to the work was a last-ditch effort. Nine years of inactivity suggest that the Quintet came very close to abandonment in that bottom drawer where dwelt the Violin Concerto, the Symphony in D Minor and many other compositions Fauré either never felt satisfied with or refused to publish. His revival and completion of the Quintet over the following two summers formed an important chapter in his life; those three years marked a passage from sterility to artistic fulfillment. In retrospect, we may also see that they marked a transition into Fauré's late style.

Here we must remember some facts of Fauré's life and especially the evidence of his letters to Marie Fauré between 1901 and 1904. These letters breathe an air of profound uncertainty and sometimes despair. In those years Fauré appears to have gone through a serious creative crisis.[66] His predicament was not simply artistic but also physical. In 1903 his hearing had begun to deteriorate noticeably, and this discovery took a great emotional toll on him. During 1903 and 1904, Fauré's personal and artistic dilemmas were so great that abstract speculations on sincerity, originality, and the nature of musical expression crept into his letters. Allusions to broad aesthetic issues and perplexities are uncharacteristic of Fauré and not to be found gathered together so frequently anywhere else in his correspondence. Two of those allusions, we may now note, provided vital documentation about sincerity (p. 12) and the ineffability of music (p. 41) in chapter 1. The quotation about "works that make progress over the preceding ones" has brought us to this correspondence again. In these unwonted speculations we glimpse the articulate outgrowths of his personal confrontation with new artistic, emotional, and physical obstacles. These letters open a window on his most general thoughts about the art of music, a kind of philosophy, but they also reflect a particular moment in his life, grounded in urgent problems.

Fluctuating and incurable, Fauré's auditory malady depressed him and exacerbated all the uncertainties he was feeling about his future. When he set out alone for a month in Switzerland in 1903, his intentions were twofold: to improve his health and to try to compose. He explained to Marie, "Like you and no less than you, I am sorry not to have composed anything for almost a year now. I hope a holiday and rest will get me going again."[67] Unfortunately, after a week of rest his hearing was worse than ever, and he seemed to lose hope. "I'm crushed by this illness that has attacked me in the very faculty it would have been absolutely imperative to keep unimpaired . . . This morning I put some music paper on my table; I wanted to try to work. But I feel only a horrible cloak of misery and discouragement on my shoulders. . ."[68]

Two weeks later, around 20 August 1903, a new piece of music began to take shape in his mind. Though at first it seemed to him a violin sonata, it became a second movement, the magnificent Adagio for the stalled Quintet. With new impetus at last, Fauré reported to his wife, "The second movement will force me to take up the first again."[69] We need not retrace the steps of Fauré's patient compositional progress over the next two years any further to understand its significance. He ended his period of frustrated silence by immersing himself in a major work, a work which had refused to speak to him for a long time and yet which he would try to "hear" through his terrifying new sensory impairment. It was, at the same time, a moment of spiritual and artistic self-renewal.

In March 1906, a few months after the Quintet was finished, and on the occasion of the dress rehearsal with Eugène Ysaÿe, Fauré wrote his wife:

> Ysaÿe finds the style of the Quintet finer and loftier than that of my quartets, more completely free of any search for effect: absolute music. I'm very happy that he had this impression, the more so because, at the moment, music is

striving to be everything *but* music. Maybe [Roger-]Ducasse will not approve of this work, which stands completely on its own, but that's all the same to me. Deep down, I have the feeling that my methods are not within *everyone's* reach![70]

The sense of conviction in this paragraph is altogether different from the pained self-questioning of the letters written two and three years before. And in this account it is not a matter of Ysaÿe's opinion alone; we infer from these words Fauré's own perception of the finished work. In transmitting Ysaÿe's opinion, Fauré was especially honored by his friend's high appraisal of music that represented the labor of many years and much self-searching. To have attained something "finer and loftier" in the Quintet than in the preceding quartets, to have forged an art "more completely free of any search for effect," was this not to have written a work "en progrès sur les précédentes"? The First Quintet appears to have fulfilled that craving for self-renewal Fauré announced in the letter he wrote in 1904, during the second summer of its creation. Today, its pivotal standing in Fauré's stylistic development is clear: Nectoux has rightly considered the First Quintet a portal to the masterpieces of Fauré's final period.[71] Even in 1910, only four years after the première, Joseph de Marliave astutely identified "the new style inaugurated by the master in his Quintet."[72]

Let us consider the reception of the work in 1906. Remarkably, I have been unable to locate a single negative review of the First Quintet, and only Georges Servières offered a mixed review. Troubled by "dampened sonorities" and a certain "severity" in thematic development, he opined nonetheless that "study and repeated hearing" would "undoubtedly clarify the seemingly cloudy polyphony of this composition." He added that its "nobility of bearing and the thread of its style never once weaken."[73] Fauré's critics, even the ambivalent Servières, spoke of the beauty and spiritual elevation of the work. The general public was also enthusiastic. When the Quintet made its Paris première in the Salle Pleyel, Louis Vierne reported that "frenetic bursts of applause" broke out after the first two movements, and at the end of the work "an immense uproar, prolonged, ringing with enthusiasm," obliged Fauré to take at least five bows. "I had not seen anything like it since the first performance of Franck's Quintet."[74] Two weeks later, the Quintet triumphed again at the Société Nationale. Although Fauré's public success with this work was decisive, his "desire to write works that make progress over the preceding ones" was not necessarily a good formula for winning such success. The lingering identification of an artist's personality with the style and character of his first public triumph could lead listeners to reject deviations from that best known work. The next chapter will be the place to consider public resistance to changes in personal style; for now we need only keep in mind the potential gap between a composer's private ideal and public expectations.

Reviewing the performance of the First Quintet at the Société Nationale, Pierre Lalo started his column for *Le temps* by noting, "M. Fauré had not published a new piece of chamber music for a long time. His most recent, the Second Quartet, already dates back some twenty years. With curiosity we awaited this Quintet, whose impending appearance was no secret."[75] Such curiosity would usually greet the première of a major new work by a widely recognized composer, but in this case the curiosity verged on restlessness and seems to have prompted a careful interrogation of Fauré's whole creative direction. This apprehension is unmistakable in Vierne's review:

> What newness, after all, could he bring us who has already said so many new things? what methods would he use? what would be the means brought into play? what would be the nature of his ideas? Before the concert I found myself turning over these disquieting questions.[76]

Vierne's worries about innovation were answered by what he called the "long enchantment" he experienced while listening to the new Quintet. But these worries, like Lalo's curiosity, help us to understand what was at stake in the première of a new work – and what Fauré knew to expect of admirers and detractors. Concern with self-renewal was both a personal and a public issue. Critics' keen consciousness of the interplay of novelty and originality meant that composers did not earn public triumph lightly.

Indeed, in self-renewal, these listeners were looking for a very particular, balanced combination of novelty and continuity. The essence of an artist's past musical style, his "most original originality," would always remain in place but ever imbued with fresh ideas and new means of realization. This was the double ideal: never to let innovation break the personal, identifiable thread connecting past works to present, yet never to let self-reliance lapse into mere repetition. Fauré's First Quintet succeeded in this task; it revealed a voice transformed, enhanced, renewed, but not altered out of recognition. The critics, to their credit, understood and stressed the intelligible relations between this new work and Fauré's previous ones. They admired his knack for discovering change within continuity and isolated an underlying homogeneity behind the changes in his style. (We shall see, in the next chapter, that the critics did not do so well by Debussy.)

Of the first three concerts featuring the Quintet, two were entirely devoted to Fauré's music. Thus, as public events, these concerts could and did become a test of the norm just described. Where did the new work stand in relation to old ones? What were its influences? What future did it promise? In Brussels, the First Quintet ended a recital that also included Fauré's Second Quartet and eight songs from various periods. At the Société Nationale, the program began with the First Quintet and ended with the Violin Sonata, op. 13, thus drawing together the latest and first of Fauré's chamber compositions. *La bonne chanson*, the Sixth Nocturne, the Third Barcarolle and the *Thème et variations* filled out the span between the Sonata and the Quintet.[77] These concerts elicited reviews focused on the simultaneous progress and continuity of Fauré's art. From Brussels, Octave Maus observed, "What is striking in Fauré's work when we see its past to its present thus joined, is the *unity* that presides over the development of his personality."[78] Both Lalo and Laloy marveled at this same kind of homogeneity in Fauré even as they expressed the sense that something in the style had changed:

> His most recent work stood by some very early ones and others dating from the middle of his career. There was no disparity from one piece to another. This art has undoubtedly changed, become deeper and more subtle; the feeling, thought and inspiration, though, have remained the same.[79]

> Better than ever by bringing [earlier and later works] together could one appreciate that unity of style of a music which was always sure of itself and which did not let itself be turned aside by Wagner or César Franck from the road which it was making for itself with smiling, tranquil assurance.[80]

Laloy raises the question of influence, which is, of course, tied to the questions of originality and innovation. The reviews by Laloy, Vierne and Lalo all name Franck, because Franck's Piano Quintet was the first and most celebrated French work in this medium.[81] But significantly, they bring up Franck only to emphasize Fauré's independence from him. Laloy describes Fauré's footing on a personal path apart from Franck or Wagner. Vierne, implicitly recalling the cyclical structure of Franck's Quintet, pointed out that in Fauré's, "each movement has two themes of which we find no traces in the following one."[82] And for Lalo, Franck directly or indirectly instructed every other subsequent French composer in chamber music, but Fauré's "innate originality, at once delicate and invincible," allowed him to find a path apart from Franck.[83]

Lalo chalked up the absence of Franckian traces in the First Quintet to Fauré's originality. But absence is only a negative attribute. Originality is positive, and Lalo was interested in illuminating qualities that were Fauré's alone. Why was Fauré an original composer and one capable of self-renewal? Lalo argued that Fauré's originality was based on sincerity and self-realization:

> From the time of his earliest efforts to the present moment, [Fauré] has
> listened to the music he had inside himself and has not been troubled by
> what others wrote; in his beautiful quartets as in his priceless songs, he said
> what he felt, as he felt it: he was himself.

Lalo then connects this originality, whose triumph comes from self-reliance,
to the vitality of *self-renewal*. The artist's original qualities gain in worth and
intensity according to their capacity for controlled self-transformation.

> [Fauré's] art has gradually become more complex, and he has used more and
> more intricate means of expression. But its complexity, delicate and
> seemingly transparent, mars neither its clarity nor its subtle engagement with
> sensibility. Here, indeed, increasing complexity and exploration do not have
> their sources in artificial study but in the natural evolution of an art that has
> never ceased to be in intimate accord with thought and feeling.[84]

Lalo lavishes his greatest praise on the balance between sameness and innovation in Fauré's unfolding œuvre. Beneath this praise, as we have so often
found, lies the firm demand that stylistic explorations remain grounded in
personal sensibility – that they arise, as Lalo put it, "in intimate accord with
thought and feeling."

Lalo concludes this review by making explicit the relation between
progress and permanence in Fauré's style. Lalo joined many others in
admiring a kind of sameness, a homogeneity, persisting through Fauré's
long career. This cherished sameness was intimately bound up with the idea
of originality: the full expression of inner life and feeling which allows originality to show itself in a single piece has equally powerful implications for
the consistency of an entire life's creative accomplishment. "Originality so
strong and deep-seated," says Lalo, "not only shelters the composer who
possesses it from outside influences, it ensures *the unity of his work*." Fauré's
First Quintet affirmed this larger unity by taking its place in an expanding
personal canon; it "tallies with his previous work and continues it harmo-
niously."[85] The dialectic of self-renewal and homogeneity was vital to the
musical aesthetics of Fauré's period, especially to the understanding of style
and self-renewal. Therefore I have devoted the next chapter to the implications of homogeneity for compositional practice.

4 Posterities: to Boulez and back

In chapter 2, we considered novelty as an outward manifestation of originality. Now we have studied originality itself. We have also investigated its
role as the root of artistic self-renewal and a powerful idea about an
artist's vocation. We may again summarize the relation between novelty and

originality by saying that radical originality, the kind Dukas affirmed and
Fauré applauded, esteems novelty but always insistently points to a primary,
unique origin located in the creator.[86] This relation of ideas is easy to understand but, inasmuch as it differs from views on innovation closer to our own
time, it is unfamiliar, or muffled by louder voices. I cannot write an integral
history of originality in the twentieth century in this study or pretend to
address important but very complicated questions of national difference in
aesthetic values. I have spoken in detail of two or three decades, only in
France. Nevertheless, the fate of novelty and originality since 1900, both
within and across national boundaries, is worthy of thorough consideration. Leonard B. Meyer almost alone in historical studies of music has
shown us what the foundations of such an inquiry could be.[87] Within the
narrower context of this chapter, however, I would like to extend historical
consequence to the idea of originality. Here is an occasion for a shift forward
in time, even to the work of living composers. We shall consider Boulez,
whose changing convictions render a vivid picture of the rivalry or interplay
between technical and personal bases for originality. Through the distinction between the technical and the personal – between novelty and originality – we may show how some composers reacted against the old values
toward the middle of the twentieth century. As we reach the 1970s, however,
ideas and attitudes begin to return to originality in ways that compel us to
recognize the enduring relevance of its radical meaning.

The decline of originality

In the United States, writers on music and art have become so accustomed
to measuring originality by the evidence of novelty that few even bother to
warrant the connection. Middle and late twentieth-century "originality,"
tending toward the technical or the "made" quality of the work, almost
ceased to be a property of personality at all. Thus it became easier to equate
boldness or rebellion with originality. Moreover, at the historiographic
level, today's received ideas become confused with yesterday's; late twentieth-century originality was imposed on late nineteenth-century originality.
Some of our most self-conscious historiographers have consented to reproduce superficial images of nineteenth-century originality, as in Mary
Devereaux's recent reference to romantic "originality" as an artist's capacity
"for breaking with tradition and making his or her own rules."[88] However,
Devereaux only verges on identifying novelty with originality here; she does
not actually erase the distinction. Hers is still a relatively generous conception of originality, for it embraces the creative subject and thus supposes
a personal shaping of art. But she meant to show the difference between

nineteenth-century views of artistic originality and our own by summarizing the former, and in this she fails by binding radical originality to concern for "rules" and their transgression. The thesis mistakes more recent concerns for those of a century ago. Such a limited idea of originality reflects deep-seated presuppositions shaped by aesthetic circumstances in the past fifty years.[89]

Radical originality lost its ideological priority to novelty toward the middle of the century, though not universally. Curiously, the idea of self-renewal seems to have suffered no parallel decline; critics and composers today continue to defend and discuss artistic growth and self-renewal in terms Fauré or Dukas would have found intelligible.[90] But "renewal" would operate not so much upon the self and its artistic expression as upon the means of making, or technique. As a result of displacing originality from the fundamental position it held at the start of the twentieth century, we have shifted away from talking about the originality of a given composer; we tend to speak of the originality of a work of art. Thus, the word "originality" is often used for precisely what would have been called "novelty" in 1895. For many later twentieth-century artists and critics, the ties between radical originality and a romantic cult of personality and poetic enthusiasm tainted the concept. A rearrangement of priorities allowed personal originality to be absorbed into the neutral, impersonal realm of novelty. The "modernist" places aesthetic satisfaction in the objective results of originality, in the "skillfulness of the combinations and their effect."[91] The *subjective* origin of these combinations is effaced rather than represented.

The least generous interpretation of originality will reduce it to a mere claim on the technical precedence of a particular work. A focus on breaking and making rules, as in Devereaux's definition, already points in that direction and turns the old priority of originality over novelty upside-down. By 1950 a significant number of composers and critics had succeeded in carrying out this inversion and made a philosophy and practice of compositional objectivity. This emphasis on technique was shared, on different grounds, by composers working in total serialism, electronic music, and experimental (or, to borrow Meyer's term, "transcendental") music. Few of these composers would ever openly admit to prizing novelty above originality. Most of them, especially the serialists, affected a masterful silence about originality, accompanied by a tendency to affirm compositional progress through organizational complexity and scientific jargon. In extremely reflective artists, we occasionally find an ambivalent awareness of the prevailing winds and an acknowledgement of their dangers. In 1948, John Cage put the matter with some eloquence as he tried to describe his own position:

> In spite of these [anti-materialistic] convictions [of mine], I am frankly embarrassed that most of my musical life has been spent in the search for new materials. The significance of new materials is that they represent, I believe, the incessant desire in our culture to explore the unknown . . . This desire has found expression in our culture in new materials, because our culture has its faith not in the peaceful center of the spirit but in an ever-hopeful projection on to things of our own desire for completion.[92]

But for all this judiciousness, Cage was no believer in the value of original expression (which is, after all, more a spiritual than a material value). He would later criticize Varèse for honoring the needs of his own artistic imagination, taste, and personality – as if those needs prevented Varèse from pursuing his acoustic and experimental goals. "'Rather than dealing with sounds as sounds, he dealt with them as Varèse.'"[93] The remark speaks directly to the ideological change at hand. To cultivate impersonality consciously, to abolish expression, to deal with sounds as sounds (rather than to deal with them as a person), renders originality not just secondary, but irrelevant. Deprived of its roots in personal translation, originality loses all purchase.

Leonard Meyer has accurately evaluated this shift as marking the repudiation of "belief in the value and importance of personal-cultural expression (originality and uniqueness)" in favor of the idea that "creation consists of the impersonal invention of means and relational systems and the discovery of their implications."[94] Some of the later serialists (who are traditional composers compared to a transcendentalist like Cage) reassigned "originality" to a narrow, fully inverted interpretation, which, far from putting novelty in the service of something essentially personal, reduced originality to half the idea it once was. Originality came to be equated with the fabric of composition, the outer raiments that, however brilliant, earlier composers would not have thought self-sufficient. Meyer summarized both the old and the new views of creativity and suggested their concomitant implications for critical evaluation. Until the end of World War II, he wrote, "to create was to embody . . . unique and personal insights and affects in pigment, in words, or in tones. If this embodiment truly reflected the inner being of the artist, his work would be original and idiosyncratic."[95] In contrast, of the period after 1945 he writes,

> The ideal of individualism and the goal of intense personal expression have now been repudiated by two of the important ideologies of our time and have been derogated by some traditional artists. In their place has been substituted the concept of the work of art as an objective construct. *Originality is no longer tied to the discovery of means expressive of the artist's*

inner experience, but to the ordering of materials; and creativity is seen not as an act of self-revelation, but as a species of problem solving . . . Form and technique have thus superseded inspiration and expression.[96]

This ideological transposition asserted itself so well that its assumptions soon gained the upper hand in critical work dealing with music from *any* part of the century. Over the past four decades, a diminished view of originality has left its mark on many studies of twentieth-century music. And with regard to the period before 1945, the resulting blind spots would certainly have troubled some of the composers whose contributions I am seeking to illuminate.

We find the post-war ideological constraints described by Meyer embodied in even a work as recent and catholic as Robert Morgan's *Twentieth-Century Music*.[97] The book is by no means unsophisticated and quite consciously orients its discourse toward the pluralistic concerns of our own *fin-de-siècle*. But Morgan falls into a kind of ambivalence in the face of different attitudes toward material novelty and personal originality. On the one hand, he implicitly signals the difference between originality and novelty. Noting the changes that have occurred since Meyer wrote *Music, the Arts, and Ideas*, Morgan ventures the opinion that composers in the past two decades "have changed direction, effectively giving up on technique as the primary ground of newness" even though – and this is quite correct – "the change in viewpoint does not necessarily mean the end of technical innovations in musical language; novelty will still grow out of original sensibilities."[98] Morgan's language has a surprising affinity with some statements from the opposite end of the century. It is isolated in the book but is held out with conviction – a conviction, I suspect, that comes from Morgan's experience as a composer rather than as a historian. Unfortunately, this present-day insight throws open no windows on the past in Morgan's historical gallery. "Originality," in name or conception, is notable in all the chapters for its absence, and taken as a whole, the book becomes an account of donations to the technical till. Morgan has a great deal to say about "the evolution of twentieth-century musical language" (p. 35), but his primary interest in staking the trails of "language" means snubbing many individual contributions – in particular (as we should expect) those that are difficult to link up with the technical "main line" (Janáček, Fauré, Vierne). This, admittedly, is the kind of survey many readers would expect from the outset, "a survey that concentrates mainly on new developments" (p. 481), and one that also parallels the course of the century in its increasing turn away from personalities and toward technical assets. But we must remember the cost of this kind of exclusion. For instance, if we treat Ravel primarily from the point of view of advancing "musical language," we might well sum up his contribution to the technical repository as Morgan does: "not major" (pp. 126–27). However, there are good reasons to ask whether Ravel's contribution might not be greater when seen from another point of view – perhaps the *aesthetic* point of view Morgan contrasts with a technical one earlier in the book (p. 17).

How aware was Morgan of his equivocal treatment of originality or the effects of that treatment on the stated importance of a given composer's achievement? Is his defense of this treatment, in the preface to the book, a kind of apology for his warrants?

> Musical modernism has defined itself more through emphasis on the new, on what was musically unprecedented and thus distinct from the older tradition, than through any other single attribute – an important reason for the concentration on *technical issues* in the study of twentieth-century music. (xiv, emphasis mine)

Morgan shows some awareness of the historiographic dilemma his project has come up against. But he resolves it by ideological fiat. What *is* "musical modernism" – the subject of the sentence cited above and, ostensibly, the whole book? Morgan never bothers to give us a definition, historical or systematic, or even justify his usage; such want of distinction has a direct bearing on the problems I have begun to point out.[99]

Dispossessing originality, I would suggest, had real consequences for the kind of internal evolution imagined for music earlier in the century. Meyer pithily noted that "novelty, often mistakenly confused with 'originality,' from which it sprang, gradually became a criterion for judging works of art."[100] One-sided exaltations of novelty affected not only criticism and historiography, but also the very possibilities of composition. In the late 1940s and 1950s, an aesthetic of impersonality and objectivity, which found expression both in aleatoric procedures and the quest for rigorous new principles of order, coincided with the rejection of expressive originality. Meyer cites three examples of this trend:

> The composer who works with predetermined formulas for the pitch, time, timbre, and dynamic series of his piece, and then merely follows these, is not involved in the configurations and combinations which result . . . Similarly, the composer who allows random events to choose for him is being objective and impersonal. And, of course, the final stage of impersonality takes place where the musician programs rules for a computer and allows the computer to do the composing.[101]

In every case the artist's personal, lyric afflatus has been jettisoned together with other salient elements of traditional composition. "If the individuality and personal will of the artist is no longer considered significant and central, if making an art work is a discovery rather than a creation, then it becomes more or less irrelevant who created a given art work or when it was created. Art becomes anonymous."[102]

This was an extreme point on a line of historical development. Harbingers of a retreat from these aesthetic conditions became more and more conspicuous toward the end of the 1960s. Today a composer who grew up in that turbulent decade may "rejoice that the great technique-fixation of the post-war era is over."[103] The author of that phrase, Paul Moravec, a composer born in the United States in 1957, considers "the end of the primacy of technical innovation over all other considerations of music-making" to be "a healthy development."[104] His position, which could have appeared reactionary three or four decades ago, is today neither reactionary nor isolated. For not only has objective experimentation ceased to provide a secure foundation for originality; the very idea of technical discovery, even in the service of the traditional habits of innovation, has come into question, too.[105] In giving an account of his personal and artistic development between the 1970s and the 1990s, Moravec speaks of the need to distinguish the "what" of a composition from the "how." He ultimately registers a plea to revive the distinction between novelty and originality in creative work and therefore calls for the very difference that had been effaced in an earlier generation's quest for absolute technical modernity. The gradual collapse of technological optimism brought creative work toward a new point of departure: "finding themselves in a dilemma regarding their use of technique, composers sensibly returned it to its appropriate, subordinate role."[106] Each composer must then assume responsibility for the materials and means brought into play for a particular work but need no longer demand an intrinsic novelty of them. "I sense that a new, or rather, renewed, standard of originality has emerged and continues to gain acceptance in the post-postwar era. It may or may not concern innovation, with which it was confused for so long. But it must certainly involve an authoritative individual spirit."[107]

Moravec's skepticism will not surprise historians and critics who have paid attention to musical events over the past three decades. Not long after Moravec was born, an older generation of composers had already begun to question the viability of an unceasing pursuit of innovation in musical materials and techniques. Moravec is a latecomer in the twentieth century. What we should find remarkable in his essay, however, are its echoes and vindications of ideas Dukas tried to enjoin upon *his* contemporaries one hundred years earlier! Moravec's misgivings over "technique-fixation" are significant but need not imply what accompanies them: his earnest call for the restitution of originality in its spiritual fullness. Moravec asserts his need "to develop a satisfying *personal* common practice" and therein recognizes the fundamental aim of originality: "What makes my song new is my particular human experience and expression – whatever its worth – entirely unprecedented and forever unrepeatable."[108] Probably unaware of his Dukasian affinities, Moravec has nonetheless mustered arguments that that composer would have admired for their judiciousness and their motivations in sincerity. Although the content and concerns of Moravec's essay betray later twentieth-century concerns, he holds out an old theoretical vessel, radical originality, to renewed artistic purpose.

As the phoenix originality rises again from its century-old ashes, a postmodern and slightly skeptical creature, we witness, as so often in the history of art, the restoration of a past point of view in new circumstances.[109] Yet we would be mistaken to take the word "restoration" too seriously, for it exaggerates the degree to which originality ever vanished from Western musical culture. I do not think it is bold to suggest that the old balance of originality against novelty, despite remarkable counter-surges, never left our consciousness. If some artists accepted novelty as a premise of originality rather than its consequence, others, and not only the most conservative, held and continue to hold to the opposite view. In this light, Morgan could be reproached for allowing "1945" to become a kind of historiographic talisman, warding off any composer who failed to mingle with the avant-garde at Darmstadt or Donaueschingen. His emphasis on a historical break ultimately cherishes the convenience of an exhilarating, uniformly revolutionary spirit in post-war musical culture.[110] Like all such conveniences, however, it is a highly selective view disguised as a self-evident generalization. The wish to dichotomize a whole century, or even its modernity, around a moment of remarkable energies cannot, I think, be sustained unless we are willing to accept some rather bankrupt reductions.

In 1947 René Leibowitz categorically asserted that the serial language "was the only necessary and authentic musical art of our time."[111] This is but a specific statement of a principle which might be rephrased, "Only those composers adhering to *my* technical etiquette express themselves and their epoch authentically." Leibowitz's dictum now appears far less representative of "our time" (or even his time) than of a particular camp. Likewise, accounts of North American music that insist on an emphatic displacement of one ideological order by another toward the middle of the twentieth century seem less and less plausible as we start the twenty-first. The same is certainly true in France. To be sure, the expressive priorities favored by Fauré's and Debussy's generations were already under intense cultural pressure in Paris by the end of the First World War. Even some composers close to Fauréan priorities would partake of the upheaval, as we saw with Ravel's repudiation of the principle of artistic sincerity.[112] On the other hand, we find no sign of French composers abandoning the specific idea of originality until the 1940s. Only then, with the first creative activity of the post-serial generation, did radical originality lapse into an apparent, only scattered, neglect in France. René Leibowitz's assertion about the twelve-tone method gives us a glimpse of this new attitude. While not explicitly defying the old idea of originality, Leibowitz shows himself uniformly indifferent to it.[113] This conceptual omission is stunning; certainly I know of no earlier French discussion of progressive music that does without the ideal of personal originality in its exhortations to stylistic development. Leibowitz wants to explain the accomplishments of the Second Viennese School from "the angle of the evolution of *compositional problems*" and is willing to stop the discussion there. The resources that composers bring to the "problems" confronting them are expressly "the data of the language of their time."[114] In other words, personal sensibility and originality are not brought to bear on stylistic change. In their absence, Leibowitz expresses a technical or "linguistic" interest in the music he discusses; personal sensibility seems to play no role in constituting novelty. This account, published in 1947, already begins to resemble the kind of history Morgan and many others would write later.

Boulez: gesture, idea, realization

If the inversion of priorities was especially shallow and transient in France, no composer and thinker could better persuade us of the fact than Pierre Boulez, of his generation one of the composers most inexorably committed to *modernité*. Yet Boulez has turned out to be a passionate spokesman for originality. This would perhaps surprise those readers who identify his musical thought with the rapier provisos of his youth. Indeed, between 1948 and 1962, Boulez's remarks on serialism and modern music did Leibowitz, his tutor in serialism, one better. But with maturity Boulez began to angle his critical idiom away from dogmatic assertion and embarked on a period of open-ended exploration that continues to this day. The shift in perspective seems to have been one result of his coming to grips with the immense challenges of his own artistic ideals even as he became increasingly involved with the music of others on the podium and in analytical essays. To understand the tack and consistency of Boulez's thought across the years, we need to retrace it from its earliest manifestations (in the testy *Relevés d'apprenti*) to the wide-ranging speculations on history and composition he recently published under the title *Jalons*. In the following pages I shall attempt no

more than a blueprint of this intellectual development and restrict myself
to comparing some of the oldest and newest of his writings.

Let us begin with Boulez's famous edict on serialism – one of those statements that brought him so much attention when he was in his twenties:
"Any musician who has not experienced – I do not say understood, but truly
experienced – the necessity of dodecaphonic language is USELESS. For his
entire work brings him up short of the needs of his time."[115] This statement
(perhaps the most striking instance of a general tendency in Boulez's early
writings) makes claims for specific technical necessities above and beyond
sensibility. For Boulez, the very arena of "useless art" is defined by disparity
between personal necessities and historical ones; personal necessities, obviously, are no longer conceded the supreme office they held in Fauré's day.
From this new scale of values follows Boulez's willingness to condemn two
generations of composers on the basis of their alleged technical
insufficiency or "uselessness."[116] He most explicitly condemned Hindemith
and Leibowitz, but his negative critique also admitted such diverse figures
as Milhaud, Malipiero, Françaix, and Dallapiccola. There are those who
resorted to a false "classicism" and those who wallowed in the "dregs of
romanticism"; Boulez dispenses with them. Here, there is no question of a
unique personal voice redeeming the value of a style. Certain stylistic categories are "contaminated" from the start. As for those rare artists Boulez
enthusiastically rescues from the great post-Schoenbergian void (Webern,
Varèse, Messiaen, and, transiently, Cage), they are praised not for their personalities but in terms of their specifically technical contributions.[117] This
train of thought naturally gives a firm impression of "technique-fixation"
on Boulez's part, and in truth, he is willing to treat "musical language" as an
autonomous entity, as if it could somehow *on its own* create the crises and
problems facing a composer.

It seems fair to say that the early twentieth-century view of artistic creation, as exemplified in the thought of Fauré or Dukas, tends to essentialize
personal sensibility. Boulez, in contrast, essentializes musical technique, for
he poses compositional problems as prior to the negotiations between individual imagination and social and historical contingencies.[118] This brand of
essentialism shapes his critiques of ascendants and contemporaries, not
least of all of Schoenberg, who, for Boulez, failed to understand the logical
implications of his own discoveries. Schoenberg lost the address of his own
technique: "Beyond its role as regulator, the serial phenomenon passed vir-
tually unnoticed by Schoenberg."[119] Boulez's *Relevés d'apprenti* cover the
period from 1948 to 1962 and include his harshest rhetorical attacks. The
most militant pieces are hard to take, because Boulez allows pure pugnacity
to vitiate often splendid critical reflections. If, however, these critiques

sometimes lapse into the hateful, the intolerant, or the pontifical, certain passages already reveal another side of Boulez. The essentializing utterances are best remembered chiefly because they coincide with his most notorious polemical slashes; for all that, it is wrong to equate Boulez's vision of creativity with the limiting tendency we have just summarized. Even in "Schoenberg Is Dead" we find nuanced observations within the rodomontade. While Boulez seeks to discredit Schoenberg's serial works, he looks very favorably upon the earlier atonal works, where, significantly, "the musical thought is perfectly balanced by the purely formal aspects of the experimentation."[120] Here the phrase "musical thought" refers to what Schoenberg, in a passage Boulez has just quoted, called the "'very powerful expressive forces'" that guided the first atonal pieces. In this analysis, Boulez not only associates expression with technical means but also consciously gives expression a standing at least equal to technique. This partnership, as an aesthetic ideal, seems to be confirmed in the corollary, negative observation: Boulez writes that, with the works after opus 22, "Schoenberg seems to have been overtaken by his own innovation" and backed himself into a "no man's land of strictness." In the earlier works, "aesthetics, poetics, and technique are all in phase," but then the synergy is broken.[121]

In "Possibly …", which contains that infamous statement about "useless" composers, we find further hints of Boulez's reluctance to stand pat with his technical cards. At one point in the essay he suddenly interposes this remark:

> It may seem surprising that I say nothing at this point about the actual composition of the work. But from all that has been said about the discovery of the world of serialism, it will be transparently obvious that I refuse to describe creativity as simply a mechanism for setting these initial structures in motion; any account would be unsatisfactory which gave the act of writing the appearance of a conditioned reflex.[122]

What a striking modulation coming from someone who claimed in preceding pages that the "first object" in serial technique "should be to give [it] its autonomy."[123] Unlike Cage, Boulez is not content to "deal with structures as structures," at least not for long. But neither is Boulez yet prepared to air the creative process whose importance he already grasps. His chief intellectual concern lies in integrating all the structural elements of a new work – what he himself is struggling to create. At the end of the essay he offers a self-defense that speaks to the problem more directly:

> But why should I be ashamed of my technique? On the contrary, I retaliate by saying that this allegation of intellectualism is ill-founded since it starts from a false conception . . . of the interlocking roles of sensibility and intelligence in all creative work. Do not forget that, in music, *expression is intrinsically*

bound up with language, even with the technique of language. Music is perhaps the least dissociable of all expressive media, in the sense that it is its actual morphology, before all else, which expresses the emotional development of the artist.

I . . . tend to the view that imagination needs the various springboards of formal resource placed at its disposal by a technique which dares tell its name.[124]

Looking back over Boulez's career, we may see these two passages as presages of themes to be developed later in his criticism but already active in his aesthetic practice. Troubled by the mirage of formalism early on, Boulez tried to be honest with himself and his readers. Without denying that his primary object of speculation was currently technical, he insisted, in this last passage, that technical resources serve imaginative needs. He does not seek to wipe out imagination and expression but stresses their necessary, reciprocal relationship with technical responsibility:

It is the need to pin down what one wants to *express* that directs the evolution of technique; this technique reinforces the imagination, which can then project itself toward the previously unperceived; and in this way, in an endless play of mirrors, creativity pursues its course; a living and lived organization, allowing every discovery, enriched by every new experience.[125]

Boulez was already on a path to a carefully integrated vision of creativity.

In an insightful introduction, Robert Piencikowski captured the transition (or fluctuation) in Boulez's critical work over the fourteen years chronicled by the *Relevés*. "One passed from the stage at which technique made do with an indefinite aesthetic, to the stage at which it is the aesthetic, made conscious by necessity, that will determine the technical means. This reversal contributes to a modification of Boulez's role in the avant-garde music of the 1950s, in relation to the tendencies which begin to emerge at that time."[126] It is only necessary to add that the development of Boulez's thought was not strictly chronological. We find different propensities in contemporaneous essays, because different essays, and even different sections of the same essay, were thought out according to different dialectical and personal needs. Nor can we ignore the sheer self-assertion that lies behind some of Boulez's most prickly statements; he was declaring what he wanted his own art to become. Like Cocteau, Boulez began his career by marking out an aesthetic territory for himself with a sharp, ironic blade. Synthesis and consistency came later.

We find both these seasoned qualities in *Jalons*, which brings together the amazing lectures Boulez gave at the Collège de France between 1976 and 1988. Published in 1989, they represent the most recent phase of his work.[127]

Jalons places his ongoing concern with technique – and most of all its aesthetic *motivations* – in a context so rich that one could never mistake his present artistic aims for those of a formalist. Boulez's lectures are an organized, literate, and extremely conscientious reflection on a composer's artistic vocation. Here, under the significant title "Idée, réalisation, métier," he does at last concern himself with "the actual composition of the work" and thus fulfills the promissory comments we found in the *Relevés*. Boulez's own artistic achievements since the 1960s have allowed him to envision music from a less combative angle, and his reflections on individuality and self-realization seem to dispel the earlier tendency to insist almost exclusively on technical means:

> Every important work – and I mean not just a particular piece, but the whole of a composer's accomplishment – is a new coalescence in which a unique volition led to a synthesis never known before . . . This synthesis has been made once and for all and thenceforth renders all syntheses of the same kind impossible, for they could only be reproductions devoid of originality and therefore not really syntheses at all.[128]

Here Boulez has not stashed the concept of originality behind a compulsory technology, serial or otherwise, but brought it into the foreground. We could even go so far as to compare his statement with one by Louis Aguettant, who, summarizing Fauré's originality, speaks to the same issue in more conventional terms: "His musical language is no mosaic of procedures but his very nature. This language could serve only once, to express a sensibility with qualities as individual as Chopin's and Debussy's."[129]

Thus the most modern of French composers seems to have come round to a point of view on musical invention surprisingly close to that of preceding generations. Two specific values in Boulez's recent writings allow us to confirm the affinity. First, he gives a prominent role to personality and homogeneity. He believes that the realization of an original achievement, a unique synthesis, depends on "a latent personal profile that only asks to be revealed, that comes into focus and takes form little by little through privileged encounters."[130] Boulez believes that historians of music have not emphasized enough this consistent "inner disposition" that reveals itself in an original body of work:

> For the most part, traditional musicology has concerned itself with showing the evolution of a personality by describing certain imitative procedures in order to reach the most absolute imprints of originality. But what this account lacks, and what would be more interesting by far, is attention to the permanent quality of *gesture* in a given composer's work; we should see how this gesture reaches toward someone else at first, then deforms the other's

gesture by increasing or reshaping in a specific way; we should see how this
gesture becomes stronger and is recognized as itself; how, finally, it is
polished, amplified, and becomes irreducible to any other class of gesture.
(pp. 44–45)

The idea of gesture, "un geste authéntiquement profond" (p. 66), has
become a critical mainstay of Boulez's. Without doubt it is the surrogate for
what Fauré's generation simply called personality. Indeed, as Boulez himself
admits, "The primordial gesture" is "the one which can only be explained
by that word, so banal, so inevitable: personality."[131] This profound
"gesture" manifests itself in the stylistic homogeneity of a body of work.

The second traditional value in *Jalons* follows directly from this clear
concern with personality (or the irreducible qualities of "gesture"): his constant attention to stylistic development. Like Dukas, Boulez is fascinated
with the process by which a composer moves from imitation to self-realization. Like Dukas, too, he refuses to grant the possibility of an absolutely
impersonal artwork: "To be sure, in every early work there is a large share
of invention that may be reduced to the model and where reference to this
model remains noticeable. But a certain irreducible quality will already exist
by which personality reveals itself" (p. 41). Boulez displays a readiness to
acknowledge the importance of these models, and thus of tradition in
general; this is what he means when he speaks enthusiastically of "privileged
encounters" – privileged in their reach across both time and space. The
providential, revelatory experiences a composer has with another artist's
music can nudge him onto a path of his own by allowing him to discover
his own "difference." Learning others' music "helps us to discover what we
are" – though at the same time Boulez wonders whether "it may be that
analysis can teach us nothing we do not already know but only reveals this
[inner knowledge] to us and makes us conscious of it" (p. 64). As for the
composer's path into maturity, Boulez presents its course in equally familiar terms. "If the composer's personality is strong enough," he writes, "he
will pass of his own accord into the next stage" because his "intuition" of
what he really wants for his own music will be continually strengthened
through his experiences with other works (p. 38). This is the stage where, in
Dukas's words, the composer begins to assert himself by shaking off the
authority of his models. In the last stage, Boulez asserts, "the composer finds
the resources his intuition calls for only in himself" (p. 39).

As we should expect, Boulez does not envision this maturity as static: it
moves repeatedly from self-realization toward self-renewal. The oscillation
between these two aims is as vital for Boulez as it was for Dukas or Fauré.
Boulez is on the lookout for "change, the sudden discovery of an unmapped
field of Invention, the imagining of new ramifications," for these are signs

of continued growth. "As surprising as the alteration may seem to us, however brusque, however unforeseen, it is nonetheless integrated in a process of evolution that always faithfully reflects . . . the composer's gesture" (p. 66). *Le geste du compositeur* – beyond it, perhaps, we glimpse through originality and those "faithful reflections" something like sincerity. It would be too much to expect Boulez, after Ravel, to use *that* encumbered word. But, in this last passage, Boulez produces a defense of self-renewal cast in the same mold as that which served Louis Laloy, in 1910, to champion Debussy's stylistic evolution after *La mer*.[132] We shall return to this very real conceptual affinity and come to understand its basis, the ideal of homogeneity, in the next chapter.

No less real, however, are certain differences between Boulez and his early twentieth-century compatriots. For all his interest in personality, Boulez still locates "the essential" inside the work, not in the imagination; this is one implication of his insistence on "réalisation." "The essential thing is buried in the work and will only be revealed through it" (p. 35). This work, nevertheless, responds directly to personality, even to sensibility: "thought and expression . . . imply stylistic traits suited solely to such thought and expression and justified only by them" (p. 47). To measure the evolution of Boulez's thinking and attest his reluctance to fetishize technical traits, we need only notice what implies what in this sentence, what justifies what. We cannot separate technical work from personal expression in Boulez's philosophy of composition without betraying his thought. For him, the "unique synthesis" embodied in a great work entails both technical progress and something irreducibly personal at once. He refuses to put originality and novelty, or what he also calls Idea and Realization, in opposition (pp. 63–65). Compared to Dukas or Laloy, Boulez, in his urges to realize originality, synthesis, or compositional progress, seems to call upon the *work* more than the *person*; at the same time, he actively invokes personal resources, the composer's "irreducible gesture" and "inner dispositions" (see pp. 44, 45). Technical adequacy and progress have always been special preoccupations for Boulez, but he has become increasingly interested in the personal qualities that contribute to the homogeneity and idiosyncrasy of a life's work. Thus he admires the secret homogeneity of an individual style: "I speak not of the form of the work but rather of the formal concepts that go into its language, constituent mannerisms that moreover allow an almost unerring recognition of its stylistic profile" (p. 38). So Boulez conceives of a "stylistic profile." He knows from experience that the composer begins his process of discovery by learning from selected "traditions" ("privileged encounters"). Finally, these are Dukasian postulates sifted through Boulezian concerns.

We began this discussion of Boulez by mentioning one of his teachers, René Leibowitz. Yet Boulez promptly and ungraciously disavowed Leibowitz's ideas for their "dogmatism" and "larval academicism."[133] So let us remember Boulez's other teacher in composition, Olivier Messiaen, whom he was certainly willing to criticize, but whom he held in devotion long after leaving the Conservatoire and whose musical influence proved lasting.[134] It is curious to recall that Messiaen's composition teacher, in turn, had been Paul Dukas. Messiaen took his First Prize in composition under Dukas's guardianship only thirteen years before Boulez matriculated into the same institution. Could we not end this whole chapter with an unexpected (and certainly "privileged") encounter: Boulez and Dukas? There is some merit to looking upon Dukas as Boulez's spiritual grandfather. But to trace a direct line between their thinking is tendentious. Rather, the continuity is oblique; I would associate it with a broad stream of beliefs about musical creativity in France. Boulez is merely the most recent representative of this tradition – but the crucible of its vitality, too.

5 Conclusion

The work of this chapter has alternated between two tasks. First, I have tried, now in plain terms, now more elaborately, to show what originality meant to Fauré, Dukas, their contemporaries, and others who came later. I have also related considerations of influence, self-renewal and stylistic evolution to the idea of originality. What we have learned illuminates how shared yet often intuitive principles supported the creation of music of lasting inventiveness and character. Second and concurrently, we find that sincerity and originality repeatedly intersect. This overlap reflects a kind of unity in French thinking about music, but also leads to some confusion. All our efforts to distinguish between them will never altogether erase this confusion. We may try to grasp these aesthetic concepts and show their interaction as explicitly as possible, but at the same time we must recognize that their basically unsystematic character does not allow for a fixed or hierarchical arrangement. Sincerity and originality are profoundly invested in one another, and qualities that suggest their individual aesthetic functions sometimes disappear as we approach ideological foundations.

Fauré, Dukas, and their artistic and critical peers called upon a radical sense of the word "originality" in order to ground their belief in a fundamentally different "something" that makes a creative testament what it is – or what it becomes in the process of elaboration. To discuss originality in this deep sense therefore would mean approaching a discussion of essences:

He possesses that originality which is definitive: the originality of his soul, and he has sought the original forms that make up his style only in order to express what he heard within himself. Originality of style soon enough surrounds a composer with a throng of imitators. Originality of soul cannot be imitated, and the master predestined for it finds but seldom in time and space those equals who make true disciples.[135]

Carraud's complementary use of the outward and inward senses of "originality" in this passage is instructive, but it is by no means unusual. He has only distinguished between Fauré's "originality of soul" and the novelty or "original forms" of his music, and he has done so in order to show the validity or truth of Fauré's novelty. In placing the greater weight on originality in the radical sense, he echoes the distinction and the preference Dukas claimed for musical genius in "La musique et l'originalité" some fourteen years earlier. On the material side of originality, the "original forms" that Carraud evokes refer not to sonata, rondo, or fugue, but to "form" in the broadest sense of the word, as any sonorous translation of imagination or Idea. In this role, the word "form," justly extensive, subordinate to originality but not pejorative, stands for all musical embodiment. Form is everything that Dukas contrasted with the prior "spark of life," but it is only through that lesser, formal light that we can sense the original fire.

4 Homogeneity: meaning, risks, and consequences

The consistency of a composer's musical style over time was one of the most important themes to emerge out of the previous chapter. The continuities that link a composer's past, present, and future work are what we shall now discuss as the *homogeneity* of his music. We can find this quality in the unique strands that run through a store of music, link it together at distant intervals, and ultimately reveal its origin within a single human imagination. Without the distinction between novelty and originality established in previous chapters, it might seem difficult to reconcile originality and homogeneity as aesthetic ideals co-existing productively. But we have seen that a composer's *sameness of voice*, for critics from Lalo to Boulez, served as a proof of originality. (Indeed, in chapter 3 we cited critics whose affirmations of musical originality converged on praises of stylistic homogeneity so often that it was difficult to defer discussion of the latter idea until this point.) In what follows we shall have more than one occasion to confirm that homogeneity depends, radically, on the concept of originality and the practice of sincerity. Sincerity, self-renewal, originality, and homogeneity were concepts bound up with one another in mutually conditional relationships.

This chapter is divided into three sections, and both the first and third call on the ideas of Marcel Proust. The first section discusses sameness in Fauré's work as perceived as a mark of superiority. I suggest reasons for this system of aesthetic values and relate homogeneity to complementary ideas, such as heterogeneity and innovation. The second section, considerably longer, discusses the negative consequences of insufficient homogeneity. We consider Debussy as well as Fauré and, for each, analyze the vagaries of public reception. The balance of sameness and innovation in a new work proves to be one touchstone of public understanding. In the third section, Proust's meditations on homogeneity prompt a new approach to forms of recurrence in Fauré's music and bring us to the concrete level of musical examples.

1 Homogeneity

While the previous chapters provide enough background for us to understand why Fauré's contemporaries would value stylistic homogeneity, we need a more specific and qualitative sense of this aesthetic category. In particular, how did homogeneity fit into what we might call the ideology of composition? Here we may turn to Proust, whom I present as the most important theoretician of homogeneity in the period of Fauré's maturity. Proust's observations about music have not merely an anecdotal or personal significance but a strong cultural one, and, with Jean-Jacques Nattiez, I believe that we must take Proust seriously as a thinker about music.[1] Proust was an amateur and a passionate listener, and like the best French amateurs of his time he heard music quite as perceptively as professional critics and musicians. Indeed, we shall later see that it was Proust, not Saint-Saëns or Debussy, who immediately recognized Fauré's *Bonne chanson* as a masterpiece.[2] Himself a creator obsessed with personal style and authentic self-expression, Proust was superbly equipped to grasp the aesthetic importance of kindred tendencies in the other arts, and his well-known love of Fauré's music makes citing him in this context that much more appropriate.

In a passage toward the end of *La prisonnière*, the narrator, Marcel, turns to one of his favorite topics, the music of Vinteuil. In the first chapter of this study we noted that Proust associated the music of this fictional artist with Fauré, and particularly his First Piano Quartet, op. 15. We may now take up the rest of a passage cited there, concerning the "perfumed silkiness" of Vinteuil's music and its "geranium scent" (p. 47). Vinteuil's personal style is the focus of the rest of the passage:

> Perhaps it was in this unknown quality of a unique world, one no other musician would ever have made us see, I said to Albertine, that the most authentic proof of genius lies, more, really, than in the content of the work itself. "Even in literature?" Albertine asked me.
>
> "Even in literature." And thinking again of the sameness [*monotonie*] of Vinteuil's works, I explained to Albertine that none of the great writers ever composed more than a single work, or rather, they refracted through various media a single kind of beauty they bring into the world.[3]

Here Marcel elegantly escorts us from originality to homogeneity. In his first sentence, the "unknown quality of a unique world" corresponds exactly to the concept of originality set forth in chapter 3. The composer's "most original originality," the "proof of genius," is beyond or behind "the content of the work itself" because the composer's native voice is its first cause, the "origin." The second half of the quotation, after Albertine's interjection, introduces "homogeneity" through the idea of Vinteuil's sameness or "monotonie." For Marcel, this *monotonie* is admirable, not irritating. We shall come to see that Vinteuil's homogeneity is evidence of true self-realization in artistic expression. The value of homogeneity is tied to the idea of originality, because the "monotonie" is the sameness of a unique inner world: a unique origin of "a single kind of beauty."

Proust's emphasis on the sameness of Vinteuil's work throws light on late nineteenth-century concepts of artistic development in general. As the following observation suggests, this emphasis is particularly suited to the case of Fauré. In 1981 James Kidd wrote, "The consistent character and craftsmanship of [Fauré's] music present special challenges to the analyst, not least being the fundamental issue of 'originality as newness' versus 'invention through sameness' it raises in the minds of listeners and scholars." Kidd recognized Fauré's propensity for the latter, "invention through sameness," but added that the significance of this aesthetic disposition "remains perplexing."[4] The concept of homogeneity helps undo the perplexity, at least from a historical point of view; it provides the most adequate category for explaining the cultural significance of Fauré's knack for "invention within sameness." The tendency toward stylistic homogeneity is not at all peculiar to Fauré's art. We may think of Monet, Fantin-Latour, Mallarmé, and perhaps even Ravel as likewise "inventing through sameness." Fauré's stylistic homogeneity betrays his participation in a more general ideology of personal growth and expression in art.

Kidd was not the first critic to remark Fauré's "invention through sameness." The composer's contemporaries responded to the continuity in his style with enthusiasm and used a variety of expressions to describe it. I have chosen the word "homogeneity" because it is apt and unambiguous. Though not often encountered in musical criticism of Fauré's time, this term was not unknown. In an article in *Mercure de France*, Jean Marnold praised the "supreme homogeneity" of Fauré's work. Marnold used a rare term, but his understanding of the phenomenon was commonplace: he cited Fauré's faithfulness to originality and personal sensibility as the source of his homogeneity.[5] Critics were acutely aware of stylistic consistency and considered it a mark of artistic superiority as a material trace of the inner, original spirit of an artist and evidence of its sincere translation.

In speaking of Fauré's homogeneity, critics ultimately referred to his remarkably continuous discovery of differences within the boundaries of stable and recognizable attitudes toward technique and expression. It is necessary to emphasize that critics admired both the *differences* and the *consistencies*. That is, their praise of homogeneity cannot be mistaken for a simple aversion to variety and change, and this fact will become apparent by the end of the chapter. Most praises of Fauré's homogeneity included praise of variety, too; hence, specific kinds of heterogeneity were subsumed in the more general "sameness." In the following statement by Joseph de Marliave, we find sameness and difference brought together this way: "The variety of this achievement is unrivalled. For more than thirty years [Fauré's] art, living off nothing more than its own substance, . . . has renewed itself ceaselessly within an absolute unity of character."[6] De Marliave stresses the variety and self-renewal of Fauré's art, but he considers these in a context of homogeneity; Fauré's art lives off "its own substance"; the music has "an absolute unity of character." Balancing these opposed categories, appreciations of Fauré's originality had as much to do with what remained the same from work to work (homogeneity) as with what was new (novelty). This reasoning would at first seem paradoxical, but, as the previous chapter shows, it was a logical consequence of a particular understanding of the word "originality."

Although French critics looked for a balance between heterogeneity and homogeneity in art, homogeneity, that peculiar "unity of character," was most captivating for them. But why should a composer's sameness of voice be so interesting? To be sure, Fauré maintained high standards in almost every work he published; the beauty and finish of his music is undeniable. One account of his homogeneity could equate it with the consistency in his workmanship. But another account, more interesting and complex by far, would get at the changing musical language beneath this alluring surface. For example, in Fauré's first works, we can already find the principles of contrapuntal expansion that led him to explore the extreme limits of tonal syntax in his late works. Indeed, two recent studies by Edward Phillips and Taylor Greer have analyzed different phases of this technical continuity in Fauré's long stylistic itinerary.[7] In abstract terms, Fauré's technical development over sixty years might be explained as a series of deductions, at once logical and inspired, from a rather small set of premises. But the musical language of Fauré's old age is drastically different from that of his youth – so drastically different that critics have suggested comparisons between late Fauré and Stravinsky's work in the twenties and thirties.[8] We look in vain for any glimmer of Stravinsky in, say, Fauré's early nocturnes, so there must be some hidden alchemy in his logical chain of deductions. Fauré, in short, presents us with a stylistic development whose seamlessness is as obvious as the distance between its starting and ending points is baffling.

Fauré composed right through an era that saw all the great musical innovations of the first half of the twentieth century. In fact, Fauré's last years were among his most productive. I suspect that Fauré's homogeneity fascinated his contemporaries in part because it allowed him to write music that continued to explore the sensibility and musical materials of his earlier works without ever sounding dated. Roland-Manuel, in a review of Fauré's Piano Trio, op. 120, of 1923, wittily acknowledged the modernity of the work: "Gabriel Fauré's recent works attest to a freshness, a versatility, a juvenile quality so marvelous that one reaches the point of wondering whether we are failing to show the proper respect due this great and illustrious

composer when we salute him with praises that are too much like encour-
agements."[9] Fauré's ability to innovate within the slowly expanding boundaries of his own originality continues to challenge critics today.[10] It would
seem, then, that homogeneity, and Fauré's success with it, are worth examining from a historical point of view.

It should be clear that homogeneity has to involve a particular understanding of musical style. Leonard Meyer has defined style as "a replication
of patterning, whether in human behavior or in the artifacts produced by
human behavior, that results from a series of choices made within some set
of constraints."[11] Fauré's contemporaries would probably have recognized
the authority and precision of this definition but would have wished to add
something else to it. To understand what style meant to them, we must consider the concept in a more diffused light and take its spiritual as well as its
material conditions into account:

> In art each individual brings two things: first a personal vision of the
> universe, then an instrument with which to make it real. The artist lives
> almost uniquely by *style*, that is, by what he invests of himself in his work, by
> the personal idea to whose realization he bends his material. He forges
> rhythms to match the rhythms of his heart.[12]

This statement from 1911 gives us a sense of the high regard for the visionary and personal facets of musical style in early twentieth-century French
criticism. For Proust's narrator, an artist's style divulges a way of seeing the
world that we would not otherwise know, and his experience of "the intimate composition of those worlds which we call individuals" is a central
affirmation in the novel. The beautiful realization of a personal style allows
us, in his words, "to see the universe through the eyes of another, of a
hundred others, to see the hundred universes that each of them sees, that
each of them is; and this we can do with an Elstir, with a Vinteuil; with men
like these we do really fly from star to star."[13]

It would, however, be a mistake to exaggerate this visionary bias in interpreting style to the point of reducing homogeneity to some purely Platonic
category. Karuyoschi Yoshikawa, in his fine study of the material in Proust's
notebooks relating to Vinteuil's Septet, comes close to this exaggeration.
Yoshikawa infers the importance of homogeneity in Proust but limits its
meaning to a metaphysical realm. Of the dialogue between Marcel and
Albertine, cited above, Yoshikawa writes, "The allusion here is not to actual
works but the profound identity that crosses them, the very essence of an
artist, the quality of his art that lies beyond the bounds of time."[14] I will
contend, on the other hand, that Proust *also* referred to a real connection
between actual works. And one simple name for this connection, its concrete correlation, is style.

The appreciation of homogeneity also led to a model of artistic growth which stressed continuity over discontinuity. This is hardly surprising, since stylistic disjunction threatens homogeneity. Fauré himself seems to have adopted a model of gradual change for artistic growth, and this was the dominant model of his time. In the following comment on Beethoven's string quartets, Fauré reconciles the claims of innovation with those of homogeneity in a way Proust and others would have appreciated:

> Let the critic show us the promises of the first quartets realized in those that follow; let him point out the composer's favored methods from the earliest movements, and then in that long series of works, all different yet poured into an almost unchanging mold; let him unveil the slow but uninterrupted ascent of this inner life, of this thought, style, and technique, from involuntary imitation to free creation.[15]

As we have seen in previous chapters, Fauré believed that a composer who is faithful to his own affective and intellectual temperament gradually makes what he inherits his own and, in the process, perfects the means of expressing what he himself feels and desires. In this statement on Beethoven, Fauré's injunctions reveal his preference for an image of stylistic change that is slow and intensifying rather than sudden or disjointed. In particular, he refers to a "slow but uninterrupted ascent." He understood Beethoven's quartets as examples of such an ascent, but this image applies just as well, indeed, better, to Fauré's own achievement. His reference to "an almost unchanging mold," while consistent with Beethoven's obsessive pursuit of forms based on the sonata and theme and variations, is not adequate to the unforeseen frameworks of some of the late quartets. But Fauré's turn of phrase squares perfectly with his own persistent "invention within sameness."

Fauré's attitude toward stylistic change is also consistent with his general aesthetic convictions. The respect for tradition, the goal of progressive self-realization, the grounding of this self-realization in the sincere translation of a native gift: all these endorse the "slow but uninterrupted ascent" of an individual style. The principle of homogeneity does not exclude the idea of different stylistic phases or periods, but it tends to identify what joins these phases or periods together rather than what separates them. Fauré's comment about Beethoven's progress from "involuntary imitation to free creation" heightens the continuity of that progress rather than breaking it into distinct periods. That Fauré is in fact completely silent about Beethoven's three periods (and in the preface to a book obviously organized around them) may be significant.[16] In a lecture given six years later, Philippe Fauré-Fremiet echoed his father's analysis of Beethoven's development and remarked, "I must say I find it completely arbitrary to define *bounded periods* in the work of an artist, and most of all when that work represents, even in its variety, an absolutely continuous creative labor."[17] Perhaps this comment renders explicit the meaning of Fauré's silence about stylistic periods. Fauré-Fremiet goes on to say that an artist's "successive stylistic periods consist in gradually stripping away borrowed elements, which at first necessarily served him as the ground-rules of a language, in order to approach that perfect *expression* he seeks."[18] This is simply a restatement of Fauré's "ascent . . . from voluntary imitation to free creation" in terms that admit the provisional convenience of periodization. "I do not deny that making distinctions of styles or periods may help us . . . to penetrate a composer's or a poet's work by representing a long, constant, and sometimes painful evolution, in simplified images, in nicely partitioned stages. But is it not true here, as with all such schemes, that we must discard them immediately after using them – as soon as we have seized the very movement, the living ascent of his thought?"[19] Fauré-Fremiet's lecture argues for a "continuous evolution" and even an "ascent" in the development of his father's chamber music. Thus he stressed the continuity of Fauré's work just as Fauré had done for Beethoven.

In a city that saw such rapid cultural change as did Paris between 1890 and 1920, a theory of artistic evolution had to make room for heterogeneity and innovation or risk irrelevance. The partisans of homogeneity valued innovation; indeed, they presumed that an individual artist would change over time. At the same time, however, they placed innovation in the context of intelligible self-transformation so that change ultimately approaches renewal *within* homogeneity. Changes in style are real traces that allow us to observe the progress of an individual artist, but this progress has as its goal the ever truer illustration of a single sensibility, the purer distillation of some inner essence. Bernard de Fallois likens this concept of the creator to "an irreplaceable universe, slowly brought to light in the work of a lifetime."[20] In French criticism after the turn of the century, Fauré's image as a composer conformed to the dominant ideal of renewal within homogeneity. The following remarks, from an important article by Gaston Carraud written in 1909, are characteristic:

> Certainly Fauré's art has changed with the passage of time and with the exercise of his own creative powers. But his evolution and his progressive enrichment of forms, ever more complex and refined, only figure as the consequences of an intelligent adaptation to different genres, ideas, and poets, not as consecutive periods or styles. . . .
>
> Only the manner of speaking changes, not the spirit, which keeps a consistency such as one rarely sees in a body of work so diverse.

Carraud adds further on, "His thought and methods were able to enlarge themselves whenever that was necessary; they are fundamentally always the same."[21] This view has been persistent in French critical thought, and we read a similar, if more opaque, observation in Jankélévitch: "Fauréan novelty is new in the same way that Bergsonian freedom is free: first, in the immanence of ceaseless becoming; second, in renewing the gains of memory and the past in manners unforeseen. Fauré is an innovator without a fetish for novelty . . . Innovation is nonetheless constant beneath the surface of his work."[22]

Therefore homogeneity does not necessarily impose a throttle on variety, as we might at first presume. For the practicing artist as for his interpreters, there was great latitude for diversity within homogeneity. We may turn again to Proust for a deeper understanding of these complementary values. We possess a curious document from the end of his life, his response to a survey on stylistic renewal. In this response, Proust embraced the notion of renewal within homogeneity; his terms are similar to those we have already encountered: "Stylistic continuity is not endangered but assured by the perpetual renewal of style. There is a metaphysical reason for that, but an account of it would unduly prolong my response."[23]

Do we really lack Proust's account because of a journalistic contingency? No. We may find it in *A la recherche du temps perdu* – in Proust's two hawthorns, white and pink, and their metaphorical relation to Vinteuil's music. The hawthorns are at the root of the narrator's speculation on the coexistence of sameness and difference in artistic style. In order to make this case, it is necessary to turn to one of Proust's notebooks, to a passage concerning the musical soirée at the Verdurins. Here, Proust explicitly connects Vinteuil's Quartet (which would become a Septet in the printed editions) to the enigma of the flowering hawthorns:

> Just as once, at Combray, when having exhausted the joys the hawthorn afforded me and not wishing to demand them of another flower, I saw a source of new joys spring up for me in the form of a bush of pink hawthorn on the path leading up from Tansonville, so also, having no new joy to espouse in Vinteuil's Sonata anymore, I suddenly felt, on hearing the Quartet begin, that I was experiencing that joy again, the same and yet still intact, enveloping and revealing to my sight another world, similar but unknown.[24]

Nattiez has already remarked on this analogy between flowers and music in the context of another argument.[25] The narrator's first hawthorn, the white, corresponds to the Sonata; its pink reincarnation, to the Septet. The Quartet (or Septet), the narrator tells us, "radiated, blazed joyous scarlet flashes; it was an incarnadine piece, it was the Sonata in pink."[26] In the published text of *La prisonnière*, Proust suppressed the explicit analogy and instead developed the allusiveness of his opposing colors. We read of "the white Sonata" and "the glowing, erubescent Septet."[27] The tonal associations bloom luxuriantly here, and other flowers appear: "The sonata opened upon a lily-white pastoral dawn, dividing its fragile purity only to hover in the delicate yet compact entanglement of a rustic bower of honeysuckle against white geraniums." The Sonata is "candid" and soothes the ear like "the cooing of a dove." The Septet, in contrast, rises in "a rose-red daybreak"; its tints are "scarlet" and "crimson."[28] The contrast of colors conveys the vivid "tonal" differences between the Sonata and the Septet. What is most interesting for the present argument, the narrator then proceeds to reconsider these differences by balancing them against common traits he comes more and more to perceive between the two pieces.

This process begins with the following passage. Here the narrator's account of his experience with the Septet clearly corresponds to the experience of "new joy" at the discovery of the pink hawthorns, as related in Proust's first draft:

> I knew now, and everything that followed only confirmed my knowledge, that this world was one of those which I had never even been capable of imagining that Vinteuil could have created, for, when weary of the sonata which was to me a universe thoroughly explored, I tried to imagine others equally beautiful but different, I was merely doing what those poets do who fill their artificial paradise with meadows, flowers and streams which duplicate those existing already upon earth. What was now before me made me feel as keen a joy as the sonata would have given me if I had not already known it, and consequently, while no less beautiful, was different.[29]

Despite this difference between the Septet and the Sonata, or perhaps because of it, the narrator feels privy to a new joy, as he did with the pink hawthorns: a joy at once "similar but unknown." His elation, drawn from his discovery of a latent unity in Vinteuil's chamber music, prompts one of the most important insights on personal style in the entire novel. Indeed, this excursus on style covers between sixteen and twenty pages of prose, depending on the edition. The narrator's first response to the Septet, with its "redness, so new, so absent from the tender, pastoral, unadorned sonata," is disorientation.[30] But soon elements from the sonata (and, Marcel later learns, other works of Vinteuil) come in and out of his observation; the Septet seems to contain dozens of minute elements of the composer's past. Marcel singles out one of these phrases, the famous "little phrase" of the Sonata, whose radical transformation in the Septet astonishes him; he emphasizes the disparity between these two occurrences of the phrase. "And yet," he says, "these very different phrases were composed of the same elements; . . . those two questions, so dissimilar, . . . were nevertheless the same prayer, bursting forth before different inner sunrises, and merely refracted through the different media of other thoughts, of artistic researches carried on through years in which he had wanted to create something new."[31] In the last section of this chapter I shall return to the effect on homogeneity of the desire to create something new. For now, let us cut directly to the central insight of Marcel's experience. From his discovery of sameness within or behind exterior disparities, he is able to conclude, "It is indeed a unique accent, an unmistakable voice, to which in spite of themselves those great singers that original composers are rise and return, which is proof of the irreducibly individual existence of the soul."[32] The two opposing colors, paradoxically, become a vehicle for a meditation on homogeneity, the "unique accent" that is the proof of individual style.

The idea of *refraction* is important in Proust's explanation. We just read that Vinteuil "refracted" his musical style "through the different media of other thoughts" and was therefore able to produce a new masterpiece, like his previous works and yet unlike them. Later in *La prisonnière*, in the scene at the pianola, Marcel will again use the concept of refraction to explain homogeneity. "The great men of letters," he insists, "have never done more than refract through various media an identical beauty which they bring into the world."[33] This kind of refraction enlarges on the original metaphor of the two colors, because refraction can break a source of light into its spectrum. That spectrum, in turn, corresponds to what Proust would call "the individual existence of the soul." The *visible colors* of an individual style may shift from work to work, but the *inner source of radiant energy*, revealed in its intrinsic spectrum, is unique. We may corroborate this interpretation by citing one of the narrator's observations during the soirée at the Verdurins: "The art of a Vinteuil like that of an Elstir . . . exteriorises in the colours of the spectrum the intimate composition of those worlds which we call individuals."[34] Vinteuil's successive works displayed new colors, refracting them through various media, but the "source of light," his originality, remained the same.

Proust, of course, does not present a logical argument, but his thinking permits us insights into a specific historical perspective on musical style. We have not relied on Proust's imaginative work alone for this perspective. The quotidian criticism of the period confirms the same ideal: it was important for an artist to realize a personal consistency in his work even as he exploited possibilities of variety within and around that consistency. Unity and variety do not exclude one another in this conception of artistic practice. If we return to James Kidd's opposition, one might adduce Chopin and

Brahms alongside Fauré as examples of composers "inventing within same-ness," while Varèse and Schoenberg approach "originality as newness." But in either case, we refer only to general tendencies, not absolute methods; artists who break completely with their own pasts are, if not nonexistent, surely as rare as those who never leave the boundaries of a single mode of expression.[35] The Proustian prism is an optical device for decomposing sty-listic realities. Theoretically, one could use this tool to find difference as well as sameness. But in the historical usage we have been examining, French writers and critics had certain preconceptions about what their prisms would reveal. They wanted evidence of homogeneity.

2 Disputing and defending homogeneity: Debussy, Fauré, and the responses to self-renewal

I have argued that Fauré, Proust and others attached great importance to artistic homogeneity as evidence of personal style. But since artists seldom if ever can abandon their pasts, the fact of homogeneity finally seems to describe only an ordinary condition of artistic production. Why should we bother with something so ordinary? We must remember that judgments of homogeneity are judgments of style, and, as such, are volatile. Like any other aesthetic value, homogeneity was subject to debate and redefinition; atten-tion to it was intense and constant; its evidence was ambiguous. Interpretations of a composer's progress sometimes resulted in misunder-standings, and these could have serious effects on the reception of a work or a series of works. To understand the creation and reception of French music in this period, it is necessary to understand the prestige of homogeneity.

We have seen that those who valued homogeneity also welcomed a certain amount of heterogeneity as well – and in particular any kind of change rec-ognizable as "self-renewal." However, the balance between homogeneity and heterogeneity was absolutely critical. To strike it successfully was, for the composer, a formidable task. This balance also made for a fragile and sub-jective criterion. If a critic found the heterogeneity of a composer's recent works suspect or excessive, he could raise thorny questions: Is the composer betraying his own voice by mimicking others? Is he whoring after fashion or cheap success? Is he groping aimlessly, having spent all his creative energies on his previous compositions? All these questions ultimately cast doubt on the composer's sincerity. Let us consider Jules Combarieu's impassioned warning, written in 1909:

> Lack of unity is like a reef where vast poems are wrecked, and this lack, we
> may say without hesitation, *always* results from a breach in sincerity, which

itself is brought on by lack of faith in a particular ideal and a failing of
creative strength. The creator who does not possess – by lack of culture or
irremediable deficiency – adequate resources inside himself, falls back on
what is external, on various sidelines; he wanders by adventure, seeking
assistance or borrowing a mask that will hide his weakness. And since this
domain of the non-self has no limits, he roves here and there without a
compass and has no particular reason to prefer this to that; in other words,
he soon falls to anthologizing, arranging miscellanies, whence the
incoherence of useless whims, and when we try to follow him, we are worn
down by fatigue. On the other hand, a creator who . . . has been excited by a
strong feeling from within, before taking pen to paper, by means of lived
experience and imagination – he is sure never to lack the first of all
principles: unity. I speak not of the sort of unity we *prove* by comparing
themes and parts, but of that which we *feel* and which surpasses
demonstration.[36]

Combarieu was speculating on homogeneity as evidence of unity within a
single work, but his remarks speak directly to the homogeneity of successive
works as well – the "faith in a particular ideal" that binds separate creative
efforts together.

In the culture of sincerity, criticisms alleging the dispersal of a creative
personality, that is, fragmentation or lack of integrity in self-expression, had
disastrous consequences. It was imperative that a perception of artistic
homogeneity emerge out of the interaction between creator and audience if
works of art were not to wreck on that reef of confusion painted by
Combarieu. Fullness of self-translation, which we have identified as one of
the practices of sincerity, should result in homogeneity. But several questions remain about how such an accomplishment can be understood. How
will homogeneity manifest itself in a given work of art? How will anyone
know where sincerity ends and self-deception begins? What allows listeners
to distinguish self-renewal from arbitrary extravagance? Jean Cocteau
understood the ideological foundation of these related quandaries, and he
had a courageous answer for his fellow artists: "The sincerity which may be
packed into each separate minute, even though giving rise to a series of
apparent contradictions, traces a line deeper and straighter than any of
those theoretic lines to which one is often obliged to sacrifice what is best in
oneself."[37] Thus, what to the superficial observer looks like excessive heterogeneity, even self-contradiction, is often proof of an artist's most profound
self-translation. The "deeper and straighter line" indicated by Cocteau
traces a homogeneity that paradoxically shows itself through incongruities
at first, but then ultimately renders a true and consistent picture of the
artist's soul. But let Cocteau's statement collide with Combarieu's, and it is

easy to see the grounds for misunderstanding. That is, there is nothing to prevent an honest critic from taking "a series of apparent contradictions," the stuff of Cocteau's higher sincerity, for "the incoherence of useless whims" that Combarieu disparages as resulting from a "breach in sincerity." Anything that casts doubt on the subjective unity of a work can be taken (or mistaken) for insincerity. Cocteau was aware of this danger, as was Gide, another defender of maximal sincerity. Both writers knew that belief in one's own "apparent contradictions" is not a guarantee of public success. Therefore, since an artist's inner sense of triumph might find no outer echoes (or ones delayed by years or decades of debate), self-renewal could become an occasion for risk and frustration.

We turn now to historical examples of misunderstandings that were created by different perceptions of stylistic change. We begin with Debussy, whose orchestral works after the première of *Pelléas et Mélisande* (1902) created an increasingly fractious dialogue in the Parisian press. In particular, the first two *Images* – *Ibéria* and *Rondes de printemps* – stirred up what would turn out to be the most serious journalistic spat of Debussy's career.[38] Why is it necessary to turn to Debussy? Fauré's stylistic evolution was less controversial than Debussy's and never provoked a major critical fracas, whereas the quarrel over Debussy's *Images* provides an opportunity to observe the claims of homogeneity raised to a very high pitch. We shall nonetheless return to Fauré at the end of this section and see that the critiques visited on his stylistic progress were, if less contentious than the arguments about Debussy's *Images*, marked by the same assumptions.

It is interesting to note that Fauré and Debussy shared similar attitudes toward self-renewal and personal style. Differences in their music have sometimes prevented historians from discerning the aesthetic premises they held in common. "The composer or artist of today who has achieved a major reputation has but one concern," said Debussy: "to produce *personal works*, works *renewed* as much as possible."[39] We recall a number of comparable statements by Fauré.[40] For Debussy as for Fauré, the composer devotes himself to a quest for individual accents grounded in personal sensibility. In the wake of the premières of *Ibéria* and *Rondes de printemps*, the two pieces that will concern us here, Debussy insisted,

> There is . . . no greater pleasure than plunging down into oneself, stirring up one's whole being, searching for new and hidden treasures. What a joy it is to find something new there, something that surprises and pleases even the composer. Doesn't it seem one who repeats himself is like one who imitates others?[41]

With Debussy's "plunge" into himself, we come up against the paradox of homogeneity described earlier, for his continuous reorientations of style toward an "essential self" ensure homogeneity in the long run but can strain the listener's ability to discover it in the short run. Debussy strives to be new; in seeking to avoid repeating himself, he sees no sign of self-betrayal but only a search for "new and hidden treasures." But this inner quest remained opaque to most French critics, for whom *La mer* and the *Images* came as unhappy surprises. Their negative reception might be summed up in a single question, however unlikely it seems: "Has Debussy betrayed himself?"[42]

In the discussion of Fauré's First Quintet in the previous chapter, we noted that the first decade of the twentieth century was a period of marked self-renewal for Fauré, and the same was true of Debussy. Indeed, the coincidence is precise, since both Fauré's First Quintet and Debussy's orchestral *Images* would be singled out by later historians as breaking new stylistic ground. The two works are also comparable for their long periods of germination and the consequent anticipation the press conjured up around them. But there the resemblance ends. Fauré's Quintet was a resounding success; the contrasts it presented with his previous style were praised as progressive and self-renewing. Debussy's work, conversely, lost him many supporters because of the difficulty they had in identifying the *Images* positively with his earlier works. The *Images* crossed the threshold of heterogeneity and suffered the consequences.

While Fauré's stylistic development was usually described as gradual, Debussy seemed to leap and pirouette unexpectedly from one work to the next. Dukas pointed out this peculiarity in 1901:

> M. Debussy seems to enjoy throwing his admirers off the scent; . . . in his work, one piece will not seem the expected consequence of the other; rather they all bring us something distinctive that represents, if not a really salient transformation of his style, at least a new and surprising point of view.

Debussy's sense of adventure, continued Dukas, "accounts for the difficulties that some people – those who like to be warned of an artist's inclinations *for good* – experience in categorizing him."[43] The remark was prescient. Debussy's habit of surprising his listeners carried considerable risks, and Dukas foresaw the cause of an imminent conflict between the composer and his critics, in particular Pierre Lalo and Gaston Carraud.

Lalo and Carraud, two of the most respected critics in Paris, had been keen admirers of *Pelléas et Mélisande*. The success of the opera sealed Debussy's reputation as a composer of the front rank, and French critics looked to his future compositions with the highest expectations. In *La mer* (1905) Debussy created a masterpiece that later critics have characterized as perhaps the greatest symphony ever written by a Frenchman, but Carraud's and Lalo's reviews were mixed.[44] From 1905 onward, an air of disappointment haunted all their comments on Debussy's music, and the *Images* for orchestra brought these dissatisfactions to a nadir. By 1910 Lalo and Carraud had come to view *Pelléas* and the orchestral *Nocturnes* (1900) as pinnacles against which Debussy's subsequent works seemed to mark a steady decline. To retrace all the details of Debussy's reception between 1903 and 1910 is far beyond the scope of this chapter. We shall focus only on the fact, a central fact, that Lalo and Carraud failed, or refused, to recognize the homogeneity of Debussy's music before and after *Pelléas*.

When *Ibéria* and *Rondes de printemps* reached the concert hall in 1910, Debussy had offered the public no major works since *La mer*. The lull of six years raised the artistic stakes, and many critics used their reviews of these two *Images* to look back over Debussy's whole career and judge his most recent work in light of that long perspective. Lalo's approach was representative: "The *Images* offer us an occasion . . . to learn more about Debussy's art, about what it was at first, and what it seems to be becoming now."[45] One already detects the premises of homogeneity behind Lalo's critical operation.

While Debussy, "searching for new and hidden treasures," thought he was bearing his art to a logical and worthy fruition, Lalo and Carraud were unconvinced. One might take their resistance to Debussy's later work as mere resistance to innovation – the eternal cause of critical invective. But Debussy's deviations from traditional musical materials, including his free treatment of form, tonality, and vertical dissonance, were not the bone of contention. On the contrary, Lalo and Carraud reproached Debussy for the opposite of innovation: for conventionality of form, for reliance on external sources of inspiration, and for a loss of spontaneity and creative nerve.

In order to understand this surprising critique, let us begin by looking to Carraud's and Lalo's common warrants. First, there is the matter of sensibility and its seeming absence. Lalo and Carraud suggest that Debussy lost contact with the emotional core of his own music and, for lack of it, substituted sensation for sensibility. The sensations themselves, Carraud thought, lacked the spontaneity and delicacy of his earlier work:

> Indeed, the emotion has disappeared, this emotion of a kind altogether unique in the whole art of music and that enveloped in its mysterious unity a multitude of sensations; . . . it was mind and soul concentrating the testimony of the senses. And now, here the sensations alone still continue, and it seems they are at once shrunken and heavier, that they have lost something of their freshness and their originality.[46]

Carraud's review asserts that the loss to Debussy's music lies in the domain of the spiritual or mental: *l'âme*. As I observed at the end of chapter 3, this is perhaps the most powerful word a critic could choose to designate the source of an artist's potential. In *Rondes de printemps*, "l'âme" has ceased to "concentrate the testimony of the senses," which are left to the whim of unsupported "sensations," thus cold or feebly motivated.[47] Here Combarieu's earlier comment on the "shipwreck" of inner unity comes to mind again: "The creator who does not possess . . . adequate resources inside himself, falls back on what is external, on various sidelines; he wanders by adventure, seeking assistance or borrowing a mask that will hide his weakness" (above, p. 137). Lalo bemoaned this same lack in Debussy, and it was evident to him on the very surface of the music. "The sense of style is no longer the same. Instead of a perfect balance, instead of a manner effortless, light and spare, we find emphasis and excess in *Ibéria*; the art which once expressed itself so simply, almost in an undertone, today shouts and gesticulates."[48] For these critics, Debussy's powers of self-expression, through which he could make his unique sensibility sing, had failed him. Lalo discerned in *Ibéria* "an external agreeableness, which has nothing living, penetrating, or unusual about it, an agreeableness that is superficial, almost on the level of rhetoric . . . Is this, then, all we can ask today of the music of Debussy, the man who composed *Pelléas*?"[49] Lalo's and Carraud's first criticism, then, calls on the distinction between sincere *inner* sensibility and *outer* sensation, superficial effect.

Their second criticism proceeds to the related issue of self-realization. Lalo and Carraud charge Debussy with abandoning his creative destiny – whose "true" promises lay slumbering in *Pelléas* and the *Nocturnes*. In 1900, Carraud had hailed Debussy as "one of the most original artists of the day," but now he depicted him as wandering through brambles of self-deception.[50]

It is possible to come to terms with these critiques once we understand the power of homogeneity in shaping responses to new works of art. The reception of Debussy's music after 1905 suffered from a basic failure on the part of his critics: their failure to grasp the connections between his old works and his new ones. Unable to pick up the thread of Debussy's style, Lalo and Carraud presumed that the composer had lost faith in himself. Blindness, insight and polemical disturbances are tangled up in this conclusion.

I do not want to claim that stylistic homogeneity was the sole factor in the negative reception of Debussy's music after 1905. Reception itself is hardly homogeneous, and different critics rejected Debussy's music for different reasons. Before turning to the question of style, I would like to indicate two other issues that influenced responses to Debussy's music in this period. The first was Debussy's cruel abandonment of his first wife, Rosalie Texier, whom he divorced in 1904 in order to marry Emma Bardac. The second was the cultural phenomenon of "debussysme." It is true that Debussy's desertion of Rosalie Texier sent waves of shock and disapproval through Parisian musical circles and lost him some friends. However, I think historians have been too quick to assume that Debussy's personal immorality and selfishness tainted the reception of all his subsequent music. Two letters from this period by Albert Roussel will help show that the two things could be kept apart. In the first letter, dated 16 November 1904, Roussel describes, in his usual poker-faced style, the circumstances of Debussy's divorce to Jeanne Taravant:

> Have you heard about Debussy's divorce? . . . Poor Mme Debussy at first wanted to starve herself, then she took a revolver and shot herself twice in the stomach. She is being treated at Rue Blomet, where Tout-Paris musical and extramusical has been to bring her the assurance of their sympathies.[51]

A letter Roussel wrote to Taravant eleven months later concerns the pre- mière of *La mer*. Roussel begins, "Perhaps you have heard that Debussy's stock in the musical marketplace has been much jeopardized," and one would think he is referring to collective antipathy toward the cad who left Rosalie Texier. But it turns out that *La mer* itself is the cause; disappoint- ment was not a foregone conclusion at all. After the concert, Roussel heard the talk on the street:

> Cunning retreats were effected, critics shook their heads, dilettantes held forth with big gestures; the atmosphere was that of a rout . . . What was most amusing were the faces of certain journalists who wrote their reviews in advance and would very much have liked to take back their praises![52]

Although this is only one account, it comes from a remarkably perceptive, sympathetic, and honest composer. If critics were ready to praise Debussy *pro forma* in 1905, we cannot discount their ability to distinguish between a man's domestic affairs and his art.

Between, on the one hand, the upheavals of Debussy's personal life and, on the other, *debussysme*, the latter was a more significant factor in the reception of his music. The powerful influence that *Pelléas* and Debussy's works in general exercised over his juniors and contemporaries seems to have muddled perceptions of his own later music. But in contrast to the questions of form and style we are about to discuss here, the strength of Debussy's image as a creator in relation to his followers has less to do with the principle of stylistic homogeneity than the related question of original- ity. Lalo and Carraud, among others, suggested that Debussy was starting to sound more like his imitators than himself. In this, Debussy's critics suffered from a kind of auditory illusion whereby imitators become (to use Dukas's phrase) "prejudicial to the model" (above, p. 84). Some works by *debussystes* brought out what was most easily imitable in Debussy's style, especially its external traits of harmony and timbre. In response to these stylistic echoes, critics probed Debussy's new compositions with increasing intensity and skepticism for the signs of a "deeper" originality. *Debussysme* was an aggravating factor in the negative reception of the *Images*, but it was not the only one, and it does not explain the earlier criticisms of *La mer*. The present discussion, by following the strand of homogeneity, is able to isolate a common factor spanning the criticisms of both works. After carefully weighing the responses and values of Carraud and Lalo, I believe that stylistic homogeneity, of all the possible issues, best allows us to understand why Lalo and Carraud responded as they did to the *Images* as well as *La mer*.

The heart of the problem lay in a formal feature: both *La mer* and the *Images* use cyclical repetition and development. Within the French musical world of the first decade of the twentieth century, form had a much more than merely formal meaning: cyclical forms carried a political charge. The Schola Cantorum tried to make this technique its special property in France. Teachers at the Schola, in encouraging their students to use cyclical form for their large-scale works, thought to honor the spirit of Franck. Because Debussy mercilessly ridiculed the formal protocols taught at the Schola, his seeming adoption of its chief compositional method led to suspicions of artistic perjury. An important pretext for this suspicion goes back to 1904, the year before *La mer* appeared, when Debussy was interviewed by Paul Landormy. In response to Landormy, Debussy surely infuriated the *scholistes* by insisting that Franck, their spiritual father, was not a French composer. "Oh, César Franck isn't a Frenchman, he's Belgian," Debussy told his interlocutor; "[his] effect on French composers really doesn't amount to much." With characteristic aplomb, Debussy displaced his admiration to Massenet, who – unlike Franck and the composers at the Schola – understood the true character of French art: he knew that "music should humbly seek to *please*." Debussy claimed that this hedonistic aesthetics better represented French nineteenth-century art, and indeed, French culture and taste in general, than the austere disciplines of the Schola. "Extreme complication is the opposite of art. Beauty must be sensuous and palpable [*sensible*]; it must stir an immediate delight in us, it must imprint or insinuate itself in us without our having to make the least effort to grasp it."[53] To dispense with César Franck so highhandedly was bad enough, but to put Massenet in his stead as the champion of modern French music rubbed salt into the *scholiste* wound. Debussy made his own position clear. But having articulated this opinion, why would he resort to cyclical techniques in *La mer* and the *Images*? This contradiction inspired suspicion and confusion, and Debussy's cavalier comments about the "extreme complication" of the Schola's art would haunt him for the rest of the decade.

Carraud's attacks on *Ibéria* and *Rondes de printemps* clearly drew on this background. Ironically, Carraud was sympathetic to the music of Franck, to d'Indy's work at the Schola, and originally to Debussy's music as well. But he objected to *scholiste* incursions into Debussy's musical language. Carraud had always praised the freshness and spontaneity in Debussy's music rather than its formal dexterity, and, even though Carraud had no objection to *scholiste* formal etiquettes in their proper place, he seems to have believed that Debussy had been right to reject them for his own art. Hence the following sentence is at the heart of Carraud's critique:

> What creates unity is no longer feeling but musical technique and its artifices: *Rondes de printemps*, built upon a single theme and practically according to the principles – *horresco* . . . ! – laid down for the nurslings at the Schola, does not give the same impression of cohesion as did the works of Debussy's "first style," when a number of different themes was used.[54]

Carraud saw Debussy as belatedly and errantly tempted over the *scholiste* threshold. More recent critics have praised Debussy's fresh, almost coloristic approach to cyclical principles (insofar as they even recognize the network of cyclical ideas at all). But for Debussy's contemporaries these formal annexations smacked of hypocrisy. Why would *he* have any truck with the legacy of a school he privately declared to be "consecrated to Boredom"?[55] The truth is, Debussy did not need the Schola to teach him these techniques. Lalo and Carraud were too quick to forget that Debussy had been interested in cyclical processes before the Schola Cantorum even existed. In his *Fantaisie* (1889–90) and the String Quartet (1893) in particular, Debussy had approached the possibilities of these formal strategies with great individuality. Unfortunately, the polemical atmosphere of 1910 prevented Carraud and Lalo from making a more rational examination of these technical continuities in Debussy's music.[56]

Louis Laloy, who wrote one of the few positive Parisian reviews of the first two *Images*, probably could have made this rational examination, but he chose not to do so. He probably realized that the argument would lack force in 1910, when the link between cyclical form and the Schola had become so strong as to make a composer's past practices all but irrelevant. We turn to Laloy, a trusted friend of Debussy's, because he developed a cogent defense of the composer against Carraud and Lalo in a series of remarkable essays dating from between 1907 and 1910.[57] In all these essays Laloy stressed a "progress of style" in Debussy's music and depicted this change as vital to the complete translation of Debussy's artistic vision. When Carraud and Lalo, reviewing *Ibéria* and *Rondes de printemps*, proved their continuing resistance to such "progress," Laloy responded with "Claude Debussy et le Debussysme."

Laloy knew what was at stake. He sought to re-establish the essential homogeneity of Debussy's music through nothing less than the principle of sincerity. On the one hand, Laloy openly acknowledged that Debussy's music had changed. But he insisted on the validity of this new direction through its origins in Debussy's continuing self-realization. On the other hand, Laloy underlined the continuities in Debussy's music and took pains to reveal links between his "new manner" and his old one. Laloy proposed that Debussy never really left behind the manner he had cultivated before 1904; rather, this earlier work supplied the composer "with the material from which he would build another world, more solid and definite."[58] Debussy did not, as Carraud and Lalo seemed to have wished him to do, stand pat with *Pelléas*. But this restlessness did not mean that Debussy lost his way. Rather, Laloy says, the composer pursued and grappled with an aesthetic ideal maturing within himself. "Having left the sure harbor of the style he had established . . . , he was seeking *to realize an idea of beauty ripened in his mind*."[59]

Carraud and Lalo were in no position to object to self-searching growth. The principle of self-realization in art – the idea at the heart of Laloy's essay – was as dear to Lalo and Carraud as to Laloy. The power of Laloy's counter-argument springs from the return to a common ground. He turned basic beliefs about creative development against Lalo and Carraud in order to show up their judgments of *La mer* and the *Images* as garbled. The two reluctant critics saw their reproaches of Debussy equated with a denial of his very right to evolve. "It seems," Laloy remarked, "that they bear a grudge against the artist for having passed beyond the limits they imagined for him – *as if this were somehow a betrayal*."[60] Laloy maintained that Debussy had no reason *to stand still*; this kind of docile fixity does not befit a great creative mind.

Laloy's indictment of Debussy's detractors was forceful and elegant. The final sentences of "Claude Debussy et le Debussysme" savor of triumph:

> [Those critics] confine themselves to the *Nocturnes* and consider themselves finished with Debussy. The *Nocturnes* are indeed wonderful poems, but they stand at the beginning of a career that has been productive both in the number of works and in the fact that each, compared to the ones before it, is new. How easy it would have been for the composer, after his first successes, to win popularity by spending the rest of his days copying himself! He must be forgiven: *for him sincerity is not a virtue; it is a necessity*.[61]

Laloy's sudden recourse to sincerity depends on strong ideological ties between originality, self-renewal, and personal translation. Debussy, as rescued by Laloy, must be "forgiven" his desire to write works transcending what he has already accomplished because in doing so he only realizes "an idea of beauty ripened in his mind"; he translates an inner and *evolving* self sincerely.

Toward the end of 1910, Debussy stepped into the space Laloy had helped clear for him by asserting his artistic prerogatives, emphasizing the satisfactions of "plunging down into oneself" in the "search for new and hidden treasures" (see the quotation cited at the beginning of this section, p. 138). Debussy made no pretense of pleading for his right to artistic evolution; when questioned about his future work, he took change for granted. He observed, "It seems to me that the main failing among most writers and artists is not having enough courage and willpower to break away from success and look for new ways and ideas."[62] If we wonder about what kind of novelty Debussy had in mind, we may find the answer in an interview he gave two years before: "The composer or artist of today who has achieved a major reputation has but one concern: to produce *personal works*, works renewed as much as possible" (cited above, p. 138). Thus Debussy, as we should expect, articulates self-renewal in personal expression as a supreme goal. If his critics supposed that he lost his way after *Pelléas*, Debussy turned the tables on them and proposed that "the courage to leave the certain for the uncertain" had to be the basis for any discussion of artistic growth.[63]

A seemingly sudden change in Debussy's style brought beliefs about homogeneity onto the critical battlefield. Laloy's task as a critic was to show that Debussy's music bore the mark of higher homogeneity by surpassing, through radical self-renewal, a homogeneity that would be superficial or uninventive. Hence the first two *Images* are an exception that proves the rule. The argument between Laloy and his opponents is now forgotten. Who today criticizes Debussy's works after *Pelléas* for lacking perceptible connections to his earlier ones?[64] But between 1904 and 1910, journalistic contention over the degree of continuity in Debussy's musical style brought him considerable grief.

Though Fauré, too, launched his art in new directions at the beginning of the century, he enjoyed much greater public approval than Debussy. In 1900, the critic Paul-Louis Garnier expressed his astonishment over Fauré's *Prométhée* – but also satisfaction:

> This was an almost thrilling surprise for me, and I would never have thought the composer of so many songs and rapt quartets could suddenly reveal himself as a symphonist of incomparable power and wield orchestral masses with such unifying breadth. In this music Gabriel Fauré has revealed a new expression of his musical aesthetic, and the composer celebrated for so many slow and nostalgic songs, and sober and melodious choruses, has in a single stroke burst the bonds of his usual inspiration.[65]

Prométhée, an open-air *tragédie lyrique* written for the amphitheater at Béziers, was a work no one expected from Fauré. Its dramatic power, block-like construction, and performing forces – including an array of choruses and solo singers against a massive orchestra of full strings, three wind bands, and eighteen harps – put it worlds away from anything Fauré had written before. Most critics reacted as Garnier did: with surprise and enthusiasm.[66] Yet if we consider the style and presentation of *Prométhée*, we might say that the distance between it and any of Fauré's previous works was greater than that between Debussy's *Nocturnes* and *La mer*, or even the *Images*. Thus, Debussy's negative reception is ironic from a historical point of view, but this irony is evident to us because we are no longer haunted by the concerns over cyclical forms and invidious comparisons to *debussyste* imitators that blocked more objective judgments from audiences in 1905 and 1910. *La mer*, to my mind, marks a powerful advance in Debussy's creative develop-ment; similarly, *Prométhée* and the First Quintet mark the boundaries of a critical period in Fauré's life. In this chapter and others, we have also spoken of the affinities between Fauré's and Debussy's aesthetic principles, their common belief in sincerity, their common search for "works that make progress over preceding ones" (Fauré) or "something that surprises and pleases even the composer" (Debussy). But these common artistic bearings never guarantee an even-handed reception in the short term; stylistic details and external circumstances, then as now, bend the first impressions of an individual work.

"In our political country, everything is up for debate, and practically everything becomes a pretext for mobilizing a group. Quarreling is in our blood." Thus Laloy, already engaged in the debate over Debussy's style, began one of his essays in 1907.[67] Laloy states an obvious truth for anyone who reads French cultural history. But the great volume of Parisian editori-al activity in this period made the potential for such quarrels especially staggering. An informal count for the year 1905 will yield nineteen daily newspapers, over a dozen journals of culture and opinion (covering theater, the fine arts and literature, and each retaining a music critic of some distinc-tion), and at least nine periodicals devoted exclusively to music. French critics of the early twentieth century spilled a lot of ink in these quarrels.[68]

Given this contentious atmosphere, it really is remarkable that Fauré's music, whose style did change, courted so little misapprehension. Fauré was an obscure figure until the turn of the century, when the success of a big theatrical work, *Prométhée*, and the performance of the Requiem at the Trocadéro as part of the Universal Exposition, brought him belated national attention. If the press had noticed Fauré's music only sporadically before 1900, attention to him was constant thereafter. There was plenty of opportunity for debate, but Fauré's work evidently rendered a comprehensible curve of development to the mind of his contemporaries. We have already seen critics like de Marliave speak to this stylistic poise. The following remarks by Bruneau on Fauré's *Pénélope* provide another example. One can hardly imagine more definitive praise for a balance of innovation and homogeneity:

> While many other composers are freezing themselves into the formula that earned them success, trying to stop or check the natural motion of art, M. Fauré, without hesitation or fear, searches out new paths . . . Despite such metamorphoses, he still keeps his deep originality [*originalité profonde*] intact. If there is nothing in this most recent score to bring to mind his first songs, everything in it allows us to recognize him, to admire the force of his noble personality.[69]

The difference between this response and Carraud's to *Rondes de printemps* is readily apparent. There were forces beyond the intrinsic qualities of Fauré's music that contributed to this kind of success. His adroitness in separating himself from any identifiable camp and the resistance his style posed to imitation both complemented the perception of stylistic homogeneity and favored the possibility of critics writing about his music unpolemically.

However, Fauré's music was by no means universally admired. Indeed, there are a number of reviews indicating a misunderstanding or refusal of stylistic change in particular works, though none involved the scale of debate aroused by *La mer* and the *Images*. Let us take the example of *La bonne chanson*, composed between 1892 and 1894; this work caused real dissension and displeased even Fauré's admirers, including Saint-Saëns and Camille Bellaigue. The self-renewal in this work resulted in a degree of outward novelty too great for most of Fauré's listeners. The review Bellaigue wrote for *La revue des deux mondes* is particularly revealing. Bellaigue treats Debussy's *Proses lyriques* in this same article, and his rhetorical transition from one work to the other is worth transcribing:

> Reading M. Debussy's music, I cursed liberty.
>   Reading M. Fauré's most recent collection, *La bonne chanson*, . . . I doubted in progress.

He continues:

> I compared these new songs . . . to the ones he composed in years past, or only yesterday, and I could not bring myself to like the new ones; I could barely understand them . . . It is hard to know whether this music is the work of a decadent or a primitive. Practically the whole of M. Fauré's volume leaves us in doubt, too, for beyond a certain point, cunning looks like ignorance, and an excess of refinement leads to barbarism.[70]

Bellaigue knew Fauré personally from the early 1870s and, as ably as any critic, he might have viewed *La bonne chanson* as the culmination of three decades of the composer's song-writing. But the musical language was too shocking for him (though he was thirteen years Fauré's junior), and its new qualities suggested just the opposite of progress: "I would allow that this kind of beauty, the play of prismatic reflections, can be seen on the iridescent neck of a pigeon, but we also find it on the surface of things in the process of decomposition and corruption."[71] Bellaigue ends his review with a nostalgic appreciation of Fauré's earlier songs. He singles out "Au bord de l'eau," "Après un rêve," and the three songs of *Poëme d'un jour*, all composed between 1875 and 1878. In preferring Fauré's earlier songs, Bellaigue was in good company. Saint-Saëns felt the same way. Albert Bertelin said that Saint-Saëns told Fauré to burn *La bonne chanson*.[72] Emmanuel Fauré-Fremiet remembered Saint-Saëns's simply declaring, "Fauré's gone completely out of his mind!"[73]

Georges Servières, Jacques Méraly, and Paul Ladmirault, all critics for distinguished journals, praised *La bonne chanson* and made defensible qualitative distinctions between the different songs.[74] But it was a man of letters – Proust – who took this music at its true worth from the start. Did Proust's profound understanding of the relation between originality and self-renewal help him grasp Fauré's transformation of his own style? We do not know the exact cause for the novelist's enthusiasm. In a letter that Philip Kolb dates to September 1894, Proust wrote:

> Did you know the young composers are almost unanimous in disliking *La bonne chanson*? It would seem the work is uselessly complicated, etc., very inferior to the rest; Bréville, Debussy (said to be a great genius high above Fauré) hold this opinion. That's all the same to me; I adore this volume, and on the contrary, it's the early songs they feign to prefer which I don't like.[75]

Some would say that Proust could insist on the superiority of this work over Fauré's earlier ones because he was free of the technical scruples that made its innovations problematic for Saint-Saëns and Bellaigue. But this is a little too easy. Surely Proust, who loved Verlaine's poetry, also admired *La bonne chanson* because he recognized the appropriate complexity of Fauré's realization of poetic form and meaning, and also because the work, compared to Fauré's earlier songs, offered testimony to the kind of self-renewal that brings us closer to an artist's "most original originality."

We end this section by returning to Fauré's First Quintet, whose history and reception occupied us in the previous chapter. The near unanimity of critical opinion about Fauré's Quintet gives us another example of his knack for capturing a plausible balance between novelty and homogeneity in his music. The auspicious reception of the work gives little evidence of the risks of self-renewal Fauré himself experienced in composing it; the Quintet stood apart from Fauré's earlier chamber music, but critics understood and honored this change. Moreover, in contrast to Debussy's orchestral works in the same decade, Fauré's Quintet ran little risk of censure on the basis of encumbered formal alliances. That is, Fauré's work has no trace of the cyclical procedures that became so fraught with ideological implications in the reception of Debussy's music. To show the significance of this difference, we need only return to the succession of reviews cited in the last chapter. Louis Vierne compared the brilliant acclaim of Fauré's Quintet to that of Franck's, and thus he placed a new masterpiece in the light of an old one. Lalo and Laloy, too, both raised the ghost of César Franck. Franck's Quintet, after all, was the first great French (or, if you prefer, Belgian) work in the medium; it also happened to be resolutely cyclical in structure. But Vierne, Lalo, and Laloy brought up Franck only in order to point out Fauré's independence from him, and Vierne specifically mentioned the technical distinction: "Each of [Fauré's] movements has two themes whose traces cannot be found again in the following movements."[76] Vierne could compare only the triumphant receptions of the two works, not their forms; he offered no further analogies. Finally, Octave Maus singled out the absence of what he called "technical pedantry" and "verbiage" in Fauré's Quintet. These terms almost certainly allude to thematic procedures favored by post-Franckian composers at the Schola.[77] There is no question, however, that the mere absence of a trait, in this case cyclism, could ever suffice to institute homogeneity. Works by Fauré that did make use of cyclical themes, such as *La chanson d'Ève* and the Second Violin Sonata, prompted no accusations of *scholiste* pedantry, and this suggests that other stylistic and historical factors came into account. We would be surprised if the opposite were true.

In chapter 3, we cited a lone exception to the general praise for Fauré's First Quintet: a mixed review by Georges Servières. We passed over this review rather quickly there. Let us now look at the content and coherence of Servières's objections:

> Is it . . . by some calculated will to sobriety and discretion that the work dwells almost throughout in dampened sonorities and tonalities; that its developments sometimes have a character of labored severity; that, compared to its forerunners, it is less illuminated with the tender and melancholy "Fauréan" smile? Study and repeated hearings will undoubtedly clarify the seemingly cloudy polyphony of this composition.

Servières continues by praising the quality of Fauré's ideas and invention but nonetheless ends his review with a doubt: "The handling of these excellent elements lacks the decisiveness, the perspicacity, the suppleness of coloring that we find in M. Fauré's two Quartets."[78] Again we see that cyclical form was not the only reason for bringing a composer's homogeneity into question around 1905. At the same time, both of these complaints are founded on negative comparisons with Fauré's earlier works, the deficiencies that the Quintet presents in relation to Fauré's two earlier Quartets. Polite as it is, Servières's critique fundamentally resembles the critique Lalo and Carraud leveled at Debussy. Had Servières's views of the Quintet typified those of the majority of French critics, Fauré's work might well have required the services of a Louis Laloy to rescue its homogeneity and prove its proper place in Fauré's ongoing development.

It is amusing to observe that while Laloy and Lalo disagreed bitterly over the quality of Debussy's music after *Pelléas*, their views of Fauré's work in the same period do not differ in the least. With reference to the recital at the Société Nationale in May 1906, which included the First Quintet alongside other works of Fauré, we may refresh our memory by citing these two quotations, the first by Laloy, the second by Lalo, side by side:

> Better than ever by bringing [earlier and later works] together could one appreciate that unity of style of a music which was always sure of itself and which did not let itself be turned aside by Wagner or César Franck from the road which it was making for itself with smiling, tranquil assurance. A concert for which his works furnish the entire program is a severe test for a composer. Fauré came out of it, not only victorious, but triumphant and younger than ever.[79]

> Originality so strong and deep-seated not only shelters the composer who possesses it from outside influences, it ensures the unity of his work . . . [On this program] his most recent composition stood by some very early ones and others dating from the middle of his career. There was no disparity from one piece to the other. This art has undoubtedly changed, become deeper and more subtle; the feeling, thought and inspiration, though, have remained the same. And nothing has become dated . . . Among composers of our day, how many could come out of such a test victoriously?[80]

How remarkable that these statements, almost identical and both demonstrating a strong perception of stylistic homogeneity, came from two critics who clashed bitterly over Debussy's contemporaneous works. We also may recall from the previous chapter that the balance between sameness and innovation in Fauré's successive works was the object of Lalo's broadest praise. Lalo's was an exemplary recognition of homogeneity:

> [Fauré's] art has gradually become more complex, and he has used more and more intricate means of expression. But its complexity, delicate and

seemingly transparent, mars neither its clarity nor its subtle engagement with sensibility. Here, indeed, increasing complexity and exploration do not have their sources in artificial study but in the natural evolution of an art that has never ceased to be in intimate accord with thought and feeling.[81]

Lalo was unable to muster a comparable understanding of Debussy. The contrast is striking. What is more important than this contrast, however, is a basic similarity. Lalo defends Fauré's art and its increasing "complexity" in the same language, using the same warrants, that Laloy used in his defense of Debussy's "new manner." The aesthetic ideology is the same; the individual responses diverge.

In a detailed consideration of the concept of style, James Ackerman has observed, "Our image of style is not discovered but created by abstracting certain features and combinations from works of art for the purpose of assisting historical and critical activity."[82] French artists and thinkers around 1900, in favoring such ideas as "originality" and "homogeneity," shaped a particular conception of style, and undoubtedly one whose biases treated some creative projects better than others. Ackerman also observes, "For the artist and for his audience, style is a protection against chaos; it serves the same purpose as do cultural patterns and institutions in society."[83] Homogeneity is an aspect of style; it answers this need for order and has real implications for compositional practice. But the protection it affords against chaos may not be valued by audiences and artists in the same ways, or to the same degree. Artists and audiences may not agree upon the limits of change.

3 Fauré's homogeneity in a Proustian mirror

Homogeneity emerges as a problematic critical category, to be sure, but one necessary for understanding the terms of musical reception in early twentieth-century France. Now we return to Proust to pick up the threads of speculations only half woven in the first section. In order to distinguish between different forms of unity and homogeneity and to approach the possibility of using these forms as a way of understanding the development of a composer's work, we begin with Vinteuil. Then we turn to Fauré, one of the composers whose music Proust subsumed in this fictional figure and whose work reflects aspects of Proustian homogeneity more exactly than the novelist ever knew.

In the previous section our critics alighted repeatedly on the question of unity: "the unity of a style," "the unity of a work." What kind of unity? Combarieu, Carraud, Laloy and Lalo were certainly all concerned about the unity or organic integrity of a composition, but they were perhaps even more concerned about the unity that makes a *series* of works recognizable as the achievement of a single imagination. In three substantial passages from *La prisonnière*, we shall see Proust speculate on different manifestations of this latter kind of unity.

One theory of unity, the most difficult to apply to Fauré's music, appears in the first third of Proust's book. Marcel amuses himself by playing through Vinteuil's Sonata and, caught up in the tributaries of speculation awakened by it, considers the ways in which composers and writers have "discovered" a kind of retrospective unity in their own works. Marcel thinks of masterpieces by Wagner, Hugo, Balzac, and Michelet which were organized or reconceived in a kind of grandiose afterthought. Under the spell of such retrospection, nineteenth-century writers, to be sure, sometimes achieved a unity more claimed than felt, more manufactured than real. Admitting a certain ambivalence toward Hugo and Michelet, Marcel settles on Balzac's *Comédie humaine* as an example of a true unity. Superficial evidence to the contrary, Marcel argues that when Balzac, "casting over his books the eye at once of a stranger and of a father, . . . suddenly decided, shedding a retrospective illumination upon them, that they would be better brought together in a cycle in which the same characters would reappear [i.e., *La Comédie humaine*], and touched up his work with a swift brush-stroke, the last and most sublime," he created "an ulterior unity, but not a factitious one, otherwise it would have crumbled into dust like all the other systematisations of mediocre writers who with copious titles and sub-titles give themselves the appearance of having pursued a single and transcendent design." Balzac's unity, he continues, is "not factitious, perhaps indeed all the more real for being ulterior, for being born of a moment of enthusiasm when it is discovered to exist among fragments which need only to be joined together; *a unity that was unaware of itself,* hence vital and not logical, that did not prohibit variety, dampen invention."[84]

It is difficult to parlay these considerations into our understanding of Fauré's music for two reasons. First, Fauré composed no works like Wagner's tetralogy or Berlioz's *Épisode de la vie d'un artiste* (i.e., the *Symphonie fantastique* and *Lélio*), works self-standing yet explicitly linked, which would lend themselves to "retrospective brush-strokes." Second, it is not at all evident that Fauré ever applied such retrospective illuminations even to sections or movements within his individual works. Though it is certainly possible that he may have done so, he did not speak of working in this way, and his surviving manuscripts yield no evidence to that end. The one exception, perhaps, is the Ballade, op. 19, which apparently began its existence as a group of separate pieces. We will recall Fauré's statement to Marie

Clerc that "by using methods at once *new* and *old*, I have found the means to develop, in a sort of interlude, the phrases of the second piece and at the same time to give the premises of the third, in such a way that the three parts have become a whole."[85] Yet there is a qualitative difference between this "local" effort at unity and the grand "ulterior unity" of a Balzac or a Wagner; it is a question not only of scale but of time. The "pieces" of the Ballade were composed over a matter of months, not decades, and Fauré's invention and reconsideration of his material were almost simultaneous in comparison to the strokes of reinvention Marcel attributes to Balzac. What we shall take away from Marcel's observation most profitably is rather the detail I have stressed through italics: the notion that unity may be the more authentic for being "unaware of itself" – instinctive or unconscious.

Proust treats this theme, the question of the artist's self-awareness, in a subsequent passage from *La prisonnière*. The occasion for Marcel's speculation is again a work of Vinteuil, this time the Septet, which the narrator hears for the first time at the soirée held by the Verdurins. We must remember that the Septet is a work of Vinteuil's old age, posthumously deciphered by a friend of the composer's daughter. Because Marcel is able to compare this late work to the Sonata he already knows, he discusses a kind of unity different from Balzac's "retrospective illumination." Marcel turns to the form of unity I have called homogeneity:

> Every artist seems . . . like the citizen of an unknown homeland that he himself has forgotten, different from the one from which another great artist will set out for this earth . . . Composers do not remember this lost homeland, but every one of them always remains unconsciously harmonized in a kind of unison with it; a composer is delirious with joy when he sings in tune with his homeland; he sometimes betrays it for love of glory, but then in searching for glory he flees it, and it is only in disdaining such gain that he finds it again, when he intones that individual song whose singleness of tone [*monotonie*] (for, whatever subject he treats, he remains identical to himself) proves the constancy of the elements that make up his soul.[86]

In pondering the mystery of artistic style, Marcel again isolates the positive quality of "monotonie" (see above, p. 127). Marcel summons up this "monotonie" both as "that individual song whose singleness of tone . . . proves the constancy of the elements that make up [the composer's] soul" and as the idea that composers "always remain unconsciously harmonized in a kind of unison" with their homeland. Loyalty to this "unknown homeland" seems to be a prerequisite for the kind of homogeneity ("singleness of tone," "constancy") that the narrator admires in Vinteuil.

But why is the composer's homeland numinous, "unknown"? The quotation about Balzac has already suggested at least one answer: for Proust, a composer's relation to his own style would seem to be largely unconscious. The composer feels a magnetic attraction toward his stylistic "homeland," but he does not "know" it in an objective sense; that is, he could not map its boundaries or topography. But there may be a second reason, perhaps more important, for describing this homeland as "unknown": it cannot be located in particular works but only, so to speak, in between them. It is, however, somewhat misleading to describe the space between works as "unknown," for it is charged with meaning for a sensitive listener like Marcel. It is the listener who can in fact "know" and recognize the composer's homeland. If this homeland were literally unknown, even Marcel could not bring it up for scrutiny, much less associate it with the kind of work Vinteuil has created. On this point, nevertheless, Proust's peculiar attitude toward art is consistent: his great artists are intellectually innocent of their creative destinies. Their stylistic homogeneity is instinctive, while it is left to Proust's fictional proxies to discover it and describe its peculiarities for the reader.[87]

Now we turn to Marcel's third and most specific consideration of homogeneity in *La prisonnière*. Here he advances to the stage of trying to distinguish between different kinds of homogeneity in Vinteuil's art:

> It was precisely when he was striving with all his might to create something new that one recognised, beneath the apparent differences, the profound similarities and the deliberate resemblances that existed in the body of a work; when Vinteuil took up the same phrase again and again, diversified it, amused himself by altering its rhythm, by making it reappear in its original form, those *deliberate resemblances*, the work of his intellect, necessarily superficial, never succeeded in being as striking as the disguised, *involuntary resemblances*, which broke out in different colours, between the two separate masterpieces; for then Vinteuil, striving to do something new, interrogated himself, with all the power of his creative energy, reached down to his essential self at those depths where, whatever the question asked, it is in the same accent, that is to say its own, that it replies. Such an accent, the accent of Vinteuil . . .[88]

This is a powerfully unifying text for the themes of this chapter. First, we see that Marcel is concerned with the intermediary space I described a moment ago: "the resemblances, which broke out in different colours, *between the two separate masterpieces*." If we think back to Balzac's ability to realize a true "ulterior unity," we can now see that he was able to do so not through any artifice but through his faith in a particular ideal: his constant attraction to the same artistic "homeland" which assured the unity of his work from start to finish. Second, Proust renders the differences between Vinteuil's two masterpieces through his favorite metaphor of "different colors," whose significance we analyzed earlier. Third, this metaphor of colors and refraction leads us back to a source of light: the singular "creative energy" emanating from the composer's "essential self," which we may now safely identify as the stopping point in Proust's analysis. Fourth, and this is the detail that will concern us for the remainder of this chapter, Marcel believes that the "involuntary resemblances" produced by Vinteuil's "essential self" are more striking than the "deliberate resemblances" through which the composer consciously tried to unify his work.

Although Nattiez, in his fine study of Proust, is not concerned with the varieties of unity, he recognizes the great importance of unity in Proust's aesthetics. Nattiez does not examine the "unknown homeland" or cite the passage on Balzac but, for his own reasons, he does probe the quotation just cited. He remarks that the narrator "distinguishes between two types of similarity . . . Deliberate resemblances are the result of industrious toil; the rest, of the composer's desire to look only towards the future . . . What is of crucial importance in the Septet, then, is not the effort of will, the 'analytical forms of reasoning,' but the specificity that the work displays in relation to all the others at one and the same time as it shares a stylistic relationship with them."[89] Here Nattiez has neatly isolated the two different forms of homogeneity the narrator tries to describe. This basic distinction may be made more specific: we may oppose thematic working-out, motivic recrudescence and the like, on the one hand, to the essential sameness of personal style on the other. We call the latter "essential" because it in some sense transcends technique. Alternatively, we might explain this difference as that between unity acquired through material means and the unity an artistic personality confers on a life's work. However we describe it, the difference offers us a starting point for reconsidering homogeneity in Fauré's music.

The fact that Fauré returned again and again to certain melodic fragments over the course of his life is well known. It was not long after his death that the most attentive students of his music, particularly Jankélévitch and Philippe Fauré-Fremiet, noted this phenomenon in print. Building on these occasional insights, Nectoux devoted a more systematic, but by no means exhaustive, essay to the question of Fauré's self-quotations in 1979. Nectoux summarizes his findings, which he describes as providing "elements for a Fauréan catalogue," at the start of his article:

> The melismatic cells with which [Fauré] seems to be obsessed fall into
> distinct groups, tending to link works to other works in a sort of musical
> chain. The richest of these motives develops over a period of some fifty years,
> while other, less sophisticated cells have a more ephemeral life, as though
> their substance were more rapidly exhausted. Occasionally these reuses of
> themes are voluntary, as when Fauré purposefully borrows material from

abandoned works, but often they seem to be unconscious and thus all the more meaningful to the study of his thematic idiom.[90]

More recently, Robin Tait carried the identification of some of these self-quotations further and reached similar conclusions:

> My aim [in these examples] is to show that Fauré's themes recur not necessarily as the main motive of a work, but often in the course of the music as a subsidiary motive, or even incidentally, in a melodic curve. No doubt, not all of these recurrences were intentional; all we can say with certainty is that they are present, and that the effect of recognising them adds to the music a dimension of memory to which Proust surely responded in his love for Fauré's music.[91]

Both Tait and (elsewhere in the article just cited) Nectoux associate the recurrence of ideas across Fauré's music with the figure of Proust. Tait even goes so far as to speak of one of Fauré's intermittent motives as a "musical madeleine." Unfortunately, Proust's letters, rich though they are in musical references, strongly indicate that he did not know enough of Fauré's works to have encountered these allusive repetitions. Yet the relation between Proustian homogeneity and recurrence in Fauré's music is worth pursuing. References to "madeleines" and "time regained" are suggestive, but the concept of homogeneity, which Nectoux and Tait overlook, is a general one through which Fauré's and Proust's aesthetic ideals may be connected to one another with real historical warrants.

We must acknowledge that literary critics who have studied the role of music in Proust's work have likewise neglected the potential of homogeneity as an interpretive tool. Georges Piroué, for example, proposes the cyclic and leitmotivic techniques of Franck and Wagner as sources for Proust's ideas about the power of musical analogies.[92] It is certainly true that Proust was interested in these techniques, but his ideas about musical affinities are far from exhausted by such a narrow explanation. The passages quoted earlier from Proust demonstrate that his image of stylistic unity went beyond the motivic content of a single composition. The conscious manipulation of themes and motives, the "deliberate resemblances" Marcel hears in Vinteuil's Septet, are less striking to him than the "involuntary" ones that connect it to Vinteuil's style as a whole. Better than any cyclical machinery, the kinds of casual likenesses Nectoux and Tait have identified in Fauré would seem to match Marcel's image of a higher homogeneity. In Fauré we can find resemblances between or across, not merely within, separate works. The idea that at least some of these resemblances seem to be "unconscious" or "incidental" is important, too, and we shall come back to the problem of determining their "unconscious" nature. It is clear, however, that the

Example 9. The "Lydian" lineage.
  a. "Lydia," op. 4, no. 2 (*c.* 1870), mm. 3–6 (vocal melody).
  b. *La bonne chanson*, op. 61, no. 3: "La lune blanche" (1893), mm. 9–11 (piano).
  c. *Prométhée*, op. 82 (1900), Act III, no. 4, mm. 3–4.
  d. *Messe basse*, Kyrie (1906), mm. 19–25 (organ and voices).

recurrence of certain melodic figures in Fauré's work is, in a positive sense, *gratuitous*. Unlike leading motives or cyclical themes, these Fauréan repetitions have no technical function – like the lilies of the field, they toil not, neither do they spin. Such gratuity is an important criterion in Marcel's typology of homogeneity.

Nectoux has dealt with Fauré's recurring ideas in some detail, and it would be pointless to retrace his steps here. Two examples, however, will help to make this discussion more tangible for a reader unfamiliar with Nectoux's work. Let us look over the series of related melodies that may be traced back to "Lydia," one of Fauré's earliest songs (Example 9). Nectoux and Orledge overlooked the last instance cited above, from the *Messe basse*, but Kœchlin noticed its filiation with "Lydia" long ago.[93] These four compositions span thirty-six years of Fauré's creative life, a span suggesting that this common melodic content responded to some persistent expressive need in Fauré. Two elements of Fauré's style come to mind. First, the special quality of this melody, the way it rises against a kind of bland resistance while doubling back on itself, becomes more and more characteristic of Fauré's mature melodic style.[94] Second, "Lydia" bears within it the seeds for two related tendencies in Fauré's later music: his fondness for the raised fourth degree and his habit of making sequences by whole-tones. These converging tendencies eventually led him to extend the basic pattern in "Lydia" by one whole-tone, then another. The resulting whole-tone collection subsequently served as the structural basis for extravagant harmonic detours in works from "Pleurs d'or" (1896) and "Le parfum impérissable" (1897) onward. "Lydia," the first composition by Fauré in which the raised fourth degree assumes a prominent position, is not just the mother of the three sibling tunes of Example 9 but an origin of this more general stylistic evolution.[95] The Lydian phrase, whether expressed melodically or composed out as a harmonic structure, seems to have become for Fauré a kind of mental template for spurring melodic and harmonic fantasy.

Our second example, rather different, has its origins in Fauré's musical characterization of Ulysses in *Pénélope*. After inventing the theme for Ulysses in 1907, Fauré described it as "heroic, almost joyous."[96] First heard in the orchestral prelude to the opera, the whole idea is eight measures long. It is, however, the first constituent motive of the theme, shown in Example 10a, that proved peculiarly malleable for Fauré and begot a progeny of related melodic patterns. As in the previous example, these citations are arranged chronologically. Nectoux quotes two of them (Examples 10a and 10d).[97] The other four examples, all from Fauré's chamber music, are ones I have newly identified. With this motive, even more than in the case of "Lydia," we are dealing with a flexible pattern. Example 10a is an elementary structure around which Fauré realized variations. We may describe this basic structure as an octave, usually rising, and always embellished by neighboring whole-tones. The possibility of treating the octave less as an intervallic displacement than as an elastic, singing profile, seems to have intrigued Fauré. The expressive quality of this gesture ranges from resolve and self-confidence, personified in the aplomb of Ulysses, to the radiant happiness of the *Fantaisie*, op. 111. In the finales of the First Cello Sonata and the Second Violin Sonata, Fauré expands what was once a terse motive into buoyant, even frisky, themes of considerable breadth.[98] In the finale of the String Quartet, the last piece of music Fauré wrote, the Odyssean material appears as an accompanimental design in the second violin. This choice is rather surprising; indeed, by dint of its peculiar jumpiness, this open pattern seems to become a terse countersubject. In general, let us observe that the chronology of the examples is not particularly significant; it is not a question of some continuous movement away from a rudimentary form. The "derivative" in the String Quartet is even more compact than its prototype in *Pénélope*.

Example 10. The "Odyssean" lineage.

a. *Pénélope* (1907–12): "Prélude," mm. 42–43 (first trumpet).
b. Second Violin Sonata, op. 108 (1916–17): III, mm. 34–42 (violin).
c. First Cello Sonata, op. 109 (1917): III, mm. 24–33 (cello).
d. *Fantaisie*, op. 111 (1918), mm. 29–30 (first violins).
e. Second Quintet, op. 115 (1919–21): I, mm. 45–49 (piano).
f. String Quartet, op. 121 (1924): III, mm. 1–2.

a [Andante moderato]

b [Allegro non troppo]

c [Allegro commodo]

d [Allegro moderato]

e [Allegro moderato]

f Allegro

Can the passages cited in the examples above be said to correspond to Marcel's observation of "disguised, involuntary resemblances, which broke out in different colours, between . . . separate masterpieces"? In the sense that there is no evidence of a deliberate technical or symbolic connection between the compositions in each example, we may answer with a qualified yes – qualified, because one exception must be mentioned. In 1902, Louis Aguettant, trying to discuss the thematic structure of *La bonne chanson* with Fauré, unwittingly got him to acknowledge the identity between "Lydia" and the phrase cited from "La lune blanche" in Example 9. Not only was Fauré conscious of the reappearance of the Lydian melody in the later song, but the repetition seems to have been deliberate, since he added enigmatically, "[The theme] refers to a performer."[99] This comment changes what might be taken for an unconscious recurrence into a real self-quotation. But could we ever have doubted that Fauré should have repeated himself so obviously without conscious design? Examples 9a and 9b are simply too close. Now, whether this self-quotation referred to Lydia Eustis, Emma Bardac, or some other singer, remains unknown; nor, more importantly, do we know what Fauré *meant* by the repetition. Fauré's comment nonetheless raises the possibility that there may be symbolic meanings hidden behind other instances of the Lydian theme. But if their purpose is (or seems) unknown, are such recurrences not, in effect, still "gratuitous"?

We need to consider the elusive question of deliberation on the part of the composer because it seems clear that, for Proust, the highest forms of unity were marked by such gratuitousness. Indeed, Marcel is specifically troubled by the difficulty of determining whether the resemblance between two musical passages is due to conscious fabrication or to involuntary memory. Confronting instances of conscious thematic interpolation in the music of Wagner and Vinteuil, Marcel confesses, "I was troubled by this Vulcanian skill. Could *this* be what, in great artists, gave the illusion of a deep-seated, irreducible originality, apparently the reflection of some more than human reality, but in fact the product of diligent labor?"[100] Marcel will eventually answer this important question in the negative, when the existence of "a deep-seated, irreducible originality" beside and beneath the work of "diligent labor," is confirmed for him in his later encounter with Vinteuil's Septet. Although Marcel ultimately claims to perceive the difference between a homogeneity resulting from diligent labor and one resulting from an involuntary process, it is hard to see how we can reproduce his knowledge. Proust's opposition of "involuntary" and "deliberate" resemblances presents a methodological problem.

I thought, at first, to expand on Proust's insight by distinguishing two kinds of musical recurrence from one another. On the one hand: deliberate

repetitions, under which we can now include not only the laborious spin-
ning of themes and motives within a single composition but also self-quotation, however whimsical, between works, as seen with "Lydia" and "La
lune blanche." On the other hand: likenesses between compositions not
otherwise linked and which seem less like self-quotations than unconscious,
or at least casual, reminiscences. But what is to prevent the listener from pre-
suming a hidden content behind every set of affinities? It seems most
unlikely that the passages gathered under Example 10 refer to a single
signifier whose name we ignore and cannot find, but the possibility cannot
be ruled out. How can we tell the difference between stylistic essence and
diligent labor when we look at such examples? We come up against this
paradox repeatedly. The more confidence we have in the identity of two
resemblances, the more homogeneous they are, the more reason we find to
suspect them of bearing an unknown meaning, of, in the end, serving a
function, thus losing their "essential" or "gratuitous" quality. This problem
may be irresolvable. Proust's standard of homogeneity is frankly essentialis-
tic, and we have only found its cul-de-sac. The methodological problem
does not, however, erase our real perception of homogeneity in Fauré's
music or lessen the importance of an attempt to understand homogeneity
in the culturally pertinent terms Proust provides.

For a final time, let us return to those terms, expressed by Marcel in a
splendid metaphor:

> They were phrases of the sort which, without our being able to understand
> what affinity assigns to them as their sole and necessary abode the past of a
> certain composer, are to be found only in his work, and appear constantly in
> his work, of which they are the spirits, the dryads, the familiar deities.[101]

It is not clear which type of homogeneity Marcel means to represent in this
remark on the Septet. The sentence, on its own, speaks to the most abstract
form of homogeneity – of affinities "unaware of themselves," compelling us
to recognize an "irreducible originality." The appearance of metaphorical
"spirits," "dryads" and "familiar deities" deepens this interpretation. These
are genii: in the ancient sense, they are Vinteuil's guardian deities; in the
modern sense, they are the constituents of his musical genius. Conversely,
however, we must also observe that this metaphor develops out of Marcel's
observation that, in the Septet, "again and again one phrase or another from
the sonata recurred, but altered each time, its rhythm and harmony different,
the same and yet something else."[102] Once we know the preamble, the passage
cited above seems only to describe "Vulcanian" motivic work and self-quotation. But we cannot be certain. As so often happens with Proust's train of
thought, we move fluidly from the specific to the general and back again.

We need to broaden our perspective. It is true that Marcel assimilates these "familiar deities" to self-quotations or traits of motivic recrudescence. But he also assimilates them to something more general. The genii are inhabitants of Vinteuil's involuntary memory and prove to Marcel the singularity of his musical "accent." Proust's account of music in *A la recherche du temps perdu*, taken *as a whole*, does not allow us to doubt the greater weight he assigns to the latter, more general meaning. To invert these values would not only trifle with Vinteuil's genii but also his genius. If we assert that the genii are only illusions created by workmanship, by Vulcanian dexterity, we obliterate precisely the "irreducible originality" that proves to Marcel the "existence of the individual soul." "If art is no more than that," he says, "it is no more real than life."[103] Were this strange but very Proustian deduction the end of Marcel's journey, his growing sense of his own vocation as a writer would wither and die. Incidentally, we should also remember that if it is difficult to determine the status of the "familiar deities" in Marcel's account of the Verdurins' soirée, that is because, at any particular moment in the novel, his stream of mental associations is changing course, evolving, and scattering in different directions.

Now I shall suggest an extrapolation, for we can respond constructively to the methodological problem outlined above even if we can never escape it. With the fullest significance of Proust's "deities" and "dryads" in mind, let us see if we can discern something in Fauré's music that would correspond to them. This does not mean changing the direction of our argument, only refining it. Instead of a phrase as obvious and striking as that of "Lydia," which in each instance cited in Example 9 occurs at a point of thematic or formal articulation, we should turn to musical ideas that are even less self-contained or that appear in inconspicuous positions. Example 10 already provides a model. Because the passages in Example 10 show more diversity than those in Example 9 and because the recurrence of the same motive is less obvious, the "Odyssean" lineage appears less likely to be deliberately or secretly coded than the "Lydian" one. We may find works by Fauré where similar repetitions occur – for instance, a passing, internal cadence in the coda of the Eleventh Barcarolle which echoes the love theme of *Pénélope* (Example 11).[104] This example is peculiarly disguised, for on the one hand, the passage in the Barcarolle is a logical extension of the main theme of the piece, and on the other hand, it corresponds to a point not at the beginning but in the middle of the love theme. Fauré started writing his Eleventh Barcarolle in 1913, that is to say, in the immediate wake of *Pénélope*; this internal echo seems therefore both understandable and spontaneous. Yet, as we noted several paragraphs ago with regard to the pieces in Example 10, one can always propose that this resemblance, though tacit, is deliberate.

Example 11.
  a. Eleventh Barcarolle, op. 105, mm. 106–09.
  b. *Pénélope*, Act I, scene 6.

a

b

Could Fauré, for instance, have intended this musical reference to convey a private message of affection to Laura Albéniz, to whom he dedicated this Barcarolle?

If even a fleeting motive has an identity too distinct for us to be able to refute the idea that its recurrence could not, in the final analysis, be due to just that "industrious toil" Marcel found so disenchanting, we need to rethink our strategy further. Perhaps we may better seek gratuitous self-resemblance in other kinds of musical material. Logic suggests that we turn to entities that are neither thematic nor motivic, yet a convincing case cannot be built around raw musical materials such as sequences by falling fifths, ascents by rising thirds, or a whole-tone scale, for these are grammatical units shared by many composers; they cannot bear witness to a unique personal accent.[105] Therefore I should like to cite a set of passages from Fauré's music that do not have thematic status but are nonetheless distinctively Fauréan and also bear a structural function in common. These passages constitute what, for lack of a better word, musicians often call a "gesture" (Example 12). These descending passages all mark a kind of exhalation after points of climax.[106] In Examples 12b and 12c, we may also note Fauré's impulse to "fill in" registral space by continuing a linear pattern from the right hand into the left (the Fourth Barcarolle, mm. 29–32, provides yet another example). The fact that all these passages come from Fauré's piano music may be significant. These octaves, thrown over opulent harmonic beddings, allow the pianist to unburden the preceding points of tension in an extremely satisfying way. The physicality of the gesture attests to its spontaneous quality, as if Fauré's own hands, so skilled in improvisation, knew all the possible levers of a personal mechanism for descending from musical summits. Even though none of these scalar descents has a thematic status, the content of each one echoes characteristic intervals heard earlier in the piece. Thus the passage in the Fifth Barcarolle is derived from the middle of its second theme (m. 18), the initial E-flat and C-flat in the treble part of the Eighth Barcarolle reproduce the fifth and sixth notes of its main tune (m. 2), and the long example from the Ballade is a meandering extension of the first five notes of its second theme (m. 37).

In spite of these details that bind each of the examples to its particular composition, there is a clear family resemblance between them all. In addition to the purely tactile excitement of these passages, their transitory nature, nonchalant and evasive, seems to deprive them of any potential for extramusical significance. Indeed, beneath their elegant, expansive surfaces, these are, like most descending phrases, cadences. All but the third example share a basic harmonic structure. Each begins on a subdominant or predominant harmony, which is stretched out and shifted to delay the following dominant; then the dominant arrives and dutifully resolves to the tonic. The Fifth Barcarolle presents an exception, because Fauré has used the same gesture not only as a descent from a high point but also as a transition that will prepare us for a new climax. If the other examples may be compared to full cadences, the Fifth Barcarolle presents us with something like a deceptive cadence. The sense of relaxation imparted by the gradual fall from the high F at the start of the example is quickly complicated. Instead of moving toward resolution, Fauré switches the implied tonal center from F to F-sharp. We plunge all the way to the depths and, with the dominant bass note C-sharp struck in measure 102, are on our way to the true climax of the piece, which arrives twelve measures later. Thus, Fauré is able to turn his habitual mode of descent to a new purpose, but we still recognize the gesture.

These passages, written over the course of twenty-seven years, fulfill related expressive and structural functions. In their peculiar similarities, they represent, as well as any examples I can imagine, the familiar spirits and genii of Fauré's art. Since they do not join these four separate compositions in a factitious unity or serve any conceivable illustrative or symbolic function, their common gesture also meets, or at least approaches, the formidable Proustian criterion of gratuity. This example, however, is suggestive rather than definitive; as a single illustration of casual recurrence, it is a blueprint, not a proof. Earlier I referred to this effort to find Fauré's dryads as an extrapolation. I did so because I have, in providing musical evidence that tries to match the fullness of Proust's metaphor, undoubtedly gone beyond what his prose says about the music heard by the narrator. Since

Example 12.

    a. Ballade, op. 19, (1877–79), mm. 206–10 (version for piano solo; in the later
       version for piano and orchestra, see mm. 207–11 instead).

    b. Fourth Nocturne, op. 36 (1884), mm. 56–58.

    c. Fifth Barcarolle, op. 66 (1894), mm. 99–101.

    d. Eighth Barcarolle, op. 96 (1906), mm. 69–70.

a   [Allegro moderato]

b   [Andante molto moderato]

Example 12. (*cont.*)

c   [**Allegretto moderato**]

d   [**Allegretto moderato**]

Proust's musical sensitivity was greater than his technical or analytical apti-
tude, this extension is not necessarily unfaithful to his thinking, and his
notion of stylistic homogeneity remains at the heart of our argument.

The passages we have considered are like cross-referencing entries in the
lexicon of Fauré's style. If we are willing to go beyond the yardstick of
Proustian homogeneity, the musical phrase or motive, we could also
approach Fauré's homogeneity through the recurrence of characteristic
"deep structures" in his music. To do so here would launch us into an analytical project beyond the scope of this chapter. Fortunately, the studies by
Edward Phillips and Taylor Greer, both mentioned earlier, have gone a considerable way to establishing the existence of these structures and showing
us how Fauré used them. In a series of fastidious Schenkerian and Fortean
analyses, Phillips has proven that Fauré developed, over the course of his

career, a set of consistent techniques for disrupting tonal syntax. These distortions of voice-leading occur at the foreground, middleground, and background levels. Fauré moreover forges the contrapuntal armament of his music so that alterations at different structural levels are offset from one another – a technique Phillips has aptly compared to the passage of the harmonic structure through a prism. Phillips discusses the effect of one such passage as follows: "the foreground is the result of a distortion of the structural voice leading," but this distortion "is applied to different degrees in different voices: a given bass note is often nowhere near the upper voices it is supporting."[107] Over the course of fifty years, the harmonic organization of Fauré's compositions became more and more imbued with these distortions; however, the techniques themselves did not change in kind, only in degree. These "specific techniques . . . originate near the foreground but . . . come to affect structures that are more fundamental."[108] Fauré's steadfast pursuit of the implications of a unique harmonic discourse points to another aspect of his homogeneity.

Like Phillips, Taylor Greer has brought to light habits and procedures that underpin Fauré's evolving harmonic style. Greer is particularly interested in Fauré's use of two different middleground structures, both based on fragments of the whole-tone scale. The first of these structures, which Greer calls "the linked-third span," is an example of "Fauré's unique gift for endowing a limited number of whole-tone segments with an almost unlimited number of tonal meanings."[109] "These recurring linear motives create a rich network of correspondences within Fauré's œuvre: among passages within a single song . . ., among songs within a larger cycle . . . and among independent songs written over a twenty-year period."[110] Greer's account of the second structure he isolates, based on parallel counterpoint in wholetones, takes the reader from the simple chain of rising thirds over a tonal bass at the beginning of "Lydia" (c. 1870), to an eight-measure interpolation in "Puisque l'aube grandit" (1893, at mm. 31–38) which briefly suspends the harmonic function of the bass, to a radical expansion of this same technique in the Fifth Impromptu (1909), which withholds its first strictly harmonic progression until the hundred-fiftieth measure: the last page of the piece![111] The Fifth Impromptu is especially persuasive evidence of the self-renewal and innovation Fauré found possible within the syntactic boundaries he set for himself. In this strange piece, almost purely contrapuntal in conception, he so drastically postpones the onset of a tonal syntax that its late arrival becomes, in fact, more surprising than the atonal music that preceded it. Through this paradox, Fauré reveals that tonality is no longer a law for him, but a choice. The dizzying artifice by which he institutes a tonal progression on the last page of the Impromptu distances us from tonal language in a completely modern way. It is a moment of comedy, but also a declaration of mastery.

*

We have considered homogeneity both generally and specifically: as the sameness that characterizes the art of a single individual and as real musical resemblances in particular works. After treating this aesthetic concept from an overwhelmingly positive point of view, I find it interesting to note that Fauré was frankly worried about the threshold between profound homogeneity and monotony in his own music. From Zurich in 1904, he touched on this problem in the following letter, written while he was working on the troublesome First Quintet:

> The weather has become mild and the sky has cleared, allowing views to faraway summits covered with snow. It is always glorious to see how the sunlight plays on the crags, the water, the trees and meadows. And what a multiplicity of effects, what bursts of light or velvet tinging! I could certainly wish that my music were so diverse. It seems to me that I repeat myself constantly and that I am not finding a tone [*un accent*] appreciably different from what I've already expressed.[112]

Here Fauré connects his work on the Quintet with a characteristic appreciation of nature, and he suspects that what he creates cannot measure up to the beauty of the visible world. But in a fitting coincidence, Fauré uses the same French word, *accent*, to which Proust would later resort in praising Vinteuil's profound homogeneity. What Vinteuil finds when he strives hardest to be new, we recall, is his own singular "accent" – which is to say his style or "way of singing."[113] Fauré was ambivalent toward a certain kind of sameness in his own work, but apparently there was not much he could do about it. He knew that stylistic homogeneity came to him effortlessly; as James Kidd says, "Fauré had and knew his own 'voice' to an astonishing degree."[114] He could pursue difference and innovation against the background of his dependable sameness, and he did so by trying "to write works that make progress over the preceding ones."[115] But just as Vinteuil, in consciously striving to be new, only displaces his sameness to some other point of our perception, Fauré's tendency to homogeneity produces complex resemblances between his successive works. We might say that this circle of likenesses traces *the law of style*. With such laws often comes an element of despotism. But for Fauré and Vinteuil, homogeneity appears to have been a benign regulator.

5 Fauré's religion: ideas and music

1 Preliminary: the interregnum

How does Fauré's art provide evidence of his religious beliefs? What was the role of religion in Fauré's artistic vocation? These are daunting questions. In seeking answers, this chapter employs two modes of inquiry. First, it investigates the relationship between Fauré's personal commitments and the social and religious controversies of his day. Second, it shows the effects of his beliefs on his own music, sacred and secular. The question of religion is significant not only because of Fauré's personal tendencies – as an artist of the ideal and the equivocal – but because he lived through a crucial period in the history of the Roman Catholic Church. Mallarmé, born three years earlier than Fauré, referred to their age as "the interregnum": a period between declining religion and the unknown ideological paradigms of the future.[1] For this generation, the religious organization of French society was marked by dispersion rather than unity. In a speech before the Senate, Sainte-Beuve referred to Frenchmen who had fallen outside the structures of organized religion as themselves comprising "an immense diocese . . . counting innumerable deists, spiritualists, disciples of so-called natural religion, pantheists, positivists, realists, . . . skeptics, seekers of every kind, virtuosos of common sense and votaries of pure science."[2] This rough inventory shows how many terms were, by 1868, already needed to describe the fragmenting French spiritual "diocese" and to distinguish shades of belief within it from one another.

French Catholicism faced grave challenges from modern science and from changes in social and political conditions during the second half of the nineteenth century. In the social challenge to dogma, art played a role as well. In 1834, during the noontide of French romanticism, the playwright and politician Félix Pyat cannily noted, "Art is almost a cult, a new religion that arrives most opportunely, when the Gods have gone and the kings, too."[3] Music in particular had raised its status among the arts in the wake of the canonical decline. By the end of the century music could claim victories in two overlapping domains: one aesthetic (new access to the domain of the intellect), the other spiritual (sacramental pretensions). Music, in its elevated status, became an object of quasi-religious devotion and at the same time was able to represent personal (rather than strictly ritual) belief more adequately.

Let us consider the aesthetic victory first. Quite simply, by about 1885 the art of music had gained the right of access to *thought*, which in France had hitherto been reserved to letters. This exclusion had long assured the unique spiritual and intellectual authority of the literary and biblical word in France. In one of the classic statements of the traditional French position, Victor Cousin declared that poetry "expresses what is inaccessible to every other art, by which I mean thought . . . thought in its most sublime flight, in its most refined abstraction."[4] Cousin, writing from the perspective of the first half of the century, considered poetry the most complete of all the arts, and few among his contemporaries in France would have thought to contest so ordinary a claim. The metaphor of flight is significant and appears in other French writing on verbal expression: thought has wings; the superiority of poetry lay in its singular, "lofty" access to *la pensée*. But music, too, would grow wings, and its triumphant ascent authorized Jules Combarieu to turn Cousin's meditation upside-down in 1907:

> Music . . . free from literary formalism and absorbing only the most general dynamism from reality, is more liable to cross the surface of things and penetrate further into their depths . . . Music gives plastic form to immaterial realities; without straying from fundamental laws, it constructs possible ones. It is supple, diverse, changeable; it is free, it has wings like thought; in a word, it does what it will.[5]

The daring, wordless flight of music toward intellectual abstraction unsettled traditional aesthetic categories and their literary orientation. In 1891, the composer Guy Ropartz, taking the bull by the horns, simply insisted, "One can think in music just as one can think in prose and verse."[6] To affirm the existence of a bridge between tone and idea where only word and idea had been bridged before was a serious break with French tradition. The *clarté* venerated and instituted by conservative thinkers as radically linguistic was, by the end of the nineteenth century, increasingly subject to charges of deforming by definition (Combarieu's "literary formalism") rather than revealing by intuition, of failing to penetrate beneath the surface of things.[7] Music, for a time, would occupy the highest position among the arts in France. Mallarmé, as profoundly astonished by this challenge to the Word as avid to answer it, urged his fellow poets to "recapture our rightful wealth," to take back the original, tacit music that belonged to poetry. But to articulate his meaning, to show how poetry could match the power of "the elemental sonorities of brass, strings, and woodwinds," Mallarmé had to redefine music as a category larger than any single art: "the assemblage of relations existing in everything."[8]

As for the spiritual victory, music naturally acquired a broader metaphysical value along with its new intellectual privileges. In 1906 Dujardin-Beaumetz, the undersecretary of state for fine arts, articulated his understanding of the moral role of art in modern France; his straightforward confidence probably surprised even some liberal Republicans: "It is the cult of the beautiful that will become the meeting-place of so many overturned or demolished faiths, and it is through art that sensitive and anxious souls, yearning for something outside of themselves, will find definitive satisfaction."[9] The ineffability and ecstasies of musical experience assumed greater cultural prestige as artists and art-lovers turned to it as an expressive alternative to the word and a form of higher illusion available to an increasingly wide audience.[10] In 1895 Proust would write Suzette Lemaire,

> The essence of music is to awake in us a mysterious depth of soul (one which cannot be expressed in literature or in any of the other finite modes of expression that make use of words . . . or else make use of objects that are determined – painting, sculpture –), a depth that begins where finite things, and all that arts having finite things as their object, end, and where science ends, and which may thereby be called religious.[11]

Proust, of course, was among the most musically besotted of French writers. But his musical rapture had an authentic spiritual component. At the end of his career, Proust frankly declared to Benoist-Méchin that music had brought him "incomparable joys," and "even more, a proof that there exists in this world something besides the nothingness I run up against on all sides."[12] Like Proust's fiction, Fauré's music was born in and through an attraction to the sensual but found aesthetic expression in "the pursuit and cult of the ideal." The destination of his music, whether religious or not, is often spiritual. But can we maintain a distinction between the "religious" and the "spiritual," or is doing so merely relying on verbal artifice? Can a work of art satisfy some of the same human needs as a religion? Fauré, like many of his contemporaries, faced these difficult questions. In 1903, Lionel de La Laurencie would ask, "Do not religion and art alike aspire to the pursuit and cult of the Ideal? In the final analysis, the two ideas seem closely related – not to say identical – rather than issuing from one another in cause and effect. They coincide in satisfying the same deep and irresistible need in the human soul."[13]

The redemptive swerve toward art seen in Proust's remarks is but a specific manifestation of a wider search for alternative faiths. Catholicism was losing adherents, but the aura (if not the doctrinal content) of religion remained potent and alluring. The Rosicrucian movement has often been cited in this connection. The weird flamboyance of its leading cultist, Sâr

Péladan, has however caused popular historians to exaggerate the Rosicrucian influence in late nineteenth-century France. More important for well-educated French agnostics in this period was the revelation of an ancient, exotic but living religious tradition: Buddhism. The pathbreaking work of scholars such as Eugène Burnouf, Abel Rémusat, Julien Stanislas, Philippe Foucaux, and Emile Senart, who translated and published Buddhist texts hitherto unknown to the West, opened up a new world of religious knowledge.[14] Leconte de Lisle's *Poèmes antiques* of 1852 was the first collection of French poems to take advantage of this knowledge and to embrace Buddhist themes; in its definitive form, this book included seven such poems.[15] Curiously, Leconte de Lisle, an avowed purist in his treatment of Greek and Roman themes, mingled distinct Buddhist, Vedantic, and Brahmanic traditions in these poems. But such casual or deliberate syncretism was characteristic of popular French responses to the discovery of Eastern religions. While diligent Orientalists sought, manuscript by manuscript, to reveal and sort out the nuances of sundry Buddhist traditions, most artists took their Buddhism as they liked it: a religion without a personal divinity, now atheistic, now pantheistic, excluding all traces of personal immortality but usually including some concept of an immanent life-giving energy. Bertrand Marchal writes,

> This soul or divine substance, through which every individual participates in the great allness . . . is itself hardly more than a vitalist metaphor vague enough to accommodate modern science. Indeed, it replaces the creationist model – its dualistic universe and personal, transcendent God – with the vision of a world in perpetual evolution, an organic model, and this new metaphor found a timely scientific warrant in the new theory of evolution proposed by Darwin in 1859.[16]

Later we shall find a striking historical illustration of the link between Darwinian theory and the displacement of the traditional Christian theological model in the beliefs of one of Fauré's poets, Charles Van Lerberghe.

Where did Fauré stand in the religious interregnum? This chapter offers a series of answers. In the context of this first, preliminary section, Fauré's narrow but notable contact with Buddhism and its popularizers is already worth airing. It is often tempting to isolate Fauré from his contemporaries since his artistic independence was so marked, but his social life in Paris was in fact extremely active, and he read widely. Fauré knew Renan personally from 1872, when the young composer began frequenting Pauline Viardot's salon:

> There we played charades, with Turgenev and Saint-Saëns as actors, Flaubert, George Sand, Renan and even Louis Blanc as spectators. George Sand was

then a kindly old lady. Turgenev was the big gun, good-looking, and with a gentleness that was even more attractive. I remember the timbre of his voice so well that when I read one of his books it seems that I hear him. Gustave Flaubert very much enjoyed our joking around, but it was Renan who had the most fun, and we would watch him for the pure joy of seeing him shaken by his own indulgent mirth.[17]

Owing to these early liaisons, Fauré always read Flaubert and Turgenev with particular interest. The sentences above suggest that Fauré pulled Turgenev's books off the shelf from time to time, and in 1913 Fauré wrote his wife a postcard from Lugano which said merely, "I am here passionately reading Flaubert's letters."[18] One imagines Fauré read Renan with similar interest. But given Renan's immense influence as a popularizer of religious history, it is just as likely that Fauré would have read Renan without any personal acquaintance. Renan's two famous essays on Buddhism probably introduced more lay readers to exotic religious traditions than the erudite translations of Burnouf or Senart. Paul Desjardins spoke to this influence (for him, negative) when he criticized "charming doubters like M. Renan and his melodious disciples, somber Buddhists and nihilists, those to whom M. Leconte de Lisle lent the resonance of his clanging cymbal."[19] Renan's literary career was launched on a crisis of faith; he turned his back on the priesthood to devote himself to the study of world religions. A complex man whose character, like Fauré's, combined deep introspection with religious doubt and an indulgent, forgiving humanity, Renan could not have failed to impress the young composer – the more so because Fauré's own faith, even as early 1872, was at best tentative.[20] That Fauré might have discussed religion with Renan is unfortunately an unprovable proposition. But everything we know about Fauré's later beliefs suggests that he would have been sympathetic to Renan's simultaneous defiance of both Catholicism and pure positivism.[21]

It is fascinating to remember that Fauré once contemplated writing an opera about Buddha. The late nineteenth-century interest in alternative faiths did not fail to touch his creative milieu. In 1892 the Princesse de Polignac, seeking a suitable large-scale project for Fauré, suggested a stage work about Siddharta Gautama. Maurice Bouchor was approached for the libretto, but he was already writing a play on the subject for a marionette theater; he recommended his friend Albert Samain.[22] For better or worse, the literary quality of Samain's *Tentation* [or *Vocation*] *de Bouddha*, fragments of which survive in manuscript, fell below Fauré's fastidious standards. Nectoux has examined the surviving textual fragments and concluded that, aside from the quality of the verse, "Samain had no idea what was required for a stage work."[23] This defect is hardly surprising in a poet who made his reputation with diaphanous, lyrical miniatures and who had never written for the stage before. Léon Bocquet, Samain's biographer, referred to *Bouddha* as "a sort of mystery play based on Hindu religion."[24] Fauré's musical realization was never to be, but it is significant that he accepted the project and puttered with Samain's libretto for a year or two. Of course, Fauré need not have thought seriously about Buddhism merely because he was contemplating a *Buddha.* Nothing suggests that Fauré sought spiritual enlightenment in Eastern religions, but we shall see that there is a more general case to be made for Fauré as a pantheist.

Moments when art and religion cross force us to confront basic human questions. We shall begin by studying Fauré's opinions on sacred music and some of his avowals and disavowals of faith, all interpreted in the context of contemporary French religious categories. Beyond that, our ultimate goal is to find out how his ideas about art, humanity, and the world might be reflected in his music. Obviously, Fauré's sacred music provides a foundation for understanding his expression of religious beliefs in music. In his sacred songs and choral works we find clues to his beliefs as soon as we pay close attention to his musical and textual choices. At the same time we have seen that music in general, the art of music, assumed a distinctive spiritual value during his lifetime. In these circumstances, a secular work might hold just as revealing a place in a composer's religious and ideological development as a sacred work, and I shall attempt to make that argument for Fauré's *Chanson d'Ève.*

2 "Quelle musique est religieuse? Quelle musique ne l'est pas?"

In four of the finest pages of his recent biography, Jean-Michel Nectoux assembled nearly all the outward acts and statements of Fauré's religious life.[25] Nectoux contends that Fauré's personal beliefs, characterized from the start by general indifference to the established Church, tended toward agnosticism or a limited personal theism. We may describe either of these attitudes in the language of Fauré's contemporaries by using the term *libre pensée* (freethought). In France, this woolly term marked the domain of all those who found themselves somewhere between the territory of organized Christian sects on the one side and absolute atheists on the other.[26] Yet if Fauré may be considered a *libre penseur,* this category still includes diverse forms of theism, pantheism, or agnosticism. Which describes Fauré? Or rather, which describes him when? This simple point cannot be overemphasized: Fauré's religion changed over the course of his lifetime. We cannot sort out our spiritual categories once and for all. He was raised and educated in Catholicism, the traditional theism of his society, moved through free-thought and pantheism, and then seems to have approached atheism in the last fourteen years of his life.

Fauré was brought up by Catholic parents and, at the age of nine, sent away to the École de Musique Classique et Religieuse in Paris. The purpose of this school, founded by Louis Niedermeyer in 1853, was to train organists and choirmasters, and religion naturally played a significant role in the formation of the students. They were required to attend a nightly religious reading and go to mass on Thursdays and Sundays. Alongside Fauré's exhaustive musical training, which included the singing and accompaniment of plainchant, he studied general literature and history under the clergy of Saint-Louis-d'Antin and Sainte-Elizabeth. When he was twelve years old, he won a prize for religious knowledge, as he would for general literature two years later.[27] But Fauré's initial religious obedience is unremarkable. As a student and boarder, his compliance was compulsory and carefully monitored. That his participation in the rites of the Church soon grew lukewarm, however, there seems to be no doubt.

Fauré left the École Niedermeyer in 1865 and assumed his first position the following year, when he became organist at Saint-Sauveur in Rennes. Fauré reported meeting with the hostility of the parish priest, "who," he later commented, "harbored some doubts about me as a practicing Catholic."[28] One would guess that Fauré's habit of "going down to smoke cigarettes under the vestibule during the sermon" did not inspire the priest's confidence in him. In an unpublished letter to Dukas in 1916, Fauré recalled his years in Rennes with wry humor:

> While you're in Rennes, please go remember me to the Church of Saint Sauveur, where I was organist for four years, from 1866 to 1869. I had a lot of fun there – not in the church, but around town. There I led a happy-go-lucky existence [*j'y ai fait une fête allez gaie*] with Dalimier's father, who was a professor in the lycée, and many of his colleagues, one of whom, Jules Tannery, a wonderful human being, later became director of the École Normale Supérieure. Perhaps I might have remained there my whole life if my bad behavior hadn't decided the parish priest of St. Sauveur to pull the organ out from under my fingers. *Felix culpa!*[29]

The "fortunate misconduct" to which Fauré referred was an incident that caused him to lose his job at Saint-Sauveur in March 1870: one Sunday morning he came directly from a municipal ball and was seen climbing the staircase of the organ loft in white tie and tails.[30] Fauré had, in any case, already exposed himself to public criticism in his leisure hours, for he was often seen conversing with mathematicians, chemists, and lawyers in cafés. In pious provincial communities any young scientist fresh from normal school was all but presumed to be a miscreant.[31] One of these scientists was Fauré's next-door neighbor, the mathematician Jules Tannery (1848–1910), whom he remembered so fondly in the letter to Dukas we just read. After Fauré left Rennes, he kept up a correspondence with Tannery for a time. J. Barrie Jones has published two letters that Tannery wrote Fauré in the spring of 1870, and their content is arresting. In his first letter Tannery lets drop a casual reference to the theory of evolution and goes on to discuss his own ongoing "moral crisis," a crisis of faith aggravated by the "despotic" measures of the First Vatican Council. In his second letter, Tannery complains of the revisions he has been forced to make in a paper on mechanical distributors, so that he "is not called by the population of Rennes an atheist of materialist inclinations, a pantheist, a chemist, a humbug."[32] If these letters exemplify the topics Fauré enjoyed discussing with his young friends in the lycée, the Catholic community of Rennes was not wrong to be suspicious of their choirmaster's secular hours. More generally, we shall find reasons to believe that what Fauré called his "felix culpa" was not just superficial irreverence but a sign of more profound indifference.

One might argue that Fauré's casual contempt of the forms of the Church does not necessarily imply an indifference to its values. In Fauré's case I think we must concede this point, but only provisionally; for the later part of his life we have an increasingly positive record of his unbelief. Until 1905, nonetheless, Fauré continued to occupy posts as a choirmaster and organist; he spent more than half his life as a church musician. Since participation in the old Catholic rites was a fact of his livelihood, and his livelihood was never bountiful, perhaps he felt he could not afford to make his deepest beliefs too manifest. After 1883 he had a family to support, too, and could no longer afford the lighthearted conduct that lost him his position in Rennes and then again at Notre Dame de Clignancourt in Paris.[33]

For signs of Fauré's thinking, let us first look to his statements about religious music. By the time he wrote his Requiem and later motets, he articulated a firm independence of opinion in his private letters and spoke of bringing something "different" to religious music. This difference was, quite simply, the mark of his own sensibility. We shall see that the composer to whom he felt closest in his conception of modern religious music was Gounod. At the same time he distanced himself from what he considered either excessively ascetic or excessively theatrical styles, the former associated with conservative, ultramontane Catholicism, the latter with popular taste. In general, Fauré avowed that his ideal in religious music was an expression of *human feelings* rather than divine or institutionally purified ones. In a letter to the Princesse de Polignac in 1894, he thus defended some of his recent motets: "I have also composed four short religious pieces, but

(I'm sorry to say) not in the spirit of the new Society for Sacred Music! Into these pieces, whatever they're worth, I've put the human feelings I felt like putting in them!"[34] Here, as so often in his letters, Fauré revealed himself in an offhand, apparently self-dismissive remark. He underlines the subjective, humanistic nature of his own conception of religious music. This statement identifies a positive value in Fauré's religious style, but it also suggests an opposition – "the new Society for Sacred Music" that Fauré referred to with ironic, parenthetical regrets ("j'en suis désolé").

The Société de Musique Religieuse, also known as the Schola Cantorum, had been organized for the study and performance of early religious music; its leaders, Charles Bordes (conductor of the Chanteurs de Saint-Gervais), Vincent d'Indy, and Alexandre Guilmant had held their first meeting five days earlier, on 6 June 1894, in the company of several priests, including the parish curate of Saint-Gervais. What was the "spirit" of this group, from which Fauré chose to stand apart? Its official mission, announced repeatedly, was "to return to the Gregorian tradition in the performance of plainchant," "to return Palestrinan music to its place of honor," "to create a modern religious music respecting the text and laws of the liturgy and taking inspiration from the Gregorian and Palestrinan traditions," and finally, "to improve the organist's repertory with a view to binding it to the Gregorian melodies."[35] Two years after this first meeting, Bordes, d'Indy, and Guilmant would enlarge the mission of the Société de Musique Religieuse by founding the famous school built around these ideals: the Schola Cantorum, which would become the chief rival to the state Conservatoire by 1900.

Fauré's letter betrays the composer's, if not the choirmaster's, desire to detach himself from the Palestrinan and Gregorian agendas of the future Schola. Why would Fauré adopt this position? His indifference cannot be attributed to his affiliation with the Conservatoire; he was not to be hired there until 1896. Moreover, far from scorning the old music promoted by Bordes, Fauré admired it deeply. He explicitly asserted how much composers could enrich themselves by frequent contact with both plainchant and sixteenth- and seventeenth-century polyphony (chap. 2, p. 71).

We may approach Fauré's opposition to the Schola from three directions: institutional, artistic, and political. He acquired his knowledge of early music at Niedermeyer's École de Musique Classique et Religieuse, and he felt allied to that institution for the rest of his life. He had studied plainchant and classical polyphony during his years as a student, and he repeatedly acknowledged his debt to Louis Niedermeyer for this valuable training. Indeed, in a late interview Fauré would comment that at the École Niedermeyer "a choir of students performed everything that Saint-Gervais sings today."[36] From this remark we can infer that Fauré perhaps saw a historical injustice in the nearly exclusive acclaim bestowed on the Chanteurs de Saint-Gervais for having discovered and resurrected the performance of early vocal music. The Schola Cantorum, increasingly successful, went about its mission with a self-importance and self-righteousness that irked Fauré.[37] In 1902, René de Castéra, a pupil of d'Indy's, wrote a history of the Schola in which he mentioned that "some professionals and choirmasters" had seen fit to remind that institution of the precedent set by the École Niedermeyer. De Castéra then dismissed this and other efforts in sweeping and malevolent terms. "One must truly love an art and give oneself over to it *completely* in order to have any hopes of an enduring accomplishment, and those who boasted of having known and performed the Palestrinan repertory before Saint-Gervais and who admitted, in their broad eclecticism, ephemeral works beside immortal ones, were far from pure."[38] Fauré kept an almost filial admiration for his first mentor, and it is not hard to imagine his outrage at de Castéra's broad contempt for Niedermeyer's work and the school he founded. It was probably *scholiste* propaganda for artistic "purity," with its selective historical memory, that encouraged Fauré to uphold "eclecticism," the artistic attitude attacked by de Castéra in this quotation and abominated by the Schola in general. For de Castéra, as for d'Indy, "eclecticism" was a bad word, but Fauré did not hesitate to take it up for himself: "You see, I am eclectic, in the province of music as in all others."[39] It is possible that Fauré would not have resorted to this word if the Schola's disdain for the alleged "eclecticism" of Niedermeyer, Gounod, Saint-Saëns, and other colleagues had not charged it with personal significance for him.

Fauré's distance from the Schola may also be measured in artistic terms. His early study of chant and polyphony had contributed a great deal to the formation of his style. We would therefore expect him to be sympathetic to the *stylistic* aims of the Schola. But while the structure of some of Fauré's most beautiful melodic lines betrays a latent assimilation of plainchant, Fauré never once quoted a chant, whereas composers at the Schola explicitly concerned themselves with the task of integrating real chants into original music.[40] We recall that one of the four founding principles of the Schola was to create modern liturgical music taking inspiration from plainchant and to foster a repertory for organ "bound to the Gregorian melodies." Some composers at the Schola, including d'Indy, took the further step of using plainchant as a symbolic Christian element in secular works. Fauré disliked literalism and found the symbolic and dogmatic facets of the Schola's inculcation of plainchant unpalatable.

What might be called the "politics" of liturgical music provides a third way of understanding Fauré's position. Part of his desire to stand apart from any movement for the purification of sacred music stemmed from his liberal politics and aloofness to ecclesiastical authority. The leaders of the Schola worked vigorously to enlarge and perpetuate the authority of the Roman Catholic Church in France. The initial establishment of the school, indeed, would have been nearly impossible without a timely and generous gift from the archbishop of Paris, Cardinal Richard. Two years later, in 1898, the Institut Catholique de Paris incorporated the Schola into its section for the fine arts by the unanimous vote of its members.[41] And in 1904, support came from the highest authority: in a personal breve to Charles Bordes, Pope St Pius X praised the labors of Bordes and the Schola on behalf of liturgical music. Amédée Gastoué, a professor of chant at the Schola, was then invited to join the Pontifical Commission for the Vatican Edition.[42] In matters of plainchant, the founders of the Schola stood firmly on the side of the Benedictine revival, and at the end of the first academic year a trip was arranged for students to go the abbey of Solesmes to hear the monks sing plainchant under Dom Pothier and Dom Mocquereau. The Benedictine scholars reciprocated their support of the Schola. They contributed articles to its official organ, *La tribune de Saint-Gervais*, and Dom Mocquereau and Dom Delpech traveled to Paris to lecture and direct choral performances at the Schola in 1897. In short, the pedagogical orientation and activities of the school reflected the strong religious views of its founders, and their efforts to serve the Church can be considered immensely successful. This religious attitude was not merely official; it was fundamental. Bordes, d'Indy, and Guilmant intended their institution to serve the music of the faithful and the faith at once; for them art and Catholicism were intertwined. In an inaugural address, d'Indy charged the students and faculty to accept faith, hope, and charity as the indispensable foundations of their vocations: "These three virtues that the catechism calls 'theological' can, with good reason, be called 'artistic,' for speaking of God they thereby speak of Art, divine emanation."[43]

Fauré harbored no ultramontane sympathies. He knew that the music heard in French churches was often banal or uninspiring, but he also thought that soliciting rules from Rome to define religious music according to certain historical and stylistic criteria would, in the end, check the independence of composers to write religious music according to their individual sense of the sacred. Individualism, we shall see, lies at the heart of Fauré's explanation of his own sacred style.

In an insightful paper given in 1989, Susan Richardson described Fauré's Requiem as an aesthetic affirmation of "independent ideology," meaning that Fauré invested the work with a certain kind of religious feeling, but one that knowingly stood apart from the institutional codes for sacred music which were competing for priority at the time it was written.[44] Richardson isolates Fauré from the partisans of the Schola, but she neglects to indicate another important contemporary practice – the most widespread of all. If Fauré rejected the ultramontane asceticism of the Schola Cantorum, he also deplored the vapid taste that prevailed among both the clergy and laity of most Parisian churches, including La Madeleine. Speaking to this taste in 1892, Gounod evoked "the marshmallowy romances and sweetmeats of piety that have abused our stomachs for too long now."[45] The co-existence of sugary and ascetic musical styles allows us to identify the undeclared referents of the following statement:

> As aloof from the insipid specialists of worldly religiosity as from the Jansenists of parochial counterpoint, Gabriel Fauré developed a religious music whose style is sincere, a style of calm nobility and confident renunciation, a style animated by hope and charity, if not by a more formal faith.[46]

Thus René Paroissin knowingly plotted Fauré's path between complacent routine and *scholiste* severity. "Worldly religiosity" had had one of its most famous exponents in a former organist of La Madeleine, Lefébure-Wély, whose style had prompted Fétis to write an indignant essay in 1856 entitled "L'Orgue mondaine et la musique érotique à l'église."[47] Saint-Saëns's efforts to raise musical standards when he succeeded Lefébure-Wély sometimes met with obtuse resistance:

> One of the curates of the parish set about indoctrinating me one day . . .
> "The overwhelming majority of people who come to La Madeleine," he said to me, "are rich people, and rich people often go to the Opéra-Comique; they have acquired musical habits there that we are well advised to respect."
> "Dear Father," I answered, "when I hear dialogues from the Opéra-Comique coming from the pulpit, I shall provide appropriate music, but not before."[48]

From what we know of Fauré's tenure at La Madeleine, musical taste there had changed only slightly. Publishers still dealt in arrangements of operatic arias outfitted with Latin words, and parishioners demanded these pieces for weddings and important ceremonies.[49] As Camille Bellaigue wryly observed, "The rite of burial is merely the last concert or opera the deceased will attend."[50] Ease, convenience, and the satisfaction of an affluent congregation were the touchstones of the clergy's approach to music in La Madeleine. In an interview with Auguste Mangeot, Fauré mentioned "the formidable range of troubles that choirmasters in Paris face when they restrict themselves to executing music worthy of the church."[51] Mangeot had solicited Fauré's opinion on the reform of sacred music, as promulgated by Pius X in the famous *motu proprio* of 22 November 1903. Fauré was skeptical:

> The [papal] instructions . . . will not modify established habits one whit, at least as far as churches in Paris are concerned. First, because, with the best faith and the worst taste in the world, the clergy is convinced that it was already in compliance even before said instructions were published. Second, because an unconscious complicity exists between the faithful and the clergy to find everything for the best.[52]

Fauré did what he could to assert his taste, but he was working against an establishment whose inertia was so powerful that, at least in his mind, even instructions from the pope would be of little avail. Whatever Fauré conducted and played on demand for burials and weddings, however, he made few concessions to an insipid style, and none at all to an operatic one, in his own religious music.

Let us turn to Fauré's general views on religious music, its modern varieties and its function in the cult. We just cited his response to the papal instructions of 1903, but we stopped short of a third reason Fauré gave for doubting their efficacy. "Finally," he said, "it is rather difficult to establish a demarcation between what is a truly religious style and what is not. That will vary according to individual judgment."[53] This comment encapsulates Fauré's whole attitude toward music for the Church. Fundamentally liberal, he refused to condone efforts to establish a single "sacred style" for modern religious music. This refusal to draw a definitive boundary is entirely characteristic of Fauré. But in this case the refusal does not leave us with unanswerable questions. He explains:

> The religious faith of a Gounod is completely different from that of a Franck or a Bach. Gounod is all heart and Franck is all spirit. Did not the faith of Saint Theresa express itself in words so ardent, so passionate, that they are at times licentious? And yet she was a saint and no one thinks of tossing her out of the church.
>
> The truth is that the ruling is not radical enough. We ought only to sing plainchant in the churches, and only in unison, considering that it dates from an era with no forethought of polyphony. To take the sacred music of the sixteenth century as an unalterable model is simply impossible. When that music was composed it represented an absolutely *luxurious* art, which only seems simple to us today owing to everything that happened to music in the meantime.[54]

There are several points to note here. First, Fauré draws a contrast between the music of Gounod and Franck in order to suggest a legitimate breadth of

expression in religious style. Fauré will develop this opposition, only suggested here, in a later text, and we shall reconsider it then. Second, Fauré
calls upon the example of Saint Theresa in order to challenge the notion that
asceticism is a precondition of true religious expression. He implies that, in
the right circumstances, sacred music can be voluptuous. His shrewd characterization of sixteenth-century polyphony likewise supports this point.
Third, Fauré's allegation that "the ruling is not radical enough" and "we
ought only to sing plainchant" is unexpected and remarkable. We need to
give it more detailed attention.

In this statement, I believe that Fauré made a rhetorical gambit rather
than a practical suggestion. He did so under the cover of a real appreciation
for chant and a sudden rigor as liturgically irreproachable as it was feigned.
It is important to recall the content of the *motu proprio* in this regard,
specifically its second section. The first article of the second section recognizes Gregorian plainchant as the "proper song" of the Roman Catholic
Church and the "supreme model of sacred music." The second article rec-
ommends the polyphony of Palestrina and his contemporaries as the most
commendable offspring of plainchant. The third article sanctions contemporary music in the church, but only so long as it contain "nothing profane"
in either form or content.[55] There is really little in the *motu proprio*, aside
from a subsequent direction concerning strict adherence to the order and
texts of the liturgy, that would have excluded Fauré's own religious music.
But Fauré was apparently more concerned with the authority the Schola
would be able to draw from these instructions than with their intrinsic
moderation or restrictiveness.[56] He therefore attacked the pope's stance
where it was most vulnerable: in its successive steps away from its own
"supreme model." Fauré's calculated call for chant and chant alone
outpontificates the pope, but it does so less to enhance the established role
of the liturgy's "proper song" – which needed no more protection than Pius
X, Dom Pothier, and the Schola were already giving it – than to defend the
rights of stylistic freedom in all the music that comes after. As Nectoux
observes, "Fauré thought, not unreasonably, that the nature and the style of
religious music presented a false problem as soon as one left the province of
plainchant, the authentic repertory of the Roman Catholic Church, and
took up music written by any individual, named composer."[57] The remarkable French distinction between the words "plain-chant" (or *cantus*) and
"musique" (*musica*), still current in the nineteenth century, lent further
authority to Fauré's conception; indeed the *motu proprio* itself referred to
singing sacred words either "to their Gregorian melodies" or "to music."[58]
A parallel distinction between "liturgical music" and "religious music" may
also stand behind Fauré's argument. As André Cœuroy observed, "If any

sort of music can be *religious*, only Gregorian chant is *liturgical*: a mass sung to non-Gregorian music is considered but a low mass so far as the liturgy is concerned."[59] Fauré's proposition may be summarized: It is fatuous to make rules for religious music, so if the pope cannot accept the full range of human expression in music, let us hear only the liturgical melodies.

The gambit is cunning, but it is also circumstantial and therefore cannot match the significance of Fauré's broader ideological statements on sacred music. Faced with ultramontane meddling, Fauré spoke his mind about the privileged status of plainchant as "liturgical music," but elsewhere he continued to think about "religious music," for it was in that realm that he had contributed something and there, too, that he admired the works of certain other composers. Fauré included an important paragraph on religious music in his "Souvenirs" of 1922. The passage first of all proves that his beliefs about freedom of expression in religious music had not changed:

> The music we hear in churches daily often gives rise to harsh criticism. Certain church choirs in Paris and others in the provinces nonetheless stand out by their selection and performance of works truly worthy of their intended purpose. Yet this superiority is not decisive for every comer. Some musical composition, loftily conceived and purely written, can seem, according to individual opinion, adorned with religious character or destitute of it. What music is religious? What music is not? To try to resolve the question is rather risky when you consider that however sincere religious feeling may be in a musician, it is through his personal sensibility that he expresses himself and not according to laws that cannot be made to stick. All classification in this field of thought has always seemed arbitrary to me.[60]

For Fauré, individualism and personal sensibility still serve to justify diversity in sacred music. In the last sentence, Fauré again dismisses regulatory measures such as the pope's instructions. But now, instead of Gregorian polemics, Fauré launches into a justification of his convictions about modern religious music:

> Would you hold, for example, that certain religious compositions of Franck's, among the ones that reach the highest, to the very quivering of seraphic wings, are, by reason of their very suavity, absolutely free of sensuality? On the other hand, in the *Messe solennelle* by Gounod, is not the effect of the child's voice, which rises up alone to sing "Gloria in excelsis Deo," one of wonderful purity? The text of the Agnus Dei in this same Mass inspired Gounod to accents of ineffable tenderness; would you therefore say that he profaned the text? If I take these two great musicians for my example, it is, first, because their religious styles have often been set against one another in opposition, and second, in order to try to prove that when we are faced with truly musical and beautiful works, separating the religious ones from those that "savor of heresy" is practically impossible.[61]

Here we learn more about Fauré's personal taste. For once he names a religious work by Gounod that he admires. Yet even here the composer presented his examples in such a way as to invite a polemical interpretation. Fauré admits seeking to dismantle a traditional opposition between Gounod and Franck. He does so in order to suggest a continuum in religious feeling that cannot be hedged in by official forms of sanctity. Gounod's religious music was often criticized for its worldliness and theatricality. Even a critic sympathetic to Gounod's achievements would avow, at the time Fauré wrote his article, "Gounod's religious art is too often worldly. In his music the expression of divine love finds no accents other than those of profane love."[62] Franck, having been instituted as the spiritual father of the Schola, had acquired a very different posthumous reputation. D'Indy, who all but built a reliquary for Franck's skeleton in the foyer of the Schola, called him "an artist whose form appears to us as if encircled by a halo, like the saints in fifteenth-century frescoes."[63] But even Vincent d'Indy knew that Franck's religious music is no less fraught with moments of theatrical pretension than the most melodramatic works of Gounod, and moreover, a significant number of Gounod's religious works are self-consciously austere. Gounod was even an early supporter of Bordes's Chanteurs de Saint-Gervais. Fauré understood this range of styles and intentions in the two composers, both of whom he knew personally. Ignoring their historiographic stereotypes and saying nothing about the ultimate value of their contributions, he only sought to bring them together, to take Franck down from his shrine and pull Gounod out of the pit. Fauré does not rate one above the other but instead touches on just those aesthetic qualities that were significant for his own religious style. The three that he cites with implicit admiration – sensuality, purity, and tenderness – are the hallmarks of his own Requiem. Fauré enters a general plea for personal expression in religious music through a convincing revision of received ideas. But in speaking about Franck, Gounod, and sacred music, Fauré naturally also begins to tell us about himself.

Let us then return to Fauré's views of his own religious music and, in particular, how those views manifested themselves in his Requiem, op. 48. This work, composed between 1887 and 1891, is incontestably his most important contribution to sacred music.[64] Richardson and Nectoux both point out that Fauré knew the conventions of a Requiem Mass but consciously chose to depart from them.[65] We have Fauré's own admission on that count. "Perhaps instinctively I sought to break loose from convention," he told Louis Aguettant in 1902. "I've been accompanying burial services at the organ for so long now! I've had it up to here with all that. I wanted to do something else."[66] The independence Fauré expressed in his desire to invest his motets with "the human feelings I felt like putting in them" informed his approach to the Requiem, too.

We may first look at the texts Fauré chose to set to music. Recent writers, comparing Fauré's Requiem to other settings, have noted his omission of the Sequence ("Dies iræ") and the Benedictus and his inclusion of the texts "Pie Jesu," "Libera me," and "In paradisum." Today these five choices might appear equally important and idiosyncratic. However, in Fauré's time, three of them attracted no notice at all. In order to understand which of Fauré's choices seemed out of the ordinary to his audiences, we must put them in the context of liturgical traditions in late nineteenth-century Paris, not the jumble of traditions reflected in the modern repertory of Requiems. It is also misleading to consult the Vatican editions of the *Graduale* and *Cantus missæ*, for the diocese of Paris did not officially adopt the Roman rite until 1873. This fact is not widely known. Until about 1840, each French diocese practiced its own version (or versions) of the Gallican rite. In the capital, which was last to adopt the Roman rite, elements of the superseded "Parisian" uses persisted to the end of the nineteenth century, and Saint-Saëns recalled that La Madeleine adopted the new rite only "unwillingly and incompletely."[67] More work needs to be done on the individual liturgies of French churches and their relation to the music composed for them, but the evidence I have gathered thus far suggests that, of the five choices noted above, two may be said to mark the real singularity of Fauré's conception: his inclusion of the "In paradisum" and exclusion of the "Dies iræ." These same two choices garnered the most notice from contemporary critics, a coincidence that seems to back up inferences I make on liturgical grounds.

What about the other three choices? In Paris, and at La Madeleine in particular, the "Pie Jesu" could stand in place of the Benedictus in a Requiem Mass. Thus, Fauré's omission of the Benedictus was not a lapse, and, in Parisian use, the "Pie Jesu" was in its proper place as a song for the Elevation.[68] As for the "Libera me," independent settings of both it and "Pie Jesu" were extremely popular in Fauré's time; both were heard regularly in churches as motets or accompanied songs. The appearance of these texts within a Requiem Mass (a familiar context for the "Pie Jesu," less expected for the "Libera me") raised no objections among Fauré's critics. Yet this silence is somewhat surprising in the case of the "Libera me," since neither it nor the following "In paradisum" are part of the Mass for the Dead. The "Libera me" is a responsory in the act of absolution, performed after the mass is over. The antiphon "In paradisum" is usually sung outside the church, as the casket is being carried to the cemetery. In a country where critics prided themselves on contesting points of nomenclature and generic propriety, it is surprising that none of them objected to the presence of either the "Libera me" or "In paradisum" on liturgical grounds. It is no doubt significant that while Fauré's final movements exceed the boundaries of the Requiem Mass, they do so in a way that is both emotionally satisfying and obedient to the physical sequence of the liturgy. Fauré's decision to join the mass to the burial in a single musical conception apparently made sense to his contemporaries.

The "In paradisum" attracted attention for other reasons. It was a marginal text in the history of religious music; before Fauré there are almost no polyphonic settings.[69] Fauré not only took up a little-known text but used it to end his Requiem in an unforgettable atmosphere of stillness and light. By ending with this text, Fauré also endowed his work with a unique circularity: it begins and ends with the same word, *requiem*. Norman Suckling first pointed out this detail and also remarked that the word *requiem* "appears in all but two of the seven movements" and "is thrown into strong relief wherever it occurs."[70] On the other hand, to exclude a text so strongly associated with the post-Mozartian Requiem Mass as the "Dies iræ" was a startling decision. Fauré's must be the only nineteenth-century Latin Requiem to omit this text. The general critical reaction to these choices may be summarized by citing the beginning of Louis Laloy's review:

> M. Fauré has conceived and handled his work in a completely personal way: the "Dies iræ" does not appear, divine wrath has no place, and the antiphon "In paradisum," serving as conclusion, offers a glimpse of eternal blisses . . . Is the religious tone missing? No, no more than tenderness and compassion are excluded from the Gospel. But here we find only one of the faces of religion, the gentlest, the most human.[71]

By putting aside the Sequence with its cavalcade of judgment, sin, horror, and desperation, Fauré rejected the most graphic, picturesque text of the Requiem. Louis Vierne thought that Fauré had nonetheless "penetrated the correct meaning" of the ceremony as a whole:

> His predecessors treated it as a drama, thus preferring external appearance to the mystical, consoling poetry that thoroughly dominates this description of the future life. Only the "Dies iræ" seems to have struck composers' imaginations, and its dramatic color spilled over into all the other parts of their settings; these rendered chiefly terror, hopeless fear, the sensation of the awful. Fauré, on the other hand, saw in his text our final rest, the end of human miseries, the blessing of men of good will.[72]

Fauré represented the element of divine judgment briefly in the "Libera me," where Vierne found it "simply indicated, without commentary or development."[73] Nonetheless, by lightening the stress on fatal judgment, Fauré's Requiem often induced confusions:

> It is the music of Elysian fields; the tender gravity and soft sadness of [the music] remind me more of Athenian tombs than of the edifying sculptures of the portals of our churches. For here is a Paradise without a hell, where the soul, without being judged, is admitted by right of innocence or by right of beauty – it is hard to decide which – or rather it is because of a beauty so pure that it signifies innocence. And this conception of Paradise is not so far removed as one might believe from orthodox Catholicism; certainly it is more Catholic than Protestant since it is somewhat pagan in character.[74]

Here Laloy's denominational uncertainties foreshadow what seem to have been some of Fauré's own.

Instead of the Sequence, Fauré made a page of perfect tranquility the heart of his Requiem: the "Pie Jesu." Not only is it the middle movement of the work, but it bears relation to two different parts of the liturgy; it replaces one and effaces the other. We have already seen that the "Pie Jesu" is a functional surrogate for the Benedictus. But it also evokes a text we would have expected to hear earlier in the Requiem; as Susan Richardson notes, the words of the "Pie Jesu" coincide with the final line of the Sequence: "Pie Jesu, Domine, dona eis requiem." Fauré's "Pie Jesu" thus reminds us of "the only line in the Sequence that deals with peace or rest."[75] But this serene evocation negates the dominant sentiment of the "Dies iræ" – terror. The center of Fauré's Requiem, through a minimal textual reminiscence and complete sentimental opposition, reminds us of what it is not.

Fauré was as free in his treatment of the internal structure of his texts as in their selection. He repeated, suppressed, and added words where he wished. In the Kyrie, for instance, he fails to respect the traditional threefold acclamation. Nectoux has discussed a number of these textual irregularities.[76] By far the most interesting one comes in the Offertory, where Fauré changed "libera animas omnium fidelium defunctorum" ("deliver the souls of all the departed faithful") to the significantly less specific "libera animas defunctorum" ("deliver the souls of the departed"). Why did he omit "omnium fidelium"? He could easily have included the two missing words in his musical setting if he had wished. We might wager that the omission betrays the scruples (or hopes) of a man who was no longer sure he could be counted among "the faithful." Even if Fauré suppressed "omnium fidelium" accidentally, that kind of oversight is meaningful. Whichever explanation we prefer, Fauré managed to eliminate the only reference to "the faithful" in the entire text of his Requiem.

These details may seem insignificant. If Fauré drew on the liturgy in ways he found most suited his personal vision and aesthetic intentions, he obviously did so without overstepping the bounds of what was acceptable or tolerable for a funeral service in La Madeleine. We know that he conducted the

Requiem in services there at least four times between 1888 and 1893. His willful hand with sacred texts, however, was by no means too subtle to go unnoticed. The Belgian reviewer François Verhelst, who found the work "imprinted with real religious sentiment," nonetheless reproached Fauré "for taking too many liberties with the words of the liturgy," and especially in the Offertory.[77] These sorts of liberties took on a significance that was more than just personal and artistic for members of the Schola Cantorum, who, as we know, demanded that modern religious music "respect the text and laws of the liturgy." In 1894, the Congregation of Rites issued a decree on sacred music which forbade "musical settings that leave out a single word belonging to the liturgy, or in which the text is transposed or imprudently repeated," and the pope's future *motu proprio* would likewise explicitly forbid the kinds of alterations Fauré made within the texts of his Requiem.[78]

As with its arrangement of liturgical texts, the music of Fauré's work revealed a personal vision of the afterlife which stood apart from conventional Christian views of death and judgment. Unpretentious, translucent and serene, this Requiem was sober but not heavy; its beauty was perfect rather than sublime or terrible.[79] When Fauré's publisher at last agreed to print the work, its success was immediate and widespread: the Requiem finally took Fauré's name beyond coteries and connoisseurs to the greater public. To probe the appeal of this music, we may think back to considerations from earlier in this chapter: Fauré's Requiem, radiantly confident in eternal rest and notably cool about eternal damnation, was good religious music for the "interregnum." Here was a spiritual reverie in which agnostics as well as believers could find consolation. In a conversation preserved by Louis Aguettant, Fauré spoke of his Requiem and his attitude toward death in 1902:

> People have said my Requiem did not express the terror of death; someone called it *a lullaby of death*. But that's the way I perceive death: as a happy release, an aspiration to the happiness of beyond rather than a grievous passage. Gounod's religious music has also been censured for leaning too heavily on human tenderness. But his nature predisposed him to feel that way; religious emotion took that form in him. Must we not accept an artist's nature?[80]

Fauré defends the gentle, affectionate nature of his Requiem indirectly, by reminding Aguettant of a precedent in Gounod's sacred music. Fauré has nothing to say about those Gregorian and Palestrinan models of sacred music the *scholistes* would have advocated as best serving the "laws of the liturgy." Self-expression and individual human feeling, not orthodoxy, lie at the center of his explanation. "Must we not accept an artist's nature?" is

Fauré's classic rhetorical question. In 1916, he would voice it again in the form, "Isn't every artist free to translate his thought, his sensibility, by the means it pleases him to choose?"[81]

It is perhaps significant that Fauré chose to speak of "religious emotion" rather than "religion" in this self-defense. Aguettant seems to have harbored certain doubts about the work, even after his conversation with the composer. He fancied Fauré's work a Requiem for "some ephebe, baptized very late, whose light soul floated off to rest under a grove of myrtles where mourners with beautiful gestures consoled it with smiling plaint."[82] Fauré's realization of his own "religious emotion," bountiful in human tenderness and sometimes "voluptuously Gregorian" in its elegant contours, touched a point of profound receptivity in his contemporary listeners, but it also raised questions.[83] What was the innermost creed of this officially Catholic and Parisian Requiem? In 1888, Camille Benoît, its first reviewer, spoke of it as "half pagan, half Christian," "a work in the spirit of Antiquity."[84] This denominational ambivalence was a constant topic in subsequent reviews (as we already saw in Laloy's comments) and the Requiem, though greatly admired, did not always meet with thoroughgoing approval for this reason. Even Benoît, otherwise enthusiastic, warned, "It would not be good to tarry overlong in these regions of enchantment, . . . for the joys we taste there are sometimes mortal, and the *eternal feminine* does not always lead to heaven."[85] A certain Catholic sensibility found, or felt it had to find, something suspect in Fauré's disinclination to severity. Toward the end of Fauré's life, an interviewer broached this longstanding perception with the composer and remarked, "Certain people found the Requiem a bit pagan." Fauré, who had heard his Requiem described as "Attic" or "pagan" for thirty-four years, only begged the question by way of response: "'Pagan' does not necessarily mean 'irreligious'!" He knew that this provocative defense would never redeem him in Catholic eyes, nor did he care to deny the perception of paganism. He added more candidly, "Besides, I can't deny that pagan Antiquity has always exerted a strong pull on my imagination."[86] If some Catholics found the Requiem too pagan, too delightful, perhaps their mistrust was justified, for Fauré never made any claims for its immanent orthodoxy, only for its sincerity.

However individual Fauré's Requiem may be, we also know that it was liturgically functional. Indeed today, even as the Requiem enjoys frequent performance in concerts, it also continues to serve the liturgy (and, more broadly, the faith).[87] The endurance of the work's original liturgical role is intriguing. The Requiem has contributed to a popular image of Fauré as a devoutly religious composer. But some practicing Catholics who have inferred or recognized Fauré's spiritual non-conformity have not therefor thought less of his Requiem. Their acceptance of the work raises a speculative question: How can an artist create an inspiring musical realization of a faith he does not fully share?

It is true that the values attributed to any work of art may, in different historical circumstances, surpass or abridge the beliefs of its maker. But for a community of believers, the values of a religious work – a work that renders them the very elements of their faith – are not historically contingent but immanent and eternal. Moreover, the Roman Catholic Church, dependent on central rulings for musical usage, must make determinations about the spiritual authenticity of the music it sanctions; thus a speculative question becomes a practical choice in the institution of the liturgy. With respect to Fauré's Requiem, the only approach to this spiritual and aesthetic quandary known to me comes from René Paroissin. Paroissin, a believer, asks how it is that certain unbelieving artists and musicians, including Schumann, Berlioz, Wagner, and Fauré, create music worthy of Christian praise. He proposes that the inner lyric enthusiasm of a great artist is a manifestation of divine beauty and a "sort of natural charisma" that allows him to write divinely. In this way, believers may embrace the work of gifted mortals whose art was, literally, more faithful than they knew. After making this point, Paroissin adds a curious aside, "Who will prevent me from thinking that Debussy, obedient to the fundamental idea of his theme [the martyrdom of Saint Sebastian], attains an utterly Christian simplicity? And Fauré's Requiem!"[88] Paroissin's awareness of Fauré's uncertain faith, indicated in this exclamation, may be confirmed in a passage we cited earlier from another of his books. There he granted Fauré two of the three theological virtues: hope and charity, but not faith (p. 181).

It is uncertain how Paroissin reached his conclusions about Fauré's beliefs. Fauré's reputation as a doubter was subject to gossip during his lifetime, as we shall see below. Whether Paroissin formed his judgment of Fauré's faith through hearsay, through profound contemplation of his music, or by reading Fauré's then recently published *Lettres intimes*, we do not know. What remains significant is that charisma and spirituality, in the absence of explicit belief, may suffice in the mind of a modern Christian to endow a beautiful work of art with religion. Thus we might conclude that Fauré's liberal view of what constitutes a "religious style" in music, his willingness to include sensuality and tenderness beside purity, has "paid off" in two ways. First, the "human feelings" he put into his Requiem have proven their ability to speak persuasively to both Christian and non-Christian audiences in innumerable concerts and recordings. Second, and more unexpectedly, his "Pie Jesu" may be heard in some modern liturgies as part of the official music of the Church. In other words, Fauré's music has earned a place beside the chants whose revival the Schola promoted so zealously.[89] Ironically, the compositional efforts of Fauré's contemporaries at the Schola, "taking inspiration from the Gregorian and Palestrinan traditions," do not figure in the modern liturgy.[90] Without the literal recourse to plain-chant recommended by his more obeisant contemporaries, Fauré's sacred music somehow managed to find a place next to that "supreme model," the "proper song" of the Church. Not everyone will be as confident as René Paroissin in concluding that Fauré's music was therefore "more faithful than he knew." But we have every reason to ascribe the continuing liturgical pros-perity of Fauré's Requiem to its winning qualities as a work of art.

3 "Désir de choses inexistantes, peut-être . . ."

If we wish to understand Fauré's personal doubts, we cannot ignore the pos-itive spiritual destination of his religious music. Fauré's Requiem reaches and radiates back what Fauré called *l'émotion religieuse* – that basic, per-sonal religious sensibility that he spoke of in reference to Gounod's sacred music. Fauré's conception of "religious emotion," being completely open to personal feeling and persuasion, could draw on the widest possible spec-trum of spiritual thought to reflect the artist's temperament. Such "religious liberalism" (the term is Marchal's) goes right back to the first French roman-tics. Benjamin Constant once declared, "Yes, there is undoubtedly a revela-tion, but a universal one; it is permanent; its source is in the human heart. Man need only listen to himself, he need only listen to nature speaking to him in a thousand voices, in order to be carried inexorably into religion."[91] Marchal has described the commonplace of such variants of nineteenth-century freethought as a search "to recognize . . . the most authentic voice of the human soul, released from all dogmatic formulas or established Churches in order to open out into a cosmic reverie that joins love and nature and a desire for the infinite."[92] Whether or not these terms describe Fauré's religious sensibility is an open question, but they resonate deeply with his statements about art and the human imagination. Here we may recall that Fauré once associated the "proper domain of music" with the "desire for nonexistent things, perhaps."[93]

Fauré's assertions of illusion and the unreal as a zone for creative freedom may have a genealogical relation to the residual Catholicism he soon enough ceased to practice. His aims as an artist tended strongly "upward," away from the mundane. This transcendent view of art, whose exact relationship to religion and reality merits another chapter in itself, is evident in the fol-lowing passage. Fauré was writing his son Philippe about the art of compo-sition, at which Philippe was making his first efforts:

To *imagine* consists of trying to give expression to everything we could want in the way of something better, everything that goes beyond reality. So risk what later on might seem absurd to you. You won't have wasted your time for all that. For me, art, and music especially, consists of raising ourselves as far as possible above what is.[94]

Marchal's book on Mallarmé's religion has shown us that an artist's spiritual condition, even when characterized by a traumatic loss of faith, continues to mark creative activity at many levels. The idea that religion could be dismissed once and for all in the wake of human sciences is a cliché of overconfident positivism. Mallarmé's atheism, being hard won, was profoundly haunted. Fauré, the artist with the slightly veiled smile, the dreamer and skeptic, the epicurean and melancholic, was not one to forswear the uses of illusion and the beauties it can offer an artist beaten down by publishers, musical juries, and priests with terrible taste in music. His yearning for "nonexistent things," his assertion of imaginative acts that give expression to some transcendent reality, these mark the eloquence of illusion in his artistic ideal.[95]

Illusion, in its reach for the beyond, approaches the domain of religious belief. "On hearing Fauré's music," wrote the critic Henri Collet in 1919, "how often have painters, sculptors, or poets told us of experiencing a 'religious' emotion, but one without the bitterness of sorrow!"[96] They might rather have said, more pointedly, "without the burden of sin." We shall soon discuss a period in Fauré's life when the end of his duties at La Madeleine and release from its religious conditions provoked a kind of spiritual reevaluation in him. What remains to a man who turns his back on the faith – its dogmas, miracles, and sacraments – but is by no means hostile to the ideal? Fauré confronted this question with thousands of other Frenchmen at the end of the nineteenth century. In *L'irreligion de l'avenir*, a book whose popularity took it through many editions and translations, Jean-Marie Guyau spoke for a great throng of European agnostics and atheists who were seeking a vision of optimism and social progress that did not depend on religious faith. Guyau insisted that abandoning Christian faith had nothing to do with abandoning its metaphysical and moral concerns. The problems to which religion provides its answers remain objects of profound speculation for those who do not believe, just as for those who do. Hence the pursuit of the ideal is not closed to the atheist:

To be *non-religious* or *a-religious* is not to be *anti-religious*. Indeed . . . the non-religion of the future will be able to retain what was purest in religious feeling: on the one hand, admiration for the cosmos and the infinite powers unfurled in it; on the other, the pursuit of an ideal that is not merely individual but social and even cosmic, an ideal that goes beyond momentary reality.[97]

Guyau predicted that "what will surely subsist of the sundry religions in the non-religion of the future" is the ideal of establishing ever closer social connections between living beings.[98] It is hard to say how Fauré might have responded to this specifically sociological interpretation of religious feeling. The evidence seems to suggest that, for Fauré, what would subsist of old religion in the non-religion of the future is rather man's incurable and touching need for illusions; in short, "the pursuit of an ideal," as Guyau said, but in the realm of fiction in the largest sense. If we are to stay among French *libres penseurs* of Fauré's era, we find a spirit closer to him in Ferdinand Buisson, who described what he called the basic "religious emotion" as "the feeling of the Beyond which escapes our grasp; the ideal we are so unhappy never to reach, and which we should be more unhappy yet not to pursue for ever."[99] Through this "feeling of the Beyond," Buisson marks out a vague, overlapping realm of religion and illusion. We may speculate that it was this ambivalent domain that Fauré never entirely abandoned.

We should now return to that "pagan" religiousness Fauré alluded to in defending his Requiem and ask if it could not be the sign of more specific spiritual affinities. We may rule out a literal paganism, that is, the polytheism of antiquity. However, paganism had also been closely linked to *pantheism* since the beginning of the nineteenth century, and we may begin to make a case for a pantheistic "moment" in Fauré's religious thinking between 1906 and 1910, if not longer. One of the most interesting testimonies of Fauré's later attitude toward religion comes to us from Eugène Berteaux:

> For him – and I have it from his lips – the word "God" was merely an immense synonym for the word "Love." This belief . . . by its sheer breadth . . . sooner or later must have worn down the protests of slack epicurean indifference and irreligiosity which various musical camps heaped upon him, really out of partisanship, though some would claim that "such an attitude of philosophical neutrality was unbefitting a former organist of La Madeleine."
>
> "Those poor people [*Les pauvres gens*]" was all Fauré would say, marking this utterance with his best, indulgent smile.[100]

In equating "God" with "Love," Fauré made a statement characteristic of pantheism rather than theism or atheism. As a metaphysical and religious position, pantheism may be distinguished from theism, including Catholicism, by its denial of personal immortality. It may be distinguished from both theism *and* atheism in rejecting the idea of God as a divine Person but not the *idea* of God. For the pantheist, the Love of which Fauré spoke may be equated with God because both are aspects of a single natural and supernatural process engendering and sustaining the universe.

Yet we may rightly hesitate to speak of Fauré's pantheism until we know how the word was used in nineteenth-century France. And even then, our most conscientious efforts at defining religious typologies may prove beside the point. To distinguish pantheism from panentheism, for instance, requires extended philosophical argumentation, but such systematic work is unlikely to help us in our goal of understanding Fauré.[101] Fauré was an artist, not a philosopher: he was reticent about his beliefs, and he left no trace of having thought out his own position in theoretical or speculative terms. Nonetheless, we have the means to define the range and development of ideas that went by the name of "pantheism" in nineteenth-century France, and this task proves instructive. Victor Cousin touched the issue of pantheism in his *Cours de l'histoire de la philosophie* of 1829. In a discussion of John Locke, Cousin observed that "[sensualism] recognizes no God but the aggregate of natural phenomena and the assemblage of things in this world. Thence pantheism, the indispensable theodicy of paganism and sensualist philosophy." He added, in a later passage referring to Locke's followers, "and the natural theism of Locke's wavering sensualism will end in an open pantheism, which is to say, atheism."[102] Cousin's assertion that pantheism implies a particular relation to the natural world seems reasonable, as does his association of pantheism with "paganism and sensualist philosophy." But his blunt equation of pantheism with atheism is surprising. Further study, however, proves that a whole series of nineteenth-century French writers, particularly those hostile to pantheism, likewise refused to accept pantheism as anything but an imperfectly avowed atheism. In 1862 the Goncourt brothers would testily claim, "The most foolish thing in the world is a system of skepticism – pantheism, for example. When unbelief becomes a faith, it is stupider than a religion."[103] This denial begins to change toward the end of the century, probably due to the influence of Renan and the serious study of Eastern religions. Paul Bourget, a writer of Fauré's generation, acknowledged the distinction between pantheism and atheism and more generously defined the former around "the communion of the soul and nature"; he suggested the potential of pantheism for "profound joy . . . intoxicated and almost ecstatic."[104] We shall see that these very qualities characterize Fauré's settings of poems from Charles Van Lerberghe's *Chanson d'Ève*. But it is still important to remember that some nineteenth-century thinkers conflated pantheism and atheism, for those who later recognized the difference between them also remembered their alleged overlap. The ideological contact between the two systems may have influenced the gradual and uncertain development of Fauré's own thinking.

For this discussion, the general premises of "pantheism" outlined two paragraphs ago remain intact, but now complemented by an awareness of historical controversies. Pantheism proclaims an all-encompassing unity of the world and its creatures and considers this unity divine, but the most important difference between atheism and pantheism lies not in the concept of unity but in divinity. An atheist may envision the same oneness as a pantheist, but the atheist attributes it to natural forces. The cardinal difference between the *divine* and the *natural* marks the point where Fauré's position eludes final analysis and returns us to the basic nineteenth-century doctrinal confusion outlined in the last paragraph. The confusion undoubtedly stems in part from the fact that the founding denials of pantheism can shade into atheism so easily. While it is difficult to fix Fauré's position, his drift in the same direction is clear. In 1921, at the age of seventy-six, Fauré spoke with René Fauchois about the possibility of another opera. When Fauchois responded with a *Jérusalem délivrée*, Fauré wrote back a letter of great candor:

> Unfortunately I feel . . . I would be utterly lacking in all *conviction*, I feel I don't even have the words to *begin* to express my utter indifference to the fate of Jerusalem, and in the circumstances I would bring absolutely no life to the work. Such religious illusions as I was ever able to hold all went into my Requiem, which is, moreover, marked from start to finish by this rather human feeling: confidence in eternal rest.[105]

Fauré again speaks of the importance of "human feelings" in his Requiem. But by associating his work with past "religious illusions," Fauré now sounds like an atheist glancing back to a time when he clung to reassuring vestiges of faith. In another letter, written to his wife a year later, Fauré dismissed original sin as a convenient fable invented to explain human misery, and he equated eternal rest not with salvation or redemption, but total oblivion.[106]

In suggesting that Fauré had come close to atheism by the end of his life, I go further than any of his biographers, who have ascribed to him beliefs ranging from agnosticism to a secret or passive Catholicism. Fauré's pupil Emile Vuillermoz, for example, declares him an "indulgent philosopher" whose "agnosticism was complete," while Jean Vuaillat calls him "a Christian unaware of his own faith" ["un chrétien qui s'ignore"].[107] Fauré's younger son devoted more than a few paragraphs in his writings to his father's religion; these passages are all interesting but do not pretend to any certainty. Fauré-Fremiet's personal experience with his father, it seems, revealed nothing too certain about this aspect of Fauré's mind. However, Fauré-Fremiet, proceeding from fact to speculation, makes a case for his father as a kind of agnostic idealist.[108] Fauré-Fremiet has great insight into the potential interaction of artistic transcendence, illusion, and residual faith; he rightly asserts that Fauré could aspire to an ideal without being a believer.[109] However, he also tends to ascribe a latent faith to Fauré on the basis of the creative and personal optimism he senses in Fauré's music and personality. In making this leap, Fauré-Fremiet imposes a certain supernaturalism on what may be a purely human quality. Often Fauré-Fremiet speaks of an "aspiration to the beyond" comparable to that ambivalent, overlapping zone of religion and illusion that we identified with Buisson. But at other times Fauré-Fremiet defines optimism as "confiance," and *confiance* verges on faith and a divine presence. At one point he writes, "Gabriel Fauré always had confidence in a supreme mansuetude that can only be divine, and this confidence is fully and absolutely attested by his Requiem."[110] Now, Fauré's outlook on life, his attitude toward humanity, might be well characterized by the "confidence" of which Fauré-Fremiet speaks. But there is a difference between temperament and faith, between a sturdy optimism and a belief in something divine. Fauré-Fremiet's statement is understandable as a reflection on the "In Paradisum" at the end of Fauré's Requiem. But to say that Fauré "always had confidence" renders his beliefs homogeneous over the course of his whole lifetime, and to claim that the serenity to which his music aspired "can only be divine" is stipulative; he begs the question. It is likely that some of Fauré-Fremiet's free meditations on Fauré's religion reveal more about his own spiritual concerns than those of his father.

More recently, Jean-Michel Nectoux has given considerable attention to Fauré's religious doubts. He acknowledges them but concludes that it "would, even so, be quite wrong to regard him as an atheist." Nectoux seems to believe that Fauré's sensitivity to the beauty of the natural world, evident in many of the composer's private letters, rules out the possibility of atheism.[111] But atheism and a profound love of nature are not in the least mutually exclusive. The beauty of nature is often the *common* element across which the believer and the atheist argue their opposing views of the world, and it is certainly wrong to equate atheism with a hatred of the created world or with pessimism. Let us recall the "admiration for the cosmos" that Guyau foresaw for a practice of "non-religion" profoundly respectful of human beings and nature. Michel Faure, who recently exaggerated Fauré's pessimism to the point of representing him as a nihilist, commits the errors of simplification Guyau warned against long ago. If Nectoux stops too short in refusing to take Fauré's atheism seriously, Michel Faure goes too far by half.[112] Fauré seems to have nurtured what might be called an "optimistic fatalism"; he was resigned in the face of human folly but too tender-hearted and forgiving to join the ranks of reliable pessimists like Flaubert and Leconte de Lisle.

The historical evidence does not permit us to know the precise nature of Fauré's religion once and for all; we are left with deductions and approximations. His life seems to trace a path from belief to unbelief. But he himself significantly admitted, in a late letter to his wife, "You are categorical about everything. Not me. I will die as I have lived, with my mind not made up."[113]

4 Versions of Eve

Fauré composed *La chanson d'Ève* between 1906 and 1910: the years are significant. Having assumed his new position as director of the Conservatoire in October 1905, Fauré immediately quit his job at La Madeleine. No longer beholden to the Church in any way, he left the organ, his improvisations, and all his ecclesiastical duties behind. At the same time, a new contract with the firm of Heugel encouraged him to clean house and revise a few old pieces for publication, including an *Ave Maria* for two high voices and the *Messe basse*. With these two works, his production of sacred music came to an end. At this same moment, in the fall of 1906, he began to write *La chanson d'Ève*. I shall argue that this cycle of songs marks the turning point between Fauré's waning Catholicism and his incipient atheism. Given the nature of Van Lerberghe's book and Fauré's very individual approach to it, we may describe this moment as more than just abstractly transitional. In discussing *La chanson d'Ève*, the term "pantheism" is entirely appropriate, though here we must speak of an informal pantheism: poetic, not systematic. Both Fauré and Van Lerberghe sometimes leave us to wonder whether the all-embracing "oneness" of Eve's world is natural or divine. Such a basic uncertainty lacks philosophical rigor but is defensible in a work of art.

Van Lerberghe and Fauré published their respective works in 1904 and 1910, and this timing is again significant. Both were brought to life during one of the most crisis-ridden decades in the history of French Catholicism. The period from 1880 to 1905 was one of almost continuous secularization in France, and the anticlerical measures that Waldeck-Rousseau and Combes proposed between 1901 and 1904 culminated in a divorce from the Vatican and the separation of Church and State in 1905. Ironically, at the peak of all this secularizing activity, Pope St Pius X, who succeeded the more open-minded Leo XIII in 1903, began to issue increasingly frequent and hostile proclamations against religious liberalism (then called "modernism"). Between 1903 and 1910, the Vatican and Third Republic were moving in opposite directions, and the resulting flurry of polemical literature in France, as well as genuine attempts at internal reorganization and discussion among the liberal Catholics, led only to a stream of condemnations from the Holy See.

An artist who rewrites the story of Genesis will have to disclose his acceptance or refusal of certain received doctrines. While there may be no direct connection between the political events of the first decade of the century and Fauré's or Van Lerberghe's achievement, it is clear that both of them created a new universe for a biblical figure, a universe in harmony with the secular, revisionary tendencies of their time rather than the reactionary ones. Fauré shed no tears over the separation of Church and State in France. His attitude is clear from a letter he wrote from Vitznau in 1906 in which he complained that the Vitznauerhof only subscribed to "reactionary French newspapers":

> If I don't go out and get myself *Le Matin* or *Le Temps*, I only hear one bell. And when it's *Le Gaulois* that rings the changes, the tune is outrageous. You've got to see how it's ordering the government, under penalty of being expeditiously pulverized, to beg the pope's forgiveness. What wonderful impudence! And wonderful, too, the naïveté, or vanity, or stupidity or bad faith of the people for whom all that is written, printed, and circulated.[114]

Van Lerberghe, for his part, was anticlerical, and by 1904 an avowed atheist who admired Christian myth as a poetic source but declared himself on the side of "the only acceptable theology from Heraclitus down to our own time: [the theory of] Evolution." He added in the same letter, "I put Poetry and Art above everything. Philosophy and Religion were and will always be their humble servants . . . We have returned today to the right path, that of true poetry, of nature's universal symbolism, of its free and infinitely multiple interpretation according to the liking of each mind and soul."[115]

Van Lerberghe's book of ninety-six poems, *La chanson d'Ève*, offers a striking mixture of selective biblical allegory and imaginative pantheism. The pantheism particularly struck the first readers of the poem. Jacques Rivière, in a letter to Alain-Fournier, not only identified Van Lerberghe's work as pantheistic but also suggested that its pantheism was somehow modern, not simply a neoclassical paganism:

> How exquisite [the poem] is . . . above all this delightful pantheism, purer, more naive, and also deeper than pagan pantheism. Eve is conscious of being in a more direct communication with Universal Substance since she recognizes it in herself, while the pagans found it only in beings outside themselves.[116]

Van Lerberghe plays out a perpetual confusion of Eve with the world, a sense of all-inclusive oneness that scatters her personal identity across the animate and inanimate forces of nature. In "Premières paroles," the first chapter of Van Lerberghe's book, we encounter this brand of pantheism at every turn. We may take the sixth poem as an example:

Ne suis-je vous, n'êtes-vous moi,
O choses que de mes doigts
Je touche, et de la lumière
De mes yeux éblouis?
Fleurs où je respire, soleil où je luis,
Ame qui penses,
Qui peut me dire où je finis,
Où je commence?

Ah! que mon cœur infiniment
Partout se retrouve! Que votre sève
C'est mon sang!
Comme un beau fleuve,
En toutes choses la même vie coule,
Et nous rêvons le même rêve.[117]

[Am I not you, are you not I,
O things I touch with my fingers
and with the light
of my dazzled eyes?
Flowers in which I breathe, sun where I shine,
O thinking soul,
who can tell me where I end,
where I start?

Ah! let my heart be found
everywhere without bounds! Your sap
is my blood!
Like a beautiful river,
the same life flows in all things,
and we dream the same dream.]

Eve, through all her senses, professes a total identification with the world around her. This dazzled confusion continues into the next poem, "Roses ardentes," which Fauré set as his third song. In the first strophe, Eve addresses the roses of Eden as a source of her being and her song ("C'est en vous que je chante | Et que je suis"). She suffuses herself and her senses in the roses, the stars and the sea, and she in turn is suffused by them. In the last strophe she turns to the sun itself and affirms her intuition of personal divinity: "And in you, supreme power, | radiant Sun, | my very soul | attains its god!"[118]

The next poem in Fauré's cycle, "Comme Dieu rayonne," is Van Lerberghe's twelfth poem: "How God beams today, I how he exults, how he flowers I amid these roses and these fruits."[119] The first line suggests traditional theism, yet hardly do we hear the name of God before Van Lerberghe's imagery and language conspire to identify the "divine beaming" with that of the sun, to diffuse His Person in fountains, birdsong, and the scent of springtime. We realize that this god is one with the world:

Comme il se baigne dans la lumière
Avec amour, mon jeune dieu!
Toutes les choses de la terre
Sont ses vêtements radieux.

[How he bathes in the light
lovingly, my young god!
all things on earth
are his shining raiments.]

The change from "Dieu" (majuscule) at the beginning of the poem to "dieu" (minuscule) at the end betrays this effect whereby God is absorbed into his creation. The identification of God and the world is a basic tenet of pantheism.[120] In a lecture given one year after Fauré completed La chanson d'Ève, the critic and novelist André Beaunier cautiously observed that the deity in this song was far from the stern figure of the Old Testament. Rather, he suggested, "there is a prodigious joy in the young universe, a joy like a blithe, charming, beaming god. This is the divinity of nature."[121] In the same paragraph, Beaunier points out the identification of Eve with nature, the mysterious communication between them that had likewise fascinated Rivière.

Let us draw back to consider Van Lerberghe's book as a whole. He places Eve alone in Eden. There is no Adam. God awakens her to a beautiful garden and tells her, "Go human daughter, I and give to all the beings I I have created, a word from your lips, I a sound to know them by."[122] Eve identifies herself with all the elements and sensations of her world, then gradually becomes aware of her subjective difference from them.[123] In Van Lerberghe's Paradise, Eve's "temptation" consists in deepening her sensual and intellectual involvement with these elements. Once she has named and sung the Garden, she gradually comes to desire to know its secrets and observe the whole from a position of detachment and timelessness. In one of the early poems, the Lord counsels Eve to "Turn a deaf ear to the voice that calls I in the shadowy depths, the tempting voice, I the voice of the serpent, or the voice of the sirens, I or that of the passionate doves I in Love's dark groves. I Remain ignorant" (pp. 29–30). She is tempted by knowledge, as in the Bible, and thus perhaps by power, too. But Eve's greatest desire is for *self-knowledge*, and in "La tentation," the second chapter of the book, this search draws her through the enchantments of her garden into philosophy and finally a reeling glimpse of a silent, impassible Elsewhere at the threshold of Eden. The transgression is deadly. She calls on her angels; they rescue her. Eve is returned to life: "Come back," the angels say. "The error was human; God forgives. | All Paradise awaits you as before" (p. 146).

In the third chapter, "La faute," Eve transgresses differently. While her angels sleep, she tastes the golden fruit of a forbidden tree; her eyes are opened to the truth and she feels equal to God. Yet, curiously, the angels pay her homage; she is not punished. She enjoys Eden again with new comprehension. From the start, God and the angels let her play and explore the world. They try, in vain, to shield her from knowledge, which will bring unhappiness. "Leave the fruit on the branch, | do not deepen your happiness," God advises in the ninth poem of the book. "Ne pense pas; chante," "Don't think; sing" (p. 30). Eve's error is simply self-consciousness; for Van Lerberghe this is an "innocent" error; thus there is no punishment, only understanding.[124] Eve was never promised immortality, and her experiences in the final chapter, "Crépuscule," confirm that growing consciousness of death she already felt as early as "La poussière m'a dit," a poem in the first chapter (p. 58). Having perceived mortality in the world at many levels, from the fading of flowers to the solar tragedy of nightfall, she finally fathoms her own mortality, and this is how she leaves her paradise.

In looking to Fauré's work, drawn from Van Lerberghe's poem but distinct from it, it would be reckless to "fill in" the Van Lerberghe that Fauré left out in order to submit the musical content to some more complete meaning. Rather, let us take Fauré's omissions and choices as artistically and personally significant. His selection and handling of ten poems from Van Lerberghe's book provide a starting point for analyzing his departures from a traditional theological model.

We may see the pattern of Fauré's selections and omissions in Table 1. First, observe that Fauré drew the majority of his songs from "Premières paroles," the most joyous and innocent chapter of the poem. Second, "La faute" ("Error" or "Sin") turns out, significantly, to be the only chapter from which he drew no poems at all, and from the preceding "Tentation" he took only one poem. Fauré left aside precisely those sections of the book most influenced by the moral lessons of the Old Testament. The single poem Fauré did take from "La tentation" appears out of order in his cycle; he inserted it back in between two poems from "Premières paroles" and thus lifted it out of the context of temptation into the less morally charged atmosphere of Van Lerberghe's first chapter. Fauré's decision to close with

"O mort, poussière d'étoiles," Eve's invocation to death, is his starkest revision. Van Lerberghe's book continues with two other poems that abandon Eve's voice for an omniscient narrator. In his penultimate poem, the angel Azraël "descends the staircase of clouds" and gently blows out Eve's life-breath as she sleeps. In the last poem, her soul fades into a pale dawn, "she evaporates into the clear air; | in a smile she returns | to the universe she sang." We find none of these soft, melting tones in Fauré: he deliberately ended with Eve at night, awake and alone, offering herself to death without angels, smiles or the reassuring light of a new day.

Van Lerberghe adorns his Paradise with fairies, sirens, spirits of the air and water, but under all these pagan garlands retains the Christian elements of temptation, the serpent, and, after Eve's death, a vague but luminous apotheosis. Fauré departs from the old ideology more abruptly; he excludes all reference to the serpent, temptation, and sin. Above all, he forfeits the gentle ending. His *Chanson d'Ève* culminates in an earthbound, unflinching acceptance of death. Is it possible that through Eve, and through his rearrangement and treatment of Van Lerberghe's poem, Fauré articulated a kind of eschatology? *

To measure the distance Fauré and Van Lerberghe alike traveled from an orthodox interpretation of Genesis, we can turn to Massenet's setting of Louis Gallet's poem *Ève*. In the French repertory this "mystère" in three parts, composed in 1875, stands as the nearest musical precursor to Fauré's work. Massenet's Eve cuts a very different figure. Once Gallet's and Massenet's "Voices of Night" seduce Eve and arouse in her a thirst for knowledge and power, her fall is inexorable, and she drags Adam in her wake. In contrast to the confused pantheism of Van Lerberghe's heroine, this Eve lusts for raw dominion over nature and man. "Tu marcheras l'orgueil au front" ("You will go with pride on your brow"), the chorus sings to celebrate her newly gained knowledge. She soon tempts Adam into the obscure delights of eros; he succumbs easily. In "La Malédiction," the final section of the work, the "Voices of Nature," a choral channel for God's wrath, denounce the fallen couple against gaudy orchestral counterpoints fashioned from the "Dies iræ." Choral cries of "Soyez maudits!" ("Be accursed!") resound against a massive five-octave descent through the G-minor scale on the last page of the score. The symbolic import of this "fall" is unmistakable – and very loud. Massenet and Gallet, shouting their message at the French public, render the moral content of the Old Testament with little subtlety and no ambiguity.

Fauré, in contrast, completely excluded the idea of original sin from his work. This was no oversight but a willful disregard of biblical allegory. Fauré's portrait of Eve, more than Van Lerberghe's, defies Christian

* branch of theology concerned ɛ final events, or death

Table 1. *Van Lerberghe's book compared to Fauré's op. 95. Distribution and selection of poems*

VAN LERBERGHE	[96 POEMS]	FAURÉ	[10 SONGS]
Prélude	<2 poems>	< none >	
PREMIÈRES PAROLES	<28 poems>	<7 poems>	
[3]		1. "Paradis" (Fauré's title)	
[7]		3. "Roses ardentes"	
[8]		2. "Prima verba" (Fauré's title)	
[12]		4. "Comme Dieu rayonne . . ."	
[16]		5. "L'aube blanche"	
[22]		6. "Eau vivante" (Fauré's title)	
[29]		8. "Dans un parfum de roses blanches . . ."	
LA TENTATION	<36 poems>	<1 poem>	
[39]		7. "Veilles-tu, ma senteur de soleil . . ."	
LA FAUTE	<18 poems>	< none >	
CRÉPUSCULE	<12 poems>	<2 poems>	
[86]		9. "Crépuscule" (Fauré's title)	
[94]		10. "O mort, poussière d'étoiles . . ."	

theology and ignores Genesis. While the poet casts more than one backward glance on the ancient Roman Catholic edifice, Fauré turns away and keeps going. Evidence that Fauré abhorred the idea of fatal damnation is not lacking. In a letter to his wife from 1922, he responded to her scorn for mankind with a remarkable plea for compassion and tolerance. We must quote from this letter at length:

> In one of your recent letters you spoke to me of your admiration for the created world and your disdain for its creatures. Is that fair? The universe is order, man is disorder. But is that his fault? He was thrown onto this earth,

where everything seems harmonious to us and where *he* goes lurching, stumbling from his first day to his last; he was thrown here weighted down with a burden of physical and moral ailments (to the point that *original sin* had to be invented to explain this phenomenon!). All his life on earth he retains the mentality of a child who wants to try so hard to be good, though it is difficult and irritating, on the understanding that he will be rewarded for it! And what is the reward promised this childlike soul? The satisfaction of having been beaten and bruised for the future of humanity? Could you find one human being in ten thousand who would be content with that? And what proves our sorry state more than anything else is this promise, the best that could be made to man: total oblivion, the Hindu nirvana, or for that matter our *requiem æternam.*

No, this poor bundle of miseries that is man, this being condemned to *struggle for life* and whose first and most ghastly duty is to devour another or be devoured himself, deserves more indulgence. There! For years and years I have wanted to use this reasoning, banal as it is, to rebut the immeasurable bitterness of your judgments![125]

It would seem Fauré might have agreed with one of Santayana's observations, which reveals a similar frame of mind: "It is pathetic . . . to observe how lowly the motives are that religion, even the highest, attributes to the deity, and from what a hard-pressed and bitter existence they have been drawn."[126] The end of Fauré's letter concerns us further on. Right now the first paragraph is most relevant. Fauré imagined man "thrown onto this earth" like a die, "lurching, stumbling from his first day to his last" and weighted down with such a burden of miseries that original sin had to be "invented" to explain them. This explanation of the human condition differs fundamentally from the conventional Catholic attitude I take Massenet's and Gallet's work to represent. In Christian theology, original sin is much more than a convenient invention, a fiction; it is practically a cosmogonical imperative. How would the concept of redemption come into play without it?

Fauré abolishes original sin from the garden of Eden and forces us to imagine Eve's relation to the world anew. Unredeemed because never guilty, Eve does not transcend the world through personal immortality but rather returns to the world, is absorbed by it, becomes it. Fauré specifically suggests the inseparability of life and death through Eve's immersion and reflection in nature, in which joy and suffering are part of the same mortal mystery. This outlook may help to explain a structural aspect of Fauré's cycle which has puzzled critics. I refer to the fact that two different recurring musical ideas run through *La chanson d'Ève*, but Fauré does not ask them to fulfill the function of opposed symbols. Both Jankélévitch and Philippe

Fauré-Fremiet tried to assign each theme a distinct set of symbolic values, but their efforts at distinction tended to collapse into sameness.[127] Fauré-Fremiet himself finally decided that the two themes, though musically distinct, resist symbolic differentiation since they are so unstable in the contexts of their reappearances.[128] His scruples were just. First, Fauré's use of thematic material gives a greater role to fantasy than design. Second, the permeability Fauré built into the work is the sign of a larger symbolic objective, one related to its pantheism. If all that exists constitutes a unity, if God cannot be separated from the world, then on what basis should we decide that one musical idea represents the divine, the other the worldly? This is why Fauré's cycle is bithematic but not dialectic. Fauré, like Eve facing her new world, relishes the confusion of the mind and the senses. His thematic oscillations seem to pose her eternal question again and again: "Who can tell me where I end, | where I start?" (above, p. 200).

Fauré's *Chanson d'Ève*, however, is not so enigmatic in other ways. Its large-scale symbolic design seems clear: Fauré arranged the songs in a curve leading from dawn to night. This "solar drama" or "tragedy of nature" was one of the great archetypes of late nineteenth-century French poetry, and one especially associated with the interpretation of myth. In *Les dieux antiques*, Mallarmé referred expansively to the endless remaking of a single human myth, "the many narrations of the great solar drama realized before our eyes every day and every year": the setting and rebirth of the sun, the yearly cycle of the seasons.[129] In a private letter, Van Lerberghe himself drew a parallel between the successive chapters of his poem and morning, noon, afternoon, and nightfall.[130] Fauré, even as he left aside nine-tenths of Van Lerberghe's poems, observed this pattern and cast Eve's drama as the rise and decline of sunlight. The morning of the first song, "Paradis," and the evening of "Crépuscule," the next to last, are both set in twilight, and Fauré's similar treatment of the initial theme reflects this common lighting (Examples 13a, 13b). The noon of Eve's radiance arrives in the middle of the work. Her approach to a solar apogee is first expressed at the end of "Roses ardentes": "Et c'est en toi, force suprême, | Soleil radieux, | Que mon âme elle-même | Atteint son dieu!"[131] In this and the following two songs, Fauré breaks with the general sobriety of the cycle as a whole for incandescent registral and timbral effects ("Roses ardentes," mm. 34–36; "Comme Dieu rayonne . . .," mm. 13–25; "L'Aube blanche," mm. 5–7). Evening descends in the seventh song, "Dans un parfum de roses blanches," as the sun tinges the blue garden with afternoon's gold: "Le soir descend, le bosquet dort; . . . Sur le paradis bleu s'ouvre un paradis d'or."[132] Then, after "Crépuscule" (literally "twilight"), comes the final song, "O mort, poussière d'étoiles," Eve's call to death. The sun has gone below the horizon to reveal the stars and the

Example 13a. *La chanson d'Ève*, op. 95, no. 1: "Paradis," mm. 1–6.

Example 13b. *La chanson d'Ève*, op. 95, no. 9: "Crépuscule," mm. 1–4.

emptiness of space. Eve dies with the sun, and the journey from the first song to the last traces a great eschatological cycle from first awakening to final sleep.

5 This enigma, death

The solar myths of the West are usually allegories of resurrection. Van Lerberghe hews lightly to this tradition in his final poem, "Une aube pâle . . .", where he returns Eve to the skies in a vague aerial sublimation. But Fauré offers Eve no new morning, only an abyssal plunge into elemental reintegration. His ending poses several questions. Where Van Lerberghe's ninety-six poems give ample occasion for scattered premonitions of dust, mortality, and darkness, "Crépuscule," Fauré's next-to-last song, provides the sole adumbration of Eve's death. The first eight songs are so steeped in life and joy that the sadness of "Crépuscule" seems to come from nowhere:

> Ce soir, à travers le bonheur,
> Qui donc soupire, qu'est-ce qui pleure?
> Qu'est-ce qui vient palpiter sur mon cœur,
> Comme un oiseau blessé?

Est-ce une plainte de la terre,
Est-ce une voix future,
Une voix du passé?
J'écoute, jusqu'à la souffrance,
Ce son dans le silence.

Ile d'oubli, ô Paradis!
Quel cri déchire, cette nuit,
Ta voix qui me berce?
Quel cri traverse
Ta ceinture de fleurs,
Et ton beau voile d'allégresse?[133]

[This evening, through happiness,
who is that sighing, who cries?
What comes beating upon my heart
like a wounded bird?

Is this a moan from the earth,
is this a future voice,
a voice from the past?
To the point of pain, I listen
to this sound in the silence.

Isle without memories, O Paradise!
Tonight what cry rends
your voice that quells me?
What cry crosses
your girdle of flowers
and your beautiful veil of gladness?]

This song represents Eve's first contact with suffering in the world. Yet the poem, beyond the disturbance of a mysterious cry in the dying light, is strangely indeterminate: a series of questions.[134] For the last poetic line, Fauré effaces the minor mode, and the piano answers Eve's words with a warm halo of rising major scales. "Crépuscule" thus ends calmly and radiantly in D major, the key of Fauré's "In paradisum." For a moment it seems possible that the next song will fulfill or draw out this happier vision. But our glimpse of a second Jerusalem, as Jankélévitch notes, "is swallowed up in the black, telluric shadows of the final song."[135] The "veil of gladness" was indeed a veil, and there will be no Christian resurrection as in the Requiem. The tonality drops a half-step to D-flat, and we hear these momentous words: "O death, stardust, I rise beneath my tread!"[136] "O mort" provides an answer to the questions posed in "Crépuscule," which was indeed a presage of death. But what death is this? In the complementary images of Van

Lerberghe's "O mort," stars and earth, at opposite ends of the cosmic pole, are brought together: the glittering dust above Eve's head and the dark dust beneath her feet. She is part of both; to die between them is to be enveloped in the pantheist fold.

Since Fauré draws Eve's existence through the path of the declining sun, the end of the cycle is a natural place for her to meet death. But we may still ask why this death, which she faces without resistance, has no evident cause or explanation. The question persists because Fauré's fundamental rejection of the traditional pretext for human suffering, original sin, leaves us searching for other causes. He finally seems to have posed death in its suddenness and inexplicability to remind us that the bounty of nature is fatally linked to its sorrow. The law itself is beyond our command. "Crépuscule," with its indefinite ache and its questioning receptiveness, was the perfect poem to convey a sense of foreboding without the reassurance of explanation. It is also important to observe that Eve's own recognition of mortality in no way breaks her identification with the forces of nature. "O mort, poussière d'étoiles," like the songs of flowers, sun, and water, manifests her intimacy with the elemental world. Her previous surrender to joy has now turned into a grave compliance with the destructive claims of nature:

O death, stardust,
rise beneath my tread!

Come, O gentle wave shining
in the darkness.
Carry me into your void!

Come, dark breath wherein I waver
like a flame drunk on wind!

In you would I stretch out,
be blown out, melted,
death, where my soul aspires!

Come, break me like a flower of foam,
a flower of sunlight on the crest of the waters!

And as from a golden amphora
a wine of flame and divine aroma,
pour my soul into your abyss,
so that it might embalm
the dark earth and the breath of the dead.[137]

Water, wind, fire, and earth: the four elements await Eve in her imminent diffusion into the body of the world. Fauré strengthens the elemental imagery of Van Lerberghe's poem through some sensitive cuts (Table 2). He eliminates lines sixteen and seventeen, which refer redundantly to night, shadow, and space, and also lines eleven and twelve, where Eve evokes death as a "strong god." This sudden personification, with its shadow of divinity, undercuts the purely elemental imagery of the poem, in which Fauré must have seen the strength of Van Lerberghe's overall conception. By distilling the elemental essences of the poem, perhaps Fauré even improved it. In any case he strengthened its pantheistic affirmation of impersonal unity with the world. We are reminded of a comment Renan made in his first essay on Buddhism: "When man, this amalgam of four elements, comes to the end of his days, earth returns to the store of earth, water to the store of water, fire to the store of fire, and wind to the store of wind."[138]

On the last page of the last song Fauré was able to draw together Eve's birth and her death, her awakening vision of the garden and her last glimpse of it. He did this through his choice, ordering, and transformation of Van Lerberghe's poems. He also transposed his vision of Eve into musical terms through his treatment of the second theme, whose last appearance in the cycle is momentous. In measure 18 of "O mort," at the last stanza, this theme slides quietly into the accompaniment. The theme had first appeared in "Paradis" immediately after the words "Un jardin bleu s'épanouit" to suggest the misty emergence of the garden of Eden. Its reappearance at the end of the cycle is subtle but did not escape some of Fauré's first listeners. In a review of the première, Joseph de Marliave, for one, recognized Fauré's symbolic design with admiration: "Nothing is so moving as, at the end of this sublime page, the distant recollection of the melody that greeted the young, divine Eve being awakened by God at the beginning of the work."[139] Through this transformation, Fauré bends the waxing light of "Paradis" (Example 14a) into utter night – the broken descent of the same theme at the end of "O mort" (Example 14b). It is even more interesting to consider Fauré's use of this same theme at the end of "Comme Dieu rayonne," where Eve's innocent wonder at the beauty of the world creates a sense of glowing happiness. In the middle of the song, the second theme enters high on the keyboard in a wash of undulating harmonies (Example 15, m. 15).[140] When the vocal part re-enters, the second theme begins a slow descent on the piano, and the singer responds with her largest and most ecstatic leaps in the whole cycle: "How he lovingly bathes I in the light, my young god! I All the things of the earth I are his shining raiments."[141] Both "Comme Dieu rayonne" and "O mort" share a bass governed by a cycle of falling minor thirds (Example 16). Fauré gave the two songs this same, audible structure despite their patently different poetic themes. While we saw that he also uses the second theme in "Paradis," there it is laid over a completely different

Table 2. *"O mort, poussière d'étoiles . . .": Fauré's revisions*

Van Lerberghe's poem	Fauré's song
O mort, poussière d'étoiles,	O mort, poussière d'étoiles,
Lève-toi sous mes pas!	Lève-toi sous mes pas!
Viens, souffle sombre où je vacille,	Viens, ô douce vague qui brille
Comme une flamme ivre de vent!	Dans les ténèbres.
	Emporte-moi dans ton néant!
Viens, ô douce vague qui brill[es]*	
Dans les ténèbres;	Viens, souffle sombre où je vacille,
Emporte-moi dans ton néant!	Comme une flamme ivre de vent!
C'est en toi que je veux m'étendre,	C'est en toi que je veux m'étendre,
M'éteindre et me dissoudre,	M'éteindre et me dissoudre,
Mort, où mon âme aspire!	Mort, où mon âme aspire!
Dieu fort qu'elle attend	
Avec des chants et des rires d'amour.	
Viens, brise-moi comme une fleur d'écume,	Viens, brise-moi comme une fleur d'écume,
Une fleur de soleil à la cime	Une fleur de soleil à la cime des eaux!
Des eaux,	
Que la nuit effeuille, que l'ombre efface,	
Et que l'espace épanouit,	
Et comme d'une amphore d'or	Et comme d'une amphore d'or
Un vin de flamme et d'arome divin,	Un vin de flamme et d'arome divin,
Épanche mon âme	Épanche mon âme en ton abîme,
En ton abîme, pour qu'elle embaume	Pour qu'elle embaume
La terre sombre et le souffle des morts.	La terre sombre et le souffle des morts.

Note:

* In the 1904 edition of the poem, "-es" was omitted – a typographical error. Fauré amended it to "brille." The 1952 edition of Van Lerberghe's *Chanson d'Ève* more correctly gives "brilles."

harmonic foundation in the bass, which rises rather than falls.[142] The structural likeness between "Comme Dieu rayonne" and "O mort" is undeniably stronger. While "O mort" throws its shadow back over Eve's birth in "Paradis," the burst of joyous light in "Comme Dieu rayonne" incurs this retrospective shading even more vividly. In either case, with the conclusion of the work, the listener realizes that the strange harmonic glimmer of Fauré's second theme bore within it a seed of death.

Fauré also represented the relatedness of life and death without recourse

Example 14a. *La chanson d'Ève*, op. 95, no. 1: "Paradis," mm. 19–22.

Example 14b. *La chanson d'Ève*, op. 95, no. 10: "O mort . . .," mm. 18–21.

to the two recurring themes. We find such a likeness between two phrases from "L'aube blanche" and "O mort, poussière d'étoiles" (Example 17). "L'aube blanche" is a song of warmth and whiteness: Eve opens her eyes to a blaze of morning sunlight. What could be further from this image than her surrender to the deepest sleep of all in "O mort"? Yet though the images, ideas, and musical colors are opposed, the striking likeness of these two phrases reminds us of a greater unity. The treble pitches are the same, and

Example 15. *La chanson d'Ève*, op. 95, no. 4: "Comme Dieu rayonne," mm. 13–18.

in each case they descend by whole tones through appoggiaturas or suspensions. Fauré's path of escape diverges after the sixth tone, so that each phrase ends on a different cadence. "L'aube blanche" is relaxed and resolved; "O mort," tense and inconclusive, and this difference is appropriate to the emotional content of each song.

The fact that this analogy does not involve a theme, however, may make us wonder if it is not a coincidence. The possibility of mere coincidence is impossible to gainsay, but it is undermined by the discovery that the melodic and harmonic similarity of these two phrases extends to other parameters. First, "L'aube blanche" and "O mort" are the only two songs in the key of D-flat major. Second, the passages in Example 17 contain the registral climaxes of each song, both on the same pitch (D-sharp or E-flat). Third, the phrase cited from "L'aube blanche" marks the very center of the

Example 16. *La chanson d'Ève*, op. 95. Comparison of minor thirds outlined in the bass in the fourth and last songs: "Comme Dieu rayonne . . ." (no. 4), mm. 15–20; "O mort, poussière d'étoiles" (no. 10), mm. 18–21.

"Comme Dieu rayonne . . . " (no. 4), mm. 15–20

"O mort, poussière d'étoiles" (no. 10), mm. 18–21

entire work. This series of relationships, especially the last, suggests a kind of formal symmetry and permits further speculation on Fauré's large-scale design. The first nine songs may be grouped into three "triads" marked by the tonal identity of their outer elements (Figure 1). The tenth song, with its cold starlight, stands outside this sequence of triads, for, as we have already noted, the entry into night in "O mort" sets it apart. It seems possible that Fauré, aware of the relative isolation of his tenth song, chose to link it back to the middle one at different levels, including key, climactic phrases, and pitch. ("O mort" was in fact composed after "L'aube blanche.") Joining the midpoint to the end, these two songs in D-flat thus become a formal pair thrown across the bundles of three. The correspondences between the fifth and tenth songs seem less a coincidence than a token of Fauré's desire to draw the cycle together and reflect life and death into one another.

Poetic content, too, can foster coherence, and Fauré matched up certain words and symbols in his selection from Van Lerberghe. Like the similarity of two distant musical phrases, lexical recurrences can create a sense of unity, or a nonsequential harmony of thoughts and images. In "L'aube blanche" the awakening sun is compared to "a flame . . . a breath," touching and quickening Eve's sleeping body. In "O mort," fire is still an image of life, but the relation is reversed. Eve now becomes a flame that death will extinguish: "Come, dark breath wherein I waver, I like a flame drunk on wind! I In you I would stretch out, I be blown out and melted."[143] In another example, the verb "embalm" creates a link between "O mort" and the seventh song, the exuberant "Veilles-tu, ma senteur de soleil?" A word associated with either the luxury of perfumes or the preparation of the dead,

Example 17. *La chanson d'Ève*, op. 95. Comparison of climactic phrases in the fifth and last songs: "L'aube blanche" (no. 5), mm. 16–19; "O mort, poussière d'étoiles" (no. 10), mm. 15–17.

"L'aube blanche" (no. 5), mm. 16–19

"O mort, poussière d'étoiles" (no. 10), mm. 15–17

Figure 1. *La chanson d'Ève*, op. 95: Schematic interpretation.

"embaumer" first appears at the end of "Veilles-tu" as the perfume of lilies in Eve's voice. In "O mort" the association is again drastically transformed: Eve offers her own soul "to embalm | the dark earth and the breath of the dead." The verb is the more memorable for appearing in the last sentence of both poems.[144]

Just as "L'hiver a cessé," the last song of *La bonne chanson*, is Fauré's most radiantly joyous, "O mort" is his darkest. Fauré's younger son, Philippe, once referred to "O mort" as "a sort of funeral march toward an open-armed nirvana."[145] He cited the last two lines of Fauré's setting but offered no further explanation. Did he grasp the poetic and lexical validity of his own remark? Nirvana is the fundamental spiritual ideal of Buddhism, and in its Hindu adaptations in particular it is often likened to a blowing out of the flame of life and an overthrow of all continuing personal passions and identity. Such extinction is the central image of "O mort." The third and fourth strophes of Fauré's rearrangement come closest to translating the Hindu image: death is a "souffle sombre" ("dark breath") extinguishing Eve's mortal flame. Fauré knew what nirvana was and even used the word in the same letter where he explained the fiction of original sin to his wife and remarked on the sadness of humanity. He concluded, "What proves our sorry state more than anything else is this promise, the best that could be made to man: total oblivion, the Hindu nirvana, or for that matter our *requiem æternam*."[146] Fauré thus touches a profound question – whether there is any final compensation for human suffering. His answer bears little trace of Christian faith. For him, the only promise to be taken seriously, eternal rest and oblivion, was at the same time the proof of our miserable state. So we are left to wonder further: was the dissolution of any continuing personal identity after death, a condition common to pantheism and Buddhism, a matter of consolation or pessimism for Fauré?

With reference to the end of *La chanson d'Ève* it seems impossible to arrive at a definitive answer because so much depends on how each listener hears its final page. The relation of our subjective impressions to Fauré's attitude is open to question. For Philippe Fauré-Fremiet, "O mort" was a moment of tragic pessimism, and Fauré's decision to pass over Van Lerberghe's brighter ending tantamount to a crisis of faith. "Only once, it seems to me, was Fauréan confidence conquered and disarmed," he wrote, "the end of *La chanson d'Ève*."[147] "O mort" is probably Fauré's most profound song, but it is not necessarily an expression of philosophical anguish. It is worth remembering that Fauré set this song of death in the major mode! It may seem, to start with, the darkest D-flat major ever written, but the harmonic palette gradually infuses Eve's sorrow with nobility and calm. When the second theme softly emerges at measure 18, the music, though resigned, gathers itself into a kind of wisdom, and the final measures suggest a strange, burnished darkness. Jankélévitch rightly insisted, against Philippe Fauré-Fremiet, that "O mort" is "far, very far, from being a song of desperation." Jankélévitch significantly defended this view by reminding us not to confuse pantheism with nihilism. Thus he calls "O mort, poussière des étoiles" a "méditation quiétiste et panthéiste" and a song of ecstasy, "that cosmic ecstasy which is a plenary communion with nothingness, or better, a fusion into total presence."[148] Here we have reached a point of extreme speculation. Whether Fauré's ending seems optimistic or pessimistic will, I believe, ultimately depend on each listener's own expectations of the afterlife. What is certain and striking is that Fauré, finding so much to admire in Van Lerberghe's book, chose to end his own work so differently. Alain-Fournier compared Van Lerberghe's book to a spring whose waters change as we plunge deeper but remain calm, cool, and clear to the very bottom.[149] Rather than a spring, Fauré's ending suggests waves breaking hypnotically on an invisible shore under a starlit sky. We are left with a feeling of peace, near-silence, and expanding distance.

Considering the cycle as a whole, the last song comes as a kind of revelatory vision of the world and human existence: the lucid consequence of man's identification with nature. This book of secular songs has a kind of eschatology, or strongly suggests one, and Fauré's ideological choices seem too decisive not to reflect his continuing drift away from the Catholic doctrine of personal resurrection. This pantheistic reverie reflects, as clearly as we can seem to know, Fauré's own beliefs at this particular moment in his life. Still, we cannot remind ourselves too often that his philosophical position was intermediate and non-categorical. In his memoirs of the composer, Eugène Berteaux put it this way:

> Having some foreboding of the divine through the unfathomable qualities of the universe, Fauré, upon whom the pagan poetry of ages past had cast its spell, resisted all preconceived denials and deemed it more noble, and above all, more modestly human, to bow before the majesty of the Unknown.[150]

Similarly, Van Lerberghe himself would confess to Albert Mockel in 1898, "I'm no mystic, . . . but I am not an irreligious man in the ideal sense of the word. *Could any poet be?*"[151] Van Lerberghe would, however, answer that question affirmatively within two years, when he began to declare his atheism with no apologies. But the poet's moment of ambivalence, when he felt unfaithful but not irreligious, or wavered between religious illusion and poetic fiction, captures something of Fauré's situation in the first decade of the twentieth century.

Fauré left us a good number of statements about the nature of religious music and his own goals as a composer of such music. Of his actual beliefs he wrote much less, but the evidence of his creative work goes some way to redress the lack. Nonetheless, we must admit that he never described or defined in words what "religion" meant to him, nor did he ever go so far as to declare, "I am an atheist," "I am a believer." His discretion allows for prudent guesses, but we can never be certain of wholly understanding his personal conception of humanity in relation to divinity at any point in his life. Through his views of nature and society, through the formation of his vocation, through his artistic taste and his statements about sacred music, and through his music itself, we can measure his thinking against the spiritual tendencies of his time. But to study Fauré's religion is finally to approach the private thoughts of a man who himself was probably never quite sure.

check

nor did he announce his 'political views e.g. re Dreyfus the litmus test of its time

6 Fauré the elusive

" ... les trajectoires illimitées et sûres, tel état opulent aussitôt évasif, une
inaptitude délicieuse à finir ..."[1]

Mallarmé, "La Musique et les Lettres" (1894)

Fauré's religious beliefs leave historians a generous margin of uncertainty.
The same may be said for his attitude toward his own compositions, about
which he revealed little. And some technical aspects of his art seem to escape
our grasp repeatedly: how does his music make its effects, and does it build
on a consistent set of methods or habits?

After describing Fauré's artistic and personal beliefs, his teaching, his stylistic tendencies, and his influence, one quality always remains: his elusiveness. Fauré loved a threshold, an evanescence, or a point of instability; his
art cannily resists exact determinations and categories. This closing chapter
seeks to consider Fauré's elusiveness from two perspectives: as an aspect of
his technique and as an aspect of his personality as an artist. This double
approach will move from the concrete to the abstract but will also allow for
reflection between them. Within the discussion of technique, I have chosen
to focus on certain aspects of Fauré's rhythmic practice since it has been
neglected in favor of harmonic analysis of his music. To amplify the value
of this focus, I place it in the context of some rudimentary observations
about the most elusive traits of Fauré's style in general. The second half of
the chapter turns to a discussion of what the French philosopher Etienne
Gilson calls "poiesis," a term more recently employed by Jean-Jacques
Nattiez.[2] Poiesis speaks to the making of art, in contrast to its reception or
interpretation, and embraces all the deliberations, intentions, and labor a
creator invests in producing a work. Poiesis also includes an artist's attitude
toward the physical evidence he leaves behind, and what limitations he
places on the aims and elucidation of his creativity. In these areas we shall
again find Fauré making a practice of evasion.

In *Style and Music*, Leonard Meyer includes a quick, masterful "sketch-
analysis" of Wagner's music which shows how its various traits re-enforce
one another to produce a distinctive style.[3] Such "interdependent" traits
may also be observed in Fauré's mature treatment of melody, harmony,
texture, and rhythm; indeed, the ways they re-enforce one another make
Fauré's musical style distinctive. If I could do for Fauré what Meyer does for

Wagner in a mere five pages, I would. But since some of the individual parameters of Fauré's style, in contrast to Wagner's, have yet to be studied in depth, it would be more difficult to summarize their salient features and form a global impression. In this chapter, instead, I wish to examine one of those features, metrical multivalence, in some detail while making reference ⟩ to other, reinforcing parameters.

Nonetheless, an overview of those elements of Fauré's musical language which seem most distinctive will help to put his metrical style in perspective. The list, of course, is provisional, incomplete, and personal:

1. He compromises major–minor tonality with modal usages in both melody and harmony. But rather than building pieces or sections out of a single modal collection, he takes advantage of common scalar segments as well as chromaticism to move freely between the eight diatonic modes, the whole-tone scale, and other collections.

2. He is largely able to replace the dynamism of tonal modulation with fleeting tonicization. The free modal interchange mentioned above provides for a multitude of scales built on the same tonic. By shifting nodal points within these scales, Fauré is able to refocus our perception of the tonic while retaining a constant center in the background. The effect is to reconcile rapid inflections on the surface with tonal unity at a deeper level.[4]

3. He allows weak harmonic progressions founded on linear part-writing to predominate over strong progressions and root movements by fourth and fifth.

4. Within continuous figurations of a constant pulse, he treats metric groupings as servants of the phrase so as to deny the regular, cyclic recurrence of the same metrical unit.

To generalize further, these elements of Fauré's style work together to lower the level of tension or dynamism on the surface of his music. Some of the strategies and traits listed above may be found in the music of other composers, especially among Fauré's contemporaries. But their interaction, I believe, sets his music apart and makes it immediately identifiable. The combination is peculiar, and it yields peculiar results.

1 Scattering stars: Fauré's diffusion of meter

In a little essay from 1943 entitled "French Rhythm," Virgil Thomson asked the question, "What makes French music so French?" His answer was surprisingly specific: "Basically, I should say it is the rhythm."[5] He cited no particular composition or composer in support of his pronouncement. Thomson seems to have so internalized his knowledge of French musical culture and its habits as part of his own personality that he felt comfortable airing authoritative generalizations about a whole national tradition without any definite reference to specific works. Moreover, the article, at least in its later paragraphs, is concerned with interpretation rather than composition, and so Thomson mentions performers rather than pieces. Yet Thomson's insights, as we shall see, speak to compositional technique as well as to interpretation. He warrants his understanding of "French rhythm" on a national tradition, which he sets in contrast to those in Italy and Germany:

> In the Italo-German tradition, as practiced nowadays, the written measure is likely to be considered as a rhythmic unit and the first count of that measure as a dynamic impulse that sets the whole thing in motion. In French musical thought the measure has nothing to do with motion; it is a metrical unit purely. The bar line is a visual device of notation for the convenience of executants, but the French consider that it should never be perceptible to the listener.[6]

Thomson goes on to say that a special duality of accent and meter, by which they are conceived as independent from one another, "lies at the basis of French music" and is the source of a rhythmic life he finds unmatched in any other style except jazz:

> The French conceive rhythm as a duality of meter and accent. Meter is a *pattern of quantities*, of note lengths. *Its minimum unit in execution is the phrase.* Accent is a stress that may occur either regularly or irregularly; but in any case, it is always written in. It may occur on the first note of a measure, but in well-written music it will usually appear more frequently in other positions, since any regular marking off of metrical units tends to produce a hypnotic effect. French music, unless it is written for the dance or unless it aims to evoke the dance, has no dynamic propulsion at all. It proceeds at an even rate, unrolls itself phrase by phrase rather like Gregorian chant.[7]

Although I wish to emphasize the strengths, not the weaknesses, of Thomson's insights for the following discussion, some readers will be troubled by at least three points in the passage above. Let us begin by airing some objections that will allow us to separate the wheat from the chaff.

First, we need not accept Thomson's characterization of Italian and German music, which is blunt. Likewise, his reification of a single "French rhythmic tradition" from plainchant to the twentieth century must be understood as a journalistic convenience.[8] Second, Thomson's notion of *accent* is excessively limited. It is difficult to take seriously his assertion that accents need always be "written in," unless he meant "written in" in the more general sense of "composed." Accentuation may occur as an effect of voice-leading, harmonic structure, textural density, duration, register, or, indeed, "any perceptible deviation from an established pattern."[9] Expanding our understanding of "accent" to meet the norms of modern theories of rhythm only deepens the potential of Thomson's broader idea of French rhythm as a duality of meter and accent. Third, Thomson associates the repetition of regular metric patterns with dance music and what he calls a "hypnotic effect." But one could argue that the lack of "dynamic propulsion" he notes in French music, "unroll[ing] itself phrase by phrase," is equally susceptible to a hypnotic effect. Musical hypnosis may be produced by a number of methods, some of them apparently contrary (dance and chant, for example, or beating and droning), but we need not concern ourselves with categorizing perceptual effects of rhythm on this basis. It is more meaningful to discuss perceptual effects in the context of specific compositions.

Over and above these shortcomings stands Thomson's pivotal definition: he calls meter a "pattern of quantities" whose "minimum unit of execution is the phrase." This definition is, to my knowledge, unique, and it is remarkable on two counts. First, it omits the standard assumption of *regularity* in those patterns, and, second, it takes the *phrase*, not a divided pulse, as the perceptible span through which performers and listeners might sense metrical boundaries. We may fruitfully bring this conception of meter to bear on the music of Fauré in particular. The following analyses are partial but seek to latch onto details that demonstrate the complexity and elusiveness of Fauré's metrical practice.

In our general histories of music, Fauré's legacy is usually linked to harmonic innovation when it is evaluated at all. His use of rhythm or meter has attracted little attention and passes for conservative. Even specialized books and articles on Fauré's music have overlooked his use of rhythm and meter, though recent studies by Robin Tait and Timothy Jackson have gone some way to breaking new ground.[10] Part of the problem is that his compositions present an appearance of perfect regularity on the page (as a glance ahead to the musical examples will attest). Fauré almost always uses ordinary time-signatures, and he only occasionally changes time-signatures within the larger sections of his works. As if to re-enforce the semblance of regularity and repetition, Fauré often carries a single rhythmic pattern across extended sections of his music. These patterns seem to be cast in conventional, not to say banal, figurations: repeated chords, arpeggios, scales, and the like. There is nothing in the outward appearance of Fauré's music to suggest metrical complexity, and indeed, there is a great deal to suggest dullness.

Yet anyone who undertakes to perform this music realizes, if only viscerally, that something peculiar is afoot. A singer who prepares her part in Fauré's Requiem in solitary study will experience a disjunction between the straightforward metrical appearance of the music on the page and her experience of performing for the first time amid the other choral and orchestral lines. Singers and pianists encounter similar difficulties in performing Fauré's songs, particularly the late ones, when they first meet in rehearsal. These difficulties crop up with regard to both pitch and duration. The singer suddenly finds that a falling minor third, an interval so innocent on the page, becomes hard to pitch within the harmonic context of the accompaniment, while the pianist can no longer feel his downbeats in a series of simple measures in $\frac{3}{4}$ time.

As Robin Tait observes, Fauré's "apparent conservatism . . . hides a flexible rhythmic technique which constitutes a prime element of his musical language."[11] Tait tackled the question of Fauré's rhythmic style in a substantive chapter of his doctoral dissertation in 1984. He discusses a range of examples from different periods of Fauré's creative life and shows how deliberately Fauré's harmonies and rhythms conspire to "cross the barline." He also rightly emphasizes Fauré's tendency, especially in his later songs and chamber music, "to establish pulse without meter."[12] However, Tait does not bring his observations of rhythmic complexity to bear on a specifically metrical analysis. The discussion offered here bears out Tait's general observations. I also intend to show that Fauré's music is even more "equivocal" and flexible than Tait suggests.

The metrical structures of Fauré's songs are of particular interest, for not only do they frequently ignore the barline, but do so multivalently. That is, implicit metrical patterns cross barlines in different ways at the same time. Thus, the series of beats making up a particular musical phrase may be perceived as different meters on different hearings. Fauré achieves this multivalence through subtle mismatches between the metrical signals contributed by duration, voice-leading, harmony, and melodic contour. He resorts much less frequently to accents produced by dynamics, register, or textural density.

In the song "Aurore," composed in 1884, the opening phrase is susceptible to a surprising number of distinct, simultaneous metrical interpretations. Yet the notation in common time and uniform chordal accompaniment conceal these subtleties behind a framework that could hardly be more conventional. This song beautifully embodies the accentual homogeneity of Fauré's style. On close inspection, the chords in the piano and the rhythms in the voice, which both appear so ordinary, prove remarkably independent of the notated meter. The whole first section of this song, culminating on the verb "trame" ("weaves") at measure 11, unfolds a seamless harmonic fabric, perhaps inspired by the diaphanous imagery of Silvestre's first stanza:

Example 18. "Aurore," op. 39, no. 1 (1884), mm. 1–5. Interpreted metrical groupings.

Des jardins de la nuit s'envolent les étoiles,
Abeilles d'or qu'attire un invisible miel,
Et l'aube, au loin, tendant la candeur de ses toiles,
Trame de fils d'argent le manteau bleu du ciel.

[From gardens of the night stars fly away
like golden bees drawn to some invisible honey,
and dawn, far off, unfolding the whiteness of her curtain,
weaves the blue mantle of the sky in silver threads.]

Indeed, there is a curious intimacy between Fauré's musical style and this stanza, whose verbs of evasion (*s'envoler*), attraction (*attirer*), expansion (*tendre*), and integration (*tramer*) seem to mirror his methods of writing. Fauré achieves a peculiar quality of motion in "Aurore," gliding through harmonic arrivals and pushing the listener ever forward. Like Silvestre's scattering stars, metrical accents lose their gravity. Between the obfuscation of meter on the fourth beat of measure 2 and the clear return to a duple pattern on the second beat of measure 5, Fauré creates a series of pulses which may be grouped in as many as five different ways. How does he avoid metrical definition within these measures despite an absolutely regular pulsation? How does he disarm the dynamism of the downbeat? The answers lie in harmonic rhythm and voice-leading.

To address these questions in technical terms, let us look to the reasons behind each of the labeled metrical groupings shown in Example 18. The numbers associated with brackets in the example indicate groupings of quarter-note beats.[13] We shall move from the lowest layers of the diagram to the top, but there is no particular significance to the ordering. Indeed,

Fauré's freely overlapping rhythmic layers are far removed from the orderly hierarchy of a classical phrase. Even the highest, "hypermetrical" layer in this example (D), which would normally reconcile or incorporate all the subordinate metrical patterns, only coincides with selected points of articulation. (In this sense, it is not really correct to call it hypermetrical.) Moreover, the groupings shown in Example 18, for all their variety, could hardly be considered exhaustive.[14]

Layers A1 and A2 are particular to the piano part. They are, of course, nonetheless heard "across" the voice and contribute to the multivalence of the phrase when it is performed with both parts. The simple alternation of tonic and dominant harmonies in the piano accounts for the first grouping of four beats. This grouping contradicts Fauré's notation, which begins with a quarter-rest in the first measure. (This upbeat effect has probably mystified many a pianist, and we shall return to it later.) In measure 2, the meter seems immediately to shift when the neighbor-tone (or dominant-eleventh) chord is sounded twice in a row, and the motion through successively weaker inversions produces a grouping of three.[15] The following groups begin with a return to the tonic chord, now in first inversion. Here, in measure 3, A1 and A2 diverge. A2 proceeds in duple groupings founded on the regular return of harmonies built on the tonic, or the two non-dominant triads with tones common to the tonic. Thus, the duple groupings, beginning with measure 3, fall on I, I, iii, I, and vi. The groupings of A1, in contrast, are triple and more attuned to the bass-line itself than to its harmonization. The division beginning on the last beat of measure 3 arrives with a triad on the subdominant, which is the first triad in root position to appear since the tonic alternation heard at the start. This grouping also coincides with the point where the vocal line reverses direction from its registral peak. The following group of four begins with another root-position triad, this time on the tonic; the two beats before it, on the dominant degree in the bass, form an anacrusis (m. 4). This cadence from dominant to tonic is the strongest progression in the phrase and produces a downbeat on the tonic in all the interpretive layers shown in Example 18 except for the hypermetric one. With the tonic chord at the end of the first vocal phrase, layers A1 and A2 effectively merge again. The last four chords are clearly duple, since the roots (F–C D–A) form a pair of falling fourths.

The remaining three layers (B, C, and D) represent alternative hearings of the vocal line. However, the piano accompaniment is so formed as to allow (and sometimes re-enforce) these alternative hearings. In other words, it is possible to hear any of the three metrical interpretations of the vocal line when the piano accompaniment is sounding. This extraordinary fact underscores how thoroughly Fauré's harmonic discourse has escaped the weight of customary metrical accents.

The downbeat that begins layers B and C is dictated by the alternation of chords we already noted in the piano part and coincides with layers A1 and A2. Layer B proceeds with another duple group, thanks to the repetition of the same rhythmic pattern. What happens next in layer B is more complicated. Are the following five beats truly continuous or subdivided? Fauré's notated barline and the prosodic accent on "é-*toi*-les" argue for three plus two. The registral reversal mentioned earlier, peaking on D over the subdominant, argues for two plus three. In either case, the larger grouping of five is controlled by conjunct and disjunct motion in the bass; the grouping is conjunct but marked off on both sides by disjunct motion. The final group of four (mm. 4–5) marks the end of the vocal phrase and is shaped by the piano accompaniment.

Layers B and C diverge only in their second and third metrical groups, which each cover seven beats: where layer B has $\frac{2}{4}$ then $\frac{5}{4}$, layer C has $\frac{3}{4}$ then $\frac{4}{4}$. The difference lies in the extension of the first grouping from two to three beats, and this extension, forming layer C, depends almost entirely on the will of the singer. A singer who is especially sensitive to the text will be conscious of the caesura in Silvestre's line, which falls between "nuit" and "s'envolent." The latter word should receive an important secondary stress within a line of Alexandrine verse. In an effort to mitigate Fauré's wayward placement of the article "les" on the registral peak of the phrase, the singer may throw back even more emphasis on the syllable "-vo-" and thus create a prosodically appropriate accent through timbre, intensity, or a slight lengthening of the note A. This overall conception of the phrase, moreover, may also lead the singer to take the initial rest in measure 2 seriously and de-emphasize the first two eighth-notes of the vocal line. Such an interpretation, in fact, could produce yet another metrical reading: beginning in the second bar, $\frac{2}{4}$, $\frac{2}{4}$, $\frac{2}{4}$, $\frac{2}{4}$, $\frac{2}{4}$ (the last pair perhaps better as $\frac{4}{4}$). This interpretation coincides with Fauré's notated barlines, or is only offset from them (at "s'envolent") by the relatively subtle difference between duple and quadruple groupings. Perhaps Fauré's seemingly casual metrical organization of his musical content is actually meant to serve the poetic rather than the musical structure – to provide a guide to declamation.[16] If so, then Fauré used his barlines to notate that which is most difficult to notate and goes beyond music itself: poetically intelligent singing. To arrange the barlines to serve this aim, particularly in a composition which seems otherwise to call for the abandonment of barlines, perhaps shows an ill-judged trust in an imperfect tool. In any event, the tension between the demands of the musical patterns and the poetic patterns only adds another form of multivalence to one's experience of the song.

If a singer might take the rest at the beginning of the second measure seriously, then might a pianist do the same in the first measure? In that case, both performers in turn would undertake to begin their parts with silent downbeats: a difficult feat at the *beginning* of any piece; the more so where harmony and melodic contour work against the attempt. The final, hypermetrical interpretation, layer D, imagines an effort by the performers to think through longer groups and builds on the prosodic accents suggested in the preceding paragraph. This layer may nonetheless be deemed more theoretical than practical. Layer D divides the total span of eighteen beats, from the initial rest to the middle of measure 5, into three groups of six, of which the second one is weakly unified and tends to subdivide into two plus four. The initial duple alternation of chords suggests that these hypermeasures be interpreted as $\frac{3}{2}$ rather than $\frac{6}{4}$. In practice, the division between the first and second hypermeasure depends on the singer's effort to articulate a downbeat on the second syllable of "jardins," the low C. The next segment follows the singer's scalar rise through the octave, overreaching the C and turning back. This second grouping can also be reinforced by the pianist: layer A2 provides for a division at the end of measure 3, which coincides with the end of the second hypermeasure.

All the metrical interpretations under consideration here, including the last hypermetrical segment, meet again in the middle of measure 5, where the continuation of the vocal part on an upbeat leads to a passage of alternating chords – duple and, at last, metrically unambiguous. The respite from complexity, however, is brief, and the meter will begin to scatter again in measure 7.

The intricacy of the first phrase and its partial analysis here hint at the major proportions a complete study of the song would assume. Here we shall limit ourselves to one more point about "Aurore." Fauré himself proves the elastic nature of his meter at the point of return to the opening melody (Example 19, mm. 32–35). The form of the song is ternary, but here the opening passage is notated in $\frac{3}{4}$, the time-signature of the middle section. Fauré only reverts to notation in common time for the last measure of the phrase (m. 35, which is the equivalent of m. 4). The inconsistency warrants the general argument that the interpreted meter can differ from the notated meter and that Fauré's malleable harmonic language readily adapts itself to regrouping. Because Fauré has chosen a ternary form, at this point he must adapt his melody to new words. Although the harmonic content and structural melodic tones are the same as in the first section, Fauré makes an important change in rhythm by lengthening the G in measure 34. This change adjusts the prosody so as to provide a longer note on the accented syllable of "astres." However, this durational change does not really justify

Example 19. "Aurore," op. 39, no. 1 (1884), mm. 32–35.

the time-signature; neither measure 33 nor measure 34 form a convincing grouping in $\frac{3}{4}$. The strongest impression is of a duple grouping, which suggests three measures of $\frac{2}{4}$ or, returning to our interpretation of this same passage in layer D, one large measure of $\frac{3}{2}$. The F and the G cling to one another as a duple grouping, but Fauré undoubtedly went against the grain of the music and separated them with a barline because he wanted the singer to observe the caesura (at the comma) and to bring the effect of a downbeat to the first syllable of "astres."[17] Once again, then, prosodic signals and actual musical shapes vie for realization in Fauré's equivocal notation.

The inconsistent notation of meters in the parallel outer sections of "Aurore" suggests several things about Fauré's compositional process. First, the discrepancy may mean that Fauré the scribe was a step behind Fauré the composer; that is, he did not notice the inconsistencies or was simply uncertain of how to notate particular metrical groupings in his music. Second, Fauré's lack of precision in this regard suggests that metrical complexity was a *byproduct*, not a goal. The locus of Fauré's experimentation in this period seems to have been a certain *quality of motion*, whose outward impression is most strongly directed by harmonic ideas. Whether this innovation had its source more in the composer's harmonic sensibility or in his increasingly discerning realizations of French poetry and its accents is not clear. More than likely, both factors led him to develop in this direction. However, it seems likely that if *meter* had been his primary object of innovation, he would have been more careful or inventive in notating his ideas.

∗

In his recent book on metrical dissonance in the music of Robert Schumann, Harald Krebs provides the foundation for a more precise understanding of rhythmic phenomena in a broad range of nineteenth- and twentieth-century music.[18] Krebs discusses two main varieties of metrical dissonance, "grouping dissonances" and "displacement dissonances," terms he adopts from the work of Peter Kaminsky. The former term designates the interaction of two or more metrical layers whose cardinalities are different: for example, a background pulse of quarter-notes interpreted as $\frac{2}{4}$ in one musical layer and $\frac{3}{4}$ in another. The latter term describes metrical layers that have the same cardinality, but in which different points of accentuation cause a displacement or "misalignment" of one or more of the layers in relation to another.[19] One need only look at the scherzo of Fauré's Second Piano Quartet, or the first three pages of his Fifth Barcarolle, to see that both these types of metrical dissonance play a role in the music of Fauré, too. However, the aspects of Fauré's metrical practice under discussion here – aspects I believe are fundamental to his mature style – stand apart from Krebs's models of metrical conflict and cannot be addressed with his theoretical categories. This analytical distance stems from at least two important differences between Schumann's and Fauré's metrical styles. First, one almost never finds more than two levels of what Krebs calls grouping dissonance in Schumann's metrical style, whereas in Fauré's music one regularly finds three or more levels of metrical superimposition (as in "Aurore"). A second distinction is far more important. Whereas Schumann's metrical layers, however displaced or superimposed, proceed by constant groupings, Fauré's implicit metrical patterns characteristically proceed by unpredictable, irregular numeric groupings.[20] This difference has major stylistic implications. Where Schumann's metrical dissonances lend his music a special rhythmic verve, beating more dynamically than ordinary, metrically accented music, Fauré's multivalence has the opposite effect of dissolving the beats and attenuating their dynamic force.

This attenuation can be observed more consistently in Fauré's music after about 1903. We shall turn now to two songs from *La chanson d'Ève* which will show a later stage of Fauré's metrical technique and allow us to evaluate its controlled interplay of strain and stasis. In these songs, as in all Fauré's later work, one no longer finds the inconsistencies in notation or prosody that we encountered in "Aurore." The workmanship leaves no room for doubt.

In "Roses ardentes" (1908), Fauré's notation in $\frac{3}{4}$ masks a metrical multivalence that is not sporadic but radical. Let us begin by taking a large view of the song. Fauré's strategy seems to have been to subordinate metrical accents to important harmonic goals. These goals take the form of cadences on the tonic which mark the end of the first and second stanzas of the poem (mm. 9 and 17). Such cadential alignments between harmony and notated meter become increasingly frequent across the rest of the song; this momentum runs parallel to Van Lerberghe's poem. Eve begins in a state of heightened perception; here the music is silvery, mysterious, and unstable, as Fauré captures the perfumes of the "immobile night." The song ends, in

Example 20a. *La chanson d'Ève*, op. 95, no. 3: "Roses ardentes," mm. 1–9.

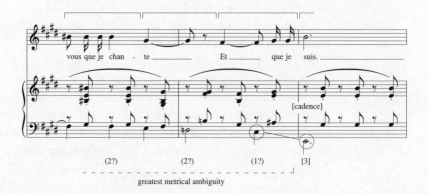

greatest metrical ambiguity

contrast, in exuberant affirmation as the harmonic and metrical structures come more and more into phase, and Eve, turning toward the sun, affirms her soul's union with a pantheistic divinity.[21] Consider the first nine measures (Example 20a). The vocal part, on its own, is consistently in $\frac{2}{4}$, a metrical dissonance against $\frac{3}{4}$ that comes back into phase with the notated measure every three groupings. This grouping of 2+2+2 imparts a structural regularity that heightens each end-rhyme. The right hand of the piano part also contributes an element of regularity, but Fauré places its chords on

Example 20b. *La chanson d'Ève*, op. 95, no. 3: "Roses ardentes," mm. 1–9, renotated.

the offbeats and thus assures himself a space without downbeats; over this weak pulsation, he can shift shapes more freely. Indeed, even this right-hand part, which seems to function as a conductor, begins to drift from the notated meter at measure 4 thanks to Fauré's manipulation of the harmonic rhythm. The left-hand part forms the most irregular metrical layer. First of all, it is an errant bass that does not keep its register; it weaves in and out of the chords of the right hand. Second, it conforms neither to the notated $\frac{3}{4}$ nor to the singer's implicit $\frac{2}{4}$, but proceeds in the following pattern:

$$\frac{2}{4} \ \frac{2}{4} \ \frac{3}{4} \ \frac{2}{4} \ \frac{5}{4} \ \frac{2}{4} \ \frac{3}{4} \ [\frac{2}{4}? + \frac{2}{4}? + \frac{1}{4}?] \ \frac{3}{4}$$

The metrical independence between this bass and the vocal line, the outer parts, is remarkable and makes this song unsettling to perform. Example 20b shows what this passage would look like if renotated polymetrically.

Measures 6 through 8 command a particular challenge: there are too many possible levels of metrical patterning for a clear beat to emerge. The piano part evades accentuation so willfully that the metrical groupings posited with question marks in Example 20a seem almost arbitrary to me. Perhaps if we ignore the piano part and focus solely on the duple groupings of the vocal line, we can bridge the plurisignificance of measures 7 and 8. But there is a diversion on the bridge, because Fauré at this same moment applies durational accents to two weak syllables in the poem: the mute syllable of "chante" and the word "et" at the beginning of the next line. Up until this point, Fauré confined his durational accents in the voice to the end-rhymes ("ar-*den*-tes," "nuit"), and the regular recurrence of these accents helped us to follow the duple groupings of the vocal part. The sudden shift away from the natural stresses of the poem (especially with the dotted quarter-note on "et") introduces a long value where we were not expecting one. The surprise subtly bumps us forward, like a syncopation, and adds to the general sense of metrical disorientation.[22]

What most insures the disorienting effect of the passage, however, is the way Fauré matches the moment of greatest metrical ambiguity to the moment of greatest harmonic instability. Earlier, I said Fauré subordinates metrical accents to the harmonic discourse, but it would be more accurate to say that he has co-ordinated harmony and meter in two parallel processes. In both parameters, a state of limited stability is complicated, pushed toward disorder, and then reclaimed. Consider measures 5 through 8: as the bass part begins to lose all metrical profile, Fauré likewise increases pressure on the tonal center, E major. A series of non-diatonic pitches (D-natural, B-sharp, A-sharp) are sounded: their incursion suggests a modulation. The B-sharp and A-sharp in particular surround the dominant degree of the scale and lead the listener to expect B major to be established in measure 9. In measure 8 Fauré even forms a harmony (a half-diminished seventh on A-sharp) that would function as a dominant in B major. Instead, the music proceeds abruptly, with contrary leaps in both outer voices, to the tonic E-major triad. We now hear it in root position for the first time. This tonic intervention is strangely "disengaged": it denies the preceding structures of modulation. The effect is rather like seeing a support knocked out from under an object only to understand a second later that invisible wires held the object in place all along. In retrospect, we also understand that what would have been the dominant harmony in B major (m. 8) turned out to be a Lydian subdominant in E major. This denial of modulation comes, of course, right at the end of the three measures of highest metrical multivalence. The sudden restoration of both harmonic and metrical regularity *at the same time* in measure 9 is completely unexpected. But it also comes as a great relief after Fauré has taken the singer and pianist to the verge of metrical disintegration. This process will set some listeners on edge, but it provides enough momentary stability to prepare us for a second excursion along a parallel path (mm. 10–17), where, once again, tonic "reason" rescues metrical fancy at the last minute.

Our next example, "Eau vivante" ("Flowing Water"), was composed in 1909, a year after "Roses ardentes." At first glance, this song presents a twofold metrical complication: against the notated $\frac{3}{4}$, the voice proceeds in

$\frac{2}{4}$ while the scalar pattern in the inner part of the accompaniment implies a grouping every two measures in $\frac{3}{2}$ (Example 21).[23] One could object that this arrangement of metrical layers is only complex in relation to the notation, for the double measures of $\frac{3}{2}$ in the piano can also be divided into three subsidiary units of $\frac{2}{4}$ (the eight sixteenth-notes for each scale from E to E), and their divisions match the duple groupings in the voice. This metrical arrangement is consistent for the first four measures. However, Fauré introduces two independent, complicating factors.

First, at some point between the last beat of measure 4 and the last beat of measure 5, the vocal part slips into a new metrical position, so that from measure 5 onward the patterns of $\frac{2}{4}$ in the voice no longer coincide with the half-note beats of $\frac{3}{2}$ in the rising scales, but on their offbeats. This shift, metrically dissonant with respect to $\frac{3}{2}$, now coincides with downbeats in the notated meter, the hitherto ignored $\frac{3}{4}$. Thus, this shift repays its moment of ambiguity by lending greater metrical security to the singer, whose six-beat phrases (counting quarter-notes) now begin at barlines. It is significant that this metrical slip in the vocal part occurs just where the harmonic motion begins to go astray. The tonality is ambiguous from the start, suggesting C major and E Phrygian at once. With the last beat of measure 4, Fauré leaves this bifocal modality behind and begins a process which will lead the song slowly upward in parallel, non-functional harmony. Measures 4 and 5 are hard to divide into metrical patterns thanks to this sudden harmonic distortion and the incursion of whole-steps into the bass-line.

Second, there is a more general distortion of meter at work from the very beginning of the song. I refer to the outer voices in the piano part. These verticals form seventh chords and augmented chords around the scalar ostinato at irregular intervals. The accentual interference of these verticals is so strong that it undermines our perception of the regular $\frac{3}{2}$ pattern set up by the scales in the inner part. Yet rather than producing a higher level of metrical tension, the shifting durations of the verticals neutralize the metrical organization altogether. Through the interaction of these three distinct elements – the rising scales, the singing line, and the irregular verticals – Fauré paradoxically achieves an extraordinarily homogeneous flow. Despite all these complexities, or because of them, the silences between the singer's phrases – the *rests* – become the listener's main point of reference. That is, Fauré's treatment of rhythm and meter shifts our durational perception of the song to the level of the phrase. This perception is enhanced, as in "Roses ardentes," by Fauré's use of durational accents in the voice for each of the end-rhymes ("*clai*-re," "vi-*van*-te," "*ter*-re," "*chan*-tes"). Robin Tait rightly observes that Fauré's melodic phrases "are faithful to the poetry, not to a musical metre," and writes out the entire vocal part without barlines to illustrate his point.[24]

Example 21. *La chanson d'Ève*, op. 95, no. 6: "Eau vivante," mm. 1–8.

One could go further in identifying such complementary strategies in this song. For instance, notice how Fauré combines pitch with duration in the first four measures to dilute downbeats. Both the voice and the upper part in the piano rock gently between E and G. But the two parts are so arranged that the piano and the voice never arrive on E or G at the same time; the use

Example 21. (*cont.*)

of duration here is almost perverse in its indirectness. When these two upper voices finally unite in pitch and duration, it is on F-sharp: another perverse evasion. The F-sharp should clarify the mode or key of the song, but it does the opposite: without functional direction or harmonic support, it cannot be identified as either the second degree of E minor or the Lydian fourth of C. Far from stabilizing the tonal meaning of the song in favor of one of these tonics, the F-sharp clouds the diatonic modality and pivots into a passage of non-functional parallel voice-leading which will last until measure 13. Once again, Fauré has used a point of resolution in one domain as a point of departure in another.

A moment ago I said that Fauré shifts our durational or articulative perception of the song to the level of the sung phrase. I thereby return to Thomson's point about French rhythm. Fauré's phrasal organization in these songs has three implications that Thomson, as a lover of lyric art, would perhaps have thought more important than any specifically musical processes. First, the sense of homogeneous flow in "Eau vivante" matches a poetic idea: the piano part, for all its abstract calculations in the metrical and harmonic dimensions, embodies the bubbling, endlessly changing sameness of the flowing water that Van Lerberghe's poem salutes: "you who pass by and go, unceasingly, never weary, | from the earth to the sea and from the sea to the sky …" Second, the way metrical complexity serves to focus our perception on the singer's phrase has a special result in Fauré. The evolutions of the poet's verse, unfolding phrase by phrase, ultimately seem to control the whole musical process. This control may be an illusion, since one can see how much labor Fauré expended on the accompaniment, but the resulting excellence of the lyric delivery and of its pacing cannot be denied. Third and finally, what happens within these carefully spaced, unfolding phrases is equally significant for the linguistic quality of Fauré's

setting, for the weakening of metrical downbeats within his phrases provides a solution to the notorious problem of French prosody. French tends
to equalize syllabic stress and create accents almost entirely through longer
duration at the ends of syntactic groups or phrases.[25] Fauré's deliberate suppression of the downbeat allows all those evenly spaced, unaccented French
syllables to tumble smoothly through the melodic line until they reach a
point of proper emphasis. He seems to have arrived at this individual solution only gradually over the course of his career, and he did not treat all
poems with the same pliancy.

The interdependent traits that have concerned us throughout this discussion are strongly in evidence and contribute to our experience of Fauré's
music as "elusive." In both "Roses ardentes" and "Eau vivante," Fauré ener-
vates metrical dynamism through weak harmonic progressions and parsi-
monious voice-leading. In "Eau vivante," the constant but uneven
oscillation between seventh chords a minor third apart (mm. 1–4) provides
neither a tonal center nor any sense of progress. The harmonies that follow
evade functional identity; they scatter rather than center our tonal expectations at precisely the point when metrical ambiguity could be rescued by a
clear harmonic outline. Fauré's flowing water will not be stilled to abide our
scrutiny but has already passed out of reach. The harmonic structure of the
first nine measures of "Roses ardentes," reduced to its constituent tones in
Example 22, shows minimal movement away from the tonic triad and an
avoidance of the dominant. Fauré exploits a technique of horizontal slip-
page which takes advantage of common tones and stepwise motion. Every
chord includes the mediant degree, G-sharp, and, in fact, the only disjunct
motion between successive sets is the minor third going from C-sharp to E
at the cadence. The chain of harmonies has more the character of a series
with internal symmetry than a true progression of contrasting or counter-
balanced harmonies. Even the more conventional harmonic syntax of
"Aurore" is molded from notably smooth voice-leading: across the span of
Example 18, all the dissonances but one form neighbor tones, passing tones,
or common tones, and there is far more conjunct than disjunct motion in
the bass. In all three of these songs, the rhythmic sameness and limited registral contrast only complement the harmonic and contrapuntal properties
of the music. Finally, there are no accent marks or dynamic changes notated
in these examples. Fauré seldom offers such obvious clues to metrical
multivalence.

These traits, taken together, are typical of Fauré. The result of his metrics
is a kind of floating continuity whose forward motion depends on a generally low level of tension. We may characterize this tension as low when we
compare Fauré's songs from La chanson d'Ève to contemporary works, such

Example 22. *La chanson d'Ève*, op. 95, no. 3: "Roses ardentes," mm. 1–9, harmonic content.

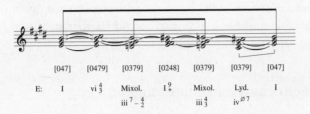

as Schoenberg's early songs and chamber music. But it is more accurate to say that the level of tension within a work by Fauré is narrowly differentiated but powerful, proceeding from one long-range tonal goal to another in waves. In an insightful analysis of Fauré's melodic style, James Kidd remarked that the composer sought a "quality of strong, undifferentiated motion, motion with an underlying forcefulness and unstoppable momentum, motion of calm intensity." For Kidd, this distinctive quality of homogeneity suggests "the sensation of walking in water, with its constant and fluid resistance demanding a constant pressure in response."[26] The comparison serves Fauré's treatment of meter almost equally well.

One could reasonably ask why Fauré notated his music within a framework of regular, equal measures. The technique we have observed is supremely fluid and ambiguous, almost, as Thomson might say, antidynamic. Perhaps the answer lies there. The avoidance of deliberate accents and the neutrality of his notation in such passages is precisely part of what makes multivalence possible. A dynamic accent, explicitly notated, can create one deviation from the notated meter but will usually not brook any competition. The notation of mixed meters, too, tends to lead interpreters to stress the beginning of each new metrical unit.[27] By hiding metrical complexity behind a bland façade of equal measures, Fauré may have sought to increase the chances of preserving distinct metrical "levels" in the different instrumental or vocal parts, and also to prevent performers from externalizing and fixing meter through strong dynamic accents. A special kind of internal tension, arising from doubt, inheres in these conflicting melodic and metrical implications. The notation of such patterns in mixed meters could encourage definite accentuation where there should be a kind of inner suspense, slipping continuously, as it were, from beat to beat. Finally, even as Fauré's music grew in metrical complexity, his habits of notation grew more and more ascetic. The plainness of his scores in the later years is yet another aspect of the poietic discretion we shall consider momentarily. A composer who could publish a four-page song without any dynamic markings in 1909 had, in comparison to almost any of his contemporaries, an uncommonly chaste approach to notation.[28] Fauré hid his novelty in plain sight, behind the barlines and meters passed down by tradition. He probably considered polymetrical notation pretentious; in any case, he seems to have done everything to avoid it.

2 Poietic evasion, aesthetic imprecision

Fauré is perhaps most elusive in his attitudes toward poiesis: his thinking and his methods. He avoided explaining or commenting on his works, he erased many of the traces of his compositional labors, and he cultivated a deliberate distance between his music and the material world around him. His silence, or what we might call his poietic discretion, usually makes it difficult to deduce his personal beliefs and exact intentions, and the evidence of his letters and criticism is surprisingly limited. Yet beyond his literary silence or disinterest, there is his music. Compared to Fauré's philosophical intentions, his music offers itself to us as an integral achievement. Yet it, too, throws up barriers to those who would seek traditional hermeneutic satisfactions. These are the themes we shall confront in the remainder of this chapter.

In the spring of 1902, Louis Aguettant went up the lift at 154 Boulevard Malesherbes to pay Fauré a visit. The ostensible purpose of the visit was to do research for an article on Fauré's songs, but the article was really a pretext arranged by a friend so that Aguettant could satisfy his personal fascination with the composer's work. He had already been introduced to Fauré and spoken with him on two previous occasions over the past three weeks. But this was his first opportunity to interview the composer without interruptions. Aguettant felt nervous and tongue-tied as he entered the composer's own study, but Fauré, with his "charmante bonhomie," so often attested by his contemporaries, soon put the young admirer at his ease.

Aguettant subsequently wrote a letter to André Lambinet that allows us to learn all these details. "I got him to do a real interview on his songs, and especially on *La bonne chanson*."[29] The interview, however, turned out to be harder work than Aguettant expected. He had not counted on Fauréan evasions:

> I asked him about certain intentions and about the full significance of certain themes, but he denied having ever looked for such things: "People often attribute to composers intentions they never had in mind."

"Did I abuse my rights of exegesis?" the interviewer asked himself, "Or is it rather Fauré, loath to dismantle the machinery of his masterpieces? But it gets better." Unabashed, Aguettant asked the composer whether the cyclical themes of *La bonne chanson* had a "literary value" or were simply "musical arabesques."

> Fauré gave me this disconcerting answer: "Themes? But there's really only one that comes back across the songs of *La bonne chanson*. It's a theme from one of my other songs, 'Lydia.'"

Aguettant was disconcerted because anyone who studies *La bonne chanson* will find at least six recurring themes (really motives), all of which are joyously drawn together in the final song:

> Only *one* theme in *La bonne chanson*? I couldn't let that go. At my request, Fauré put the score on his piano. "And this theme," I said to him, "and this one? So these recurrences are no more than coincidences?" Bit by bit, he "admitted" two or three more themes . . . But I had to put my finger on every one of these similarities, force him to recognize, one by one, all these brothers whose likeness he seemed to have forgotten. Sometimes he played over the passage as if to recall it to memory. "It's a book of songs I composed ten years ago . . ." Of course, I apologized for inflicting this vivisection on him, but I don't regret it a bit.[30]

We know that Fauré did not like to write about his own music. Apparently, he was reluctant to discuss it in private, too. His plea of ignorance is suspect. Fauré had arranged *La bonne chanson* for string quintet and piano in 1898; he himself had performed it with Maurice Bagès as recently as March 1902, three months before this interview. His protest, that he composed the songs ten years earlier, is evasive. Fauré may not have been conscious of every thematic relationship and its location, and certainly he could have "forgotten" some of them. But could this consummate craftsman have forgotten, or ignored, almost everything about the construction of a work that achieves a full-blown thematic summation in its final movement? I doubt it. Aguettant's letter is a unique document: the young enthusiast came up against Fauré's poietic discretion and wore it down. One suspects that only a few others had the pluck or persistence to make this effort.

In the introductory chapter of this book I mentioned two brief comments from Fauré's letters that likewise revealed his aversion for self-analysis. Even in the context of a private communication, Fauré cut off digressions on his own music with a kind of brusque embarrassment, going so far as to accuse himself of pedantry for writing a mere three sentences about the form of "Le don silencieux" (see above, p. 2). This aversion, always costumed in modesty or humor, seems to have extended beyond the poietic dimension: not only was Fauré reluctant to divulge his working methods, he was also reluctant to reveal himself – his inner feelings as musician. In an interview, Emmanuel Fauré-Fremiet recalled that

> my father felt embarrassed when he sensed growing emotion in his audience
> as he played the piano. He had become the center of everyone's attention; the
> moment when he felt "something was going on," he could not continue and
> abruptly cleared the atmosphere with some joke, often an outrageous one,
> such as putting his feet on the keyboard, and thus provoked general laughter.
> At such moments my mother wanted to die.[31]

One supposes that Emmanuel Fauré-Fremiet was referring to his father's
performances at home or in one of the more informal salons, as there is no
record of such behavior in Fauré's public concerts! In any case, the anecdote
reveals a man who was acutely afraid to allow his own introspection to be
observed. Rather than risk an intimacy that would have disturbed him and
perhaps broken down a carefully guarded wall of privacy, he hid the depth
of his sensibility behind a mask of lightheartedness and affability.
Fortunately, he also poured that sensibility into his compositions, where he
could shape it at will. Composition, unlike performance, provides the illusion of being unobserved.

*

If, however, poiesis becomes a performance, if the stages of composition are
exposed to the public scrutiny, the illusion of control recedes. A stranger
peers into the workshop, and a finished masterpiece suddenly returns to its
humble origins amid sandpaper, glue, and sawdust. Or worse, it becomes an
object of scholarly idolatry.

> I find it less than agreeable that just anyone (assuming anyone still cares
> about my books) will be allowed to go through my manuscripts, to compare
> them to the final text, to draw inferences from them about my working
> methods, the evolution of my thought, etc., which will always be wrong. The
> whole thing vexes me a bit.[32]

When Proust pondered the fate of his poietic residue in 1922, he was torn
between these worries and the potential profits he could reap by selling
manuscripts and corrected proofs in his own lifetime. "I have not yet been
able to form a very clear idea about this matter," he added. For the moment,
he instructed his publisher to suspend any negotiations and to keep all the
proofs and manuscripts. Proust, however, had made up his mind about his
notebooks, if not his proofs, before. Between 1916 and 1917, he had asked
Céleste Albaret to burn thirty-two of his oldest notebooks: "He gave them
to me to destroy one or sometimes two or three at a time, as he came to have
no further need of them."[33] It was natural for Proust to begin with the materials whose destruction would emancipate his literary legacy from its most
primitive compositional layer. Nattiez believes that "if only [Proust] had

time to experience the feeling that his work was finally complete," he would have done away with all his later notebooks, drafts, and papers.[34]

Proust's idealism, his extreme scruples over privacy, and, most importantly, the very philosophy of the novel whose compositional states were in question, all suggest that Nattiez is right. Here we will recall the distress of Proust's protagonist, Marcel, over the signs of "diligent labor" and fabrication that seemed to bring the existence of individual genius and its "more than human reality" into question (chap. 4, p. 161). If Proust's novel was to fulfill its own thematized ideal, Nattiez observes, it had to offer the reader a work "perfect, self-contained and independent of the conditions (both biographical and technical) in which it was created."[35]

Here again, Fauré and Proust meet, but without either knowing the other's intentions. In 1924, two years after Proust wrote the letter cited above, Fauré wrote his wife:

> [When I am back] in Paris, each day I shall set about giving you, so that you may *burn* them, all my sketches, all my rough drafts, all those things of which *I wish nothing to subsist after I am gone.* This worry haunted me while I was ill. You will help me to appease it.[36]

Perhaps nothing is so revealing of Fauré's attitude toward poiesis than this directive: the last paragraph of the very last letter he wrote. His final artistic trace is one of erasure. Nectoux attributes Fauré's destruction of his sketches, drafts, and disavowed works to a combination of motives: "not to leave to posterity pages which he considered to fall short of his aspirations" and not to be "surprised by anyone in the most tormenting parts of his creative activity."[37] Both Fauré and Proust were acutely aware of living in a culture that collected artifacts and resurrected dead works and fragments; the twin cults of historicism and celebrity had combined powerfully in the nineteenth century to produce an eager market for manuscripts and personalia. A well-known public figure, whether an artist or a politician, eventually had to confront these posthumous possibilities.

Ironically, except for the thirty-two early notebooks mentioned above, Proust's sketches and manuscripts survived, and in great profusion. More than eighty notebooks and hundreds of pages of drafts and proofs were found after his death. Because Proust was both relatively young and perpetually ill, he may never have reached a moment of final determination on the matter of all the different states of his literary materials. Fauré, however, largely succeeded in his aim. As Nectoux writes, "the large number of manuscripts that survive include very little in the way of drafts, sketches or unpublished items."[38] Only seven of Fauré's sketchbooks escaped incineration. In truth,

Fauré is an exceptional case: very few artists who have wished to obliterate their preparatory materials have succeeded, for the conditions of destruction are exacting. In Fauré's case, everything fell into place: he had finished his last work, the String Quartet, he knew death was near, and yet he had enough time to come to a decision about his estate. Proust, in contrast, had not brought the final books of his novel to a comparable state of completion before his final illness laid him low.

Perhaps most important of all, Fauré had in his wife, Marie, an ideal angel of destruction. It is no accident that he asked her, not his sons, to aid him in his final task. Marie Fauré had never realized her aspirations as an artist and felt it bitterly, living in the shadow of her husband and her father, the sculptor Fremiet. She never hesitated to express her fits of rancor and resentment to Fauré. "You once accused me of wanting to puff myself up at your expense," he wrote her after receiving one of her irate letters in 1921. "I only hoped that the growth of my reputation . . . brought you some comfort and alleviated a little the bitterness and vexation that the man, such as I am with all my failings, has caused you."[39] Fauré's final plans for the destruction of his materials were exquisitely conceived, for we may imagine what Marie Fauré might have felt at burning page after page of her husband's work. In this act, Fauré may have meant to offer Marie a symbolic compensation for some of the failures of their marriage and the emptiness of her own artistic career. She would more than stoke the cleansing fire when he grew weak and tired.

In Fauré and Proust, at the most general level, we find the same motivation: a "utopian effort to efface the poietic dimension" of creativity, to transcend the material labor of craftsmanship and leave as little trace of it as possible in the finished work.[40] Whether the destruction of sketches constitutes an act of modesty or of pride is difficult to decide. Schoenberg meticulously preserved his working materials for the benefit of posterity; he assembled an archive whose "usefulness to history" was for him a foregone conclusion. This sense of historical importance reveals Schoenberg's enormous self-regard, but his willingness to open the cabinets of his workshop to the public bespeaks his humility, too. Fauré never presumed to identify with a particular historical destiny, and insofar as he destroyed his sketches to preserve his privacy, he cuts a figure of refreshing modesty. But his act of destruction also shows his desire to control the shape of his legacy, to lock the doors of his workshop and fashion his own future image, and here we see his pride and his consciousness of his own achievement.

*

We may size up Fauré's evasion of poietic scrutiny from the kind of evidence given above. The elusiveness of his music is harder to explain because its qualities stem from an intermingling of technical properties and Fauré's general orientation as an artist. To understand the technique, we may analyze such features as metrical irregularity, part-writing, tonality, and so on. To the broad aesthetic dimension of his elusiveness, all matters, practical or philosophical, make their contributions, but it would seem particularly pertinent to ask how his music construes its relationship to the material world that surrounds the composer. The most profound and abstract statements Fauré committed to writing seem to converge on this very question. We recall these two exceptional utterances from earlier in this study. In "thoughts of a sort so imprecise that in truth they are not thoughts," in things "untranslatable by literary means," Fauré recognized the stuff of musical imagination. Imagination, in turn, "consists of trying to give expression to everything we could want in the way of something better, everything that goes beyond [*dépasse*] reality." Thus, "art, and music especially, consists of raising ourselves as far as possible above what is."[41]

These sentences are brief but profound. They seem to distill years of thought into a few words and suggest that Fauré more than once pondered the relation between his art and the world around him. A propensity for distancing, *dépassement*, and elevation in Fauré's aesthetics is unmistakable. It is less apparent how Fauré thought music moved from reality to "something better" and whether reality in some form might still be seen or felt from that elevated position. Here, perhaps his music again provides the best answer. Recall that Fauré's comments on "thoughts of a sort so imprecise that in truth they are not thoughts" formed part of his attempt to describe the path that led from "something external" (reality or, here, the recollection of reality) to art. The childhood memory of bells in a French village, ringing across a "vague reverie" in the composer's imagination, found expression in their musical echoes, and echoes of echoes, in the slow movement of his Second Quartet (see chap. 1, pp. 41–46). But does Fauré exalt reality or reject it? On this more specific point he seems to elude analysis. I can offer not much more than limited speculations. On the one hand, Fauré's evocation of something "better," "beyond," and "as far as possible above what is" suggests a desire for escape that overwhelms what is present and real. On the other hand, in Fauré we find nothing like the wholehearted rejection of the world and human society which marks the lives and works of some of his contemporaries, such as Villiers de l'Isle-Adam, Huysmans, and even Proust. Further, Fauré's belief in an artistic quest for "something better" and "nonexistent things" did not entail a repudiation of nature, as it did for Ravel; on the contrary, Fauré's letters show that nature provided him with moments of delight which resembled those accorded by art. In order to imagine some zone of coherence in which Fauré's relation to reality existed, we might consider an analogy with the aesthetic theory of Jules Combarieu. Combarieu believed that music, in "thinking without concepts," does not discard the objects that otherwise would be represented conceptually but rather penetrates them more profoundly.[42] In the same way, perhaps, Fauré's music, "going beyond reality," does not discard reality, but places it at a spiritual extreme that allows us to escape and then to return to reality in a new light. Thus an idealized art could, if we wish, renew our contact with the beauty of the world.

We may leave the thin atmosphere of speculation for lower ground. The relationship of art to reality in Fauré's work may also be approached through those observable elements of his artistic "program" which disclose his ideal of beauty. For if art could exalt or transform reality, Fauré's artistic preferences placed limits on that reality in advance of the transformation. It is clear that he did not think music should try to capture the squalid, the banal, or the ugly. In 1908, when Fauré enthusiastically reviewed the revival of Lalo's ballet *Namouna*, he included this revealing comment:

> [*Namouna*] lacks for nothing: neither brilliance nor verve nor merriment, and yet its artistic dignity remains perfectly intact. To translate vulgarity with vulgarity would undoubtedly have been more in keeping with the doctrines of *verismo*; at any rate, it would have been easier. But Lalo thought – as certain of our musicians still do, too – that music is not suited to every task.[43]

Everything we know about Fauré (including his reviews of *Zazà* and *I Pagliacci*) indicates that he counted himself among those who still agreed with Lalo. No quality could be more foreign to Fauré's music than vulgarity. His work has been described as subtle, reserved, and formally balanced, in his own time as well as today. Perhaps these terms have been overused, limiting his style in attempting to epitomize it. We need to remember the other faces of his music: the unbuttoned Valse-Caprices, with their almost frantic alternations between verve and languor, or *Pénélope* and the First Cello Sonata, which contain some of his most violent music. Yet the epitomizing qualities of reserve and subtlety are more than platitudes: they capture a dominant strain in Fauré's artistic ideal.

His highly cultivated sense of style forged a barrier between his musical imagination and any lurid colors, broad humor, or scenes of modern life or naturalistic details. Significantly, all of his dramatic works are set in the past, and most of them in the distant past. He could not, of course, tailor every artistic detail to his liking in collaborative works for the stage. Thus, Fauré's letters reveal to us that a banal couplet for one of the suitors in *Pénélope* caused him a whole day of musical struggle; such was the deadening effect a single detail could have on his sensibility.[44] It is not surprising that he avoided or eliminated such literary material when he could. His songs allowed him more control in this respect, and, as a whole, though there are a hundred of them, they are not particularly varied in their emotions, moods, objects, and settings. He gravitated toward intimate, lyrical poetic texts whose impressions could be reflected through a state of soul, rather than through realistic or descriptive details. "I try above all to bring out the general sentiment of the poem in preference to the details," he told Louis Aguettant.[45] There is very little word-painting in his music. He saw no need to re-create musically those external features of reality already expressed in the poem. The following excerpt from his response to a journalist's survey ("What should be set to music?") captures the essence of his approach:

> Verlaine is exquisite to set to music. Look, there's that short poem by him, "Green," which contains a cool, melancholy landscape, but the landscape is only the atmosphere, an environment. The harmony should apply itself to *underscoring* the deep feeling only *sketched* by the words. Likewise, in "Il pleure dans mon cœur comme il pleut sur la ville . . ." the sound of the raindrops is only an accessory. The lamentation, lovesick and troubled, is the essential thing.[46]

The poets he chose to set to music most often were Silvestre, Verlaine, and Van Lerberghe. He did not represent them in their fullness, but he did not strip them of human feeling either. Fauré's ideal was a poem that made its emotions felt through a kind of screen: a surface of sensual details that blurs but also deepens the undercurrent of passion, loss, or reverie.

To Fauré's mind, conserving this unimpeded interplay of surface and depth required a balance between the general and the specific, a balance that certain kinds of external details could easily dislocate by bringing the listener permanently to the surface. Thus, he consistently expunged references to the commonplace, the local, or the modern when he encountered them in an otherwise suitable poem. He aimed to place human emotions in as timeless and universal a context as possible. In *La bonne chanson*, for instance, he is delighted to find the lover's joy embodied in the soft light that "dances from the earth to the clear firmament," "the green return of sweet florescence," and "the unchanging azure where my love laughs"; these images in "L'hiver a cessé" take his music to the heights of passion. But Verlaine's second strophe finds no place in the song; the entire quatrain is omitted:

> Même ce Paris maussade et malade
> Semble faire accueil aux jeunes soleils,
> Et comme pour une immense accolade
> Tend les mille bras de ses toits vermeils.[47]

[Even this sullen and sickly city of Paris
Seems to welcome the youthful sunbeams,
and as if in an immense embrace
extends the thousand arms of its red roofs.]

There were a number of reasons Fauré omitted this strophe. First, Nectoux has rightly mentioned Fauré's wariness of epithets; the composer believed that a musical setting tends to magnify them to absurd proportions.[48] Second, he did not need an element of contrast at this point in the song. The only other negative image in the poem, the "saddest heart" named in the first strophe, did not move Fauré to darken the general sunshine of the song even for a moment. That sad heart, as Verlaine says, "must yield | To the immense joy strewn through the air," and this injunction abetted Fauré's custom of "bringing out the general sentiment of the poem in preference to the details." But the paired adjectives "maussade et malade" would be difficult to absorb into a song of unbridled happiness without making some sort of expressive contrast, and Fauré wanted "L'hiver a cessé" to have unstoppable momentum until the sudden, intimate relaxation of the final address to the beloved ("ô Toi . . ."). Third, the very naming of the French capital in the poem reminds the reader of the autobiographical context of Verlaine's poem and intrudes the only modern, urban note into a song whose imagery is otherwise drawn from timeless nature. This is the most important reason for Fauré's deletion and brings us back to our general observations: Fauré wanted to free the song from any specific indication of time or place. He probably would have omitted a reference to Paris even if it were not attached to a personification or gloomy adjectives.

It is even less surprising that Fauré's *Bonne chanson* bears no trace at all of Verlaine's sixteenth poem, which describes the poet's path through Parisian squalor: "the noise of the cabarets, the filth on the pavement," and soon "the creaking omnibus," "police agents," "smashed-in asphalt" and gutters draining into "overflowing sewers."[49] He also excludes any line or stanza whose tone is anecdotal. Finally, as part of his avoidance of the naturalistic detail, Fauré was extremely sensitive to colloquial language. He omitted the first strophe of "N'est-ce pas?" and the third of "Puisque l'aube grandit," both of which refer to "des sots et des méchants," a phrase one is more likely to hear from an angry nursemaid than a lyric poet.[50] The mixture of the banal and the refined is typical of Verlaine's vocabulary but was not to Fauré's taste. The composer told Aguettant that the mere words "on veut croire" were enough to stop him from setting "Le son du cor s'afflige," a poem he otherwise liked.[51] The phrase, which occurs twice in the poem, is slack and colloquial, but hardly vulgar.

In order to avoid upsetting the magical balance between sensuous surfaces and inward emotion in his songs, Fauré erased details that clashed with his vision, and the result is a persistent vagueness of time and place. This general tendency explains Fauré's fondness for poems set in gardens or other centers of quiet observation, settings which usually solve in advance the problems that arise from the sorts of external specificity that worried him as a composer. Gardens have served as spiritual centers from the earliest times. From their protected spaces we may direct our gaze inward, toward our thoughts and feelings, or outward, toward a beautiful detail: light shining through the calyx of a flower, a lover's hand, the sky between the leaves, the crossing of clouds and stars, whatever is serene and desirable. Jankélévitch calls this attitude of contemplation "l'élan de l'âme vers l'indétermination."[52] Fauré's music so often seeks to find this place of contemplation, to create a landscape unto itself, which cannot be precisely fixed in time or space.

If we are too quick to equate reality in art with the kind of treatment of external details sought by the practitioners of realism and naturalism in the later nineteenth century, we are bound to find an "absence of realism" in Fauré's music. But realism and naturalism, as movements in art and literature, conceived a narrow definition of reality, too. "Reality does not mean realism until the nineteenth century when the realistic school proclaims that the only way to transcribe reality is to make a faithful human copy of it."[53] Fauré, of course, felt out of sympathy with the aims of naturalism and realism, though he made a sincere effort to appreciate the works of Bruneau and Charpentier. If we remember that there are worlds of reality beyond realism, we can acknowledge both the limits and the presence of reality in Fauré's art.

*

Because Fauré believed that "music is not suited to every task," the limits he placed on the interaction between music and reality in his lyric works might be explained as an exclusion of the "unmusical," or what he deemed unmusical. In his instrumental works, he shunned not only the "unmusical," but more generally, the "extramusical." With only two exceptions, the only titles he gave these works were generic ones. He made no use whatsoever of "programs" in his music. In presenting and describing his own music, even in conversation, he refrained from alluding to anything extramusical with astonishing consistency, so that no images, stories or "traditions" became attached to his instrumental works, even after his death. His letter to Marie Fauré about the slow movement of the Second Quartet is perhaps the only exception. In general, he seemed to believe his listeners should approach his music as free of "literature" or premeditated analogies as possible.

Fauré sometimes had to struggle with a publisher, Edgard Hamelle, who believed that titles improved sales. Hamelle was perhaps genuinely baffled by his composer's unwillingness to co-operate over such a small matter. Thanks to these difficulties, we have detailed evidence of Fauré's attitude toward titles. Fauré wanted the set of eight short piano pieces, op. 84, to be published without even generic designations. He wrote Hamelle in 1902:

> I assure you that it is impossible to give these pieces specific titles, and I am sure that, at this point in the development of music, there is no longer any need. The title "Piece" is perfectly acceptable, and a numeral will suffice to designate it.
>
> There are many works which have not suffered in the least from the lack of a title.[54]

We sense impatience in these two paragraphs, as if Fauré had to repeat himself on this question too many times. He picks up the theme yet again in a postscript: "Saint-Saëns completely agrees with what I am telling you about titles." There is almost a touch of desperation to a fifty-seven-year-old man appealing to the authority of his former teacher for support, though it may be explained by the fact that Saint-Saëns and he actually were together in Béziers at the time. But Fauré was right to worry: Hamelle was a stubborn businessman, and the composer lost this battle. The pieces were published with titles (mostly generic, "Capriccio," "Improvisation," but also "Allégresse," and in any case the genres were mostly ones Fauré did not use in other pieces). That Fauré in no way sanctioned these titles and even resented them is proven by a letter to Micheline Kahn from fourteen years later, in which he deliberately refers to them by numbers and adds, "These pieces did not have titles; it was Hamelle who baptized them."[55]

In the list of Fauré's chamber works, with all their classical and generic designations, one is puzzled to come across a single exception, a short work entitled "Papillon," op. 77, for cello and piano. Once again, the publisher had his hand in it, as Nectoux has explained. This piece, composed in 1884 but only published in 1898, testifies to another pitched battle between Fauré and Hamelle:

> The composer wanted to call it *Pièce pour violoncelle*; the publisher, with an eye on sales, preferred *Libellules* (Dragonflies), which appears on the contract dated 14 September 1884. [Julien] Hamelle had to wait fourteen years before Fauré would agree to it being published as *Papillon*, and even then the composer was angry: "Butterfly or dungfly," he declared in exasperation, "call it whatever you like."[56]

Fauré's missives to his publisher show his kinship with Chopin, whose loathing of titles is well-known, but Fauré's purism placed him at a considerable distance from the vast majority of his own contemporaries. Even the high-minded Saint-Saëns did not despise descriptive and picturesque titles in his non-programmatic music. Fauré's attitude toward titles was not a matter of chance or habit, but reflects a deeply considered aesthetic position intimately related to his whole understanding of musical experience. Fauré's student Louis Aubert reported to Bruneau that Fauré "went so far as to deplore certain titles that he found disrespectful to music."[57] This frame of mind shows that Fauré viewed the question of titles in a broader aesthetic context.

There are only two instrumental works for which Fauré himself chose distinctive titles. These are the two exceptions mentioned earlier: *Dolly*, a suite for piano duet, whose six movements also carry titles, and *Une châtelaine en sa tour …*, a late work for harp. Both pieces have two significant traits in common which have not, to my knowledge, been pointed out and which may explain their exceptional treatment by Fauré. First, *Dolly* and *Une châtelaine* were conceived as gifts for a particular person: Emma Bardac's daughter, Hélène, called Dolly; and the young harpist, Micheline Kahn. Second, the titles Fauré chose largely derive from personal names or private, whimsical allusions. Some of the titles in *Dolly* are clear enough on their own ("Berceuse," "Tendresse"), but others would be unintelligible to listeners outside of a private circle. For example, the second movement, "Mi-a-ou," as Nectoux discovered by looking at the original manuscript, has nothing to do with cats, but is a portrait of Hélène's older brother, "Monsieur Raoul," in a child's pronunciation. (On the manuscript it is written less cryptically as "Messieu Aoul!")[58] The title of the suite as a whole is more forgiving of public scrutiny: "Dolly" serves equally well to honor its dedicatee and suggest a world of childhood. As for *Une châtelaine en sa tour …*, the title is actually a quotation, the second line of Verlaine's poem "Une Sainte en son auréole," which Fauré set as the first song in *La bonne chanson*. This poetic borrowing has sent many commentators down the wrong path, for, contrary to various claims, there is no common thematic material between the song and the piece for harp. Nectoux comes closer to my view when he muses: "It is not impossible that the work has some hidden significance, or that it is a musical (and ironical) portrait of its dedicatee."[59] The answer lies, I think, in a pedestrian detail. As we learn from a letter in verse that Fauré addressed to Micheline Kahn in 1916, she lived in "a lovely but rather high fifth-floor apartment," whose ascent a man in his seventies would well have remembered and probably gave rise to much facetious grumbling.[60] Thus, it seem to me that the charming Micheline herself, in her high apartment, is the "châtelaine" of the title, "a lady in her tower." As with *Dolly*, the title serves a private and a public function at once, for the delicate and distant quality of the music accords well with an image of "nobles Dames d'autrefois" (borrowing another line of verse from the same poem) suggested by the title.

It is certainly good to be reminded of Fauré's sense of humor in the context of this discussion of lofty artistic ideals. From these two works, we may also draw a more general understanding of Fauré's exceptional use of titles. The violinist Hélène Jourdan-Morhange drew a comparison between the brand of wit behind Fauré's numerous letters in verse and Mallarmé's famous postcards, in which the recipient's name and street address are worked into an ingenious quatrain.[61] It is a happy comparison, as it suggests how we might see *Dolly* and *Une châtelaine* as an extension of Fauré's private communications. They are, in some sense, occasional pieces that stand in a special relationship to the main line of his production. Occasional art is not necessarily unworthy of a wide audience, however. Mallarmé identified his occasional works (which also included verses inscribed on visiting cards, fans, pebbles, and Easter eggs) as *vers de circonstance*, a body of work distinct from his *poésies*, but whose level of invention and craftsmanship was high enough to merit resurrection in printed form. He even gathered the texts from some of his postcards into a small publication, an expanded edition of which he was still planning at the time of his death. Likewise, Fauré was willing to allow these two occasional pieces, whose circumstantial qualities are not so obvious as those of a literary work, to join his catalogue of published works. It would seem that the special, personal nature of the relationship between the composer and the dedicatee in both cases licensed the use of titles in Fauré's mind.[62] We might even say that the titles in these two works are an extension of the dedications at the head of the work – and printed dedications are a public gesture of friendship. Of course, Fauré could have removed the titles if he wished to disguise the origins of the pieces, but then he would have been taking back part of the gift.

Outside of these special circumstances, Fauré preferred, from the beginning to the end of his career, to publish his music with such titles as sonata, nocturne, barcarolle, ballade, impromptu, fantasy and prelude. This practice stamps him as a conservative. Specifically, he conserves and continues Chopin's aesthetic attitudes. The same practice, however, also ultimately marked him out as modern. By 1918, his preference for generic titles put him in harmony with the anti-impressionist reaction that made descriptive titles seem old-fashioned. Moreover, Fauré seemed to find even generic titles too definite. Had he not begun a series he wished to continue (his last works for piano were a thirteenth barcarolle and a thirteenth nocturne), and had his first publisher given him full control over the publication of his pieces, he very probably would have called his later nocturnes and barcarolles "pièces" and simply identified them by number or key. On this point, however extreme it may seem, we have the testimony of Philippe Fauré-Fremiet and the pianist Robert Lortat, and Fauré's letters to Julien and Edgard Hamelle give us every reason to believe their reports of his druthers.[63] In this respect, too, Fauré's thinking accorded with more recent tendencies: the German equivalent of "Pièce pour piano," whose neutrality Fauré thought would have best served his later music for piano, is "Klavierstück," used repeatedly by Schoenberg.

3 Fauré and Mallarmé

Fauré did not merely avoid titles. He created his mature art with contemplation in mind and lent it a syntactic density and homogeneity that demands singular attention to its sonorous content. The instrumental pieces not only leave aside imagery or literary fantasy, they are so aloof to imitative possibilities that they often seem positively discharged of concrete associations; they rebuff dramatic or prosopopoeic interpretations. Fauré's tendency to preserve the separation of instrumental music from elements that might, on another view, "come to its aid," was not a matter of indifference to him. The standards to which he held his own forms of musical expression, at least in chamber music, are known to us from the letter he wrote to his wife concerning the First Quintet, op. 89, and which we cited in chapter 3:

> Ysaÿe finds the style of the Quintet finer and loftier than that of my quartets, more completely free of any search for effect: absolute music [*de la musique absolue*]. I'm very happy that he had this impression, the more so because, at the moment, music is striving to be everything *but* music. Maybe [Roger-]Ducasse will not approve of this work, which stands completely on its own, but that's all the same to me. Deep down, I have the feeling that my methods are not within *everyone's* reach![64]

Behind this high-minded avowal lies a personal detachment from contemporary tendencies in music whose descriptive or coloristic qualities Fauré found overwrought. Fauré did not exempt even his own student, Ravel, from such criticism, and he was particularly put off by "lavish profusion" and "big effects" if he did not believe them to be justified on expressive grounds.[65] One must hasten to add that it would be wrong to think that Fauré's devotion to absolute music became exclusive or obsessive. In his review of Strauss's *Heldenleben*, he begins by admitting that he had "more than once been disconcerted by the excessive dimensions of M. Richard Strauss's symphonic poems, by the nature and number of exterior and psychological phenomena he tried to express in them," but that he finds himself "today absolutely won over by his *Heldenleben*, absolutely seduced by this work in which a fabulous orchestral efflorescence unfolds, by pages of vigor, dazzling luxuriance and exquisite charm."[66] Fauré never barred any musical medium from fully manifesting beauty and greatness: "There is no living form or medium to which a persistent, sincere genius cannot accord the eternity of Beauty."[67]

But in his own, very particular, compositional world, Fauré consciously exploited the potential of instrumental music to represent a domain of human thought which he specifically deemed "untranslatable by literary means." In an age of confessional lyricism, scenic suites, tone poems, polemical symphonies, and a hyperactive press, Fauré's works managed to keep their secrets well. Or perhaps it would be more precise to say that his compositions were conceived on the premise that the only secrets music has to keep are the ones built into our experiences of the medium itself.

Seldom has a composer of instrumental music in the past two hundred years succeeded so well in tying the tongues of his interpreters, and this state of muteness raises questions for some listeners. It might be tempting to equate the muteness of Fauré's instrumental music (or, for that matter, Chausson's or Magnard's) with a kind of intellectual or ideological emptiness, particularly if we take as our point of comparison music like Mahler's or Strauss's, so vividly charged with waves of personal and cultural associations and conscious reference to earlier models of mimesis. It is not as if program music solves the question of symbolic communication in music: the problem of signification persists. There is a difference, however, whose reasons go right back to style and syntax. Where the perplexing, heterogeneous structure of Mahler's music seems to compel the listener to ask how or what it means, the flowing, iridescent evolutions of Fauré's music seldom even provoke the question. Once Fauré's music ceases, though, the listener may be left wondering not so much *what* the music means, as *whether* it means. Mahler sometimes addresses and manipulates the sign through music, a brave act that Fauré eludes, for he saw that music is badly armed on the field of signification. His *musique pure* makes its home in that more peaceful domain of human endeavor which Valéry assigned to "les modes purs," which are the arts of sensation and sensibility. Deprived of exchange value through their lack of signifying address, their purpose lies rather in creating and awakening a particular state of consciousness.[68]

Rather than treating pure music as a medium of verbal indigence, unable to reach goals it never set for itself, I want to bring out its broader intellectual destiny by delineating aesthetic issues Fauré shared with a number of his contemporaries. In particular, one may begin to cast some new light on

Fauré's attitude toward pure music, with its natural inaptitude to reproduce reality, by listening to the reverberations that such music had on a poet of his own generation, Stéphane Mallarmé. This comparison will suggest that Fauré's preferred mode of presentation in his *musique pure* offers a rare intellectual freedom, even though it offers nothing in the way of literature, painting, geography, or politics.

For Mallarmé the experience of listening to music, and particularly the "mute" art of instrumental music, provided a key to his vision of a new poetry that instead of imitating reality would create transformative fictions whose beauty, depth, and intensity might rival reality. In music the poet beheld such fictions: a distilled essence, flashing and mobile – "a line, some vibration: synoptic, and everything is marked out." This allusive sublimation was for him "the antithesis of lyric art as it was, elocutionary by dint of the strict need for signification."[69] By this "strict" or narrow need for signification, Mallarmé referred to the explicit pointing functions of language, which stir poets to "elocution," literally, "speaking out," usually with gestures. We may see this elocution personified in Hugo, Racine, or Malherbe; it does not matter. The art of music opened up another direction, suggesting how poetry might emerge from a set of habits and functions that in Mallarmé's view had too long confined it. Instrumental music in general provides a strong model of a transformative, non-mimetic "fiction" along Mallarméan lines. Instrumental music as Fauré conceived it offers one of the strongest exemplars imaginable of such fiction. Beyond Fauré's more general poietic silence, his attempts to eliminate from his music times, places, or preordained images whose precision would allow it to signify manifest his concern, independent of Mallarmé's but parallel to it, to abolish the creator's elocutionary persona from the finished work.

Abolishing the elocutionary persona, however, does not mean abolishing the personal. (Who would seriously maintain that Mallarmé's poems lack a personal style?) If music seems capable of offering the contemplative modes of lyricism without the anecdotal presence of a speaking author, it does so through a "language" which is not language, a distinctively musical syntax. Mallarmé recognized this. His vision of a poetry that creates itself in the image of a superior "music" is pledged to a guarantee: syntax, which is like an invisible thread on which the verbal music winds and plays:

> The pure work implies the elocutionary disappearance of the poet, who yields the initiative to words, mobilized by the shock of their inequality; they light up with mutual reflections like a virtual trail of fire on precious stones, replacing the inhaling and exhaling perceptible in the old lyrical breath or the enthusiastic personal direction of the phrase.[70]

The *elocutionary* disappearance of the poet meant an investment in expressive syntax at the expense of naturalism and self-presentation, or a focus on the words to the greatest possible exclusion of the speaker. But Mallarmé's injunction to the poet has often been reduced to some sort of call for anonymity. Perhaps literary critics have gravitated toward this extreme until recently because they did not give as much thought as Mallarmé did to how music works through an abstract syntax. For what is most musical (and Fauréan) about Mallarmé's ideal is its preference for words – rather than rhetoric, narrative, or description – as a vehicle for a personal sensibility. There could hardly be a more personal and specific literary trait than Mallarmé's own syntax, which has nothing anonymous about it. Henri Meschonnic trenchantly supports this assertion: "How astonishing that those who took the 'elocutionary disappearance of the poet' literally glorified the syntax-maker without recognizing that, for Mallarmé, syntax is subjective."[71] Mallarmé, far from denying all subjectivity, declared that "every individual brings his own prosody, new, drawing something from his breath."[72]

Mallarmé's poetics would not forgo all subjectivity. But his poetics would evade mimesis, and particularly the elaborate naturalism of his contemporaries: "Things exist; we have no need to create them; we have only to seize their relations. And the threads of these relations are what verses and orchestras create."[73] Fauré likewise felt little need to create reality again. This "untranslatable" music invited listeners, under the challenging condition of imagining without images or words, to engage in the task of re-creating content from the ground up. Mallarmé specifically, and somewhat oracularly, called this act of re-creation "the divine transposition, for whose accomplishment mankind exists."[74]

While applying terms imagined for language too literally or extensively to music can lead the critic astray, Fauré and Mallarmé meet in their lofty regard for this transposition or re-creative task. It follows that both artists worried about the power of titles to abridge the reader's or listener's act of re-creation, or merely to inhibit reverie. In "Le mystère dans les lettres," Mallarmé asks us to imagine reading without remembering "the title that would speak too loud."[75] Likewise, the pianist Robert Lortat, one of Fauré's favorite interpreters, wrote:

> Fauré's piano music deliberately refrains from specifying anything: it would displease him to impose the constraint of an initial pretext on our imaginations. Even such titles as "barcarolle," "valse-caprice," "nocturne," "impromptu," already rather vague in any case, were extracted from the composer by a publisher worried about getting a title. Smiling, Fauré almost apologizes for it: "For my part," I often heard him say, "I would have just numbered them and left it at that."[76]

Everything in Fauré's attitude toward titles, genres, and "extramusical" allusions suggests that he wanted to prevent his instrumental pieces from being weighed down with objective meaning *before they were heard*.

The terms of the Mallarméan or Fauréan "transposition," with or without titles, are precarious and demand much of the reader or listener. Such an ideal may be dismissed as inaccessible or exorbitant. But Mallarmé's conception of poetry was no more unearthly than another, and the same may be said of Fauré's conception of pure music. Indeed, both Fauré and Mallarmé were not sworn enemies of reality and nature, but keen participants in their social milieu and even lovers of typical bourgeois recreations in the French countryside. These artists sought to institute experiences of music or of language "in which reality is as far transformed as it may be."[77] Mallarmé did not want to capture what he called the "virtual trail of fire on precious stones" or "the flower absent from every bouquet" in order to deny the qualities of real jewels and real flowers. Nor did he do so "in order to give language a forbidding autonomy," but rather, as Judy Kravis observes, "to grant language the expressiveness of reality itself."[78] At the end of a piece by Fauré or a poem by Mallarmé, the reader or listener is left with much the same thing: "some illusion equal to the gaze," an aesthetic return proportional to the effort and intensity invested in the experience.[79]

Fauré was content to compose in that fluid domain between the real and the unreal without theorizing about it. Mallarmé, who pushed his poetic project to the edge of all possible realization, was certainly a more extreme artist than Fauré and one far more inclined to theorize, however enigmatically. Whereas Fauré had the advantage of being a musician who wished to compose music, Mallarmé was a poet who wished to do much more than write verse. He set himself the task of rendering music back to its original domain, as it had been on Mount Parnassus, by subsuming its most abstract expressive abilities in Poetry, the supreme Music. Mallarmé never forgot that among the arts of the Muses in ancient Greece, the sounds of the lyre had been wedded to the word. This lyre, virtual and unheard, exists in his own poetry as "the air or song beneath the text, guiding the [reader's] divination from one point to another."[80] Fauré never set any of Mallarmé's poems to music; he thus rendered his poetic contemporary a respectful sign of understanding. Fauré once commented that certain poems by Hugo and Leconte de Lisle resisted music "because their lines of verse are too full, too rich, and too complete [in themselves] for music to be able to adapt itself to them usefully."[81] Fauré may not have known that Mallarmé considered that his poems, as written, were already "set to music," but the composer's observation about Hugo and Leconte de Lisle shows that he would have immediately recognized why Mallarmé's poems did not need more music than the poet already gave them.

Fauré's attitude toward aesthetic predisposition, then, bears comparison to Mallarmé's, but it also isolated his music from that of his contemporaries. Ravel and Debussy were not so reluctant to meet listeners further down the path of communication and offered them hints and allusions to spark, if not satisfy, their imaginations. Fauré often refuses us the reassuring support of any words or explanations emanating from the author. His pure music stands at a disadvantage before a listener who has no inclination to engage in re-creation from the abstract, syntactic level. But Fauré's silence also liberates us by yielding the initiative to the music; it opens a more generous space between the work and the composer and thus brings the responsibility of the listener to the fore. It is in this attitude, perhaps, that Fauré most closely approaches Mallarmé, that other elusive bourgeois innovator.

Notes

Introduction

1 Gustave Flaubert, *Bouvard et Pécuchet* (Paris: Lemerre, 1881), p. 157.

2 Fauré to Marie Fauré, 22 Aug. 1906, Fauré, *Lettres intimes*, ed. Philippe Fauré-Fremiet (Paris: La Colombe, 1951), p. 121.

3 Fauré to Lalo, 1 Aug. 1907, Fauré, *Correspondance*, textes réunis, présentés et annotés par Jean-Michel Nectoux (Paris: Flammarion, 1980), p. 269.

4 Even here, nonetheless, a distinction might arise when comparing the aims of critical texts (reviews, for example) to speculative ones (philosophical essays) by the same writer. If there are significant differences between these two kinds of writing, do we favor the latter as better representing "aesthetic thought" apart from "practical criticism"?

5 I am grateful to Tracy Fernandez for insisting on this point and generally helping me sort out some methodological questions that faced me at the beginning of this project.

6 Louis Aguettant, "Gabriel Fauré," *La vie intellectuelle* (Nov. 1949): 395.

7 Aaron Copland, "Gabriel Fauré, a Neglected Master," *Musical Quarterly* 10, no. 4 (1924): 576.

8 *Nineteenth-Century Piano Music*, ed. R. Larry Todd (New York: Schirmer, 1990); *Twentieth-Century Piano Music*, ed. David Burge (New York: Schirmer, 1990).

9 Robin Holloway, "Master of Hearts," *Musical Times* 136 (Aug. 1995): 396.

10 *Ibid.*

11 *Ibid.*, 395.

12 André Messager, "Gabriel Fauré," *Le Figaro* (7 June 1922): 1.

13 Louis Aubert to Louis Guitard, "Entretien avec Louis Aubert," *La table ronde* 165 (Oct. 1961): 145.

14 René Dumesnil, *Portraits de musiciens français* (Paris: Éditions d'Histoire et d'Art, 1938), p. 79.

15 As Fauré himself called them (letter to Marie Fauré, 23 March 1908, *Lettres intimes*, p. 160).

16 Jean-Michel Nectoux, "Deux interprètes de Fauré: Émilie et Édouard Risler," *Études fauréennes* 18 (1981): 21. The remark comes from a letter Fauré wrote Édouard Risler in December 1904.

17 Camille Le Senne, "Période contemporaine: France," in *Encyclopédie de la musique et Dictionnaire du Conservatoire*, ed. Albert Lavignac, 1st part (Paris: Delagrave, 1913–[1914]), 3: 1774. Emphasis mine. Le Senne is quoting a letter Saint-Saëns wrote him for the entry on Fauré.

1 The question of sincerity

1 See Émile Littré, *Dictionnaire de la langue française* (Paris: Hachette, 1882), s.v.

2 Fauré, *Lettres intimes*, ed. Philippe Fauré-Fremiet (Paris: La Colombe, 1951), p. 77. I shall explain why Fauré assigned a special role to chamber and symphonic music at the end of section 4.

3 See Littré, *Dictionnaire*, who begins his first entry for "sensibilité" with "qualité de sentir." Also compare the more elaborate entry in *Le grand Robert de la langue française* (1985).

4 Fauré, preface to *La musique française d'aujourd'hui* by Georges Jean-Aubry (Paris: Perrin, 1916), p. x. Emphasis mine.

5 Kœchlin, "Du rôle de la sensibilité dans la musique," *La revue musicale* 10 (1 Jan. 1929): 205. At the beginning of this essay Kœchlin explains that it was written in 1927.

6 Kœchlin, *Gabriel Fauré* [1927], 2nd ed., tr. Leslie Orrey (London: D. Dobson, 1946), p. 82, n. 2.

7 Paul Dukas, "Adieu à Gabriel Fauré," *La revue musicale* 6 (1 Dec. 1924): 8.

8 Kœchlin, "Les tendances de la musique moderne française" [1921], in *Encyclopédie de la musique et Dictionnaire du Conservatoire*, ed. Albert Lavignac and Lionel de La Laurencie, 2nd part (Paris: Delagrave, 1925), 1: 126. Kœchlin also referred to this "strange miracle" of self-transformation in the first part of his lecture "Gabriel Fauré," published in *Le ménestrel* 83, no. 21 (27 May 1921): 221.

9 Carraud, "L'âme harmonique de Gabriel Fauré," *Musica* no. 77 (Feb. 1909): 19.

10 Claude Debussy, interview in *Excelsior* (18 Jan. 1911), reprinted in his *Monsieur Croche et autres écrits*, rev. ed. (Paris: Gallimard, 1987), p. 318. Emphasis mine.

11 Debussy, reprinted from *La revue blanche* (1 April 1901) in his *Monsieur Croche et autres écrits*, p. 27. Ravel remarked the same failing in Witkowski's Second Symphony (1910); see "Concerts Lamoureux," *S.I.M.* (12 Feb. 1912), reprinted in *A Ravel Reader: Correspondence, Articles, Interviews*, ed. Arbie Orenstein (New York: Columbia University Press, 1990), p. 341.

12 Octave Maus, "Le Théâtre des Champs-Élysées," *L'art moderne* 33 (25 May 1913): 163.

13 Carraud, "L'âme harmonique," 20.

14 Henri Duparc, response to Paul Landormy, "L'état actuel de la musique française," *La revue bleue* (26 March 1904): 396.

15 Kœchlin, "Le théâtre," *La revue musicale* 4 (1 Oct. 1922): 239. Also see Kœchlin, "Gabriel Fauré," *Le ménestrel* 83, no. 22 (3 June 1921): 234.

16 Nadia Boulanger, interview with Jean-Michel Nectoux (19 January 1974), *Études fauréennes* 17 (1980): 4.

17 Émile Vuillermoz, *Gabriel Fauré* [1960], tr. Kenneth Schapin (New York: Chilton, 1969), p. 27.

18 Aubert, quoted in Alfred Bruneau, *La vie et les œuvres de Gabriel Fauré* (Paris: Fasquelle, 1925), p. 28. Aubert provided this account of Fauré's teaching at

Bruneau's request in 1925. For related descriptions of Fauré's teaching, see Jean-Michel Nectoux, *Gabriel Fauré: A Musical Life*, tr. Roger Nichols (New York: Cambridge University Press, 1991), pp. 263–67.

19 See Vuillermoz, "La Schola et le Conservatoire," *Mercure de France* (16 Sept. 1909): 234; Louis Laloy, "Les partis musicaux en France," *La grande revue* (25 Dec. 1907): 792; and Henry Prunières, "Portraits et médaillons de musiciens," in *Cinquante ans de musique française de 1874 à 1925*, ed. Ladislas Rohozinski (Paris: Librairie de France, 1925), 2: 370.

20 I transcribe and translate this text from a facsimile of the autograph letter reproduced on a plate between pages 48 and 49 of Jean Vuaillat's *Gabriel Fauré, musicien français* (Lyon: E. Vitte, 1973). This letter does not appear in any of the printed collections, but Nectoux, in his selection of Fauré's *Correspondance* (Paris: Flammarion, 1980), p. 361, identifies the addressee as Madame de Chaumont-Quitry and dates the letter to the summer of 1899.

21 Kœchlin, *Correspondance*, ed. Madeleine Li-Kœchlin, La revue musicale nos. 348–50 (Paris: Richard Masse, 1982), p. 45.

22 See *Le grand Robert de la langue française*. Both words obviously postdate Littré's dictionary and its supplements.

23 Marcel Proust, *Le côté de Guermantes* in his *A la recherche du temps perdu*, ed. Pierre Clarac et André Ferré (Paris: Gallimard, 1954), 2: 265–66 (my translation). This volume of *A la recherche* was first published in 1920. Cf. *In Search of Lost Time*, tr. C. K. Scott Moncrieff and Terence Kilmartin, rev. by D. J. Enright (New York: The Modern Library, 1993), 3: 359.

24 Albert Bertelin, "Quelques souvenirs sur Gabriel Fauré," *Musique et théâtre* (1 April 1925): 14. I thank Edward Phillips for providing me with a photocopy of this article.

25 Fauré to his near namesake, Gabriel Faure, August 1910, Faure, *Gabriel Fauré* (Grenoble, Paris: B. Arthaud, 1945), p. 41. (I deduce the month and year of this letter from Fauré's geographical location and the circumstances recounted in the letter.)

26 Fauré, *Lettres intimes*, p. 295. The curious emphasis is Fauré's.

27 Debussy, review in *S.I.M.* (Nov. 1912), reprinted in his *Monsieur Croche et autres écrits*, pp. 214–15.

28 Edouard Dujardin, "'La revue wagnérienne,'" *La revue musicale* 4 (1 Oct. 1923): 157.

29 Paul Landormy, *La musique française après Debussy* (Paris: Gallimard, 1943), p. 41.

30 Max Jacob to Yvon Belaval (undated letter), in Belaval, *Le souci de sincérité* (Paris: Gallimard, 1944), p. 153.

31 Fauré, preface to *La musique française d'aujourd'hui*, p. xii.

32 I am indebted to Jean-Michel Nectoux for helping me trace Fauré's enigmatic reference. Gounod had addressed himself to young artists, warning them, "Do not be taken in by all those grand, hollow words: Realism, Idealism, Impressionism – and, who knows, maybe one day we shall also have

Intentionism. These terms all form part of the nihilistic glossary of what we may agree to call *Modern Art*" (quoted in Léon Vallas, *Claude Debussy et son temps* [Paris: Albin Michel, 1958], p. 48).

33 Charles Gounod, "De l'artiste dans la société moderne," in his *Mémoires d'un artiste* (Paris: Calmann Lévy, 1896), pp. 284, 286.

34 Sincerity comes up in several of Gounod's articles and speeches. His preface to *Les soirées parisiennes de 1883* by Arnold Mortier (Paris: E. Dentu, 1884), for example, explicitly construes "the search for effect" as a false compensation for lack of sincerity (see pp. vi–vii).

35 Pierrot, *The Decadent Imagination, 1880–1900,* tr. Derek Coltman (Chicago: University of Chicago Press, 1981), pp. 16–24.

36 This aphorism occurs twice in Wilde's work. It is given as "Dorian Gray's opinion" in *The Picture of Dorian Gray* (*The Portable Oscar Wilde* [New York: Viking Press, 1947], p. 300) and as Gilbert's in Wilde's philosophical dialogue "The Critic as Artist" (*Intentions* [London: Unicorn Press, 1945], p. 149).

37 Wilde, *Dorian Gray*, p. 158.

38 Kœchlin, "Les tendances," 119.

39 See above, p. 19, or Kœchlin, "Les tendances," 65.

40 Kœchlin, "Les tendances," 61.

41 Camille Bellaigue, "Gabriel Fauré," *La revue hebdomadaire* 34 (7 March 1925): 8. Louis Aubert gave similar testimony in his letter on Fauré's teaching in Bruneau, *La vie et les œuvres*, pp. 27–28, and quoted in part above, p. 17.

42 Jean Marnold, "Gabriel Fauré," *Mercure de France* 176 (1 Dec. 1924): 499–500.

43 The article by Hugues Imbert was published under the title "Profils de musiciens: Gabriel Fauré," in *L'indépendance musicale et dramatique* 14–15 (15 Sept. and 1 Oct. 1887): 393–401 and 425–39; it was soon reprinted in his *Profils de musiciens* (Paris: Librarie Fischbacher et Librairie Sagot, 1888). I quote from pages 57 and 78 of the latter.

44 Camille Benoît, "La Messe de Requiem de Gabriel Fauré," *Le guide musical* 34 (9 and 16 Aug. 1888): 196.

45 Alfred Bruneau, "La direction du Conservatoire," *Le matin* (13 June 1905): 2.

46 Pierre Lalo, "Le *Quintette* nouveau de M. Gabriel Fauré," *Le temps* (13 July 1906): 3.

47 Kœchlin, "Le théâtre," 239. See also the lecture "Gabriel Fauré" (*Le ménestrel* 83, no. 21 [27 May 1921] and 83, no. 22 [3 June 1921]: 223, 234), where Kœchlin presents Fauré's example most explicitly as a model for the young.

48 Kœchlin, "Le 'Retour à Bach'," *La revue musicale* 8 (1 Nov. 1926): 11. The passage cited refers both to Fauré and to J. S. Bach.

49 Kœchlin, *Gabriel Fauré* (Paris: Félix Alcan, 1927), p. 208.

50 Kœchlin, "La mélodie," in *Cinquante ans de musique française*, 2: 23–24.

51 Vuillermoz, review of Fauré's Second Piano Quintet (*Le temps*, 2 Dec. 1921), reprinted in his *Musiques d'aujourd'hui* (Paris: Crès, 1923), p. 19. Vuillermoz's use of the plural "musiques" in his title again reminds us how diverse musical styles had become by 1923.

52 Darius Milhaud, "Hommage à Gabriel Fauré" [1923] reprinted in his *Notes sur la musique: Essais et chroniques*, ed. Jeremy Drake (Paris: Flammarion, 1982), p. 115. Also see Georges Auric, "Gabriel Fauré," *La revue musicale* 6 (1 Dec. 1924): 100–03. Albert Roussel's brief but overflowing homage is reprinted in his *Lettres et écrits*, ed. Nicole Labelle (Paris: Flammarion, 1987). Honegger visited Fauré in 1923 at Annecy-le-Vieux, but most of his written opinions date from twenty years later; see "*Pénélope*, un chef-d'œuvre," *Comœdia* (20 March 1943), and "Pour la musique de chambre," in his *Incantation aux fossiles* (Lausanne: Éditions d'Ouchy, 1948), pp. 133–38.

53 Arthur Symons, "The Problem of Richard Strauss," in his *Studies in the Seven Arts* (New York: E. P. Dutton, 1906), pp. 324–25.

54 *Ibid.*, p. 323.

55 Gabriel Fauré, "André Messager," *Musica* no. 72 (Sept. 1908): 131.

56 André Messager, interview, 8 March 1928, reprinted in Michel Augé-Laribé, *André Messager, musicien de théâtre* (Paris: La Colombe, 1951), pp. 189–90.

57 André Nède, "Le nouveau directeur du Conservatoire," *Le Figaro* (14 June 1905): 4. Emphasis mine.

58 Despite Saint-Saëns's intransigence about newer musical styles after the turn of the century, he admired and recognized the virtue of sincerity earlier in his career. In a eulogy of Henri Reber written in 1881, Saint-Saëns praised one quality more than any other: "sincerity, without which there is no true artist" (Saint-Saëns, "Reber" [1881], in his *Harmonie et mélodie*, 2nd ed. [Paris: Calmann Lévy, 1885], pp. 294–95). Saint-Saëns also opposed sincerity to the lure of easy success and identified it with self-understanding. His later crusades against modernity of style seem to suggest that he was not prepared to accept all the consequences of sincerity, especially full stylistic freedom. However, it is possible that he, like Gounod, influenced Fauré's attitude toward sincerity between 1860 and 1880, when he was most active as a mentor to the younger composer.

59 Fauré, preface to *Musiques d'aujourd'hui* by Émile Vuillermoz, p. vii.

60 Albert Bazaillas, *La vie personnelle* (Paris: Alcan, 1905) and *Musique et inconscience* (Paris: Alcan, 1908); Gabriel Dromard, *Essai sur la sincérité* (Paris: Alcan, 1910), *Les mensonges de la vie intérieure* (Paris: Alcan, 1910), and *Sur la sincérité en amour* (Paris: Picard, 1920). One could also include Jacques Rivière's *De la sincérité envers soi-même* (Paris: Les cahiers de Paris, 1925), written in 1912.

61 Dromard, *Essai*, pp. 4–5. Further references are parenthetical.

62 Verlaine, who resolved in the 1880s to make sincerity the central tenet of his poetic ideal, stands apart in this respect. In practice, however, Verlaine's erratic adherence to this tenet ultimately brought the possibility of literary sincerity back into question again by introducing dilemmas of self-consciousness, motivation, and duplicity. I might also mention Gide, though his attitude toward sincerity was rarely confident and never blind. For Gide, sincerity became a crucial yet relentlessly ambivalent category in literary creativity. Far more

critical than Verlaine of his own sincerity, and always cognizant of Wilde's quarrel with the idea, which greatly influenced him, Gide confronted the conceptual intricacies of sincerity even as he refused to abandon its value for his literary ideals. To discuss Gide's or Verlaine's personal and artistic sincerity in the present context is tempting but would lead us too far from the arguments at hand, which may be substantiated more succinctly by reference to Valéry. In passing, we may note that Gide himself found the perfect aphorism to express the fundamental ambivalence of sincerity in self-representation: "Whoever asserts too much that he is sincere makes others suspect his sincerity." This observation is as germane to Gide's own concerns as to the troubling case of Verlaine. See Gide, *Un esprit non prévenu* (Paris: Kra, 1929), p. 20.

63 Paul Valéry, "Stendhal" [1927] in his *Œuvres*, ed. Jean Hytier (Paris: Bibliothèque de la Pléiade, 1957–60), 1: 570.

64 *Ibid.*, pp. 570–71.

65 *Ibid.*, p. 570.

66 Interview for the *New York Times* (7 Aug. 1927), reprinted in *A Ravel Reader*, ed. Arbie Orenstein, p. 449. (All citations from this book are in Orenstein's translations.)

67 "Memories of a Lazy Child," *La petite Gironde* (12 July 1931), reprinted in *A Ravel Reader*, ed. Arbie Orenstein, p. 395. Here I have altered the translation because Orenstein always translates "conscient" as "conscious" (and "conscience" as "conscience"). Although this is literal, it is not correct. In French, "conscience" may mean "conscience," "self-conscience," "consciousness," and even "conscientiousness"; to find the best English rendering often presents a dilemma to the translator. I have tried to indicate these shades of meaning according to the context, but the reader should bear in mind that the various senses of the word may be conveyed simultaneously in French.

68 However, Ravel seems to have held a different view of sincerity when he was younger. In a pattern of thought perhaps held over from his years with Fauré, Ravel had even aspired to the condition of artistic sincerity. In a letter of 1907, for instance, he referred, with obvious commitment, both to "the sincerity of one's impressions" and "the hidden but tenacious will to attain the goal of one's pursuits." Here sincerity and art, including craft, are not in opposition but grouped into a single intention (*A Ravel Reader*, ed. Arbie Orenstein, p. 86). Likewise, in a review written five years later he defended himself against "the most serious accusation which can be brought against an artist: the lack of sincerity" (*ibid.*, p. 342, n. 2). This is a clear concession to the power of sincerity, but Ravel apparently instructed the editor to delete this paragraph before it was printed (see the facsimile of the surviving manuscript, plate 14 in *A Ravel Reader*). Did Ravel retract the phrase in order avoid looking defensive, or rather because, on second thoughts, the accusation no longer seemed to him worth warding off? Whether or not the suppression of this remark represents a turning-point in Ravel's attitude toward sincerity, it seems likely that his growing resentment of allegations of insincerity and his difficulties with

making critics understand his stylistic intentions ultimately contributed to his revolt against sincerity.

69 "The Great Musician Ravel Talks About His Art," interview with André Révesz, *ABC de Madrid* (1 May 1924), reprinted in *A Ravel Reader*, ed. Arbie Orenstein, p. 433.

70 Wilde, "The Decay of Lying," in his *Intentions*, pp. 46, 47. Although Ravel definitely knew *Salomé*, we can only guess at what else he read from Wilde. We do know that he would have had ready access to Wilde's "Decay of Lying" in either of two French translations of *Intentions* which appeared almost simultaneously – that of the novelist Jean-Joseph Renaud (Paris: P.-V. Stock, 1905), in which we find "La décadence du mensonge," or that of Hugues Rebell (Paris: C. Carrington, 1906), who rendered Wilde's title as "Le déclin du mensonge." It is also worth noting that Wilde's popularity in Paris was such that the publisher Hachette issued *Intentions* in English in October 1891 – only a few months after the first London edition.

71 Ravel, "Memories of a Lazy Child" and "An Interview with Ravel" [1931], both reprinted in *A Ravel Reader*, ed. Arbie Orenstein, pp. 395, 470.

72 Jacques Rivière, *De la sincérité envers soi-même* [1912] (Paris: Les cahiers de Paris, 1925), p. 8.

73 A comment by Ravel's close friend Roland-Manuel implies that the *abuses* of the word sincerity rather than sincerity itself irritated Ravel. See Roland-Manuel, "Des Valses à 'la Valse', 1911–1921," in *Maurice Ravel par quelques-uns de ses familiers*, ed. Roger Wild (Paris: Éditions du Tambourinaire, 1939), p. 144.

74 Valéry, "Svedenborg" [1936], in his *Œuvres*, 1: 880 (the emphases are Valéry's).

75 Dumesnil, "Le centenaire de Gabriel Fauré," p. 35. See also Jean-Aubry, *La musique française d'aujourd'hui*, p. 237: "Words indeed are tricksters and knaves . . . But music is inevitably and necessarily sincere."

76 Jules Combarieu, *La musique, ses lois, son évolution* [1907] (Paris: Flammarion, 1924), pp. 8–9.

77 *Ibid.*, 7. This definition also appears on the front cover.

78 Bazaillas, *Musique et inconscience*, pp. 81–82; see also pp. 167–68. Those who know Schopenhauer well will find that even Bazaillas, in spite of himself, is not always loyal to Schopenhauer's principles.

79 Combarieu, *La musique*, pp. 20–21. It was precisely this "excess" that endlessly fascinated one of Bergson's followers in France, Vladimir Jankélévitch, who wrote extensively on music. Curiously enough, Jankélévitch offers a streak of insight into one aspect of what Combarieu might have meant in claiming that music can "think without concepts." According to Jankélévitch, the "unexplainable" element in musical experience, its resistance to discourse and propositions, leads to a subjective disposition in the listener which induces speculation – a "féconde perplexité" – and thus a kind of thought. Music allows the reciprocation between intelligence and sensibility which Combarieu perceived because it provokes exceptional forms of awareness belonging to both

faculties at the same time. See Vladimir Jankélévitch, *La musique et l'ineffable* (Paris: A. Colin, 1961), p. 106.

80 Edouard de Hartmann, *Philosophie de l'Inconscient*, tr. D. Nolen (Paris: Ballière, 1877). The first French translation of *Die Welt als Wille und Vorstellung* appeared in 1886 in a translation by Cantacuzène, *Le monde comme volonté et comme représentation*. Bazaillas used this translation as his primary source for *Musique et inconscience*. Hartmann's conception of the unconscious was that of an impersonal "Un-Tout" circulating through all the physical and spiritual beings of the world. The conflation of this impersonal unconscious with a personal one was understandable; with a few exceptions, French writers tended to draw philosophies inspired by Indic or Buddhist sources back into a Western, individualist tradition.

81 Adolphe Boschot, "Confidences sur l'expression et la beauté" [1901], reprinted and slightly revised in his *Chez les musiciens* (Paris: Plon, 1926), 3: 206. For references to Schopenhauer and Nietzsche, see pp. 211–13 and 226.

82 Henri Bergson, *Durée et simultanéité* [1922], in his *Mélanges*, ed. André Robinet (Paris: Presses Universitaires de France, 1972), p. 103. A beautiful counterpart, fluently elaborated, to Bergson's somewhat abstruse distinction between a melody "congealed in space" and a melody "invested in pure duration" appears in a passage from Proust's *Du côté de chez Swann*, in his *A la recherche du temps perdu*, 1: 209.

83 The phrase is from Will Durant, *The Story of Philosophy* (New York: Simon and Schuster, 1943), p. 347.

84 "Bergson à Lionel Dauriac" (19 March 1913), in Bergson, *Mélanges*, p. 990.

85 For various examples in Bergson's writings, see *Durée et simultanéité* in his *Mélanges*, pp. 98–99, 103 (this last passage is given above, p. 39); *Essai sur les données immédiates de la conscience* in his *Œuvres*, ed. André Robinet (Paris: Presses Universitaires de France, 1970), pp. 69–70; and "La perception du changement," in *Mélanges*, pp. 905–06, 907, 909.

86 Bergson, *La pensée et le mouvant*, in his *Œuvres*, p. 1312. I am not the first to think that Bergson's discursive style aims to realize musical effects; his contemporaries often emphasized the musical and even hypnotic qualities of his eloquence. Jacques Morland observed that "by his way of communicating his philosophy, in suggesting what he has to say rather than saying it, he charms sensitive minds fond of nuances. Some enthusiasts attend his course as if it were an especially good concert. Bergson himself readily compares philosophy to music" ("Une heure chez M. Bergson," *L'opinion* [19 Aug. 1911], reprinted in Bergson, *Mélanges*, p. 943). Y.-G. Le Dantec also cited the musical or "harmonic" persuasion of Bergson's metaphysical discourse but considered it a danger to established social and religious institutions; see his "Réflexions d'un philistin sur la Métaphysique," *La grande revue* (10 July 1910): 1–16.

87 Bergson, *La pensée et le mouvant*, in his *Œuvres*, p. 1384.

88 Fauré to Marie Fauré, 29 Aug. 1903, *Lettres intimes*, p. 78. It was only two days

beforehand that Fauré had referred to chamber music as "the sincerest translation of a personality."

89 Fauré to Marie Fauré, 11 Sept. 1906, *Lettres intimes*, 132 (emphasis Fauré's).
There are two minor errors in this paragraph. The actual tempo marking of the
movement is not "Andante" but "Adagio non troppo." Second, as Fauré's
younger son has pointed out, the village was probably not Cadirac, which
appears never to have even had a chapel, but Ganac (Philippe Fauré-Fremiet,
Gabriel Fauré, 2nd ed. [Paris: Albin Michel, 1957], p. 156).

90 After I wrote this chapter, Basil Smallman, in *The Piano Quartet and Quintet*
(Oxford: Clarendon Press, 1994), published a similar and very perceptive analytical paragraph on this movement (p. 81), though he does not offer an explanation for Fauré's treatment of the tolling figure.

91 See above, p. 36.

92 Reynaldo Hahn, "Préambule," *Journal de l'Université des Annales* 8 (9 April
1914): 116. Hahn, of course, knew Fauré personally, but no one but Marie
Fauré had any opportunity to read what Fauré wrote of his "vague reverie."
Fauré's letters to his wife were not published until 1951.

93 Proust, *La prisonnière*, ed. Pierre-Edmond Robert (Paris: Gallimard, 1988),
pp. 360–61 (my translation); cf. Proust, *The Captive*, in *In Search of Lost Time*,
5: 505–06. Earlier in the same volume, Vinteuil's music had likewise prompted
the first mental associations between two of these three experiences – the bell-
towers of Martinville and the row of trees near Balbec (*La prisonnière*, p. 249,
quoted below).

94 Benoist-Méchin, *Avec Marcel Proust* (Paris: Albin Michel, 1977), pp. 155–56.

95 Proust, *La prisonnière*, p. 360 (my translation); cf. *The Captive*, p. 504.

96 Proust, *La prisonnière*, p. 249 (my translation); cf. *The Captive*, p. 347.

97 Proust, *La prisonnière*, p. 361 (my translation); cf. *The Captive*, p. 505. In the
present context, I should mention that these impressions of "perfumed silkiness" were specifically inspired by Fauré's First Piano Quartet, op. 15.
Alongside the beautiful simile of the geranium, Proust wrote the following in
his third notebook: "Such is the case when I first heard Vinteuil's Quartet (actually, here I'm thinking of a bit for violin as played by Capet in Fauré's First
Quartet in C Minor, no doubt in the third movement)." See Karuyoschi
Yoshikawa, "Vinteuil ou la genèse du septuor," *Études proustiennes* 3 (1979):
305, and Proust, *Correspondance*, ed. Philip Kolb (Paris: Plon, 1987), 15: 83.
Here we must recall that Proust originally conceived of Vinteuil's great work as
a *quartet* and only later transformed it into a septet or sextet (as Yoshikawa
demonstrates, which of the latter two would have represented Proust's final
intentions cannot be determined). Proust's phrase, "no doubt in the third
movement," has an air of uncertainty, and there is no need to decide exactly
which phrase of Fauré's First Quartet the novelist had in mind. Proust heard
this early work of Fauré's, probably not for the first time, at a concert at the
Odéon on 14 April 1916, where the composer performed alongside Lucien

Capet, André Hekking, and Raymond Pétain. Within a month, Proust was to invite another group, the Quatuor Poulet, to his private rooms for a sequestered performance of the same work. See Proust, *Correspondance*, 15: 83–86, and Fauré, *Correspondance*, pp. 208–10.

98 Proust, *La prisonnière*, p. 361 (my translation); cf. *The Captive*, p. 505.

99 Bergson, *La pensée et le mouvant*, in his *Œuvres*, pp. 1371, 1391.

100 Boschot, "Confidences," p. 216: "la musique la plus profonde, la plus 'intérieure' qui soit."

101 Jules Combarieu, "Paderewski," *La revue musicale* 9 (1 June 1909): 286. Brian Hart kindly sent me a photocopy of this article.

102 Boschot, "Confidences," p. 216; also see pp. 209, 220–21, and 225.

103 Kœchlin, "Les tendances," 128.

104 Boschot, "Confidences," pp. 225, 214.

105 Émile Vuillermoz, "La musique de chambre de Gabriel Fauré," *Musica* no. 77 (Feb. 1909): 23.

106 Gustave Samazeuilh, "Quatuor pour instruments à cordes (op. 121) de Gabriel Fauré," *La revue musicale* 6 (1 July 1925): 68.

107 Valéry, "Fragments des mémoires d'un poème" [1937], in his *Œuvres*, 1: 1472.

108 *Ibid.*, 1473. Note especially the following passage: "Il suffit de songer aux productions que l'on groupe sous le nom général d'*Ornement*, ou bien à la *musique pure*, pour m'entendre."

109 *Ibid.* For other references by Valéry to his ideal of "composition," see his *Œuvres*, 1: 1483 and 2: 1278.

110 Valéry, "Fragments des mémoires d'un poème," p. 1473.

111 Valéry, "Au sujet du *Cimetière marin*" [1933], in his *Œuvres*, 1: 1505.

112 Fauré, "André Messager," 132.

113 *Ibid.*, 131.

114 Henri Duparc, in response to Landormy, "L'état actuel de la musique française," 397.

115 I refer to Dorian's infatuation with Sibyl Vane, an infatuation which is not love for her self but for her Shakespearian surrogates on stage. When she ceases to be Juliet, Imogen, or Rosalind – when she gives her simple-hearted soul to Dorian – he abandons her in horror.

116 Debussy, review in *S.I.M.* (1 Nov. 1913), reprinted in his *Monsieur Croche et autres écrits*, p. 246.

117 René Dumesnil, *La musique en France entre les deux guerres, 1915–1939* (Paris: Éditions du Milieu du Monde, 1946), p. 82.

118 Paul Dukas, "*Pénélope* de G. Fauré" [1923], in *Les écrits de Paul Dukas sur la musique* (Paris: Société d'Éditions Françaises et Internationales, 1948), p. 645.

119 Kœchlin, "Les tendances," 125.

120 Arthur Honegger, *I Am a Composer* [1951], tr. Wilson O. Clough with Allan Arthur Willman (London: Faber and Faber, 1966), p. 109. Valéry and Honegger collaborated once again with *Sémiramis* (1931), produced at the Opéra in 1934.

121 There seems to have been a recent revival of interest in sincerity. Work in liter-

ary and cultural studies has tended to focus on the period from 1780 to 1830 rather than the early twentieth century. The Modern Language Association had a special session on "Romantic Sincerity" in 1996 which included papers on Blake, Novalis, and Felicia Hemans. A conference at Columbia University in 1994 entitled "French Moralists in America" likewise included papers on "Rousseau and the Cult of Sincerity" and "The Toils of Sincerity: La Rochefoucauld, Stendhal, Sartre," presented by Arthur Melzer and Charles Larmore, respectively. The latter paper, which poses an important challenge to Valéry's critique of Stendhal, appears in *Op. Cit.* 6 (Spring 1996): 63–69.

122 Stanley Cavell, *Must We Mean What We Say?* (New York: Scribner's Sons, 1969), p. 188. Further references to this book in this concluding section appear in parentheses.

123 Kœchlin, "Les tendances," 123; see also p. 65, n. 2.

124 Proust, *La prisonnière*, pp. 245–46 (my translation); cf. *The Captive*, p. 342. In another context, Jean-Michel Nectoux, *Gabriel Fauré: Les voix du clair-obscur* (Paris: Flammarion, 1990), p. 494, cites this passage.

125 Vuillermoz, "La Schola et le Conservatoire," 237.

126 Kœchlin, "Gabriel Fauré," *Le ménestrel* 83, no. 22 (3 June 1921): 234.

2 Innovation, tradition

1 Throughout, I use "novelty" and "innovation" to refer to the same thing; the latter would be an exercise of artistic choice, the former its result.

2 Nectoux, *Gabriel Fauré: A Musical Life*, tr. Roger Nichols (New York: Cambridge University Press, 1991), p. 489.

3 Camille Saint-Saëns, "Une sonate (Op. 13)" [1877], reprinted in his *Au courant de la vie* (Paris: Dorbon-Aîné, 1914), pp. 39–42.

4 Th. Lindenlaub, "Mort de Gabriel Fauré," *Le temps* (5 Nov. 1924): 3.

5 Fauré to Marie Clerc, 17 Sept. 1879, Fauré, *Correspondance*, textes réunis, présentés et annotés par Jean-Michel Nectoux (Paris: Flammarion, 1980), p. 96.

6 Jean-Michel Nectoux, *Fauré*, 2nd ed. (Paris: Seuil, 1986), p. 40.

7 Parakilas's excellent analysis of the Ballade may be found in his *Ballads Without Words: Chopin and the Tradition of the Instrumental Ballade* (Portland, Oregon: Amadeus Press, 1992), pp. 168–76.

8 Fauré to Marie Fauré, 17 March 1922, *Lettres intimes*, ed. Philippe Fauré-Fremiet (Paris: La Colombe, 1951), p. 279. The composer explained the confusion to his wife, then added with some amusement, "In 1881 Debussy was eighteen years old! Who would have thought that he could already be imitated at that age!"

9 Nectoux, *Gabriel Fauré: Les voix du clair-obscur* (Paris: Flammarion, 1990), p. 485.

10 Fauré to Marie Fauré, 23 Aug. 1904, *Lettres intimes*, p. 85. This letter and the reception of the First Quintet will be discussed in chapter 3, section 3.

11 Fauré to Marie Fauré, 22 Aug. 1906, *Lettres intimes*, p. 121. Dubois had been Fauré's predecessor at the Conservatoire and at La Madeleine.

12 See Nectoux's comments in Fauré, *Correspondance*, p. 338.

13 Fauré to Singer (Princesse Edmond de Polignac), Sept. 1891, *Correspondance*, p. 187.

14 Fauré to Countess Greffulhe, late Oct. 1893, *Correspondance*, p. 192.

15 Charles Kœchlin, *Gabriel Fauré* (Paris: Félix Alcan, 1927), p. 17.

16 Fauré to Countess Greffulhe, late Oct. 1893, Fauré, *Correspondance*, p. 192.

17 The common tone F-flat (E) is indeed functional: it is the seventh in a V^7 of V in E minor.

18 Verlaine, "A Clymène" in his *Poèmes saturniens; suivi de Fêtes galantes* (Paris: Le Livre de Poche, 1961), pp. 160–61; see Baudelaire's sonnet "Correspondances" in his *Fleurs du mal et autres poèmes* (Paris: Garnier-Flammarion, 1964), pp. 39–40.

19 To see how Fauré has foreshortened the preparation of D-flat by combining two secondary dominant functions into a single chord, insert an A-flat major triad between measures 14 and 15.

20 Note the enharmonic identity of the bass-line in measure 12 with that of measure 14, in striking contrast with the fact that the melody in the right hand of the latter is a whole-step lower! The continuity or integrity of the bass-line is often the controlling feature in Fauré's music which prevents the tonal background from breaking down under the pressure of glides and detours on the surface.

21 Fauré to Maurice Bagès and Pierre de Bréville, 28 Aug. 1891, Fauré, *Correspondance*, p. 186.

22 As great a critic as Martin Cooper dismissed him as "a nonentity" without further comment (in his *French Music from the Death of Berlioz to the Death of Fauré* [New York: Oxford University Press, 1961], p. 127). Dubois's negative reputation has perhaps been built on historical prejudice rather than contact with his music. I have only examined his songs, but their charm, skill, and even originality, is undeniable.

23 It remains difficult to draw exact conclusions, however, because the chronology of Dubois's songs has not been firmly established. The standard dictionaries of music – German, English, French, and Italian – are all inaccurate. The best list of Dubois's work is to be found in Hugues Imbert, *Nouveaux profils des musiciens* (Paris: Fischbacher, 1892), pp. 67–74, though Imbert does not list songs in collections by their individual titles, and this list necessarily only covers the composer's career to the end of 1891. The dates I provide for the three songs mentioned immediately below should only be taken as provisional endpoints, which I determined by comparing Imbert's bibliography with information provided by plate numbers, publishers' advertisements, and decorative and typographical style on covers and title pages.

24 Vladimir Jankélévitch, *Fauré et l'inexprimable* (Paris: Plon, 1974), p. 195.

25 Some of Dubois's best songs resemble the ingratiating style Fauré cultivated

before 1891. For example, Fauré's "En prière," from the end of this period (1889), and Dubois's much earlier "Désir d'avril" (1871) are remarkably similar. (I take this date from Imbert's works list. The song is certainly no later than "En prière.") Dubois's anticipation of a later Fauréan manner seems worthy of investigation.

26 Nectoux, *Gabriel Fauré: Les voix du clair-obscur*, p. 489.

27 Fauré to Saint-Saëns, 24 Aug. 1896, *Gabriel Fauré: A Life in Letters*, tr. and ed. J. Barrie Jones (London: Batsford, 1989), p. 81. Fauré was finally elected, not without serious debate, in 1909.

28 These circumstances merit further investigation. Thanks to Gail Woldu's research ("Gabriel Fauré as Director of the Conservatoire Nationale de Musique et de Déclamation, 1905–1920" [Ph.D., Yale University, 1983], pp. 2–6), we know that Dubois had announced his retirement in March 1905, two months before the "scandal" of the Prix de Rome in which Ravel was refused the right to enter because of his poor qualifying examination. Therefore Dubois's resignation cannot be construed as a consequence of this "scandal," though it cast a pall on his last months of service. At the same time, we still do not know why Fauré was ultimately chosen to be director, or who were his rivals, and these questions are worthy of archival investigation. Did Fauré's courageous public defense of Ravel against the jurors of the Conservatoire have anything to do with his nomination? Indeed, it seems possible that this contrarian defense for once may have raised rather than lowered his political stock, for this was a period of liberal government keen on reform. In his biography of his father, Philippe Fauré-Fremiet claims that Maurice Rouvier's wife persistently lobbied the undersecretary of state for fine arts, Dujardin-Beaumetz, on behalf of Fauré's cause (Fauré-Fremiet, *Gabriel Fauré*, 2nd ed. [Paris: Albin Michel, 1957], p. 91). This little observation, which seems to have gone unnoticed by other writers, favors my line of reasoning. Rouvier had become prime minister of France in 1905, and his wife had participated in musical salons where Fauré was active. Would it not also be significant that Fauré chose to dedicate his Piano Trio, op. 120, to Mme Rouvier eighteen years later, not long after retiring from the Conservatoire?

29 Paul Verlaine, *La bonne chanson* (Paris: Léon Vanier, 1891), pp. 11–12.

30 "La lune blanche" is another experiment with a "double" poem by Verlaine in this same cycle.

31 Including Saint-Saëns, whose first reaction to *La bonne chanson*, we shall see, was far from enthusiastic. Regardless, Saint-Saëns was always faithful to Fauré when it came to academic votes. The final count in the Institut in May 1894 was nonetheless twenty for Dubois, four for Fauré. In June 1896, similarly, it was nineteen for Lenepveu, four for Fauré (Nectoux, *Gabriel Fauré: Les voix du clair-obscur*, pp. 507–08).

32 The passage may be reduced further to an elaboration of a neighbor-note progression on the dominant A-flat, shown in the second diagram (this is yet another third relation). The dynamics, peaking on the "neighbor" harmony,

are important in contributing to the sense of deviation and return in this passage. (This diagram borrows loosely from Schenkerian concepts but is obviously not a Schenkerian graph.)

33 Over the next two decades, Fauré would find much bolder ways to expand or hide his boundaries and thresholds. By 1909, he was composing pieces that deny the bass its traditional harmonic function for long spans; in such works tonal harmony is replaced with contrapuntally conceived parallel voice-leading. Thus in "Eau vivante" (1909), Fauré postpones the first functional harmonic progression until after the middle of the song, and in the Fifth Impromptu, from the same year, such a progression only emerges on the final page. Taylor Greer has analyzed both pieces in his dissertation, "Tonal Process in the Songs of Gabriel Fauré: Two Structural Features of the Whole-Tone Scale" (Ph.D., Yale University, 1986), pp. 178–200.

34 Fauré to Saint-Saëns, 2 Oct. 1893, in their *Correspondance (1862–1920)*, 3rd ed., ed. Jean-Michel Nectoux (Paris: Publications de la Société française de musicologie and Éditions Klincksieck, 1994), p. 59. Emphasis mine.

35 *Correspondance (1862–1920)*, p. 59, n. 5. Albert Bertelin, "Quelques souvenirs sur Gabriel Fauré," *Musique et théâtre* (1 April 1925): 14, claims that Saint-Saëns advised Fauré to burn *La bonne chanson*.

36 Camille Bellaigue, "Quelques chansons," *La revue des deux mondes* 143, no. 4 (15 Oct. 1897): 934.

37 *Ibid.*, 935. Bellaigue let the bottom system of the third page (mm. 41–43) stand for "harmonic derangement" in this song. It is symptomatic that he singled out this system not (as he claims) "at random," but largely in order to criticize Fauré for changing the key signature to D-flat major before that key is actually established (or rather, implied). Fauré's change of signature, however, here announces the start of a long-range harmonic process and is a formal division in the song. Both formal features escaped Bellaigue.

38 Fauré, *Correspondance*, pp. 221–22.

39 ". . . *la nouveauté n'étant ici que le* moyen *nécessaire, nullement ce but puéril: étonner le bourgeois.*" Kœchlin, "Les tendances de la musique moderne française," [1921] in *Encyclopédie de la musique*, ed. Albert Lavignac and Lionel de La Laurencie, part 2, vol. 1 (Paris: Delagrave, 1925), 65. This was a theme dear to Kœchlin; see above, pp. 19, 26, as well. Not all of Fauré's students consistently practiced what they were taught, and Ravel, most notably, sometimes aroused negative criticism for *forgetting* the distinction.

40 See James Kidd, "Louis Niedermeyer's System for Gregorian Chant Accompaniment as a Compositional Source for Gabriel Fauré" (Ph.D., University of Chicago, 1974).

41 Fauré, "Souvenirs," *La revue musicale* 4 (1 Oct. 1922): 198–99.

42 *Ibid.*, 199. Fauré also spoke of Niedermeyer's pedagogy and the curriculum of the school in his response to Auguste Mangeot, "La réforme de la musique religieuse," *Le monde musical* (15 Feb. 1904): 35. A hint of the extent to which Fauré carried some of the repertory he learned as a student into his first paid

position, as organist at Saint-Sauveur in Rennes, may be seen from programs and documents gathered by Marie-Claire Le Moigne-Mussat, *Musique et société à Rennes aux XVIIIe et XIXe siècles* (Geneva: Minkoff, 1988), pp. 230, 238, 241.

43 Jean Roger-Ducasse, "L'enseignement de Gabriel Fauré," in *Gabriel Fauré* (Paris: Publications Techniques et Artistiques, 1946), p. 16, quoted in Nectoux, *Gabriel Fauré: A Musical Life*, p. 265.

44 These performances were mostly done by students from the ensemble classes: collective music-making was another one of Fauré's favorite preoccupations. See Gail Hilson Woldu, "Gabriel Fauré, directeur du Conservatoire: les réformes de 1905," *Revue de musicologie* 70, no. 2 (1984): 208–09.

45 See Woldu, "Gabriel Fauré," 207, 211–13, 215–16, and appendix, 219–28, based on material gathered in the French National Archives. In her dissertation, "Gabriel Fauré as Director of the Conservatoire Nationale de Musique et Déclamation, 1905–1920" (Ph.D., Yale University, 1983), Gail Woldu has documented the striking changes in the examinations and recitals after Fauré assumed direction of the school.

46 Charles Wegener, *The Discipline of Taste and Feeling* (Chicago: University of Chicago Press, 1992), p. 217.

47 Nède, "Le nouveau directeur du Conservatoire," *Le Figaro* (14 June 1905): 4. See chap. 1, pp. 28–9.

48 Fauré, preface to *Œuvres complètes pour orgue* by J. S. Bach (Paris: Durand, 1917–20), quoted in Nectoux, *Gabriel Fauré: Les voix du clair-obscur*, p. 67.

49 Fauré to Mangeot, Feb. 1904, letter printed posthumously and fragmentarily in "Gabriel Fauré, critique musicale," *Le monde musical* 35 (Nov. 1924): 369.

50 Fauré, preface to *Musiques d'aujourd'hui* by Émile Vuillermoz, p. vii.

51 Since I mention conservatism again, it is heuristic to read a very similar statement from Varèse, whom no one has, to my knowledge, ever labeled as conservative: "However original or different a composer may seem, he has only grafted a little bit of himself to the old plant. But he must be able to do it without others accusing him of wishing to kill the plant. All he wants to do is make a new flower" (Varèse, "Le destin de la musique" [1959], in his *Écrits*, ed. Louise Hirbour [Paris: Christian Bourgois, 1983], p. 152). Also compare this comment to the indented quotation from Fauré, below.

52 In the wake of Parisian Futurism and Simultaneism, Dada shot off its first squibs in 1916 at the Cabaret Voltaire in Zurich. "I was deeply grieved to see a snow spreading colder than death. The object was to mock and destroy literature," wrote Cocteau a few years later. "This strange suicide attracted me with its blue eyes." See Cocteau, "Order Considered as Anarchy," in his *Call to Order . . . Written Between the Years 1918 and 1926 . . .*, tr. Rollo H. Myers (London: Faber and Gwyer, 1926; New York: Haskell House, 1974), p. 192.

53 Fauré, preface to *Œuvres classiques pour piano*, ed. Benjamin Cesi *et al.*; French editor, Isidore Philipp (Paris: Ricordi, [*c.* 1910]), n.p.

54 Fauré to Arsène Alexandre, Sept. 1904, Nectoux, *Gabriel Fauré: A Musical Life*,

p. 499; see the French edition, p. 495: "Ce sourire un peu voilé qui seul est judi-cieux."

55 Quotations from Bruno Monsaingeon, *Mademoiselle: Conversations with Nadia Boulanger*, tr. Robyn Marsack (Boston: Northeastern University Press, 1988), pp. 109–10.

56 *Ibid.*

57 See *ibid.*, p. 108.

3 Originality, influence, and self-renewal

1 Charles Baudelaire, "Richard Wagner et 'Tannhäuser' à Paris" [1861], in his *Œuvres complètes*, ed. Y.-G. Le Dantec and Claude Pichois (Paris: Gallimard, 1961), p. 1235.

2 Alfred Bruneau, "La direction du Conservatoire," *Le matin* (13 June 1905): 2.

3 It is worth noting that in French this usage extends beyond art into tempera-ment or even physiology. In *L'art de chanter* (Paris: Éditions Littéraires de France, 1945), p. 96, Charles Panzéra says that the only sound medical care is that of "un médecin qui a pour principe même de traiter chaque individu selon son originalité profonde."

4 Carl Dahlhaus, *Grundlagen der Musikgeschichte* (Cologne: Hans Gerig, 1977), p. 62. Almost alone among music historians in the second half of the twenti-eth century, Dahlhaus grasped the importance of investing originality with a double significance (see also *ibid.*, p. 232). Dahlhaus's discrimination is impressive but not surprising when we recall how richly immersed he was in nineteenth-century aesthetic principles. Yet, as with so many of his most prom-ising digressions, and to our loss, he never elaborated on this insight.

5 Fauré to Imbert, Aug. 1887, Fauré, *Correspondance*, textes réunis, présentés et annotés par Jean-Michel Nectoux (Paris: Flammarion, 1980), p. 128. Imbert subsequently interviewed Fauré and published "Profils de musiciens: Gabriel Fauré," in *L'indépendance musicale et dramatique* 14–15 (15 Sept. and 1 Oct. 1887): 393–401 and 425–39. This essay was reprinted in Imbert's *Profils de mus-iciens* (Paris: Librairie Fischbacher et Librairie Sagot, 1888), pp. 57–78, and constitutes Fauré's first biography. Imbert was evidently a first-rate interviewer and a perceptive critic; his long essay contains valuable and extremely detailed information about Fauré's life between 1854 and 1885.

6 The very year of Fauré's letter, Georges Servières devoted a book to the history of Wagner's reception in France: *Richard Wagner jugé en France* (Paris: Librairie Illustrée, 1887). In the *Revue wagnérienne*, Édouard Dujardin eloquently defended Wagner against those he named the "false patriots" of France. With admirable diplomacy, at once flattering Wagner *and* French national hubris, he held out Wagner's lifework as a magisterial tribute by which Germany recipro-cated the artistic gifts France had made to her ("Notes et nouvelles," [15 April 1887]: 65–66). These two texts, cited from among many, give us some sense of French concerns in 1887. Of course, the *Revue wagnérienne*, which Dujardin

founded and published between 1885 and 1888, marked the crest of Wagnermania among French artists.

7 Philippe Fauré-Fremiet, *Gabriel Fauré* (Paris: Rieder, 1929), p. 84.

8 Fauré to Marie Fauré, 23 Aug. 1907, *Lettres intimes*, ed. Philippe Fauré-Fremiet (Paris: La Colombe, 1951), p. 146.

9 Fauré to Marie Fauré, 2 Sept. 1907, *ibid.*, p. 150.

10 Fauré to Dukas, 30 July 1923, Annecy-le Vieux. Yale University, Music Library, MS. 287.

11 See Edgar Allan Poe, "The Philosophy of Composition" [1846], in his *Essays and Reviews*, ed. G. R. Thompson, The Library of America (New York: Literary Classics of the United States, 1984), pp. 13–25.

12 Paul Dukas, "La musique et l'originalité," *La revue hebdomadaire* 4 (28 Sept. 1895): 621. (Subsequent references will appear parenthetically in the text.) Thus, to read Poe's "Philosophy of Composition" *literally* was, for Dukas, to misread it. Significantly, this reading (or misreading) was precisely Ravel's and Valéry's, though neither had yet published his views on Poe's essay.

13 It is apposite to my hypothesis about Fauré's earlier letter to Imbert that worries over Wagner's influence pervade Dukas's essay on originality. In this way, Dukas's general argument relays its historical specificity. Wagner's influence is, in fact, the only influence he ever specifically names and is a central concern in both "La musique et l'originalité" and the antecedent article from two weeks before, "Poèmes et libretti," *La revue hebdomadaire* 4 (14 Sept. 1895): 307–13.

14 Clearly, we must take the absolute language of this final phrase ("all alien influence") as seeking to communicate an ideal, something aimed for but never fully realized, for one can hardly imagine an artistic practice truly freed of *all* outside influence. We shall consider this point again later.

15 Gustave Larroumet, *Nouvelles études de littérature et d'art* (Paris: Hachette, 1894), p. 236.

16 Benoist-Méchin, *La musique et l'immortalité dans l'œuvre de Marcel Proust* (Paris: Simon Kra, 1926), p. 94.

17 Dukas, "Poèmes et libretti," 308.

18 Dukas, "*Pénélope* de G. Fauré" [1923], in *Les écrits de Paul Dukas sur la musique* (Paris: Société d'Éditions Françaises et Internationales, 1948), p. 646. Here and in "La musique et l'originalité" Dukas uses the same superlative, "tout entier," to indicate an originality fully achieved.

19 Fauré, preface [1924] to *Les quatuors de Beethoven* by Joseph de Marliave (Paris: Alcan, 1925), p. ii.

20 Édouard Schuré, preface to *Profils de musiciens*, by Hugues Imbert, p. xv.

21 Albéric Magnard, *Bérénice, tragédie en musique* (Paris: Édition Mutuelle, 1909), n.p.

22 Fauré himself recognized this difference, as we may see by comparing his reviews of *Le Roi Arthus* and *Bérénice* in his *Opinions musicales*, ed. P. B. Gheusi (Paris: Rieder, 1930), see especially pp. 34, 72.

23 See Harold Bloom, *The Anxiety of Influence: A Theory of Poetry* (New York:

Oxford University Press, 1973). I refer to this discourse as moralizing because Bloom judges poetry according to a strict ethical code: poems found to be "rugged" and "immensely anxious" are exalted, while those found "judicious," "healthy," and "serene" are cast aside. This is the difference between "strong poets" and "weak poets." (The adjectives are all Bloom's.) That Bloom issues a moralizing discourse on poetic history is ironic, since he views other critics' moralizing discourses on poems as "pernicious" (p. 23).

24 Bloom, *The Anxiety of Influence*, p. 11.

25 *Ibid.*, p. 94. This deep vein of joylessness is tapped endlessly across Bloom's writings. He always gives the impression of a man gripped by the angrier books of the Old Testament. At once attracted and repelled by myths of patricide, Bloom oscillates between biblical and Freudian fathers, a compass that should also make us wonder how the neglect of a maternal presence in influence has skewed his theory. Lloyd Whitesell has questioned Bloom's abolition of the maternal in a beautifully executed critique of gender relations in Bloom's theory, "Men with a Past: Music and the 'Anxiety of Influence'," *19th-Century Music* 28, no. 2 (Fall 1994): 152–67. From within the context of early twentieth-century France, the following passage from Cocteau tersely expresses an attitude diametrically opposed to Bloom's: "Occasionally [in good music] the influence of a master is apparent. As we perceive it, we are profoundly touched. For, when thoroughly assimilated, it is a sign of love. It is a mother's voice, step, and manner reappearing in her son" (*Cock and Harlequin*, "Appendix 1924," in Cocteau, *A Call to Order . . . Written Between the Years 1918 and 1926 . . .*, tr. Rollo H. Myers [London: Faber and Gwyer, 1926; New York: Haskell House, 1974], p. 71).

26 Bloom, *The Anxiety of Influence*, p. 96.

27 This displacement (or dismissal) also bears witness to the difference between a critic's views of art and those of artists engaged in actual work, the latter being my focus in this section. Bloom's tendency to hold his theories well above the work of practicing artists reminds me of Luciano Berio's pertinent complaint against analysts of music who display "an ill-conceived superiority with regard to the composer" (Luciano Berio, "Poetics of Analysis," sixth Charles Eliot Norton lecture, Cambridge, Massachusetts, 6 April 1994). Berio's observation speaks to an excessive rhetorical practice among academic practitioners of theory – in both music and literature: the language of *mastery*.

28 Bloom, *The Anxiety of Influence*, pp. 11, 5.

29 Fauré, *Opinions musicales*, p. 70.

30 Fauré to Marie Fauré, 16 Aug. 1907, *Lettres intimes*, p. 144.

31 Vincent d'Indy, response to Jacques Morland, "Enquête sur l'influence allemande," *Mercure de France* 45 (Jan. 1903): 98.

32 See chapter 2, pp. 70–75 on tradition.

33 Whether Bloom's ideas would make the best approach to Debussy's worries is another question. Yet I suspect that the usefulness of Bloom's ideas, or their appeal, has a direct relation to the personal temperament of the artist being considered.

34 Fauré to Marie Fauré, 16 Aug. 1907, *Lettres intimes*, p. 144. The statement reflects Fauré's displeasure with his initial idea for the suitors' theme in *Pénélope*. "I am looking for something that gives an impression of brutality and total self-satisfaction," he writes in the next sentence. He probably had never had occasion to convey this particular feeling in music before and was trying to imagine its possibilities; he may have started thinking about Wagner's music and dramatic characterizations for this very reason. (Incidentally, Fauré's word "formules" does not suggest an understanding of Wagner as "formulaic"; the word here means musical figurations of a dramatic idea.)

35 Bloom, *The Anxiety of Influence*, p. 12; for Fauré's comment to Imbert, see above, p. 78.

36 Fauré, preface to *Musiques d'aujourd'hui* by Émile Vuillermoz, p. vii. "In the measure of his gifts": that second half is important – it reminds us of Dukas's similar understanding that self-realization, one of the highest conditions of artistic greatness, still does not guarantee it.

37 Yvon Belaval, *Le souci de sincérité* (Paris: Gallimard, 1944), p. 154.

38 Téodor de Wyzéwa, "Notes sur la peinture wagnérienne," *La revue wagnérienne* 2 (May 1886): 109.

39 Harold Bloom, *A Map of Misreading* (New York: Oxford University Press, 1975), p. 10.

40 Dukas, "Théâtre royal de la Monnaie, à Bruxelles: *Fervaal*," *La revue hebdomadaire* 6 (27 March 1897): 556.

41 *Ibid.*, 563.

42 *Ibid.*

43 Vincent d'Indy, "Gabriel Fauré," *Tablettes de la Schola* 24 (Nov. 1924): 2. Due to the omission of a by-line, this speech was incorrectly attributed to Dukas when it was reprinted in *Le monde musical* 35 (Nov. 1924): 363.

44 D'Indy, "Beethoven," in *Cobbett's Cyclopedic Survey of Chamber Music*, comp. and ed. Walter Wilson Cobbett (London: Humphrey Milford, 1929), 1: 99. The article was probably translated into English by M. Drake-Brockmann and is closely related to d'Indy's earlier *Beethoven* (Paris: Henri Laurens, 1911).

45 Jacques Méraly, "Gabriel Fauré, l'homme et le musicien: *La bonne chanson*," *La revue musicale* 3 (15 Nov. 1903): 623.

46 André Gide, *Caractères* [1925], tr. Justin O'Brien, in Gide, *Pretexts: Reflections on Literature and Morality*, ed. Justin O'Brien (n.p.: Meridian Books, 1959), p. 298.

47 Gide's passionate need for sincerity in literary expression may be traced back to his very first steps as a writer. One of the earliest entries in his personal journals broods over the desire "to be utterly and perfectly sincere" and to "define artistic sincerity" (Gide, *Journals*, tr. Justin O'Brien [New York: Knopf, 1947], 1: 16–17). The theme of sincerity appears again and again on succeeding pages, in succeeding volumes. See also chap. 1, n. 62.

48 Fauré, "*Werther*," *Le Figaro* (25 April 1903), reprinted in his *Opinions musicales*, p. 76.

49 Dukas, despite his sterner idealism, seems to have reached similar conclusions

about *Werther*. Like Fauré, he raises the question of Wagner's influence and concludes that *Werther* is not Wagnerian – "'not Wagnerian in the least, even though there are, particularly in the comic parts, reminiscences of *Die Meistersinger*, and even though there are characteristic motives in it and the principal role is most often entrusted to the orchestra.'" Indeed, Dukas assessed *Werther* as positively original, not just unwagnerian: "For the most part the composer, happily for him and for us, remains himself" (Dukas, "Chronique musicale: *Werther*," *La revue hebdomadaire* 2 [11 Feb. 1893]: 304–05). Dukas's reasoning, like Fauré's, can be reconciled with the principles of "La musique et l'originalité" once we understand that Massenet, for both critics, managed to imbibe Wagnerian procedures at a radically personal stratum – without superficial recourse to "formulas" or "methods," and thus without inhibiting self-expression.

Although Dukas's review of *Werther* expresses a clear opinion about the specific matter of artistic influences, it leaves some larger questions about Massenet's artistic position or overall achievement painfully open. In an extraordinary deviation from journalistic convention, Dukas cast his review as a dialogue, a transcription of a conversation supposedly overheard between the occupants of two neighboring seats in the theater, one a fan of Massenet's music, the other a skeptic. On the one hand, the enthusiastic neighbor twice praises the work's sincerity (pp. 299, 306), and even the skeptic avows the sincere emotion of its best scenes (p. 307). The skeptic, to our surprise, is also the one who confirms that Massenet, far from becoming Wagnerian, "remains himself." On the other hand, he also announces a prejudice – a sneaking suspicion that the experience of *Werther* only partially erases: "C'est de la musique opportuniste" (p. 305). Dukas leaves this comment hanging, but surely he knew that such an accusation, even in the voice of a sullen skeptic, could not be effaced merely by suspending discussion. Dukas ends his review in his own persona, suavely echoing the voice of his fictional enthusiast, but we know better than to take his (or their) concession as conclusive: "Never was the composer better inspired" (p. 309).

Is there any echo of Dukas's ambivalence toward *Werther* (and Massenet) in Fauré's review? Perhaps. What are we to make of the strange quotation marks Fauré put around the word "himself" in the third paragraph of his review ("s'y montrer 'lui-même'")? The effect, albeit subtle, raises doubt about whom or what Massenet was really revealing. After this one equivocation, however, Fauré proceeds to use the reflexive "s'y révèle" affirmatively, without tricky emphasis or punctuation. Dukas's review is more ambivalent.

50 Carl Dahlhaus, *Nineteenth-Century Music*, tr. J. Bradford Robinson (Berkeley: University of California Press, 1989), p. 279. It is highly unlikely that Dahlhaus ever read Fauré's review; the similarity between them is probably coincidental.

51 Fauré, *Opinions musicales*, p. 77: "M. Massenet s'y révèle constamment, tout entier, . . ." Note the near-identity of language with Dukas's comments on Fauré's *Pénélope* (above, p. 83).

52 *Ibid.*: "provient, sans doute, 'd'une raison de son cœur,' que ma raison, hélas! ne connaît pas!" (Fauré's phrase echoes Pascal's famous *pensée*, "Le cœur a ses raisons, que la raison ne connaît point.") Incidentally, we might think the "punch in the chest" to be Werther's broken outburst, "Un autre son époux!" which closes the act, but Fauré's reference to the thematic content of the passage, unless his memory deceived him, rather suggests an earlier moment, underlining Werther's words, ". . . sans que nul à son tour les contemple un moment! Le céleste sourire!" It is remarkable that Debussy isolated precisely the same scene in *Werther* and also praised it and criticized it for the same qualities: "What charming intimations of feeling in Charlotte's and Werther's nocturnal return in the first act! Why must so much charm suddenly be transposed by blaring trombones underscored by seismic kettledrums? I am at a loss to explain it, even as I cannot deplore it enough" (*Gil blas* [27 April 1903], reprinted in his *Monsieur Croche et autres écrits*, p. 161).

53 To recall the original text with an added emphasis, ". . . ou *qu'à défaut* d'une irrésistible vocation, il soit devenu wagnérien parce que le wagnérisme était alors à la mode . . ."

54 Fauré to Marie Fauré, 23 Aug. 1904, *Lettres intimes*, p. 85.

55 Fauré-Fremiet, *Gabriel Fauré* (1929), p. 89.

56 *Ibid.*, p. 90.

57 Charles Panzéra, *50 mélodies françaises: leçons de style et d'interprétation* (Brussels: Schott Frères, 1964), p. 117.

58 Thus I have included the setting of the previous two lines – as well as the ending – in order to give some sense of the larger melodic journey and the unusual pull in the vocal line which the last phrase releases so simply and directly.

59 Panzéra, *50 mélodies françaises*, p. 125.

60 The circular interpretation proposed here (and inspired by Panzéra) need not force us to reject a linear one, which is, of course, how the work would be experienced in a normal performance. The last song may be seen as the end of a journey, implying encroaching night and bringing closure to a linear sequence beginning with the sun and breezes of the first song. At the same time, Fauré, selecting his four poems from de Mirmont's fourteen, practically inverted their order, so that "Vaisseaux, nous vous aurons aimés" actually comes from the beginning of the poetic collection (in Fauré's order, the songs correspond to poems XIII, XIV, XII, and V; *cf.* Jean de La Ville de Mirmont, *L'horizon chimérique* [Paris: Société littéraire de France, 1920]). Fauré's arrangement again suggests a kind of circularity, and we cannot doubt that he was using the poems to answer an affective pattern of his own. Horizons, as the title of the cycle reminds us, are shifting boundaries that can be transcended by movement through space or the imagination. Deflecting the desperate hope of the last song back into the exultant hope of the first, as Panzéra did, is an interpretative act that takes its cue from the ruling, chimerical spirit of the work.

61 Vladimir Jankélévitch, *Fauré et l'inexprimable* (Paris: Plon, 1974), p. 300.

62 It is worth noting that the upward leap of a seventh is uncharacteristic in the

prosodic style of Fauré's later songs. We have to look all the way back to 1909 to find another such leap in his *mélodies*: "Comme Dieu rayonne . . ." op. 95, no. 4, m. 18.

63 This is why the work is truly a cycle, whereas Fauré's previous two collections of songs, *Mirages* and *Le jardin clos*, were really *suites* (as Fauré himself called the latter). It is also significant that Fauré chose the same key for the outer songs (the inner ones are in D-flat and E-flat major). Such rounding might seem a conventional, almost trivial, sign of tonal closure if it were not that *none* of Fauré's other cycles and suites of songs begins and ends in the same key.

64 Fauré-Fremiet, *Gabriel Fauré* (1929), p. 54.

65 For this genesis, see *ibid.*; Fauré, *Correspondance*, p. 224; and Nectoux, *Gabriel Fauré: A Musical Life*, tr. Roger Nichols (New York: Cambridge University Press, 1991), p. 95.

66 See also Nectoux's comments, *Gabriel Fauré: A Musical Life*, p. 295.

67 Fauré to Marie Fauré, 3 Aug. 1903, *Lettres intimes*, p. 72.

68 Fauré to Marie Fauré, 12 Aug. 1903, *ibid.*, p. 73. Ellipsis in original.

69 Fauré to Marie Fauré, 25 Aug. 1903, *ibid.*, p. 77.

70 Fauré to Marie Fauré, 23 March 1906, *ibid*, p. 118. Eugène Ysaÿe, the great Belgian violinist and composer, was the dedicatee of the First Quintet. He had been loyal to the project since its inception around 1890, and he often encouraged the underconfident Fauré. Fauré's playful reference to Roger-Ducasse's "approval" is explained by the fact that the latter had a strong predilection for programmatic works. Nadia Boulanger would later recall that Roger-Ducasse was one of Fauré's favorite pupils but added, "They had quite a few arguments, for, in spite of very strong affinities in their thinking [*leur si grande intimité d'esprit*], they were not always in agreement on every point" (Boulanger, interview with Jean-Michel Nectoux, 19 Jan. 1974, *Études fauréennes* 17 [1980]: 5).

71 Nectoux, *Fauré*, 2nd ed. (Paris: Seuil, 1986), p. 100.

72 Joseph de Marliave, "La musique à Paris," *La nouvelle revue* 31 (1 Aug. 1910): 378.

73 G[eorges] S[ervières], "Cercle Artistique," *Le guide musical* 52, no. 13 (1 April 1906): 254.

74 Louis Vierne, "Salle Pleyel: Concerts Ysaye-Pugno," *Le monde musical* (15 May 1906): 136. Even though Brussels had the première, the French public considered the first performance in Paris the "real première."

75 Pierre Lalo, "Le *Quintette* nouveau de M. Gabriel Fauré," *Le temps* (13 July 1906): 3. "No secret" because Hamelle had prematurely advertised the Quintet as being "in press" as far back as 1896.

76 Vierne, "Salle Pleyel," 136.

77 The dates of completion for each composition would line up chronologically as follows: 1876, 1883, 1894, 1895, 1905. For details of the program in Brussels, see Fauré, *Lettres intimes*, p. 118; for the Société Nationale, see Willy, "La revue de la quinzaine: Lettre de Willy," *Mercure musical* 2, no. 11 (1 June 1906): 514,

and Cecilia Dunoyer, *Marguerite Long: A Life in French Music, 1874–1966* (Bloomington: Indiana University Press, 1993), p. 29.

78 Octave Maus, "Gabriel Fauré," *L'art moderne* 26, no. 12 (25 March 1906): 92. Emphasis mine.

79 Lalo, "Le *Quintette* nouveau," 3.

80 Louis Laloy, "Gabriel Fauré," *Musiclovers Calendar* 2 (Dec. 1906): 79. This article was published in English without any credit for the translation. The problematic syntax and incorrect use of lower-case letters in certain passages leaves no doubt that the original was in French, but the French text seems never to have been published.

81 The only French piano quintets written between Franck's and Fauré's were an early work by Déodat de Sévérac (1898), and Widor's op. 68 (1894). Neither quintet seems to have attracted attention and both remain in the shadows.

82 Vierne, "Salle Pleyel," 136.

83 Lalo, "Le *Quintette* nouveau," 3.

84 *Ibid.*

85 *Ibid.* Emphasis mine.

86 One may refer to this originality as "radical" with double justification, calling upon its loyalty to the root of the word ("origin") and its reference to a deeply rooted (radical) substratum of personality.

87 I refer to his *Music, the Arts, and Ideas: Patterns and Predictions in Twentieth-Century Culture* (Chicago: University of Chicago Press, 1967), especially pp. 61, 155–58, 183, 187–88, 217–20.

88 Mary Devereaux, "Protected Space: Politics, Censorship, and the Arts," *Journal of Aesthetics and Art Criticism* 51, no. 2 (Spring 1993): 214.

89 A discussion of originality is not the main topic of Devereaux's essay, which succeeds on its own ground; I have done no more than isolate a detail for critique.

90 Sometimes this passion is surprising when considered alongside the experimental or anti-traditional nature of an artist's work – as when one hears Philip Glass firmly defending his "right to evolve" (interview concerning Glass's *Orphée* on "Morning Edition," National Public Radio, May 1993).

91 The quoted phrase is Dukas's "objective" definition of originality, cited above, p. 81.

92 "A Composer's Confessions" [1948], in *John Cage, Writer*, ed. Richard Kostelanetz (New York: Limelight Editions, 1993), p. 43.

93 Quoted in Michael Nyman, *Experimental Music: Cage and Beyond* (London: Studio Vista, 1974), p. 37. One of Cage's students, Christian Wolff, issued an even more extreme version of this view in 1958 (*ibid.*, p. 26).

94 Meyer, *Music, the Arts, and Ideas*, pp. 217, 183.

95 *Ibid.*, pp. 186–87.

96 *Ibid.*, p. 188. Emphasis mine.

97 Robert P. Morgan, *Twentieth-Century Music: A History of Musical Style in Modern Europe and America* (New York: W. W. Norton, 1991). At the time this

chapter was first written, a detailed critique of Morgan's book appeared: Christopher A. Williams, "Of Canons and Context: Toward a Historiography of Twentieth-Century Music," *Repercussions* 2 (Spring 1993): 31–74. Williams's polemical treatment of Morgan's historiography is harsher and more wide-ranging than my own, but our ideas coincide in the critique of what Williams aptly calls "techno-essentialism." This similarity is the more significant for the independence of our two essays. Critical challenges to received historiographies of twentieth-century music continue to gain in volume and diversity.

98 Morgan, *Twentieth-Century Music*, p. xvi. Further references are given in parentheses.

99 The same critique applies to Morgan's essay, "Secret Languages: The Roots of Musical Modernism" (*Critical Inquiry* 10 [March 1984]: 442–61), which preceded the textbook and likewise sidesteps the problem of defining a historical field for musical modernism. At the start of the essay the term "modernism" appears as a mere synonym for "twentieth century," but Morgan ultimately settles on turning it into a "collective movement" that brought an end to the old, traditional "grammar" of tonality. He places the definitive inauguration of musical modernism between 1900 and 1910. At the same time he makes little effort to sort out national differences and ignores the related fact that some of the composers he places in this "movement" would not have recognized the word "modernism" as applying to any musical style, much less their own work.

100 Meyer, *Music, the Arts, and Ideas*, p. 218.

101 *Ibid.*, p. 155.

102 *Ibid.*, p. 157.

103 Paul Moravec, "Tonality and Transcendence," *Contemporary Music Review* 6, no. 2 (1992): 39.

104 *Ibid.*

105 Note that Robert Morgan, in observing that composers in the past two decades have been "giving up on technique as the primary ground of newness," acknowledges this turn of events (see above, p. 113).

106 Moravec, "Tonality and Transcendence," 41.

107 *Ibid.*, 39.

108 *Ibid.*, 42.

109 I was reluctant to use the term "postmodern" to refer to these circumstances until Leonard Meyer pointed out to me that, in his view, this "restoration" is directly related to the demise of the idea of historical progress.

110 Though the convenience is historiographic, it also reflects, and indeed helped to create, the cultural hegemony of a post-serialist school well into the 1960s.

111 René Leibowitz, *Schœnberg et son école: L'étape contemporaine du langage musical* (Paris: J. B. Janin, 1947), p. 10. Leibowitz (1913–72), a Polish emigré whose family moved to Paris in 1913, was a composer, conductor, and teacher. In this last role, he single-handedly introduced a number of French composers, including Boulez, to Schoenbergian serialism.

112 See the discussion in chapter 1, pp. 32–5.

113 This aesthetic shift should not, of course, be attributed to Leibowitz's paragon, Schoenberg, who was a firm advocate of personal originality and indeed unmerciful toward any innovation that did not come from "inner necessity."

114 Leibowitz, *Schœnberg et son école*, p. 13. Emphasis in the previous sentence is mine.

115 Boulez, "Possibly ..." [1952], in his *Stocktakings from an Apprenticeship* [*Relevés d'apprenti*, 1966], ed. Paule Thévenin, tr. Stephen Walsh (Oxford: Clarendon Press, 1991), p. 113, also pp. 214, 303. (I use Walsh's meticulous translation throughout.)

116 See Boulez, *Stocktakings*, pp. 115 and 231. The erring generations might be roughly indicated by those born between 1880 and 1900 on the one hand, and those born between 1900 and 1920 on the other – after Schoenberg and before Boulez.

117 That is, Messiaen's "durational technique" (Boulez, *Stocktakings*, p. 133), Cage's discovery of "nontempered sound spaces" (p. 134), Varèse's preoccupation with acoustics (p. 174), or Webern's "abolition of the old contradiction between vertical and horizontal in tonal music" (p. 297) and "treatment of each phenomenon as at once autonomous and interdependent" (p. 298).

118 See especially the third full paragraph on p. 115 in Boulez, *Stocktakings*.

119 Boulez, "Schoenberg is Dead" [1952], in Boulez, *Stocktakings*, p. 212. Here Boulez has resorted to skillful one-upmanship: he blames Schoenberg for failing to understand the very system he invented. Stephen Potter has discussed this ploy in *Lifemanship* (New York: Henry Holt, 1951), p. 61.

120 Boulez, "Schoenberg is Dead," in his *Stocktakings*, p. 211.

121 *Ibid.*

122 Boulez, "Possibly ..." in *Stocktakings*, p. 133.

123 *Ibid.*, p. 115.

124 *Ibid.*, pp, 138–39. Emphasis mine.

125 *Ibid.*, pp. 139–40. Emphasis mine. See also "... Near and Far" [1954], pp. 144–45, where Boulez begins to describe the composer's personal relation to innovation, tradition, and history. A refusal to place imagination and technique in a hierarchical or dualistic relationship comes out more explicitly in Boulez's *Jalons (pour une décennie)*, ed. Jean-Jacques Nattiez (Paris: Christian Bourgois, 1989), where the two forces are systematically generalized as "Idea" and "Realization" (p. 65) and where Boulez actually tries to breach the gulf between the idealistic thinking of Dukas's generation and the materialistic reaction that followed it. In a historical sense, this facet of Boulez's thought is profoundly synthetic.

126 Robert Piencikowski, introduction to *Stocktakings* by Pierre Boulez, p. xv.

127 During 1988, Boulez revised and polished the lectures for publication and apparently preferred to eliminate a certain number of specific musical examples in favor of general speculations. Unfortunately, Boulez's lecture of 1982, "Recherche et création," is one of two omitted from the book. It would be of great interest to us here.

128 Boulez, *Jalons*, p. 39. I draw this quotation, and most of the subsequent ones, from "L'invention musicale, I: origines et antécédents," the group of lectures Boulez gave between January and April 1978 and grouped under the rubric "Idée, réalisation, métier."

129 Louis Aguettant, "Gabriel Fauré," *La vie intellectuelle* 1 (Nov. 1949): 395.

130 Boulez, *Jalons*, p. 44 (subsequent references will be parenthetical). Here there is a striking parallel with Dukas's phrases (see p. 83 above).

131 *Ibid.*, p. 52. The slightly apologetic tone in this passage is surprisingly isolated, for in another extensive passage (pp. 38–40) Boulez resorts to the words "personal" and "personality" almost constantly and with no trace of embarrassment.

132 Louis Laloy, "Claude Debussy et le Debussysme," *Revue S.I.M.* 6, nos. 8–9 (Aug.–Sept. 1910): 515–19.

133 See *Stocktakings*, p. 138, where Boulez witheringly classes Leibowitz among those who "would like us to take . . . larval academicism for intellectualism, though it is in reality nothing but a secretion of limited and unenterprising spirits." Other attacks may be found on pp. 2, 47, 188, and 200. The former pupil was clearly at pains to dissociate himself from teachings he now viewed as parasitic on Schoenberg and hopelessly attached to an objective "science" of music as opposed to an "alchemy." Curiously, Boulez likened Leibowitz's "scientific" approach to *scholiste* thinking, whereas the idea of "alchemy" comes from Debussy, whom Boulez is ever happy to acknowledge as a progenitor (p. 22).

134 In *Stocktakings*, Boulez defends Messiaen's musical thought against a critique by Leibowitz (p. 47) and warmly acknowledges the specific influence of Messiaen's teaching (pp. 133–34, 47–50), even though at one point he cannot resist a firm but friendly stylistic critique (p. 49).

135 Gaston Carraud, "L'âme harmonique de Gabriel Fauré," *Musica* no. 77 (Feb. 1909): 20. What I translate as "originality of soul" is also "originality of mind," since "âme" may mean either. Because "âme" fuses mind and soul, it is perhaps the most powerful word a critic could choose to name the origin of a composer's personal growth (not least because it was practically impossible to prove anything about it). See Proust, *La prisonnière*, ed. Pierre-Edmond Robert (Paris: Gallimard, 1989), p. 242 (the passage beginning, "Car à des dons plus profonds . . .") for a statement that matches Carraud's to a remarkable degree.

4 Homogeneity: meaning, risks, and consequences

1 Jean-Jacques Nattiez, *Proust as Musician*, tr. Derrick Puffett (Cambridge: Cambridge University Press, 1989), pp. 9–10. This work includes a useful bibliography of writings about Proust and music. Proust's speculations on artistic homogeneity have not, to my knowledge, been treated by anyone before me. Nattiez comes closest to identifying the topic in a passage (p. 61) from which I shall quote later. Jean-Michel Nectoux has written more generally on Proust's

relations to Fauré and the artistic affinities between them; see his essay and annotations in Fauré, *Correspondance*, textes réunis, présentés et annotés par Jean-Michel Nectoux (Paris: Flammarion, 1980), pp. 194–219, and in an earlier essay, "Proust et Fauré," *Bulletin de la Société des amis de Marcel Proust et des amis de Combray* 21 (1971): 1102–120.

2 Marcel Proust, *Correspondance*, ed. Philip Kolb (Paris: Plon, 1970), 1: 338.

3 Proust, *La prisonnière*, ed. Pierre-Edmond Robert (Paris: Gallimard, 1989), p. 361 (my translation). Cf. Proust, *The Captive*, in *In Search of Lost Time*, tr. C. K. Scott Moncrieff and Terence Kilmartin, rev. by D. J. Enright (New York: The Modern Library, 1993), pp. 505–06.

4 James C. Kidd, review of *Gabriel Fauré* by Robert Orledge, *19th-Century Music* 4, no. 3 (Spring 1981): 276, 279.

5 Jean Marnold, "Gabriel Fauré," *Mercure de France* 176 (1 Dec. 1924): 501–02.

6 Joseph de Marliave, *Études musicales* (Paris: Alcan, 1917), p. 33. This essay was originally published in 1909.

7 Edward R. Phillips, "Smoke, Mirrors and Prisms: Tonal Contradiction in Fauré," *Music Analysis* 12, no. 1 (March 1993): 3–24. Taylor A. Greer, "Tonal Process in the Songs of Gabriel Fauré: Two Structural Features of the Whole-Tone Scale" (Ph.D., Yale University, 1986).

8 This comparison, with specific reference to Stravinsky's music from the Piano Sonata (1924) to *Perséphone* (1934), merits serious exploration. See Robin Holloway's suggestive comments in a recent article, "Master of Hearts," *The Musical Times* 136 (Aug. 1995): 395–96, and Bayan Northcott, "Fauré Our Contemporary," *Music and Musicians* 18, no. 8 (April 1970): 36. I know of no direct lines of influence between Fauré and Stravinsky, but the likeness of certain features in their "post-tonal" idioms is all the more worthy of investigation as an unexpected confluence of twentieth-century musical techniques.

9 Roland-Manuel, "Le Trio pour piano, violon et violoncelle de Gabriel Fauré," *La revue musicale* 4 (1 July 1923): 250.

10 For example, see Holloway, "Master of Hearts," 396; Northcott, "Fauré Our Contemporary," 35–36; Phillips, "Smoke, Mirrors and Prisms," 20–21.

11 Leonard B. Meyer, *Style and Music: Theory, History, and Ideology* (Philadelphia: University of Pennsylvania Press, 1989), p. 3.

12 Paul de Stœcklin, "L'anémie," *Le courrier musical* 14, no. 13 (1 July 1911): 462.

13 Proust, *The Captive* (Moncrieff's translation), p. 343; cf. *La prisonnière*, p. 246.

14 Karuyoschi Yoshikawa, "Vinteuil ou la genèse du septuor," *Études proustiennes* 3 (1979): 308.

15 Fauré, preface to *Les quatuors de Beethoven* by Joseph de Marliave (Paris: Alcan, 1925), p. ii. Fauré's preface is dated April 1924.

16 By the time Fauré wrote this preface in 1924, the practice of parceling Beethoven's career into creative periods had been a historiographic institution in Europe for almost eighty years. In France, the practice began with Fétis, in his *Biographie universelle des musiciens* of 1837, but it was most widely popularized by Wilhelm von Lenz's *Beethoven et ses trois styles*, published in Brussels

in 1854, printed in Paris the following year, and regularly reprinted as late as the first decades of the twentieth century.

17 Philippe Fauré-Fremiet, "La musique de chambre de Gabriel Fauré," *Le monde musical* (30 June 1930): 227.

18 *Ibid.*

19 *Ibid.*

20 Bernard de Fallois, preface to *Contre Sainte-Beuve* by Marcel Proust (Paris: Gallimard, 1954), p. 33.

21 Gaston Carraud, "L'âme harmonique de Gabriel Fauré," *Musica* no. 77 (Feb. 1909): 19–20. Another important quotation from this article is cited in the final paragraph of chapter 3.

22 Vladimir Jankélévitch, *Fauré et l'inexprimable* (Paris: Plon, 1974), p. 282.

23 Proust, response to an "enquête" organized by *La Renaissance politique, littéraire, artistique* (22 July 1922). Reprinted in Marcel Proust, *Contre Sainte-Beuve, précédé de Pastiches et mélanges et suivi de Essais et articles*, ed. Pierre Clarac and Yves Sandre (Paris: Gallimard, 1971), p. 645.

24 Proust, *Matinée chez la princesse de Guermantes: Cahiers du "Temps retrouvé,"* ed. Henri Bonnet and Bernard Brun (Paris: Gallimard, 1982), p. 293. Bonnet and Brun here transcribe Proust's Cahier 57 (N.A.F. 16 697, Bibliothèque Nationale, Paris), containing material written by Proust between 1913 and 1916. I have used Derrick Puffett's translation, as found in Nattiez, *Proust as Musician*, pp. 81–82, as the basis for my own.

25 Nattiez, *Proust as Musician*, p. 82.

26 Proust, *Matinée chez la princesse de Guermantes*, p. 293 (my translation).

27 Proust, *La prisonnière*, p. 243 (my translation); cf. Proust, *The Captive*, p. 339.

28 Proust, *The Captive*, pp. 332–33 (Moncrieff's translation); cf. *La prisonnière*, pp. 238–39.

29 Proust, *The Captive*, p. 332 (Moncrieff's translation); cf. *La prisonnière*, p. 238. For "thoroughly explored," Proust's word is "épuisé," the same one he applied to the white hawthorns in the draft cited above (there translated as "exhausted").

30 Proust, *The Captive*, p. 333 (Moncrieff's translation); cf. *La prisonnière*, p. 238.

31 Proust, *La prisonnière*, p. 243 (my translation); cf. *The Captive*, pp. 339–40.

32 Proust, *The Captive*, p. 341 (Moncrieff's translation); cf. *La prisonnière*, p. 245.

33 Proust, *The Captive*, pp. 505–06 (Moncrieff's translation); cf. *La prisonnière*, p. 361.

34 Proust, *The Captive*, p. 343 (Moncrieff's translation); cf. *La prisonnière*, p. 246. Also see *The Captive*, p. 206, or *La prisonnière*, p. 149, for a very similar passage.

35 James Ackerman seems to think that either extreme is impossible: "Unlike a machine, [an artist] cannot reproduce without inventing," and conversely he "cannot invent without reproducing." James S. Ackerman, "A Theory of Style," *Journal of Aesthetics and Art Criticism* 20, no. 3 (1962): 228.

36 Jules Combarieu, "Paderewski," *La revue musicale* 9, no. 11 (1 June 1909): 286–87. This passage is part of a long, remarkable excursus inspired by Combarieu's enthusiasm for Paderewski's Symphony.

37 Jean Cocteau, "Visits to Maurice Barrès" [1920–21] in his *A Call to Order, Written Between the Years 1918 and 1926 and Including Cock and Harlequin, Professional Secrets, and Other Critical Essays*, tr. Rollo H. Myers (London: Faber and Gwyer, 1926; rpt. New York: Haskell House, 1974), pp. 93–94. We recall that Gide voiced a similar injunction to absolute sincerity, though he did so under a veil of irony (see above, p. 93).

38 Throughout this chapter, in referring to Debussy's first two *Images*, I mean the chronological order of Debussy's composition rather than the sequential ordering of the suite (which is *Gigues, Ibéria, Rondes de printemps*). The three *Images* occupied Debussy between 1906 and 1912. *Ibéria* and *Rondes de printemps* were finished by the beginning of 1910; both were given their premières that year. *Gigues* was not complete until 1912 and not performed until the beginning of 1913.

39 Debussy, interview in *L'éclair* (Feb. 1908), reprinted in his *Monsieur Croche et autres écrits*, rev. ed. (Paris: Gallimard, 1987), p. 281. Emphasis mine.

40 See above, pp. 18, 97.

41 Interview in *Azest* (6 December 1910), reprinted in Debussy, *Monsieur Croche et autres écrits*, p. 311.

42 Jane Fulcher's recent *French Cultural Politics & Music: From the Dreyfus Affair to the First World War* (Oxford: Oxford University Press, 1999), pp. 170–94, interprets this reception in political terms that richly complement the limited aesthetic facets presented here.

43 Dukas, "Chronique musicale: Concerts Lamoureux," *La revue hebdomadaire* 10 (9 Feb. 1901): 274–75.

44 David Cox, *Debussy: Orchestral Music* (Seattle: University of Washington Press, 1974), p. 24. For an insightful treatment of the initial reception of *La mer*, see Brian Hart, "The Symphony in Theory and Practice in France, 1900–1914" (Ph.D., Indiana University, 1994), pp. 368–71.

45 Lalo, "Au concert du Châtelet: Première audition d'*Iberia* [*sic*], suite d'orchestre de M. Claude Debussy," *Le temps* (26 Feb. 1910): 3.

46 Gaston Carraud, "Le mois" [review of *Rondes de printemps*], *Revue S.I.M.* 6, no. 4 (April 1910): 267. Brian Hart directed me to this review and discussed its ideological claims with me.

47 *Ibid.*, 266–67.

48 Lalo, "Au concert du Châtelet," 3.

49 *Ibid.*

50 See Carraud's review of the first two *Nocturnes* in *La liberté* (Dec. 1900), quoted in Léon Vallas, *Claude Debussy: His Life and Works*, tr. Maire and Grace O'Brien (London: Oxford University Press, 1933), p. 118.

51 Roussel to Taravant, *Lettres à Auguste Sérieyx [par] Vincent d'Indy, Henri Duparc [et] Albert Roussel*, ed. M. L. Sérieyx (Lausanne: Éditions du Cervin; Paris: E. Ploix, 1961), p. 65. Roussel goes on to cite a passage from a review of Debussy's *Danses sacrées et profanes* in which Henri Gauthier-Villars (otherwise known as "L'Ouvreuse" or "Willy") did mix art and scandal: he used the *Danses* as a pretext for a veiled reference to Debussy's taking up with Fauré's

former mistress. Gauthier-Villars, entertaining, adored and feared, never lost an opportunity for a sarcastic pun or a wisecrack. His approach, however, was unique and cannot be taken to represent critical practices in general.

52 Roussel to Taravant, 28 October 1905, in *Lettres*, p. 72.

53 Claude Debussy, interviewed by Paul Landormy, "L'État actuel de la musique française," *La revue bleue* (26 March 1904): 422.

54 "*Horresco . . .*," i.e., "*Horresco referens*" ("I shudder to tell it"). Carraud, "Le mois," 267.

55 Debussy to Vuillermoz, 17 Jan. 1913, Debussy, *Letters*, ed. François Lesure and Roger Nichols, tr. Roger Nichols (Cambridge, Massachusetts: Harvard University Press, 1987), p. 267.

56 Fulcher, *French Cultural Politics*, pp. 187–88, sees *Rondes de printemps* as both a crafty mockery of the Schola Cantorum and a realization of "cruel self-irony" on Debussy's part. Fulcher leaves this interpretation rather up in the air; it is difficult to find a coherent argument for her claim. I do not see how this music, so earnest and unruffled, bears out her suggestion. Irony, as a mode of expression, would entail that the music somehow undo its own premises or isolate objects of derision as being foreign to more "authentic" elements; I fail to perceive this multiplicity of levels in *Rondes de printemps*, whether heard alone or in relation to Debussy's other works. I suggest below that Debussy may have been trying once again to realize cyclic techniques within his own personal forms of expression. This simpler hypothesis in fact supports Fulcher's larger arguments about Debussy's cultural politics.

57 See Laloy, "Les écoliers," *Mercure musical et S.I.M.* 3 (April 1907): 367–72; "Les partis musicaux en France," *La grande revue* (25 Dec. 1907): 790–98; "La nouvelle manière de Claude Debussy," *La grande revue* (10 Feb. 1908): 530–35; and "Claude Debussy et le Debussysme," *Revue S.I.M.* 6, nos. 8–9 (Aug.–Sept. 1910): 510–19. Laloy wrote the earliest of these essays, "Les écoliers," in direct response to Vuillermoz's "Debussy et les Debussystes," *La nouvelle presse* (26 Feb. 1907). Rejoinders and counter-rejoinders by Laloy and Vuillermoz appeared under the heading "Correspondance" in the *Mercure musical et S.I.M.* 3 (June 1907): 668–70.

58 Laloy, "Claude Debussy et le Debussysme," 515–16.

59 *Ibid.*, 517. Emphasis mine.

60 *Ibid.*, 519. Emphasis mine.

61 *Ibid.* Emphasis mine.

62 Debussy, interview in *Azest* (6 Dec. 1910), reprinted in his *Monsieur Croche et autres écrits*, p. 311.

63 *Ibid.*

64 Actually, Pierre Boulez does. Incredibly, some of the original controversies still continue to color the reception of the *Images* in France. Boulez, writing with reference to *Rondes de printemps* in 1986, faulted Debussy for lapsing into "academic or repetitive methods in which he seems ill at ease and makes us feel that way too." Boulez's surrounding comments leave no doubt that the methods he

would condemn are those of a scholiste lineage – "la descendance de César Franck" – a residue that can still inspire French indignation after seventy-six years (Boulez, *Jalons*, ed. Jean-Jacques Nattiez [Paris: Christian Bourgois, 1989], pp. 222, 224, 225). Ironically, Boulez himself espouses a "higher homogeneity" in what he calls "the composer's gesture" (chap. 3, p. 123); therefore if Laloy were alive today, he would be able to fight Boulez with the same arguments he used against Carraud and Lalo in 1910!

65 Paul-Louis Garnier, "*Prométhée* à Béziers," *La revue blanche* 23, no. 115 (Sept. 1900): 142.

66 See Paul Dukas, "*Prométhée* de G. Fauré" in *Les écrits de Paul Dukas sur la musique* (Paris: Société d'Editions Françaises et Internationales, 1948), pp. 508–09; Charles Kœchlin, "Représentations de Béziers," *Mercure de France* 150 (Nov. 1901): 550–52; Pierre Lalo, "La musique à Béziers: *Prométhée*," *Le temps* (5 Oct. 1900), reprinted in his *De Rameau à Ravel* (Paris: A. Michel, 1947), pp. 353–54.

67 Laloy, "Les partis musicaux en France," 790.

68 See Hart, "The Symphony in Theory and Practice in France," pp. 1–66, on the "guerre des écoles" and the battle over French tradition in this period.

69 Alfred Bruneau, "Au théâtre des Champs-Elysées, l'altière et pure beauté de 'Pénélope' provoque un immense enthousiasme," *Le matin* (10 May 1913): 5.

70 Camille Bellaigue, "Quelques chansons," *La revue des deux mondes* (15 Oct. 1897): 933–34.

71 *Ibid.*, 935.

72 Albert Bertelin, "Quelques souvenirs sur Gabriel Fauré," *Musique et théâtre* (1 April 1925): 14.

73 See Nectoux's commentary in Saint-Saëns and Fauré, *Correspondance*, p. 59, n. 5. For corroboration of this incident from Fauré's younger son, Philippe, see also José Bruyr, "En parlant de Gabriel Fauré avec son fils," *Le guide du concert* 24, no. 23 (1938): 616.

74 Jacques Méraly, "Gabriel Fauré, l'homme et le musicien: *La bonne chanson*," *La revue musicale* 3 (15 Nov. 1903): 622–28; Georges Servières, "Lieder français," *Le guide musical* 40 (23 Dec. 1894): 1027–28; Paul Ladmirault, "G. Fauré: *La bonne chanson*," *Courrier musical* 3, no. 13 (31 March and 7 April 1900): 1–3.

75 Proust to Pierre Lavallée, Proust, *Correspondance*, 1: 338. Proust then cites "Au cimetière" and "Après un rêve" with disparagement, but in fact he was very fond of some of Fauré's earlier songs, especially "Chant d'automne."

76 Vierne, "Salle Pleyel: Concerts Ysaye-Pugno," *Le monde musical* 17, no. 9 (15 May 1906), 136. For references to all the reviews of the Quintet, see chap. 3, pp. 106–109.

77 The word "écriture" was often used in the first decade of the century to disparage the supposed pedantry of artistic instruction at the Schola; such procedures could also be associated with "verbiage" because they were customarily freighted with an allegorical significance. To quote Maus in full: "[The new

Quintet] is as 'Fauré' as you could possibly imagine, which is to say that the charm of its inspiration is never adulterated by the least technical pedantry [*pédanterie d'écriture*], nor does any verbiage [*littérature*] burden its purely musical essence" (Maus, "Gabriel Fauré," *L'art moderne* 26, no. 12 [25 March 1906]: 92). For another reference to "écriture" see Debussy, interview in *Comœdia* (4 Nov. 1909), reprinted in his *Monsieur Croche et autres écrits*, p. 296.

78 Servières, "Cercle Artistique," *Le guide musical* 52, no. 13 (1 April 1906): 254.

79 Laloy, "Gabriel Fauré," *Musiclovers Calendar* 2 (Dec. 1906): 79–80. Anon. trans.

80 Pierre Lalo, "Le *Quintette* nouveau de M. Gabriel Fauré," *Le temps* (13 July 1906): 3.

81 *Ibid.*

82 Ackerman, "A Theory of Style," 227–28.

83 *Ibid.*, 228.

84 Proust, *The Captive*, p. 208 (Moncrieff's translation, emphasis mine); cf. *La prisonnière*, pp. 150–51.

85 Fauré to Marie Clerc, 17 Sept. 1879, Fauré, *Correspondance*, p. 96. Cited in chap. 2, p. 58.

86 Proust, *La prisonnière*, pp. 245–46 (my translation); cf. *The Captive*, p. 342. This text, by emphasizing an opposition of "glory" to authentic, individual "intonation," reflects some of the principles of sincerity and was cited for that reason at the end of chapter 1. The implications of this text for homogeneity will now also become clear.

87 For another example of this perspective in Proust, see the passage on Vinteuil as leader of an "attelage invisible" in *Du côté de chez Swann* in his *A la recherche du temps perdu*, ed. Pierre Clarac and André Ferré (Paris: Gallimard, 1954), 1: 351.

88 Proust, *The Captive*, pp. 340–41 (Moncrieff's translation, emphasis mine); cf. *La prisonnière*, p. 244.

89 Nattiez, *Proust as Musician*, p. 61.

90 Jean-Michel Nectoux, "Works Renounced, Themes Rediscovered: *Éléments pour une thématique fauréenne*," *19th-Century Music* 2, no. 3 (March 1979): 231.

91 Robin Tait, *The Musical Language of Gabriel Fauré* (New York: Garland, 1989), p. 160.

92 Georges Piroué, *La musique dans la vie, l'œuvre et l'esthétique de Proust* (Paris: Denoël, 1960), p. 179. Some copies of this book, otherwise identical, carry the alternative title *Proust et la musique du devenir*.

93 Charles Kœchlin, *Gabriel Fauré* (Paris: Félix Alcan, 1927), p. 76, n. 2. With regard to these examples, the reader should be warned that the passage cited from *Prométhée* (Ex. 9c) is not the same as the one Nectoux cites ("Works Renounced," 233), but it is from the same chorus. The phrase given here seems more directly related to "Lydia" than the one Nectoux chose. Nectoux also stretches the chain of Lydian links to "Cygne sur l'eau" (1919), the first song in

Fauré's *Mirages* ("Works Renounced," 232–33), but I am not convinced that this song can be <u>assimilated</u> to the model of "Lydia."

94 For a fascinating discussion of this specific tendency, see James C. Kidd, "Tonality in a New Key," in *Explorations in Music, the Arts, and Ideas: Essays in Honor of Leonard B. Meyer*, ed. Eugene Narmour and Ruth Solie (Stuyvesant: Pendragon Press, 1988), pp. 375–92.

95 As we shall see below, Greer, "Tonal Process," pp. 16–19, treats the ascending stepwise line in "Lydia" as "the progenitor of [a] motivic legacy."

96 Fauré to Marie Fauré, 25 Sept. 1907, *Lettres intimes*, ed. Philippe Fauré-Fremiet (Paris: La Colombe, 1951), p. 154.

97 Nectoux, "Works Renounced," 233. Nectoux also quotes a passage from the "Pastorale" in *Masques et bergamasques* (mm. 4–7, first violins), but I find that this phrase has too little in common with the original motive.

98 Examples 10b and 10c serve as secondary themes in both finales. The Odyssean motive may be found elsewhere in these two movements: in the Cello Sonata, at mm. 7–8 (within the first theme); in the Violin Sonata, at mm. 13–14 (end of the first theme) and mm. 108–31 (rehearsal number 5).

99 Louis Aguettant, "Rencontres avec Gabriel Fauré" [letter to André Lambinet, 12 July 1902, containing Aguettant's transcription of an interview with Fauré on 7 July 1902], ed. Jean-Michel Nectoux, *Études fauréennes* 19 (1982): 6. In a footnote on this page, Nectoux suggests that the performer in question may have been Lydia Eustis, to whom Fauré dedicated "Dans la forêt de septembre," written in the same year the conversation with Aguettant took place (see also Nectoux, *Gabriel Fauré: Les voix du clair-obscur* [Paris: Flammarion, 1990], p. 198). I can think of no better explanation than Nectoux's. But it *is* possible that Fauré was throwing Aguettant a red herring, for it is very hard to see why Fauré would have inserted any reference to Lydia Eustis in a cycle of songs dedicated to Emma Bardac, with whom he was passionately in love when he wrote them ten years earlier.

100 Proust, *La prisonnière*, p. 151 (my translation); cf. *The Captive*, p. 209.

101 Proust, *The Captive*, p. 345 (Moncrieff's translation); cf. *La prisonnière*, p. 247.

102 *Ibid.*

103 Proust, *The Captive*, p. 208 (Moncrieff's translation); cf. *La prisonnière*, p. 151. This sentence immediately follows the passage on "Vulcanian skill" cited above.

104 Nectoux, "Works Renounced," 235, also points out this analogy.

105 It seems to me that Robin Tait falls into the trap of taking raw material for characteristic material in his extensive list of examples showing Fauré's use of descending thirds (*The Musical Language of Gabriel Fauré*, pp. 161–65).

106 Before me, Bayan Northcott, without specifying any particular piece, spoke of a "stylistic fingerprint . . . the Fauré 'swoop' in which many of the piano works celebrate their climaxes in exultant descending scales of octaves" (Northcott, "Fauré Our Contemporary," 35). Before him, Norman Suckling, *Fauré* (London: J. M. Dent, 1946), p. 129, noted the similarity between the phrases from the Ballade and the Fourth Nocturne.

107 Phillips, "Smoke, Mirrors, and Prisms," 16; see *Le jardin clos*, "Exaucement," mm. 16–21.

108 Phillips, "Smoke, Mirrors, and Prisms," 20.

109 Greer, "Tonal Process," p. 44.

110 *Ibid.*, p. 201.

111 *Ibid.*, especially pp. 71–73 and 188–200.

112 Fauré to Marie Fauré, 27 Aug. 1904, *Lettres intimes*, p. 87.

113 "Accent" from Latin *ad-* "to" + *cantus* "singing."

114 Kidd, review of *Gabriel Fauré* by Robert Orledge, p. 279.

115 Fauré to Marie Fauré, 23 Aug. 1904, *Lettres intimes*, p. 85.

5 Fauré's religion: ideas and music

1 See Bertrand Marchal, *La religion de Mallarmé: Poésie, mythologie et religion* (Paris: José Corti, 1988), p. 36. I adopt Marchal's extension of this metaphor from poetic to religious crises.

2 Sainte-Beuve, *De la liberté de l'enseignement. Discours au Sénat le 19 mai 1868* (Paris: Michel Lévy, 1868), p. 1.

3 Quoted in Marie-Claude Genêt-Delacroix, "Esthétique officielle et art national sous la Troisième République," *Le mouvement social* 131 (April–June 1985): 108.

4 Victor Cousin, *Du Vrai, du Beau, et du Bien* (Paris: Didier, 1853), pp. 216–17; see also p. 219. Théodore de Banville would still affirm the position in his *Petit traité de poésie française* [1872] (Paris: G. Charpentier, 1881), p. 9.

5 Jules Combarieu, *La musique, ses lois, son évolution* [1907] (Paris: Flammarion, 1924), p. 333.

6 Joseph Guy Ropartz, "A propos de quelques Symphonies modernes," in his *Notations artistiques* (Paris: Lemerre, 1891), p. 190.

7 For more testimony to this point of view, see the discussion of Combarieu and Bergson in chapter 1 (pp. 36–41).

8 Stéphane Mallarmé, "Crise de vers" [1886, 1892, 1896, originally called "Vers et Musique en France"], in his *Œuvres complètes*, ed. Henri Mondor and G. Jean-Aubry (Paris: Gallimard, 1945), p. 367.

9 Quoted in Charles Tenroc, "Le problème de l'Édition française de musique, I," *Le courrier musical* (1 Feb. 1917): 53.

10 See Mallarmé, "La cour," in his *Œuvres complètes*, p. 416, on music as a "new religion" whose "facile occultism with inscrutable ecstasies" could be experienced (or observed) in public concerts.

11 Proust to Suzette Lemaire, 20 May 1895, Proust, *Correspondance*, 21 vols., ed. Philip Kolb (Paris: Plon, 1970–93), 1: 386–87.

12 Benoist-Méchin, *Avec Marcel Proust* (Paris: Albin Michel, 1977), p. 155.

13 Lionel de La Laurencie, "Le 'd'Indysme,'" *L'art moderne* 23 (15 Feb. 1903): 50.

14 See Ernest Renan, "Premiers travaux sur le bouddhisme" [1852, published in

1884] and "Nouveaux travaux sur le bouddhisme" [1883] in his *Œuvres complètes*, ed. Henriette Psichari (Paris: Calmann-Lévy, 1955), 7: 746–820. Jean-Marie Guyau, *L'irréligion de l'avenir* [1887] (Paris: Alcan, 1912), p. 402, also mentioned the influence of German philosophers, namely Schopenhauer, von Hartmann, and Bahnsen, on later nineteenth-century French interest in Buddhism.

15 See Marchal, *La religion de Mallarmé*, p. 22. Leconte de Lisle ultimately grouped these exotic poems at the head of his book. Fauré, who set three poems from the *Poèmes antiques*, probably read an edition that included all of the Indic poems except "La mort de Valmiki," which was not added until 1881. It was never Fauré's practice to turn long, narrative poems like these into songs. Instead, from the *Poèmes antiques* he chose "Lydia" (composed *c.* 1870), "Nell" (1878), and "La Rose" (1890), all either pagan or amorous in their imagery.

16 Marchal, *La religion de Mallarmé*, pp. 23–24.

17 Roger Valbelle, "Entretien avec M. Gabriel Fauré," *Excelsior* (12 June 1922): 2. Reprinted in *Bulletin de l'Association des amis de Gabriel Fauré* 12 (1975): [n.p.]

18 Fauré to Marie Fauré, 1 Aug. 1913, *Lettres intimes*, ed. Philippe Fauré-Fremiet (Paris: La Colombe, 1951), p. 220. Fauré may have been reading one of the five volumes of correspondence published as part of Flaubert's complete works in 1910.

19 Paul Desjardins, *Le devoir présent* (Paris: A. Colin, 1892), p. 8.

20 See below, p. 176, on Fauré's recusancy during his period at Rennes (1866–70).

21 For an example of Renan's double attitude, see "M. Feuerbach et la nouvelle école hégélienne" [1850], in his *Œuvres complètes*, 7: 294.

22 Nectoux, *Gabriel Fauré: A Musical Life*, tr. Roger Nichols (New York: Cambridge University Press, 1991), p. 170.

23 *Ibid.*, p. 171.

24 Léon Bocquet, *Autour d'Albert Samain* (Paris: Mercure de France, 1933), p. 180. In this same period, Charles Van Lerberghe wrote in his private journal about the possibility of a new kind of opera, for which he proposed *La vie et les enseignements de Bouddha* as an ideal theme. This is a remarkable coincidence of interests, given Fauré's prolonged attraction to Van Lerberghe's poetry a decade later. See Jacques Detemmerman, "Charles Van Lerberghe et la musique allemande," in *Charles Van Lerberghe et le Symbolisme*, ed. Helmut Siepmann and Raymond Trousson (Cologne: DME, 1988), p. 229, which includes an excerpt from the poet's unpublished journal.

25 Nectoux, *Gabriel Fauré: A Musical Life*, pp. 109–12.

26 It was under the very category of *libres penseurs* that Sainte-Beuve brought together all the non-conforming creeds he listed in *De la liberté de l'enseignement* (above, p. 170). For the term itself, see Sainte-Beuve, p. 5.

27 Nectoux, *Gabriel Fauré: A Musical Life*, p. 8.

28 François Crucy, "Les grandes figures contemporaines: Gabriel Fauré" [interview], *Le petit parisien* (28 April 1922): 1.

29 Fauré to Dukas, 16 March 1916 (postmark), Menton. Yale University, Music Library, MS. 287.

30 Both of these anecdotes are told in Alfred Bruneau's reliable and well-researched memoir, *La vie et les œuvres de Gabriel Fauré: Notice lue par l'auteur à l'Académie des Beaux-Arts* (Paris: Charpentier et Fasquelle, 1925), p. 19.

31 See Fernand Bourgeat, "Festival Fauré," *Journal de l'Université des Annales* (10 June 1908): 432; Nectoux, *Gabriel Fauré: A Musical Life*, pp. 15–16; Fauré, *Correspondance*, textes réunis, présentés et annotés par Jean-Michel Nectoux (Paris: Flammarion, 1980), p. 23.

32 Tannery to Fauré, 12 April and 17 June 1870, in *Gabriel Fauré: A Life in Letters*, tr. and ed. J. Barrie Jones (London: Batsford, 1989), pp. 22–23.

33 Fauré explained to François Crucy that, after Rennes, he was fired from his next position as well: "There again I was unable to get along with my superiors, and an escapade I'd planned well in advance led to my departure: I left Clignancourt because I went to hear *Les Huguenots!*" (Crucy, "Les grandes figures contemporaines," 1).

34 Fauré to the Princesse Edmond de Polignac, 11 June 1894, Fauré, *Correspondance*, p. 224. It is not clear which four motets Fauré had in mind, but the *Ave verum* and *Tantum ergo*, op. 65, would account for two of them. See Nectoux's note, *ibid.*, p. 224, for a discussion of the question.

35 From the "numéro-spécimen" of *La tribune de Saint-Gervais* (June 1894), reprinted in René de Castéra, *Dix années d'action musicale religieuse, 1890–1900* (Paris: Aux Bureaux de la Schola Cantorum, [1902]), in appendix [n.p.]. See also p. 27 of this same book. These objectives would appear under the rubric of the monthly *Tribune de Saint-Gervais*, official organ of the Society from 1895 onward.

36 Valbelle, "Entretien avec M. Gabriel Fauré," n.p.

37 See Fauré's comments in Auguste Mangeot, "La réforme de la musique religieuse," *Le monde musical* (15 Feb. 1904): 35. George Houdard's response to Mangeot in this same article speaks to questions of historical precedence with considerable anger.

38 De Castéra, *Dix années d'action musicale religieuse*, p. 8 (this book first appeared as a series of articles in *La tribune de Saint-Gervais* from 1900 to 1902). The École Niedermeyer, incidentally, was still very much an active institution.

39 Fauré to Valbelle, "Entretien avec M. Gabriel Fauré," n.p. Fauré also used this term to praise his friend (and fellow student at the École Niedermeyer) André Messager ("André Messager," *Musica* no. 72 [Sept. 1908]: 132). For d'Indy, on the other hand, eclecticism in France sprang from "the deleterious influence of Jewish art." Among certain *scholistes*, "eclecticism" in art was tied up not just with aesthetic integrity but with ideas about ethnic and national purity. See d'Indy, *Richard Wagner et son influence sur l'art musical français* (Paris: Delagrave, 1930), pp. 15, 18.

40 For an analysis of the structural role of plainchant in Fauré's melodic style, see James Kidd, "Louis Niedermeyer's System for Gregorian Chant Accompaniment as a Compositional Source for Gabriel Fauré" (Ph.D., University of Chicago, 1974), pp. 67–122. Kidd also discusses the relation between Niedermeyer's method and certain aspects of Fauré's harmonic practice.

41 For these facts, see de Castéra, *Dix années d'action musicale religieuse,* pp. 38–41.

42 *La Schola Cantorum: Son histoire depuis sa fondation jusqu'en 1925* (Paris: Bloud & Gay, 1927), pp. 93–94, 128. I would like to thank Brian Hart for bringing this book, which contains the text of the breve, to my attention.

43 Vincent d'Indy, "Une école d'art répondant aux besoins modernes," *La tribune de Saint-Gervais* 6, no. 11 (Nov. 1900): 313. This speech was given on the occasion of the school's relocation to the rue Saint-Jacques. D'Indy repeated the same mandate in his *Cours de composition musicale,* ed. with the collaboration of Auguste Sérieyx (Paris: Durand, [1903]), 1: 16.

44 Susan Richardson, "Fauré's Requiem as Independent Ideology," paper delivered at the 55th annual meeting of the American Musicological Society, Austin, Texas, 27 October 1989. Susan Richardson very kindly provided me with a typescript of her talk.

45 Letter to Charles Bordes quoted in André Cœuroy, "La musique religieuse," in *Cinquante ans de musique française de 1874 à 1925,* ed. Ladislas Rohozinski (Paris: Librairie de France, 1925), 2: 141.

46 René Paroissin, *Mystère de l'art sacré – des origines à nos jours* (Paris: Nouvelles Éditions Debresse, 1957), pp. 151–52.

47 In *La revue et gazette musicale* 23 (1856): 105–06, cited by William J. Peterson in *French Organ Music from the Revolution to Franck and Widor,* ed. Lawrence Archbold and William J. Peterson (Rochester: University of Rochester Press, 1995), p. 60.

48 Saint-Saëns, "L'orgue," in *École buissonnière: Notes et souvenirs* (Paris: Pierre Lafitte, 1913), p. 176. The succession of organists at La Madeleine after Lefébure-Wély was Saint-Saëns, Dubois, Fauré, Dallier.

49 Examples included an Agnus Dei adapted to an *entr'acte* from *L'Arlésienne,* a *Regina cœli* on a theme from *Pêcheurs de perles,* and an *Ave Maria* adapted to the "Meditation" from *Thaïs* (Cœuroy, "La musique religieuse," pp. 158–59). For the persistence of these contrafacta and gripes about them, see Saint-Saëns, *École buissonnière,* pp. 166, 179–80; Guilmant, response to Mangeot, "La réforme de la musique religieuse," 35–36; and Pierre Lalo, "La suppression des chanteurs de Saint-Gervais," *Le temps* (11 June 1902): 3.

50 Camille Bellaigue, "La réforme de la musique d'église" [1904], in *Études musicales* (Paris: Delagrave, 1907), 3: 224.

51 Fauré to Mangeot, "La réforme de la musique religieuse," 35.

52 *Ibid.*

53 *Ibid.* In Fauré's original, private letter to Mangeot, most of which was pub-

lished posthumously in 1924, the composer immediately continued, "Only the infallibility of . . . . . could establish such boundaries! But I don't think you're about to consult that institution, which is as deadly dull as it is self-glorifying" (letter of Feb. 1904, *Le monde musical* 35 [Nov. 1924]: 369). When we collate the public letter with the private letter, it becomes clear that the institution Fauré belittled was the Schola. Is it possible that the five dots stand for "d'Indy"? After the word "infallibility" one would, of course, expect "the pope"; the substitution of d'Indy for the pontiff would reflect Fauré's mockery of *scholiste* dogmatism.

The version of the letter published in 1924 complements the comments that Mangeot published in 1904, but neither text, unfortunately, represents the whole of Fauré's original letter, which has not been found. It is quite possible that Mangeot himself substituted the ellipsis for d'Indy's name: d'Indy was still alive in 1924. While the later printing includes passages omitted from the earlier one, Mangeot also put a long ellipsis in the former to show the omission of one or more paragraphs before the salutation, and he even omits a paragraph that he had already printed in 1904. As for the original cuts (those made in 1904), Mangeot probably had no trouble getting Fauré's consent for them, since the composer had at first wanted to sidestep publication altogether. Fauré began his letter with the following reservation: "If I weren't part of the establishment [*du bâtiment*], I would write you a letter on this subject for *Le monde musical*. Between you and me, let me say . . ." Mangeot obviously convinced Fauré to allow an edited form of the letter to be published in 1904.

54 Fauré to Mangeot, "La réforme de la musique religieuse," 35 (emphasis from the version of the letter published in 1924, p. 369).

55 A complete French translation of the *motu proprio*, "Tra le sollecitudini," appears in André Cœuroy, "La musique religieuse," in *Cinquante ans de musique française*, 2:167–72. Pius X issued a second *motu proprio*, "Col nostro," concerning the new Vatican editions, on 25 April 1904.

56 Fauré was right to be concerned, to judge from the way the Schola wrote its own history. Consider the following account: "The academic year of 1903 saw the promulgation of the celebrated *motu proprio* of Pope Pius X, which ordained for the Church the adoption of religious music exactly as it was understood at the Schola" (Guy de Lioncourt, "La Schola depuis 1900," in *La Schola Cantorum*, p. 93). Saint-Saëns was likewise suspicious of the connections between the pope and the Schola; see "Musique religieuse," in his *École buissonnière*, pp. 163–64, where he comments on d'Indy's audience with Pius X.

57 Nectoux, *Gabriel Fauré: Les voix du clair-obscur* (Paris: Flammarion, 1990), p. 130. In a letter on sacred music from 1893 Gounod provided a significant precedent for Fauré's logic, but without carrying it so far: "The Church *has* and *should have* its own language, which differs from that of the greatest geniuses in being *impersonal*. . . But as soon as the Church opens the doors of its temples to resources other than voices and the organ, to resources from without, such

as the orchestra, she thereby recognizes and declares the right of *personal* expression in religious music." Quoted in J.-G. Prod'homme and A. Dandelot, *Gounod (1818–1893): Sa vie et ses œuvres d'après des documents inédits* (Paris: Delagrave, 1911), 2: 234–35.

58 Pope St. Pius X, *motu proprio*, section 4 (Cœuroy, "La musique religieuse," p. 169). The sharp distinction between plainchant and "music," at least in French sources, goes back at least as far as the seventeenth century and is probably older. For a glimpse into the nuances of this terminology, see Bénédicte Mariolle, "Bibliographie des ouvrage théoriques traitant du plain-chant (1582–1789)," in *Plain-chant et liturgie en France au XVIIe siècle*, ed. Jean Duron (n.p.: Éditions du Centre de la Musique Baroque de Versailles, Éditions Klincksieck, 1997). Both the titles and contents of these treatises attest the distinction when both words appear (see items 26, 32, 39, 50, 60, 61, and 83).

59 André Cœuroy, "La musique religieuse," pp. 149–50. Emphasis mine. This little-known usage would also account for the seemingly incongruous title Fauré gave his *Messe basse* (that is, "Low Mass") in 1906. *Petite messe* or *Messe brève* would have been customary for such a work.

60 Fauré, "Souvenirs," *La revue musicale* 4 (1 Oct. 1922): 197.

61 *Ibid.* (this quotation and the previous one are continuous in Fauré's text). Fauré is referring to Gounod's *Messe solennelle de Sainte Cécile* (1855). Fauré's sense of harmonic pacing is much more active and finely tuned than Gounod's, but with a little imagination we can see future glimmers of Fauré's "Pie Jesu" in the serene simplicity of the Benedictus of the *Messe solennelle*, or in measures 19 to 23 of the Benedictus of Gounod's posthumous Requiem.

62 Cœuroy, "La musique religieuse," p. 140.

63 D'Indy, *Richard Wagner*, p. 41.

64 Fauré wrote the first version of the Requiem in three months between 1887 and 1888, and the first performance took place in La Madeleine on 16 January 1888. Fauré soon added the Offertory and "Libera Me" and considered the work complete by 1891. But difficulties with his publisher, Julien Hamelle, delayed publication until 1900. We are completely indebted to Jean-Michel Nectoux for establishing the complex history of this work; see his *Gabriel Fauré: A Musical Life*, pp. 540–41, and the notes to his edition of Fauré's Requiem, ed. with Roger Delage (Paris: J. Hamelle, 1994), pp. x–xii, for a detailed account of the different versions and their performances between 1888 and 1902.

65 See Richardson, "Fauré's Requiem," 12; Nectoux, *Gabriel Fauré: A Musical Life*, pp. 123–24.

66 Fauré quoted by Louis Aguettant, letter to André Lambinet, 12 July 1902, published by Jean-Michel Nectoux as "Rencontres avec Gabriel Fauré," *Études fauréennes* 19 (1982): 4.

67 Saint-Saëns, *École buissonnière*, p. 179; see also pp. 164–65.

68 There seems to have been a well-developed French tradition for using the "Pie Jesu" in this liturgical position. Cherubini's two Requiems (1815 and 1836)

both include a "Pie Jesu," and even Marc-Antoine Charpentier's two *Messes des morts*, composed in the last decade of the seventeenth century, include a "Pie Jesu" for the Elevation. All of these settings, rather than taking the Latin incipit "Pie Jesu," are named so as to make their liturgical function explicit: "A l'Élevation" or "Élevation." In a *Graduel de Paris, noté pour les dimanches et les fêtes de l'année* (Paris: Aux Dépens des Libraires Associés, pour l'usage du diocèse, 1846), the "Pie Jesu" is also specifically labeled "Pour l'Élévation" (p. cxix). I have not been able to consult a Gradual closer to the period of Fauré's Requiem, but in the score of Gounod's posthumous Requiem, a work whose second performance was directed at La Madeleine in 1894 by Fauré, the "Pie Jesu" carries the printed direction "variante pour l'Élevation au lieu du Benedictus."

The further step of suppressing of the Benedictus, on the other hand, seems to have been a development of the later nineteenth century (both Charpentier and Cherubini include the Benedictus). An anonymous "Commentaire" on the *motu proprio* in *La tribune de Saint-Gervais* 10, no. 1 (Jan. 1904) specifically deplored the practice of substituting "a motet or antiphon" for the Benedictus, and the commentator believed that the pope's instructions would put an end to this practice (p. 21).

69 Such earlier masters of the motet as Josquin Des Prés and Palestrina never set this text. Cherubini's "In paradisum" (1820), a self-standing piece for four-part chorus, is the *only* setting before Fauré's I have been able to discover.

70 Norman Suckling, *Fauré* (London: J. M. Dent, 1946), p. 179.

71 Louis Laloy, "Concerts du Conservatoire," *Revue d'histoire et de critique musicales* 1, no. 4 (April 1901): 162–63.

72 Louis Vierne, "Silhouettes d'artistes: Gabriel Fauré," *L'écho musical* 1, no. 12 (5 Dec. 1912): 2.

73 *Ibid.*

74 Laloy, "Gabriel Fauré," *Musiclovers Calendar* 2 (Dec. 1906), 78. I have amended this translation slightly. See above, p. 279 n. 80, for the problems with this anonymous English translation.

75 Richardson, "Fauré's Requiem," 16. Despite the textual coincidence Richardson notes, the "Pie Jesu," when it appears as a separate chant during the Eucharist, carries an additional word, "sempiternam," at the third acclamation; Fauré's setting includes that word and therefore is clearly a piece for the Elevation, not a misplaced fragment of the Sequence.

76 See Nectoux, *Gabriel Fauré: A Musical Life*, p. 123.

77 François Verhelst, "Musique religieuse," *Durendal* 8 (Feb. 1901): 117.

78 See Article 10 in the decree of the Sacrée Congrégation des Rites (12 June 1894); this text is reprinted by de Castéra, within the "numéro-spécimen" of *La tribune de Saint-Gervais* (June 1894), appendix [n.p.]. For the *motu proprio*, see section 3, article 9 (in Cœuroy, "La musique religieuse," 169).

79 Even though many historians accept the cult of the sublime as a determining trait in the shift from classical to romantic aesthetics, praises of the sublime are

exceedingly rare in French culture, where the "serene joys of perfection" tended to be preserved against the vertiginous excess of the sublime (see Louis Laloy's critique of Beethoven's symphonies in "Les partis musicaux en France," *La grande revue* [25 Dec. 1907]: 793–94). In refusing to grant the superiority of the sublime to the perfect, many French musicians, while absorbing so many other tendencies from across the Rhine, put up an isolated but fundamental resistance to German idealism. Perhaps this refusal makes good on their pledges of classicism.

80 Aguettant, "Rencontres avec Gabriel Fauré," 4.

81 Fauré, preface to *La musique française d'aujourd'hui* by Georges Jean-Aubry, p. x.

82 Aguettant, "Rencontres avec Gabriel Fauré," 4.

83 The epithet "voluptuously Gregorian" comes from Reynaldo Hahn, "Gabriel Fauré: Préambule," *Journal de l'Université des Annales* (15 July 1914): 117, where he applies it to Fauré's style more generally.

84 Camille Benoit, "La Messe de Requiem de Gabriel Fauré," *Le guide musicale* 34, nos. 32–33 (9 and 16 Aug. 1888): 197, 195. (Benoît's name is spelled without the circumflex in this publication but elsewhere appears with it.)

85 *Ibid.*, 196. Likewise, Verhelst wondered if the "Pie Jesu" was not "perhaps too charming" (p. 118).

86 Fauré to Crucy, "Les grandes figures contemporaines," 1.

87 The Second Vatican Council changed enough details of the liturgy to render complete performances of Fauré's work exceptional in modern ceremonies, but the "Pie Jesu" has a firm place in the repertory for Catholic funerals in the United States.

88 René Paroissin, *Art et humanisme biblique* (Paris: Nouvelles Éditions Debresse, 1955), p. 43.

89 See, for example, *Hymns, Psalms, and Spiritual Canticles*, organ–choir edition, compiled, edited, and arranged by Theodore Marier, assisted by the staff of the Boston Archdiocesan Choir School (Belmont: BACS Publishing, 1974 and 1983). Fauré's "Pie Jesu" (pp. 924–25) is the only work by a "classical" composer included in the Rite of Christian Burial; the other pieces are lightly harmonized versions of Gregorian chants or modern imitations of plainchant.

90 The complete neglect of certain works by Guilmant and Tournemire is nonetheless an injustice. More recent generations of French composers with *scholiste* patrimony have fared better. The collection cited in the previous note includes a Sanctus by Jean Langlais (pp. 86–93). Although this work is not based on plainchant, Langlais may be said to represent the Schola indirectly through his inheritance from Franck and Dupré; Langlais, moreover, later became professor of organ and improvisation at the Schola. Curiously, he was not trained at the Schola, but at the Conservatoire, where Dukas, Tournemire, and Dupré were his teachers.

91 Benjamin Constant, *De la religion considérée dans sa source, ses formes et ses*

développements, in his *Œuvres*, ed. Alfred Roulin (Paris: Gallimard, 1957), p. 1406. Also quoted by Marchal, *La religion de Mallarmé*, p. 13.

92 Marchal, *La religion de Mallarmé*, p. 12.

93 Fauré to Marie Fauré, 11 Sept. 1906, *Lettres intimes*, p. 132: "Désir de choses inexistantes, peut-être; et c'est bien là le domaine de la musique."

94 Fauré to Philippe Fauré-Fremiet, 31 Aug. 1908, Fauré, *Correspondance*, p. 275.

95 Fauré applied the image of a "sourire un peu voilé qui seul est judicieux" to his own view of life and his expressive aims as an artist in an unpublished letter to Arsène Alexandre (around 3 Sept. 1904), quoted in Nectoux, *Gabriel Fauré: A Musical Life*, p. 499 (p. 495 in the French edition).

96 Henri Collet, "La musique chez soi: Œuvres nouvelles de Gabriel Fauré," *Comœdia* (26 Dec. 1919): 2.

97 Guyau, *L'irréligion de l'avenir*, p. xiv.

98 *Ibid.*, pp. 339–40.

99 Paul Sabatier, *France To-day – Its Religious Orientation*, tr. from the second French ed. by Henry Bryan Binns (London: J. M. Dent, 1913), p. 234, quoting from Buisson's debate with François-Alphonse Aulard in *L'Action* (22 Aug. 1903).

100 Eugène Berteaux, *En ce temps-là* (Paris: Le Bateau Ivre, 1946), pp. 238–39. Fauré's comment can be dated after 1905 ("*former* organist"), but no more precisely than that. Berteaux was a civil servant in the Ministry of Public Education and Fine Arts whom Fauré probably got to know in the course of directing the Conservatoire. Berteaux's obscure but valuable memoir is one of Nectoux's bibliographical discoveries.

101 Michael P. Levine, *Pantheism: A Non-Theistic Concept of Deity* (London: Routledge, 1994), pp. 11–13, explains the distinction cogently and considers panentheism a variety of theism.

102 Victor Cousin, *Cours de l'histoire de la philosophie* (Paris: Pichon et Didier, 1829), 2: 540, 551–52.

103 Édmond and Jules de Goncourt, *Journal*, ed. Robert Ricatte (Paris: Fasquelle, Flammarion, 1956), 1: 1133 (1862).

104 Paul Bourget, *Nouveaux essais de psychologie contemporaine* (Paris: Lemerre, 1886), p. 120.

105 Fauré to Fauchois, 13 April 1921, Fauré, *Correspondance*, p. 312.

106 Fauré to Marie Fauré, 6 April 1922, *Lettres intimes*, pp. 279–80. This letter is discussed below, p. 216.

107 Émile Vuillermoz, *Gabriel Fauré* (Paris: Flammarion, 1960), p. 92; Jean Vuaillat, *Gabriel Fauré, musicien français* (Lyon: E. Vitte, 1973), p. 43.

108 See especially Philippe Fauré-Fremiet, "Réflexions sur la confiance fauréenne," in his *Gabriel Fauré*, 2nd ed. (Paris: Albin Michel, 1957), pp. 133–43, and "La pensée fauréenne," in *Gabriel Fauré* (Paris: Publications Techniques et Artistiques, 1946), pp. 8–14. We may be grateful that Fauré-Fremiet was so conscientious in his writings about his father; it is always clear where facts or narration end and speculation begins.

109 Philippe Fauré-Fremiet, "Réflexions sur la confiance fauréenne," 136–37; cf. his "Pensée fauréenne," 11.

110 Philippe Fauré-Fremiet, "*La chanson d'Ève* de Van Lerberghe – Fauré," *Synthèses* [Brussels] 196–7 (Sept.–Oct. 1962): 267. The word *confiance* in French simply refers to a strong hope or sense of trust, but its root, *fiance*, is the Old French for "faith"; this embedded meaning may explain Fauré-Fremiet's penchant for this word and his glide from hope to faith.

111 Nectoux, *Gabriel Fauré: A Musical Life*, p. 111.

112 Michel Faure, *Musique et société du Second Empire aux années vingt* (Paris: Flammarion, 1985), p. 72. Faure comes closest to implying, if not stating, that Fauré was an atheist, but he is only concerned with what he considers the composer's philosophical and social pessimism. This discussion is devoid of nuance and to label Fauré a pessimist ignores evidence of his forgiving, easygoing nature. The composer wrote his wife in 1921, "You've often reproached me for defending people with bad reputations. I defended them because *I* did not believe what was said of them, because I have a stock of *naïveté* (yes, *na-ï-veté*) that has always led me to believe the good rather than the bad" (24 March 1921, *Lettres intimes,* p. 270).

113 Fauré to Marie Fauré, 24 March 1921, *Lettres intimes,* p. 270.

114 Fauré to Marie Fauré, 24 Aug. 1906, *Lettres intimes,* pp. 122–23. It was precisely at this time that Fauré conceived *La chanson d'Ève*; his first mention of the work comes in a letter written four days later (*ibid.,* p. 123).

115 Van Lerberghe to Emile Lecomte, 4 Aug. 1904, Hubert Juin, *Charles Van Lerberghe* (Paris: Pierre Seghers, 1969), p. 75. For other references by Van Lerberghe to his own atheism, see *ibid.,* p. 29; also Van Lerberghe, *Lettres à Albert Mockel, 1887–1906,* ed. Robert Debever and Jacques Detemmerman (Brussels: Éditions Labor, 1986), pp. 236–37, 252; and Van Lerberghe, *Lettres à une jeune fille,* ed. Gustave Charlier (Brussels: La Renaissance du Livre, 1954), pp. 138–39. Van Lerberghe had read Darwin at the end of 1903; see *Lettres à Albert Mockel,* p. 324.

116 Jacques Rivière to Alain-Fournier, 13 April 1906, in their *Correspondance, 1904–1914,* new edn., ed. Alain Rivière and Pierre de Gaulmyn (Paris: Gallimard, 1991), 1: 366–67. In this letter, Rivière, personally hostile to paganism, was also expressing his dislike of Leconte de Lisle's pagan visions, which he criticized earlier in the letter.

117 Charles Van Lerberghe, *La chanson d'Ève* (Paris: Mercure de France, 1904), p. 24.

118 "Et c'est en toi, force suprême, | Soleil radieux, | Que mon âme elle-même | Atteint son dieu!" Van Lerberghe, *La chanson d'Ève,* pp. 25–26; Fauré, *La chanson d'Ève,* op. 95 (Paris: Heugel, 1910), pp. 14–16. (Notes to simply "Van Lerberghe" and "Fauré" hereafter refer to their respective versions of *Ève.*)

119 "Comme Dieu rayonne aujourd'hui, | Comme il exulte, comme il fleurit, | Parmi ces roses et ces fruits!" Van Lerberghe, p. 34; Fauré, p. 17.

120 Levine, *Pantheism,* p. 2.

121 Beaunier, "Festival Gabriel Fauré: Conférence" (16 Dec. 1911), *Journal de l'Université des Annales* 6 (15 Feb. 1912): 290. Beaunier was the husband of Jeanne Raunay, the first singer and dedicatee of *La chanson d'Ève* (Nectoux, *Gabriel Fauré: A Musical Life*, p. 369).

122 Van Lerberghe, p. 18; Fauré, p. 6. Norman Suckling mistakenly took the pronoun "il" in the poem "Veilles-tu, ma senteur de soleil" to refer to the biblical Adam, and Orledge incorporated this reading into both editions of his book. A complete reading of Van Lerberghe's work shows that Adam has no role in it, and in "Veilles-tu" (Van Lerberghe, pp. 84–85; Fauré, pp. 28–33) "il" refers to "Amour," the god of Love. It is necessary to read the two surrounding poems to understand the reference. See Suckling, *Fauré*, p. 84, and Robert Orledge, *Gabriel Fauré* (London: Eulenburg, 1979), p. 141.

123 For the first time in "Entre les biches et les daims," p. 44.

124 The blatant contradiction on the title page of Van Lerberghe's third chapter betrays the poet's irony: beneath the rubric LA FAUTE, Van Lerberghe adds an epigram from Nietzsche, "Tout est innocence."

125 Fauré to Marie Fauré, 6 April 1922, *Lettres intimes*, pp. 279–80.

126 George Santayana, *The Life of Reason, or Phases of Human Progress*, one-volume ed. rev. by the author in collaboration with Daniel Cory (New York: Charles Scribner's Sons, 1953), p. 194 [from *Reason in Religion*, 1905–06].

127 Philippe Fauré-Fremiet, "*La chanson d'Ève*," 270; Jankélévitch, *Fauré et l'inexprimable* (Paris: Plon, 1974), pp. 184–86. Fauré-Fremiet associated the two ideas with Psyche and Eros.

128 Fauré-Fremiet, "*La chanson d'Ève*," 270. The character of the first theme is relaxed and diatonic; it unfolds in E minor at the beginning of "Paradis" and rises through a minor tenth: E–B–C–E–G (see Ex. 13a). The second theme is a tense, chromatic meander constrained within a falling minor third: D#–C#–D–B–C#–B#. It is first heard in "Paradis" in measures 21 to 22 (see Ex. 14a).

129 *Les dieux antiques*, translated and annotated by Mallarmé after a work by G. W. Cox, in Mallarmé, *Œuvres complètes*, p. 1257. See also pp. 1169, 1178. The myths of Persephone, Orpheus, Hercules, and Endymion may be cited among the more obvious examples. On the transmission of the phrase "the tragedy of nature" from the work of Max Müller to George Cox to Mallarmé, see Marchal, *La religion de Mallarmé*, p. 153.

130 Van Lerberghe, *Lettres à Albert Mockel*, pp. 300–301 (6 Aug. 1902).

131 Van Lerberghe, p. 26; Fauré, p. 16.

132 Van Lerberghe, p. 63; Fauré, p. 36. There are two exceptional references to the night in the middle of the cycle, but these do not efface the overall solar curve. In "Roses ardentes," Eve refers to roses in the "immobile night," but ends by directly addressing the sun. The sensory events of the sixth song, "Veilles-tu, ma senteur de soleil?" seem to take place at night, but the exhilaration Eve expresses in this nocturnal fantasy comes from her intensified sensation of all the smells of daytime persisting in the night air. In opposition to the night of "O mort," everything here is heat, joy, and fertility, and the presence of solar

symbols, including the "scent of sunshine," blond bees, honey, and Eve's own golden hair, set the poetic tone.

133   Van Lerberghe, p. 190; Fauré, pp. 38–41.

134   The fourth sentence alone is declarative, but it is also purely receptive.

135   Jankélévitch, *Fauré et l'inexprimable*, p. 190.

136   Fauré, p. 42; Van Lerberghe, p. 203.

137   Fauré, pp. 42–44; this translation represents Fauré's version of the poem (cf. Van Lerberghe, pp. 203–04). The composer dropped four lines and traded the positions of the second and third strophes. Table 2 compares the two French texts.

138   Renan, "Premiers travaux sur le bouddhisme," 758.

139   J. Saint-Jean [Joseph de Marliave], "La musique à Paris," *La nouvelle revue* 31 (1 Aug. 1910): 379.

140   Note, in the first two measures of this example, Fauré's use of the first theme, which dominates the first half of the song and is here linked to the second theme by an enharmonic E-flat.

141   Van Lerberghe, p. 34; Fauré, pp. 18–19.

142   The sequential module under second theme in "Comme Dieu rayonne" is a fifth up, then a half-step down (e.g., E–B / D♯–D); in "O mort": a third up, a half-step down (e.g., D–F♯ / C♯–C). In both songs, these modules fall through a chain of minor thirds. In "Paradis," on the other hand, the sequence is governed by consecutive rising half-steps (E–[E–E]–F–F♯–G–A♭–A, mm. 21–40).

143   For "L'aube blanche," see Example 17: "A flame awakens my mouth, | a breath stirs my hair." For "O mort," see Van Lerberghe, p. 203; Fauré, pp. 42–44. With regard to the latter poem, it is only Fauré's manipulation of Van Lerberghe's original that brings together the four lines cited here. Fauré gives the nirvanic imagery of breath, flame, and extinction a greater continuity than does Van Lerberghe's original (see Table 2).

144   See Van Lerberghe, pp. 85, 204; Fauré, pp. 33, 44.

145   Fauré-Fremiet, "La chanson d'Ève," 272.

146   Fauré to Marie Fauré, 6 April 1922, *Lettres intimes,* p. 280. Cf. pp. 204–205 above.

147   Fauré-Fremiet, "La pensée fauréenne," 11; cf. Fauré-Fremiet, "*La chanson d'Ève,*" 272. It is possible that Fauré's son attached a bit less pessimism to the poetic and musical content of "O mort" in his later article (the second cited). In 1946, the "abyss" mentioned in the penultimate line of the song suggested only "the flavor of nothingness, of abdication" (p. 12). In the second article (originally a lecture delivered to the Cercle Royal Gaulois, Artistique et Littéraire in 1954) he introduced the notion of "an open-armed [*généreux*] nirvana." But the meaning of "nirvana" is so closely related to the idea of "abdication" that it is difficult to say whether this single new element in Fauré-Fremiet's description of the song really represents a change in his view of it. He still considered it, in the later article, "an almost *black* song," Fauré's "darkest, most tragic" (p. 272, cf. "La pensée fauréenne," 12).

148 Jankélévitch, *Fauré et l'inexprimable*, pp. 190, 202.
149 Alain-Fournier to Rivière, 16 Nov. 1905, in their *Correspondance*, 1: 207.
150 Berteaux, *En ce temps-là*, p. 238.
151 Van Lerberghe to Mockel, 23 June 1898, Van Lerberghe, *Lettres à Albert Mockel*, p. 217. Emphasis mine.

6 Fauré the elusive

1 ". . . trajectories unlimited and unerring, some opulent state suddenly evasive, a delightful inaptitude for finishing." Stéphane Mallarmé, "La Musique et les Lettres," in his *Œuvres complètes*, ed. Henri Mondor and Georges Jean-Aubry (Paris: Gallimard, 1945), p. 649.

2 Jean-Jacques Nattiez, *Music and Discourse: Toward a Semiology of Music*, tr. Carolyn Abbate (Princeton: Princeton University Press, 1990), pp. 12–13. The terms "poiesis" and "poietic" are derived from the Greek verb meaning "to make."

3 Leonard Meyer, *Style and Music: Theory, History, and Ideology* (Philadelphia: University of Pennsylvania Press, 1989), pp. 44–48.

4 Fauré himself once described his own modal usage in terms that come remarkably close to the principles of hexachordal mutation; see Fauré, *Correspondance*, textes réunis, présentés et annotés par Jean-Michel Nectoux (Paris: Flammarion, 1980), p. 258. This exceptional letter, a kind of composition lesson addressed to his son Philippe, refers to the double tonal potential of a "scale made of two keys," which he compares to melodic structures found in plainchant and the music of "the ancients." Fauré's terms, by which he accounts for tonal variety in a piece that never modulates, suggest that an analysis explaining melodic and harmonic motion in terms of overlapping modal collections could address the coherence of Fauré's tonicizations without bypassing the musical surface. However, it is equally valid to show how Fauré's style operates within a framework of tonal voice-leading, and the best recent analyses of Fauré's music have preferred this emphasis; see, for example, James W. Sobaskie, "Allusion in the Music of Gabriel Fauré," in *Regarding Fauré*, ed. Tom Gordon (Amsterdam: Gordon and Breach Publishers, 1999), pp. 181–95.

5 Virgil Thomson, "French Rhythm" [1943], in *A Virgil Thomson Reader* (Boston: Houghton Mifflin, 1981), p. 241.

6 *Ibid.*

7 *Ibid.*, p. 242. Emphases mine. Thomson could have extended this cluster of stylistic traits to the sacred polyphony of the Renaissance (Josquin, Gombert, Morales, or Palestrina).

8 However, see Susan Glaser, "French Music and the French Language," *The Flutist Quarterly* 24, no. 2 (Winter 1999): 34–39. Glaser isolates specific qualities of the French language, especially its syllabic timing and relatively narrow range of durations and intensities, and relates these to music in such a way as

to suggest that the kind of metrical treatment we find in French music would come far more intuitively to a speaker of French than to a speaker of German, English, or even another Romance language. I am grateful to Keith Waters for pointing me to this remarkably concise and thoughtful consideration of accentuation in French and its relation to music.

9   Harald Krebs, *Fantasy Pieces: Metrical Dissonance in the Music of Robert Schumann* (New York, Oxford: Oxford University Press, 1999), p. 23.

10 See Timothy L. Jackson, "Gabriel Fauré's Expansions of Nonduple Hypermeter in 'La fleur qui va sur l'eau', Op. 85, No. 2," *In Theory Only* 12 (Feb. 1992): 1–27. Robin Tait, in *The Musical Language of Gabriel Fauré* (New York: Garland, 1989), exceptionally delves into Fauré's rhythmic style and provides important insights (pp. 186–225). This book reprints Tait's doctoral dissertation for the University of St. Andrews, 1984. James C. Kidd, "Louis Niedermeyer's System for Gregorian Chant Accompaniment as a Compositional Source for Gabriel Fauré" (Ph.D., University of Chicago, 1974), pp. 298–322, is less focused on meter but considers the rhythmic structure of "Au cimetière" in relation to phrase structure and harmony.

11 Tait, *Musical Language of Gabriel Fauré*, p. 187.

12 *Ibid.*, p. 218.

13 In some cases, groupings I have marked as "4" may just as well be heard as "2+2"; see, for example, the outer elements of the layer labeled A2. Most readers will best apprehend the metrical groupings by first singing and playing them.

14 Chris Morrow, who participated in my graduate seminar on French song at the University of Colorado in 1999, produced a different analysis of this song which greatly contributed to my understanding of the mechanisms behind Fauré's metrical processes. The disparity of our groupings in this first phrase underlines how open Fauré's style is to perceptual reinterpretation: the metrical layers he finds concur with mine only at the point where they all finally reunite at the end of the phrase.

15 I owe this insight to Chris Morrow.

16 Such guidance is more important in a setting such as "Aurore," where the melodic line asserts its contours over and above the words, than it is in Fauré's later, more prosodic settings.

17 The singer may act on this cue, but a syncopation will be produced, not a downbeat.

18 See Harald Krebs, *Fantasy Pieces: Metrical Dissonance in the Music of Robert Schumann* (New York, Oxford: Oxford University Press, 1999).

19 For more exact definitions, see Krebs, *Fantasy Pieces*, pp. 31–34.

20 Fauré sometimes creates regular groupings at a hypermetrical level, but sometimes he does not. Krebs's theory, while extremely sensitive to compositional nuances, centers on regular, not irregular, metrical groups; it is founded on the perception of "a succession of accents occurring at regular intervals." Such

regular intervals (of musical time) determine the "cardinality" (the metric cycle) of a given "interpretive layer" (*Fantasy Pieces*, p. 23). Confronted with "Aurore," Krebs might say that its irregular groupings, lacking cardinality, form less an "interpretive layer" (implying organization into larger units) than a "uninterpretable" or "barely interpretable" one.

21   On this poem, see chapter 5, p. 200.

22   This prosody, incorrect on the surface, is right from the point of view of poetic meaning. Drawing out the insignificant word "et," Fauré points up the following "suis" ("am"), an ordinary, neutral verb here having a strong, revelatory meaning underlined through temporal delay. The lingering pause on "et" suggests Eve's thoughtful anticipation and her consciousness of identity.

23   Taylor A. Greer, "Tonal Process in the Songs of Gabriel Fauré: Two Structural Features of the Whole-Tone Scale" (Ph.D., Yale University, 1986), p. 184, suggests instead a metric conflict between $\frac{3}{4}$ (voice) and $\frac{3}{2}$ (piano) in mm. 5–11 but does not comment further.

24   Tait, *Musical Language of Gabriel Fauré*, p. 196.

25   Glaser, "French Music and the French Language," 35–37.

26   James C. Kidd, "Tonality in a New Key," in *Explorations in Music, the Arts, and Ideas: Essays in Honor of Leonard B. Meyer*, ed. Eugene Narmour and Ruth Solie (Stuyvesant: Pendragon, 1988), pp. 388, 391.

27   Christopher Morrow, "A Look at Gabriel Fauré's Exploration of Meter in His Songs for Medium Voice," typescript, December 1999.

28   See "Dans un parfum de roses blanches" from *La chanson d'Ève*, where the only dynamic indication is an initial "dolce" in both parts.

29   Louis Aguettant to André Lambinet, 12 July 1902, published by Jean-Michel Nectoux as "Rencontres avec Gabriel Fauré," *Études fauréennes* 19 (1982): 3–7.

30   *Ibid.*, 5–6.

31   Jean-Michel Nectoux, "Entretien avec Emmanuel Fauré-Fremiet" [1971], *Bulletin de l'Association des amis de Gabriel Fauré* no. 9 (Jan. 1972): 18.

32   Marcel Proust to Mr. and Mrs. Sydney Schiff (around 21 July 1922), in Marcel Proust, *Correspondance*, 21 vols., ed. Philip Kolb (Paris: Plon, 1970–93), 21: 372–73.

33   Céleste Albaret, *Monsieur Proust*, ed. Georges Belmont, tr. Barbara Bray (New York: McGraw-Hill, 1976), p. 274.

34   Jean-Jacques Nattiez, *Proust as Musician*, tr. Derek Puffett (New York: Cambridge University Press, 1989), p. 88.

35   *Ibid.*, p. 60.

36   Fauré to Marie Fauré, Annecy-le-Vieux, 14 Oct. 1924, *Lettres intimes*, ed. Philippe Fauré-Fremiet (Paris: La Colombe, 1951), p. 295 (emphasis Fauré's).

37   Nectoux, *Gabriel Fauré: A Musical Life*, tr. Roger Nichols (New York: Cambridge University Press, 1991), p. 481.

38   *Ibid.*; see also pp. 485–86 on the sketchbooks.

39   Fauré to Marie Fauré, 24 March 1921, *Lettres intimes*, p. 270.

40 Nattiez, *Proust as Musician*, p. 88.

41 See chap. 1, p. 41, and chap. 5, p. 193. The two statements date from 1903 and 1908 respectively.

42 Jules Combarieu, *La musique, ses lois, son évolution* [1907] (Paris: Flammarion, 1924), pp. 8–9. See the discussion of this treatise in chap. 1, pp. 36–37.

43 ". . . que la musique n'est point faite pour toutes les besognes" might also be translated, with a slightly commercial overtone, "that music is not tailored to every need." Fauré, *Opinions musicales*, ed. P. B. Gheusi (Paris: Rieder, 1930), p. 63.

44 Fauré to Marie Fauré, 2 Sept. 1907, *Lettres intimes*, p. 149.

45 Aguettant to Lambinet, 12 July 1902, published as "Rencontres avec Gabriel Fauré," 5.

46 Fernand Divoire, "Sous la musique que faut-il mettre? De beaux vers, de mauvais, des vers libres, de la prose?" *Musica* no. 101 (Feb. 1911): 38. The peculiar emphasis is Fauré's.

47 Paul Verlaine, *La bonne chanson* (Paris: Léon Vanier, 1891), p. 41.

48 Nectoux, *Gabriel Fauré: A Musical Life*, p. 350. In "Sous la musique que faut-il mettre?" Fauré gives the example of "Helen with her white feet," feet which in a musical setting would "seem gigantic and altogether out of proportion" (Divoire, "Sous la musique que faut-il mettre?" 38). How much more so Verlaine's personification of city roofs, which verges on the bizarre even without being sung.

49 Verlaine, *La bonne chanson*, p. 32.

50 *Ibid.*, pp. 9, 33.

51 Aguettant to Lambinet, 12 July 1902, published as "Rencontres avec Gabriel Fauré," 5.

52 Vladimir Jankélévitch, *Fauré et l'inexprimable* (Paris: Plon, 1974), p. 299.

53 Pedro Salinas, *Reality and the Poet in Spanish Poetry*, tr. Edith Fishtine Helman (Westport, Connecticut: Greenwood Press, 1980), p. 139.

54 Fauré to Hamelle, 14 Aug. 1902, *Correspondance*, p. 247.

55 Fauré to Kahn, 3 Aug. 1916, *ibid.*, p. 295.

56 Nectoux, *Gabriel Fauré: A Musical Life*, p. 89.

57 Aubert, quoted in Bruneau, *La vie et les œuvres de Gabriel Fauré* (Paris: Charpentier et Fasquelle, 1925), pp. 27–28. In a much later interview, Aubert recalled, "[Fauré] once said to me of Ravel, whom he held in high regard, 'He's a title-lover' [*un amateur de titres*]." See Louis Guitard, "Entretien avec Louis Aubert," *La table ronde* 165 (Oct. 1961): 144.

58 See Nectoux, *Gabriel Fauré: A Musical Life*, p. 62, for private allusions in the titles of *Dolly*. Hélène Bardac (later Mme. Gaston de Tinan) herself explained two of the titles in her "Memories of Debussy and His Circle," *The Journal of the British Institute of Recorded Sound*, no. 50–51 (April–July 1973): 162.

59 *Ibid.*, 392.

60 This letter has been published in Nectoux, *Gabriel Fauré: A Musical Life*,

pp. 392–93. On Fauré's relations with Kahn, who received a whole collection of letters in verse and other musical witticisms from him, see also Hélène Jourdan-Morhange, *Mes amis musiciens* (Paris: Éditeurs français réunis, 1955), pp. 24–25.

61 Jourdan-Morhange, *Mes amis musiciens*, p. 24.

62 It is a nice coincidence that a whole category of Mallarmé's occasional verse, the poems he included with gifts of glazed fruit on New Year's Day, have their analogue in the third movement of *Dolly*, which was presented to Hélène Bardac as a New Year's gift in 1895. Two of the other movements were birthday presents.

63 See Philippe Fauré-Fremiet, *Gabriel Fauré*, 2nd ed. (Paris: Albin Michel, 1957), p. 139: "Il eût mille fois préféré désigner ses Nocturnes, ses Impromptus, même ses Barcarolles, sous la simple mention de: *Pièce* pour le piano nᵒ tant . . ." We shall encounter Robert Lortat's testimony further on.

64 Fauré to Marie Fauré, 23 March 1906, in Fauré, *Lettres intimes*, p. 118. Fauré's use here of the phrase "la musique absolue" is exceptional and may be Ysaÿe's term rather than his own. In all his other writing, Fauré speaks of "la musique pure" instead.

65 See Fauré's letter to Emmanuel Fauré-Fremiet, 17 March 1908, in Fauré, *Gabriel Fauré: A Life in Letters*, tr. and ed. J. Barrie Jones (London: B. T. Batsford, 1989), p. 129.

66 Fauré, review of 30 March 1903, *Opinions musicales*, pp. 137–38.

67 Fauré, "André Messager," *Musica* no. 72 (Sept. 1908): 132.

68 Norman Suckling, *Paul Valéry and the Civilized Mind* (London: Oxford University Press, 1954), pp. 82–83. For Valéry's discussion of "pure" modes, see chap. 1, p. 50.

69 Stéphane Mallarmé, "Théodore de Banville," in his *Œuvres complètes*, ed. Henri Mondor and Georges Jean-Aubry (Paris: Gallimard, 1945), p. 522.

70 Mallarmé, "Crise de vers," in *ibid.*, p. 366. On syntax, see "Le mystère dans les lettres," *ibid.*, p. 385: "Il faut une garantie – La Syntaxe."

71 Henri Meschonnic, "Mallarmé au-delà du silence," preface to *Écrits sur le livre (choix de textes)* by Stéphane Mallarmé (Paris: Éditions de l'Éclat, 1985), p. 46.

72 Mallarmé, "Crise de vers," in his *Œuvres complètes*, p. 364.

73 Mallarmé to Jules Huret, "Enquête sur l'évolution littéraire" [1891], in *ibid.*, p. 871.

74 Mallarmé, "Théodore de Banville," in *ibid.*, p. 522: "*La divine transposition, pour l'accomplissement de quoi existe l'homme, va du fait à l'idéal.*" Emphasis in original.

75 Mallarmé, "Le mystère dans les lettres," in *ibid.*, p. 387.

76 Robert Lortat, "Gabriel Fauré," *Le courrier musical* 24, no. 12 (15 June 1922): 203.

77 Judy Kravis, *The Prose of Mallarmé: The Evolution of a Literary Language* (Cambridge: Cambridge University Press, 1976), p. 188.

78 *Ibid.*, p. 198.

79 Mallarmé, "Magie," in his *Œuvres complètes*, p. 400: "quelque illusion égale au regard." Also cited by Kravis, *The Prose of Mallarmé*, p. 198.

80 Mallarmé, "Le mystère dans les lettres," in his *Œuvres complètes*, p. 387.

81 Divoire, "Sous la musique que faut-il mettre?" 38.

Bibliography

Ackerman, James S. "A Theory of Style." *Journal of Aesthetics and Art Criticism* 20, no. 3 (1962): 227–37.

Aguettant, Louis. "Gabriel Fauré." *La vie intellectuelle* 1 (Nov. 1949): 388–97.

"Rencontres avec Gabriel Fauré" [letter to André Lambinet, dated 12 July 1902, containing Aguettant's transcription of an interview with Fauré on 7 July 1902]. Ed. Jean-Michel Nectoux. *Études fauréennes* 19 (1982): 3–7.

Albaret, Céleste. *Monsieur Proust.* Ed. Georges Belmont. Tr. Barbara Bray. New York: McGraw-Hill, 1976.

Anderson, R. D. *France, 1870–1914: Politics and Society.* London: Routledge & Kegan Paul, 1977.

Augé-Laribé, Michel. *André Messager, musicien de théâtre.* Paris: La Colombe, 1951.

Auric, Georges. "Gabriel Fauré." *La revue musicale* 6 (1 Dec. 1924): 100–103.

Banville, Théodore de. *Petit traité de poésie française* [1872]. Paris: G. Charpentier, 1881.

Baudelaire, Charles. *Les fleurs du mal et autres poèmes.* Paris: Garnier-Flammarion, 1964.

"Richard Wagner et 'Tannhäuser' à Paris" [1861]. In his *Œuvres complètes.* Ed. Y.-G. Le Dantec and Claude Pichois. Paris: Gallimard, 1961.

Bazaillas, Albert. *Musique et inconscience.* Paris: Alcan, 1908.

Beaunier, André. "Festival Gabriel Fauré: Conférence." *Journal de l'Université des Annales* 6 (15 Feb. 1912): 284–90.

Belaval, Yvon. *Le souci de sincérité.* Paris: Gallimard, 1944.

Bellaigue, Camille. "Gabriel Fauré." *La revue hebdomadaire* 34 (7 March 1925): 5–18.

Études musicales. Vol. 3. Paris: Delagrave, 1907.

"Quelques chansons." *La revue des deux mondes* 143, no. 4 (15 Oct. 1897): 925–36.

Benoist-Méchin. *Avec Marcel Proust.* Paris: Albin Michel, 1977.

La musique et l'immortalité dans l'œuvre de Marcel Proust. Paris: Simon Kra, 1926.

Benoît, Camille. "La Messe de Requiem de Gabriel Fauré." *Le guide musical* 34, nos. 32–33 (9 and 16 Aug. 1888): 195–97.

Bergson, Henri. *Mélanges.* Ed. André Robinet. Paris: Presses Universitaires de France, 1972.

Œuvres. Ed. André Robinet. Paris: Presses Universitaires de France, 1970.

Berio, Luciano. "Poetics of Analysis." Sixth Charles Eliot Norton Lecture, Cambridge, Massachusetts, 6 April 1994.

Berteaux, Eugène. *En ce temps-là*. Paris: Le Bateau Ivre, 1946.

Bertelin, Albert. "Quelques souvenirs sur Gabriel Fauré." *Musique et théâtre* (1 April 1925): 14.

Bloom, Harold. *The Anxiety of Influence: A Theory of Poetry*. New York: Oxford University Press, 1973.

   A Map of Misreading. New York: Oxford University Press, 1975.

Bocquet, Léon. *Autour d'Albert Samain*. Paris: Mercure de France, 1933.

Boschot, Adolphe. *Chez les musiciens*. 3 vols. Paris: Plon, 1922–26.

Boulanger, Nadia. Interview with Jean-Michel Nectoux, 19 Jan. 1974. *Études fauréennes* 17 (1980): 3–5.

Boulez, Pierre. *Jalons (pour une décennie)*. Ed. Jean-Jacques Nattiez. Paris: Christian Bourgois, 1989.

   Stocktakings from an Apprenticeship. Ed. Paule Thévenin. Tr. Stephen Walsh. Oxford: Clarendon Press, 1991.

Bourgeat, Fernand. "Festival Fauré." *Journal de l'Université des Annales* 2 (10 June 1908): 426–33.

Bourget, Paul. *Nouveaux essais de psychologie contemporaine*. Paris: Lemerre, 1886.

Bruneau, Alfred. "Au théâtre des Champs-Elysées, l'altière et pure beauté de 'Pénélope' provoque un immense enthousiasme." *Le matin* (10 May 1913): 5.

   "La direction du Conservatoire." *Le matin* (13 June 1905): 2.

   La vie et les œuvres de Gabriel Fauré: Notice lue par l'auteur à l'Académie des Beaux-Arts. Paris: Charpentier et Fasquelle, 1925.

Bruyr, José. "En parlant de Gabriel Fauré avec son fils." *Le guide du concert* 24, no. 23 (4 March 1938): 615–17.

Cage, John. "A Composer's Confessions" [1948]. In *John Cage, Writer*. Ed. Richard Kostelanetz. New York: Limelight Editions, 1993.

Carraud, Gaston. "L'âme harmonique de Gabriel Fauré." *Musica* no. 77 (Feb. 1909): 19–20.

   "Le mois" [*Rondes de printemps*]. *Revue S.I.M.* 6, no. 4 (April 1910): 265–68.

Castéra, René de. *Dix années d'action musicale religieuse, 1890–1900*. Paris: Aux Bureaux de la Schola Cantorum, [c. 1902].

Cavell, Stanley. *Must We Mean What We Say?* New York: Charles Scribner's Sons, 1969.

Cinquante ans de musique française de 1874 à 1925. 2 vols. Ed. Ladislas Rohozinski. Paris: Librairie de France, 1925.

Cocteau, Jean. *A Call to Order: Written Between the Years 1918 and 1926 and Including Cock and Harlequin, Professional Secrets, and Other Critical Essays*. Tr. Rollo H. Myers. London: Faber and Gwyer, 1926. Reprint. New York: Haskell House, 1974.

Cœuroy, André. "La musique religieuse." In *Cinquante ans de musique française de 1874 à 1925*, ed. Ladislas Rohozinski, vol. 2. Paris: Librairie de France, 1925.

Collet, Henri. "La musique chez soi: Œuvres nouvelles de Gabriel Fauré." *Comœdia* (26 Dec. 1919): 2.

Combarieu, Jules. *La musique, ses lois, son évolution* [1907]. Paris: Flammarion, 1924.

"Paderewski." *La revue musicale* 9, no. 11 (1 June 1909): 285–88.

"Commentaire" [on the *motu proprio* of Pius X]. *La tribune de Saint-Gervais* 10, no. 1 (Jan. 1904): 15–26.

Constant, Benjamin. *De la religion considérée dans sa source, ses formes et ses développements.* In his *Œuvres,* ed. Alfred Roulin. Paris: Gallimard, 1957.

Copland, Aaron. "Gabriel Fauré, a Neglected Master." *Musical Quarterly* 10, no. 4 (1924): 573–86.

Cousin, Victor. *Cours de l'histoire de la philosophie.* Vol. 2. Paris: Pichon et Didier, 1829.

———. *Du Vrai, du Beau, et du Bien.* Paris: Didier, 1853.

Cox, David. *Debussy: Orchestral Music.* Seattle: University of Washington Press, 1974.

Crucy, François. "Les grandes figures contemporaines: Gabriel Fauré" [interview]. *Le petit parisien* (28 April 1922): 1–2.

Dahlhaus, Carl. *Grundlagen der Musikgeschichte.* Cologne: Hans Gerig, 1977.

———. *Nineteenth-Century Music.* Tr. J. Bradford Robinson. Berkeley: University of California Press, 1989.

Debussy, Claude. *Letters.* Ed. François Lesure and Roger Nichols. Tr. Roger Nichols. Cambridge, Massachusetts: Harvard University Press, 1987.

———. *Monsieur Croche et autres écrits.* Rev. ed. Paris: Gallimard, 1987.

Desjardins, Paul. *Le devoir présent.* Paris: A. Colin, 1892.

Detemmerman, Jacques. "Charles Van Lerberghe et la musique allemande." In *Charles Van Lerberghe et le Symbolisme.* Ed. Helmut Siepmann and Raymond Trousson. Cologne: DME, 1988.

Divoire, Fernand. "Sous la musique que faut-il mettre? De beaux vers, de mauvais, des vers libres, de la prose?" *Musica* no. 101 (Feb. 1911): 38–40.

Dromard, Gabriel. *Essai sur la sincérité.* Paris: Alcan, 1910.

———. *Les mensonges de la vie intérieure.* Paris: Alcan, 1910.

———. *Sur la sincérité en amour.* Paris: Picard, 1920.

Dujardin, Édouard. "Notes et nouvelles." *La revue wagnérienne* 3 (15 April 1887): 65–66.

———. "'La revue wagnérienne'." *La revue musicale* 4 (1 Oct. 1923): 139–60.

Dukas, Paul. "Adieu à Gabriel Fauré." *La revue musicale* 6 (1 Dec. 1924): 97–99.

———. "Chronique musicale: Concerts Lamoureux." *La revue hebdomadaire* 10 (9 Feb. 1901): 274–75.

———. "Chronique musicale: *Werther.*" *La revue hebdomadaire* 2 (11 Feb. 1893): 296–309.

———. "Poèmes et libretti." *La revue hebdomadaire* 4 (14 Sept. 1895): 307–13.

———. "Théâtre royal de la Monnaie, à Bruxelles: *Fervaal.*" *La revue hebdomadaire* 6 (27 March 1897): 555–64.

———. *Les écrits de Paul Dukas sur la musique.* Paris: Société d'Éditions Françaises et Internationales, 1948.

Dumesnil, René. "Le centenaire de Gabriel Fauré." In *Le centenaire de Gabriel Fauré.* Paris: Éditions de la Revue Musicale, 1945.

La musique en France entre les deux guerres, 1915–1939. Paris: Éditions du Milieu du Monde, 1946.

Portraits de musiciens français. Paris: Éditions d'Histoire et d'Art, 1938.

Dunoyer, Cecilia. *Marguerite Long: A Life in French Music, 1874–1966*. Bloomington: Indiana University Press, 1993.

Durant, Will. *The Story of Philosophy*. New York: Simon and Schuster, 1943.

Encyclopédie de la musique et Dictionnaire du Conservatoire. Ed. Albert Lavignac and Lionel de La Laurencie. Part 1, *Histoire de la musique*, 5 vols.; part 2, *Technique, esthétique et pédagogie*, 6 vols. Paris: Delagrave, 1913–30.

Fallois, Bernard de. Preface to *Contre Sainte-Beuve* by Marcel Proust. Paris: Gallimard, 1954.

Faure, Gabriel. *Gabriel Fauré*. Grenoble, Paris: B. Arthaud, 1945.

Faure, Michel. *Musique et société du Second Empire aux années vingt*. Paris: Flammarion, 1985.

Fauré, Gabriel. "André Messager." *Musica* no. 72 (Sept. 1908): 131–32.

Correspondance. Textes réunis, présentés et annotés par Jean-Michel Nectoux. Paris: Flammarion, 1980.

Gabriel Fauré: A Life in Letters. Tr. and ed. J. Barrie Jones. London: Batsford, 1989.

Letter to Auguste Mangeot, Feb. 1904 (fragment). In "Gabriel Fauré, critique musicale," *Le monde musical* 35 (Nov. 1924): 369.

Letters to Paul Dukas. Music MS. 287, Yale University Library, New Haven, Connecticut.

Lettres intimes. Ed. Philippe Fauré-Fremiet. Paris: La Colombe, 1951.

Opinions musicales. Ed. P. B. Gheusi. Paris: Rieder, 1930.

Preface to *La musique française d'aujourd'hui* by Georges Jean-Aubry. Paris: Perrin, 1916.

Preface to *Musiques d'aujourd'hui* by Émile Vuillermoz. Paris: Crès, 1923.

Preface to *Œuvres classiques pour piano*, ed. Benjamin Cesi, *et al.*; Isidore Philipp, French editor. Paris: Ricordi, [*c.* 1910].

Preface to *Les quatuors de Beethoven* by Joseph de Marliave. Paris: Alcan, 1925.

"Souvenirs." *La revue musicale* 4 (1 Oct. 1922): 195–201.

Fauré-Fremiet, Emmanuel. "Entretien avec Emmanuel Fauré-Fremiet" [1971]. Two interviews conducted by Jean-Michel Nectoux. *Bulletin de l'Association des amis de Gabriel Fauré* no. 9 (Jan. 1972): 12–18.

Fauré-Fremiet, Philippe. "*La chanson d'Ève* de Van Lerberghe–Fauré." *Synthèses* 196–97 (Sept.–Oct. 1962): 261–72.

Gabriel Fauré. Paris: Rieder, 1929.

Gabriel Fauré. 2nd ed. Paris: Albin Michel, 1957.

"La musique de chambre de Gabriel Fauré." *Le monde musical* 41, no. 6 (30 June 1930): 227–29.

"La pensée fauréenne." In *Gabriel Fauré*. Paris: Publications Techniques et Artistiques, 1946.

"Réflexions sur la confiance fauréenne." In his *Gabriel Fauré*, 2nd ed. Paris: Albin Michel, 1957.

Fauré-Fremiet, Philippe, René Dumesnil, and Georges Jean-Aubry. *Le centenaire de Gabriel Fauré*. Paris: Éditions de la Revue Musicale, 1945.

French Organ Music from the Revolution to Franck and Widor. Ed. Lawrence Archbold and William J. Peterson. Rochester, NY: University of Rochester Press, 1995.

Fulcher, Jane F. *French Cultural Politics & Music: From the Dreyfus Affair to the First World War*. Oxford: Oxford University Press, 1999.

Garnier, Paul-Louis. "*Prométhée* à Béziers." *La revue blanche* 23, no. 115 (Sept. 1900): 141–43.

Genêt-Delacroix, Marie-Claude. "Esthétique officielle et art national sous la Troisième République." *Le mouvement social* 131 (April–June 1985): 105–20.

Gide, André. *Un esprit non prévenu*. Paris: Kra, 1929.

Journals. Vol. 1. Tr. Justin O'Brien. New York: Knopf, 1947.

Pretexts: Reflections on Literature and Morality. Ed. Justin O'Brien. N.p.: Meridian Books, 1959.

Glaser, Susan. "French Music and the French Language." *The Flutist Quarterly* 24, no. 2 (Winter 1999): 34–39.

Goncourt, Edmond and Jules de. *Journal*. Vol. 1. Ed. Robert Ricatte. Paris: Fasquelle, Flammarion, 1956.

Goubault, Christian. *La critique musicale dans la presse française de 1870 à 1914*. Geneva: Slatkine, 1984.

Gounod, Charles. Preface to *Les soirées parisiennes de 1883* by Un Monsieur de l'Orchestre [Arnold Mortier]. Paris: E. Dentu, 1884.

Mémoires d'un artiste. Paris: Calmann Lévy, 1896.

Greer, Taylor A. "Tonal Process in the Songs of Gabriel Fauré: Two Structural Features of the Whole-Tone Scale." Ph.D., Yale University, 1986.

Guitard, Louis. "Entretien avec Louis Aubert." *La table ronde* 165 (Oct. 1961): 141–45.

Guyau, Jean-Marie. *L'irréligion de l'avenir* [1887]. Paris: Alcan, 1912.

Hahn, Reynaldo. "Gabriel Fauré: Préambule." *Journal de l'Université des Annales* 8 (15 July 1914): 115–18.

Harding, James. *Saint-Saëns and His Circle*. London: Chapman and Hall, 1965.

Hart, Brian. "The Symphony in Theory and Practice in France, 1900–1914." Ph.D., Indiana University, 1994.

Hartmann, Edouard de. *Philosophie de l'Inconscient*. Tr. D. Nolen. Paris: Ballière, 1877.

Holloway, Robin. "Master of Hearts." *The Musical Times* 136 (Aug. 1995): 394–96.

Honegger, Arthur. *I Am a Composer* [1951]. Tr. Wilson O. Clough with Allan Arthur Willman. London: Faber and Faber, 1966.

Incantation aux fossiles. Lausanne: Éditions d'Ouchy, 1948.

"*Pénélope*, un chef-d'œuvre." *Comœdia* (20 March 1943): 1, 4.

Imbert, Hugues. *Nouveaux profils des musiciens*. Paris: Fischbacher, 1892.

Profils de musiciens. Paris: Librairie Fischbacher et Librairie Sagot, 1888.

Indy, Vincent d'. *Beethoven*. Paris: Henri Laurens, 1911.

"Beethoven." In *Cobbett's Cyclopedic Survey of Chamber Music*, comp. and ed. Walter Wilson Cobbett. London: Humphrey Milford, 1929.

Cours de composition musicale. Rédigé avec la collaboration de Auguste Sérieyx, d'après les notes prises aux classes de composition . . . en 1897–98. Vol. 1. Paris: Durand, [1903].

"Une école d'art répondant aux besoins modernes." *La tribune de Saint-Gervais* 6, no. 11 (Nov. 1900): 303–14.

"Gabriel Fauré." *Les tablettes de la Schola* 24 (Nov. 1924): 2–3.

Richard Wagner et son influence sur l'art musical français. Paris: Delagrave, 1930.

Jackson, Timothy L. "Gabriel Fauré's Expansions of Nonduple Hypermeter in 'La fleur qui va sur l'eau,' Op. 85, No. 2." *In Theory Only* 12 (Feb. 1992): 1–27.

Jankélévitch, Vladimir. *Fauré et l'inexprimable*. Paris: Plon, 1974.

La musique et l'ineffable. Paris: A. Colin, 1961.

Jean-Aubry, Georges. *La musique française d'aujourd'hui*. Paris: Perrin, 1916.

Jourdan-Morhange, Hélène. *Mes amis musiciens*. Paris: Éditeurs française réunis, 1955.

Juin, Hubert. *Charles Van Lerberghe*. Paris: Pierre Seghers, 1969.

Kidd, James C. "Louis Niedermeyer's System for Gregorian Chant Accompaniment as a Compositional Source for Gabriel Fauré." Ph.D., University of Chicago, 1974.

Review of *Gabriel Fauré* by Robert Orledge. *19th-Century Music* 4, no. 3 (Spring 1981): 276–80.

"Tonality in a New Key." In *Explorations in Music, the Arts, and Ideas: Essays in Honor of Leonard B. Meyer*, ed. Eugene Narmour and Ruth Solie. Stuyvesant: Pendragon Press, 1988.

Kœchlin, Charles. *Correspondance*. Ed. Madeleine Li-Kœchlin. La revue musicale, nos. 348–50. Paris: Richard Masse, 1982.

"Du rôle de la sensibilité dans la musique." *La revue musicale* 10 (1 Jan. 1929): 200–21.

Gabriel Fauré. Paris: F. Alcan, 1927.

Gabriel Fauré [1927]. 2nd ed. Tr. Leslie Orrey. London: D. Dobson, 1946.

"Gabriel Fauré." *Le ménestrel* 83, nos. 21–22 (27 May and 3 June 1921): 221–23, 233–35.

"La mélodie." In *Cinquante ans de musique française de 1874 à 1925*, ed. Ladislas Rohozinski, vol. 2. Paris: Librairie de France, 1925.

"Représentations de Béziers." *Mercure de France* 143 (Nov. 1901): 550–53.

"Le 'Retour à Bach'." *La revue musicale* 8 (1 Nov. 1926): 1–12.

"Les tendances de la musique moderne française" [1921] and "Évolution de l'harmonie: Période contemporaine" [1924]. In *Encyclopédie de la musique*, ed. Albert Lavignac and Lionel de La Laurencie, part 2, vol. 1. Paris: Delagrave, 1925.

"Le théâtre." *La revue musicale* 4 (1 Oct. 1922): 226–41.

Kravis, Judy. *The Prose of Mallarmé: The Evolution of a Literary Language*. Cambridge: Cambridge University Press, 1976.

Krebs, Harald. *Fantasy Pieces: Metrical Dissonance in the Music of Robert Schumann.* New York, Oxford: Oxford University Press, 1999.

La Laurencie, Lionel de. "Le 'd'Indysme'." *L'art moderne* 23 (15 Feb. 1903): 49–52.

La Ville de Mirmont, Jean de. *L'horizon chimérique.* Paris: Société littéraire de France, 1920.

Lalo, Pierre. *De Rameau à Ravel: Portraits et souvenirs.* Paris: A. Michel, 1947.

"Au concert du Châtelet: Première audition d'*Iberia* [*sic*], suite d'orchestre de M. Claude Debussy." *Le temps* (26 Feb. 1910): 3.

"La suppression des chanteurs de Saint-Gervais." *Le temps* (11 June 1902): 3.

"Le *Quintette* nouveau de M. Gabriel Fauré." *Le temps* (13 July 1906): 3.

Laloy, Louis. "Concerts du Conservatoire" [Fauré, Requiem]. *Revue d'histoire et de critique musicales* 1, no. 4 (April 1901): 162–63.

"Claude Debussy et le debussysme." *Revue S.I.M.* 6, nos. 8–9 (Aug.–Sept. 1910): 510–19.

"Les écoliers." *Mercure musical et S.I.M.* 3 (April 1907): 367–72.

"Gabriel Fauré." *Musiclovers Calendar* 2 (Dec. 1906): 77–80.

"La nouvelle manière de Claude Debussy." *La grande revue* (10 Feb. 1908): 530–35.

"Les partis musicaux en France." *La grande revue* (25 Dec. 1907): 790–98.

Landormy, Paul. "L'état actuel de la musique française." *La revue bleue* (26 March and 2 April 1904): 394–97, 421–26.

La musique française après Debussy. Paris: Gallimard, 1943.

Larmore, Charles. "The Toils of Sincerity: La Rochefoucauld, Stendhal, Sartre." *Op. Cit.* 6 (Spring 1996): 63–69.

Larroumet, Gustave. *Nouvelles études de littérature et d'art.* Paris: Hachette, 1894.

Le Dantec, Y.-G. "Réflexions d'un philistin sur la Métaphysique." *La grande revue* (10 July 1910): 1–16.

Le Moigne-Mussat, Marie-Claire. *Musique et société à Rennes aux XVIIIe et XIXe siècles.* Geneva: Minkoff, 1988.

Leconte de Lisle, Charles Marie René. *Poèmes antiques.* Ed. Claudine Gothot-Mersch. Paris: Gallimard, 1994.

Leibowitz, René. *Schœnberg et son école: L'étape contemporaine du langage musical.* Paris: J. B. Janin, 1947.

Lettres à Auguste Sérieyx [par] Vincent d'Indy, Henri Duparc [et] Albert Roussel. Ed. M. L. Sérieyx. Lausanne: Éditions du Cervin; Paris: E. Ploix, 1961.

Levine, Michael P. *Pantheism: A Non-Theistic Concept of Deity.* London: Routledge, 1994.

Lindenlaub, T. "Mort de Gabriel Fauré." *Le temps* (5 Nov. 1924): 3.

Littré, Émile. *Dictionnaire de la langue française.* 4 vols. Paris: Hachette, 1873–83.

Lortat, Robert. "Gabriel Fauré." *Le courrier musical* 24, no. 12 (15 June 1922): 203–04.

Magnard, Albéric. Preface to *Bérénice, tragédie en musique.* Paris: Édition mutuelle, 1909.

Mallarmé, Stéphane. *Œuvres complètes.* Ed. Henri Mondor and G. Jean-Aubry. Paris: Gallimard, 1945.

Mangeot, Auguste. "La réforme de la musique religieuse." *Le monde musical* (15 Feb. 1904): 34–36.

Marchal, Bertrand. *La religion de Mallarmé: Poésie, mythologie et religion.* Paris: José Corti, 1988.

Mariolle, Bénédicte. "Bibliographie des ouvrages théoriques traitant du plain-chant (1582–1789)." In *Plain-chant et liturgie en France au XVIIe siècle.* Ed. Jean Duron. N.p.: Éditions du Centre de la Musique Baroque de Versailles, Éditions Klincksieck, 1997.

Marliave, Joseph de. *Études musicales.* Paris: Alcan, 1917.

——— [J. Saint-Jean, pseud.]. "La musique à Paris." *La nouvelle revue* 31 (1 Aug. 1910): 378–79.

Marnold, Jean. "Gabriel Fauré." *Mercure de France* 176 (1 Dec. 1924): 499–503.

Maus, Octave. "Gabriel Fauré." *L'art moderne* 26, no. 12 (25 March 1906): 91–92.

——— "Le Théâtre des Champs-Élysées" [*Pénélope*]. *L'art moderne* 33 (25 May 1913): 163.

Mayeur, Jean-Marie, *et al. Libre pensée et religion laïque en France de la fin du second Empire à la fin de la troisième République.* Strasbourg: Cerdic-Publications, 1980.

Méraly, Jacques. "Gabriel Fauré, l'homme et le musicien: *La bonne chanson.*" *La revue musicale* 3 (15 Nov. 1903): 622–28.

Meschonnic, Henri. "Mallarmé au-delà du silence." Preface to *Écrits sur le livre (choix de textes)* by Stéphane Mallarmé. Paris: Éditions de l'Éclat, 1985.

Messager, André. "Gabriel Fauré." *Le Figaro* (7 June 1922): 1.

Meyer, Leonard B. *Music, the Arts, and Ideas: Patterns and Predictions in Twentieth-Century Culture.* Chicago: University of Chicago Press, 1967.

——— *Style and Music: Theory, History, and Ideology.* Philadelphia: University of Pennsylvania Press, 1989.

Milhaud, Darius. *Notes sur la musique: Essais et chroniques.* Ed. Jeremy Drake. Paris: Flammarion, 1982.

Monsaingeon, Bruno. *Mademoiselle: Conversations with Nadia Boulanger.* Tr. Robyn Marsack. Boston: Northeastern University Press, 1988.

Moravec, Paul. "Tonality and Transcendence." *Contemporary Music Review* 6, no. 2 (1992): 39–42.

Morgan, Robert P. "Secret Languages: The Roots of Musical Modernism." *Critical Inquiry* 10 (March 1984): 442–61.

——— *Twentieth-Century Music: A History of Musical Style in Modern Europe and America.* New York: W. W. Norton, 1991.

Morland, Jacques. "Enquête sur l'influence allemande, VI: Musique." *Mercure de France* 45 (Jan. 1903): 89–137.

Nattiez, Jean-Jacques. *Music and Discourse: Toward a Semiology of Music.* Tr. Carolyn Abbate. Princeton: Princeton University Press, 1990.

——— *Proust as Musician.* Tr. Derrick Puffett. Cambridge: Cambridge University Press, 1989.

Nectoux, Jean-Michel. "Deux interprètes de Fauré: Émilie et Édouard Risler." *Études fauréennes* 18 (1981): 3–25.

Fauré. 2nd ed. Paris: Seuil, 1986.

Gabriel Fauré: A Musical Life. Tr. Roger Nichols. New York: Cambridge University Press, 1991. [Translation of *Gabriel Fauré: Les voix du clair-obscur.*]

Gabriel Fauré: Les voix du clair-obscur. Paris: Flammarion, 1990.

"Proust et Fauré." *Bulletin de la Société des amis de Marcel Proust et des amis de Combray* 21 (1971): 1002–20.

"Works Renounced, Themes Rediscovered: *Éléments pour une thématique fauréenne.*" *19th-Century Music* 2, no. 3 (March 1979): 231–44.

Nède, André. "Le nouveau directeur du Conservatoire." *Le Figaro* (14 June 1905): 4.

Northcott, Bayan. "Fauré Our Contemporary." *Music and Musicians* 18, no. 8 (April 1970): 32–36, 38–40.

Nyman, Michael. *Experimental Music: Cage and Beyond.* London: Studio Vista, 1974.

Orledge, Robert. *Charles Kœchlin (1867–1950): His Life and Works.* New York: Harwood, 1989.

"From a Vision of Death to The Genesis of *Pénélope*: The Gabriel Fauré Manuscript Collection." In *Perspectives on Music,* ed. Dave Oliphant and Thomas Zigal. Austin: Humanities Resource Center, 1985.

Gabriel Fauré. London: Eulenburg, 1979.

Panzéra, Charles. *L'art de chanter.* Paris: Éditions Littéraires de France, 1945.

50 mélodies françaises: Leçons de style et d'interprétation. Brussels: Schott Frères, 1964.

Parakilas, James. *Ballads Without Words: Chopin and the Tradition of the Instrumental Ballade.* Portland, Oregon: Amadeus Press, 1992.

Paroissin, René. *Art et humanisme biblique.* Paris: Nouvelles Éditions Debresse, 1955.

Mystère de l'art sacré – des origines à nos jours. Paris: Nouvelles Éditions Debresse, 1957.

Peyre, Henri. *Literature and Sincerity.* New Haven: Yale University Press, 1963.

Phillips, Edward R. "Smoke, Mirrors and Prisms: Tonal Contradiction in Fauré." *Music Analysis* 12, no. 1 (March 1993): 3–24.

Piencikowski, Robert. Introduction to *Stocktakings from an Apprenticeship* by Pierre Boulez. Tr. Stephen Walsh. Oxford: Clarendon Press, 1991.

Pierrot, Jean. *The Decadent Imagination, 1880–1900.* Tr. Derek Coltman. Chicago: University of Chicago Press, 1981.

Piroué, Georges. *La musique dans la vie, l'œuvre et l'esthétique de Proust.* Paris: Denoël, 1960. [Note: some copies of this book, otherwise identical, carry the title *Proust et la musique du devenir.*]

Poe, Edgar Allan. "The Philosophy of Composition" [1846]. In his *Essays and Reviews.* Ed. G. R. Thompson. The Library of America. New York: Literary Classics of the United States, 1984.

Prod'homme, Jacques-Gabriel, and Arthur Dandelot. *Gounod (1818–1893): Sa vie et ses œuvres d'après des documents inédits.* 2 vols. Paris: Delagrave, 1911.

Proust, Marcel. *A la recherche du temps perdu.* 3 vols. Ed. Pierre Clarac et André
    Ferré. Paris: Gallimard, 1954.

    Contre Sainte-Beuve, précédé de Pastiches et mélanges et suivi de Essais et articles.
    Ed. Pierre Clarac and Yves Sandre. Paris: Gallimard, 1971.

    Contre Sainte-Beuve, suivi de Nouveaux mélanges. Paris: Gallimard, 1954.

    Correspondance. 21 vols. Ed. Philip Kolb. Paris: Plon, 1970–93.

    In Search of Lost Time. 6 vols. Tr. C. K. Scott Moncrieff and Terence Kilmartin;
    rev. D. J. Enright. New York: The Modern Library, 1992–93.

    Matinée chez la princesse de Guermantes: Cahiers du "Temps retrouvé." Ed. Henri
    Bonnet and Bernard Brun. Paris: Gallimard, 1982.

    La prisonnière. Ed. Pierre-Edmond Robert. Paris: Gallimard, 1988.

Prunières, Henry. "Portraits et médaillons de musiciens." In *Cinquante ans de
    musique française de 1874 à 1925*, ed. Ladislas Rohozinski, vol. 2. Paris:
    Librairie de France, 1925.

Ravel, Maurice. *A Ravel Reader: Correspondence, Articles, Interviews.* Ed. Arbie
    Orenstein. New York: Columbia University Press, 1990.

Renan, Ernest. *Œuvres complètes.* Ed. Henriette Psichari. Vol. 7. Paris: Calmann-
    Lévy, 1955.

Richardson, Susan. "Fauré's Requiem as Independent Ideology." Paper delivered at
    the 55th annual meeting of the American Musicological Society, Austin,
    Texas, 27 October 1989.

Rivière, Jacques. *De la sincérité envers soi-même* [1912]. Paris: Les Cahiers de Paris,
    1925.

    Études. Paris: Gallimard, 1925.

Rivière, Jacques, and Alain-Fournier. *Correspondance, 1904–1914.* New ed. by
    Alain Rivière and Pierre de Gaulmyn. 2 vols. Paris: Gallimard, 1991.

Roger-Ducasse, Jean. "L'enseignement de Gabriel Fauré." In *Gabriel Fauré.* Paris:
    Publications techniques et artistiques, 1946.

Roland-Manuel. "Le Trio pour piano, violon et violoncelle de Gabriel Fauré." *La
    revue musicale* 4 (1 July 1923): 250.

    "Des Valses à 'la Valse', 1911–1921." In *Maurice Ravel par quelques-uns de ses
    familiers.* Ed. Roger Wild. Paris: Éditions du Tambourinaire, 1939.

Ropartz, Joseph Guy. *Notations artistiques.* Paris: Lemerre, 1891.

Roussel, Albert. *Lettres et écrits.* Ed. Nicole Labelle. Paris: Flammarion, 1987.

Sabatier, Paul. *France To-day – Its Religious Orientation.* Tr. from the 2nd French
    ed. by Henry Bryan Binns. London: J. M. Dent, 1913.

Saint-Saëns, Camille. *Au courant de la vie.* Paris: Dorbon-Ainé, 1914.

    École buissonnière: Notes et souvenirs. Paris: Pierre Lafitte, 1913.

    Harmonie et mélodie. 2nd ed. Paris: Calmann Lévy, 1885.

Saint-Saëns, Camille, and Gabriel Fauré. *Correspondance (1862–1920).* Ed. Jean-
    Michel Nectoux. 3rd ed. Paris: Publications de la Société française de
    musicologie and Éditions Klincksieck, 1994.

Sainte-Beuve, Charles Augustin. "De la liberté de l'enseignement. Discours au
    Sénat le 19 mai 1868." Paris: Michel Lévy, 1868.

Salinas, Pedro. *Reality and the Poet in Spanish Poetry*. Tr. Edith Fishtine Helman. Westport, Connecticut: Greenwood Press, 1980.

Samazeuilh, Gustave. "Quatuor pour instruments à cordes (op. 121) de Gabriel Fauré." *La revue musicale* 6 (1 July 1925): 66–68.

Santayana, George. *The Life of Reason, or Phases of Human Progress*. One-volume edition revised by the author in collaboration with Daniel Cory. New York: Charles Scribner's Sons, 1953.

La Schola Cantorum: Son histoire depuis sa fondation jusqu'en 1925. Paris: Bloud & Gay, 1927.

Schuré, Édouard. Preface to *Profils de musiciens* by Hugues Imbert. Paris: Librairie Fischbacher et Librairie Sagot, 1888.

Servières, Georges. *Richard Wagner jugé en France*. Paris: Librairie Illustrée, 1887. "Lieder français." *Le guide musical* 40 (23 Dec. 1894): 1027–28.

[signed "G. S."]. "Cercle Artistique" [Fauré, First Quintet]. *Le guide musical* 52, no. 13 (1 April 1906): 254–55.

Smallman, Basil. *The Piano Quartet and Quintet*. Oxford: Clarendon Press, 1994.

Sobaskie, James W. "Allusion in the Music of Gabriel Fauré." In *Regarding Fauré*, ed. Tom Gordon. Amsterdam: Gordon and Breach Publishers, 1999.

Stœcklin, Paul de. "L'anémie." *Le courrier musical* 14, no. 13 (1 July 1911): 462–65.

Suckling, Norman. *Fauré*. London: J. M. Dent, 1946.

Paul Valéry and the Civilized Mind. London: Oxford University Press, 1954.

Symons, Arthur. "The Problem of Richard Strauss." In his *Studies in the Seven Arts*. New York: E. P. Dutton, 1906.

Tait, Robin. *The Musical Language of Gabriel Fauré*. New York: Garland, 1989.

Tenroc, Charles. "Le problème de l'Édition française de musique, I." *Le courrier musical* (1 Feb. 1917): 53–55.

Thomson, Virgil. *A Virgil Thomson Reader*. Boston: Houghton Mifflin, 1981.

Tinan, Hélène de. "Memories of Debussy and His Circle." *The Journal of the British Institute of Recorded Sound*, nos. 50–51 (April–July 1973): 158–63.

Trilling, Lionel. *Sincerity and Authenticity*. Cambridge, Massachusetts: Harvard University Press, 1972.

Valbelle, Roger. "Entretien avec M. Gabriel Fauré." *Bulletin de l'Association des amis de Gabriel Fauré* 12 (1975). First published in *Excelsior* (12 June 1922).

Valéry, Paul. *Œuvres*. 2 vols. Ed. Jean Hytier. Paris: Bibliothèque de la Pléiade, 1957–60.

Vallas, Léon. *Claude Debussy et son temps*. Paris: Albin Michel, 1958.

Claude Debussy: His Life and Works. Tr. Maire and Grace O'Brien. London: Oxford University Press, 1933.

Van Lerberghe, Charles. *La chanson d'Ève*. Paris: Mercure de France, [1904].

Lettres à Albert Mockel, 1887–1906. Ed. Robert Debever and Jacques Detemmerman. Brussels: Éditions Labor, 1986.

Lettres à une jeune fille. Ed. Gustave Charlier. Brussels: La Renaissance du Livre, 1954.

Varèse, Edgard. *Écrits*. Ed. Louise Hirbour. Paris: Christian Bourgois, 1983.

Verhelst, François. "Musique religieuse." *Durendal* 8 (Feb. 1901): 115–18.

Verlaine, Paul. *La bonne chanson*. Paris: Léon Vanier, 1891.

    Poèmes saturniens; suivi de Fêtes galantes. Paris: Le Livre de Poche, 1961.

Vierne, Louis. "Salle Pleyel: Concerts Ysaye-Pugno" [Fauré, First Quintet]. *Le monde musical* 17, no. 9 (15 May 1906): 136–37.

    "Silhouettes d'artistes: Gabriel Fauré." *L'écho musical* 1, no. 12 (5 Dec. 1912): 1–3.

Vuaillat, Jean. *Gabriel Fauré, musicien français*. Lyon: E. Vitte, 1973.

Vuillermoz, Émile. "Debussy et les debussystes." *La nouvelle presse* (26 Feb. 1907).

    Gabriel Fauré. Paris: Flammarion, 1960.

    Gabriel Fauré [1960]. Tr. Kenneth Schapin. New York: Chilton, 1969.

    "La musique de chambre de Gabriel Fauré." *Musica* no. 77 (Feb. 1909): 23.

    Musiques d'aujourd'hui. Paris: Crès, 1923.

    "La Schola et le Conservatoire." *Mercure de France* 153 (16 Sept. 1909): 234–43.

Vuillermoz, Émile, and Louis Laloy. "Correspondance." *Mercure musical et S.I.M.* 3 (June 1907): 668–70.

Wegener, Charles. *The Discipline of Taste and Feeling*. Chicago: University of Chicago Press, 1992.

Whitesell, Lloyd. "Men with a Past: Music and the 'Anxiety of Influence'." *19th-Century Music* 28, no. 2 (Fall 1994): 152–67.

Wilde, Oscar. "The Critic as Artist." In his *Intentions*. London: Unicorn Press, 1945.

    The Picture of Dorian Gray. In *The Portable Oscar Wilde*. New York: Viking Press, 1947.

Williams, Christopher A. "Of Canons and Context: Toward a Historiography of Twentieth-Century Music." *Repercussions* 2 (Spring 1993): 31–74.

Willy [Henri Gauthier-Villars]. "Revue de la quinzaine: Lettre de Willy." *Mercure musical* 2, no. 11 (1 June 1906): 514.

Woldu, Gail Hilson. "Gabriel Fauré as Director of the Conservatoire Nationale de Musique et de Déclamation, 1905–1920." Ph.D., Yale University, 1983.

    "Gabriel Fauré, directeur du Conservatoire: Les réformes de 1905." *La revue de musicologie* 70, no. 2 (1984): 199–228.

Wyzéwa, Téodor de. "Notes sur la peinture wagnérienne." *La revue wagnérienne* 2 (May 1886): 100–13.

Yoshikawa, Karuyoschi. "Vinteuil ou la genèse du septuor." *Études proustiennes* 3 (1979): 289–347.

Index

320